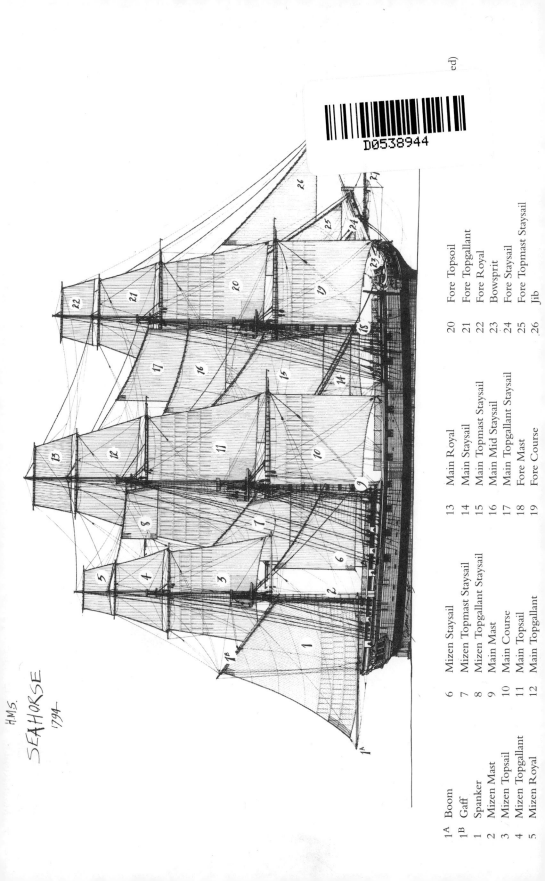

H.M.S.
SEAHORSE
1794

...ed)

1A Boom
1B Gaff
1 Spanker
2 Mizen Mast
3 Mizen Topsail
4 Mizen Topgallant
5 Mizen Royal

6 Mizen Staysail
7 Mizen Topmast Staysail
8 Mizen Topgallant Staysail
9 Main Mast
10 Main Course
11 Main Topsail
12 Main Topgallant

13 Main Royal
14 Main Staysail
15 Main Topmast Staysail
16 Main Mid Staysail
17 Main Topgallant Staysail
18 Fore Mast
19 Fore Course

20 Fore Topsoil
21 Fore Topgallant
22 Fore Royal
23 Bowsprit
24 Fore Staysail
25 Fore Topmast Staysail
26 Jib

# THE SEA WARRIORS

*Fighting Captains and Frigate Warfare
in the Age of Nelson*

*Other titles by the same author*

**Fiction:**

*The Nathaniel Drinkwater Series:*
An Eye of the Fleet
A King's Cutter
A Brig of War
The Bomb Vessel
The Corvette
1805
Baltic Mission
In Distant Waters
A Private Revenge
Under False Colours
The Flying Squadron
Beneath the Aurora
The Shadow of the Eagle
Ebb Tide

**Other novels:**

Wager
Endangered Species
The Darkening Sea
Voyage East
The Accident
Act of Terror
Waterfront
Under Sail
The Guineaman
The Privateersman
The Captain of the *Carryatid*
The Cruise of the Commissioner

**Non-Fiction:**

The History of the Ship
The Story of Sail
The Victory of Seapower, 1806–14
Arctic Convoys, 1941–45
Malta Convoys, 1940–42
Keepers of the Sea
View from the Sea

# THE SEA WARRIORS

*Fighting Captains and Frigate Warfare
in the Age of Nelson*

RICHARD WOODMAN

CONSTABLE • LONDON

Constable Publishers
3 The Lanchesters
162 Fulham Palace Road
London W6 9ER
www.constablerobinson.com

First published in the UK by Constable,
an imprint of Constable & Robinson Ltd, 2001

A copy of the British Library Cataloguing in
Publication Data is available from the British Library

ISBN 1-84119-183-3
Printed and bound in the EU

# Contents

| | | |
|---|---|---|
| *List of Illustrations* | | vii |
| *Acknowledgements* | | ix |
| *Maps* | | x |
| *Foreword* | | xv |
| | | |
| 1 | 'Post nubila Phoebus' | 1 |
| 2 | 'We dished her up in fifty minutes' | 19 |
| 3 | 'Consummate professional skill' | 35 |
| 4 | 'A very heavy gale' | 53 |
| 5 | 'Broadside uppermost' | 69 |
| 6 | 'The Devil in harbour' | 91 |
| 7 | 'I shall return' | 105 |
| 8 | 'I will lead you myself' | 119 |
| 9 | 'So daring an enterprise' | 139 |
| 10 | 'The peace which passeth all understanding' | 163 |
| 11 | 'England expects' | 187 |
| 12 | Firmness ... to the backbone' | 209 |
| 13 | 'Stand firm' | 229 |

# Contents

14   'Remember Nelson'    247

15   'My Lord, you *must* go...'    263

16   'To purge the eastern side of the globe'    279

17   'Don't give up the ship'    295

18   'The ship is safe'    323

*Chronology*    333

*Select Bibliography*    343

*An Explanation of Terminology and Glossary*    347

*Index*    357

# List of Illustrations

Admiral Lord Howe © NATIONAL MARITIME MUSEUM, LONDON
Vice Admiral Lord Collingwood © NATIONAL MARITIME MUSEUM, LONDON
Admiral Lord Gambier © NATIONAL MARITIME MUSEUM, LONDON
The Board Room at the Admiralty © NATIONAL MARITIME MUSEUM, LONDON
Rear Admiral Sir James Saumarez © NATIONAL MARITIME MUSEUM, LONDON
Admiral Sir William Cornwallis © NATIONAL MARITIME MUSEUM, LONDON
Rear Admiral Sir John Borlase Warren © NATIONAL MARITIME MUSEUM, LONDON
Admiral Sir Edward Pellew, by courtesy of the National Portrait Gallery, London
The French frigate *L'Incorruptible* © NATIONAL MARITIME MUSEUM, LONDON
A typical British frigate © NATIONAL MARITIME MUSEUM, LONDON
Captain Horatio Nelson © NATIONAL MARITIME MUSEUM, LONDON
Captain Sir Sidney Smith © NATIONAL MARITIME MUSEUM, LONDON
Rear Admiral Sir Richard Goodwin Keats © NATIONAL MARITIME MUSEUM, LONDON
To the victor the spoils, HM Frigate *Phaeton* and her prizes in 1793 © NATIONAL MARITIME MUSEUM, LONDON
Destruction of *Droits de l'Homme by Indefatigable* and *Amazon,* January 1797 © NATIONAL MARITIME MUSEUM, LONDON
*Loire*, engaged by *Anson* and raked by *Kangaroo,* off the Irish Coast, October 1798 © NATIONAL MARITIME MUSEUM, LONDON
Captain Lord Cochrane © NATIONAL MARITIME MUSEUM, LONDON
Captain David Porter (USN) © NATIONAL MARITIME MUSEUM, LONDON
Captain Sir William Hoste © NATIONAL MARITIME MUSEUM, LONDON
Captain Sir Charles Brisbane, © NATIONAL MARITIME MUSEUM, LONDON
Captain James Lawrence (USN) by courtesy of the Beverley R. Robinson Collection, United States Naval Academy Museum
Captain Sir Philip Broke © NATIONAL MARITIME MUSEUM, LONDON
Captain William Bainbridge (USN) © NATIONAL MARITIME MUSEUM, LONDON

Captain Isaac Hull (USN) by courtesy of the Beverley R. Robinson Collection, United States Naval Academy Museum
Commodore Sir Nathaniel Dance of the Honourable East India Company © NATIONAL MARITIME MUSEUM, LONDON
Commander John Wesley Wright © NATIONAL MARITIME MUSEUM, LONDON
Captain James Bowen © NATIONAL MARITIME MUSEUM, LONDON
Captain Fleetwood Pellew © NATIONAL MARITIME MUSEUM, LONDON
*Centaur* hoists a gun up Diamond Rock, January 1804 © NATIONAL MARITIME MUSEUM, LONDON
The *Speedy* rescues survivors from *Queen Charlotte* off Livorno, March 1800 © NATIONAL MARITIME MUSEUM, LONDON
Cause of war: *Mercedes* explodes, October 1804 © NATIONAL MARITIME MUSEUM, LONDON
*Shannon* captures *Chesapeake,* June 1813 © NATIONAL MARITIME MUSEUM, LONDON
*Juno* escapes from Toulon, January 1794 © NATIONAL MARITIME MUSEUM, LONDON

# List of Maps

Brest, Biscay and the Western Approaches p. x
British home waters and the Baltic p. xi
Spain and the Mediterranean p. xii
North America and the West Indies p. xiii
India, Île de France and the East Indies p. xiv

# Acknowledgements

I wish to express my gratitude to David Blomfield for his kindness in reading the typescript and suggesting a number of important structural changes; to Liz Robinson for her consummate skill as an editor; to Jan Chamier for suggesting the concept, and to Tom Pocock for suggesting the author! Thanks also to Krystyna Green for her assiduous attention to all the manifold details of book production, to Max Burnell, John Groves and John Dunne for the dust jacket, to Douglas Matthews for the index and to Tony Fernades for his splendid drawing of the *Seahorse*. The debt I owe to my wife Chris remains enormous.

Richard Woodman

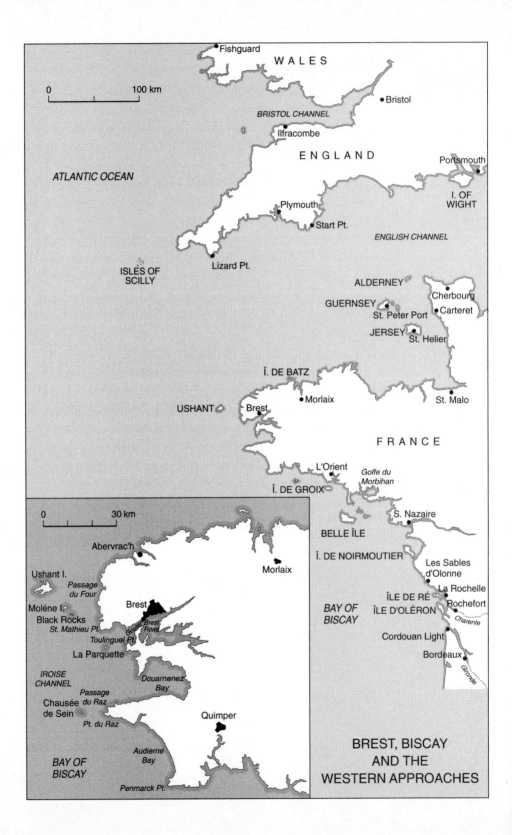

Fishguard

W A L E S

0          100 km

BRISTOL CHANNEL

Bristol

Ilfracombe

E N G L A N D

Portsmouth

ATLANTIC OCEAN

I. OF
WIGHT

Plymouth

Start Pt.

ENGLISH CHANNEL

ISLES OF
SCILLY

Lizard Pt.

ALDERNEY

Cherbourg

GUERNSEY

St. Peter Port

Carteret

JERSEY

St. Helier

Î. DE BATZ

USHANT

Brest

Morlaix

St. Malo

F R A N C E

L'Orient

Golfe du
Morbihan

Î. DE GROIX

S. Nazaire

BELLE ÎLE

Î. DE NOIRMOUTIER

Les Sables
d'Olonne

La Rochelle

ÎLE DE RÉ

Rochefort

ÎLE D'OLÉRON

Charente

BAY OF
BISCAY

Cordouan Light

Bordeaux

Gironde

0          30 km

Abervrac'h

Morlaix

Ushant I.

Passage
du Four

Moléne I.

Brest

Black Rocks

St. Mathieu Pt.

Goulet

Brest
Road

Toulinguel Pt.

La Parquette

IROISE
CHANNEL

Douarnenez
Bay

Passage
du Raz

Chausée
de Sein

Pt. du Raz

Quimper

Audierne
Bay

BAY OF
BISCAY

Penmarck Pt.

BREST, BISCAY
AND THE
WESTERN APPROACHES

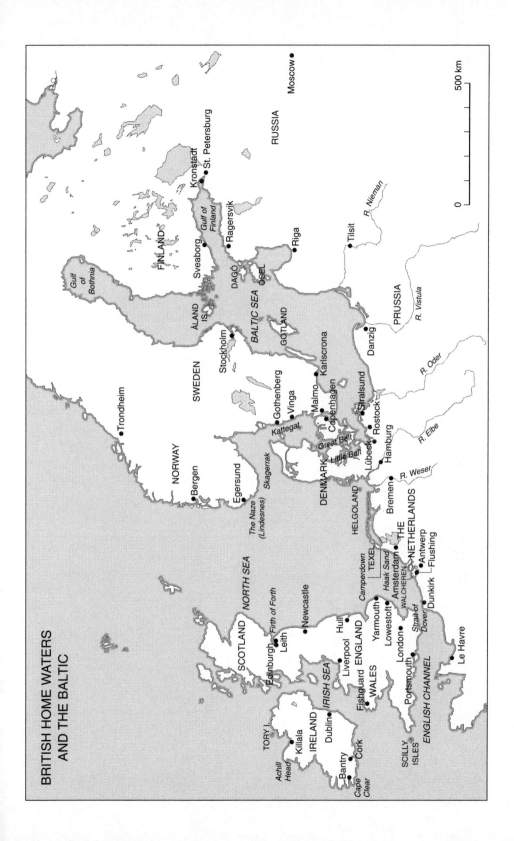

BRITISH HOME WATERS
AND THE BALTIC

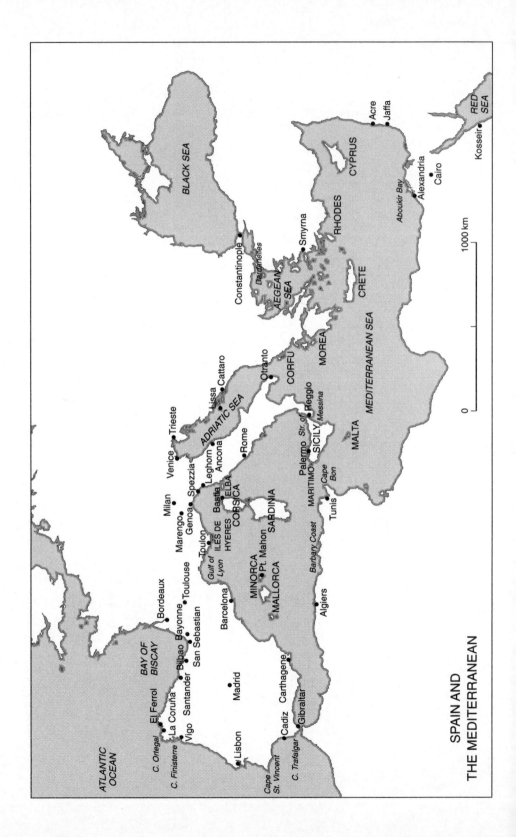

SPAIN AND
THE MEDITERRANEAN

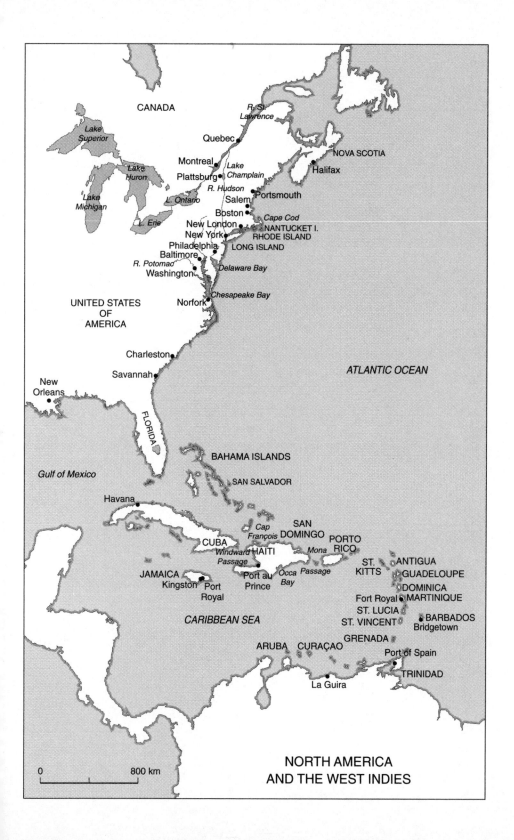

CANADA

*Lake Superior*

*Lake Huron*

*Lake Michigan*

*L. Ontario*

*L. Erie*

*R. St. Lawrence*

Quebec

Montreal

Plattsburg

*Lake Champlain*

*R. Hudson*

Salem

Portsmouth

Boston

New London

New York

Philadelphia

Baltimore

*R. Potomac*

Washington

*Cape Cod*

NANTUCKET I.

RHODE ISLAND

LONG ISLAND

*Delaware Bay*

NOVA SCOTIA

Halifax

UNITED STATES OF AMERICA

Norfork

*Chesapeake Bay*

Charleston

Savannah

New Orleans

FLORIDA

*Gulf of Mexico*

*ATLANTIC OCEAN*

BAHAMA ISLANDS

SAN SALVADOR

Havana

*Cap François*

SAN DOMINGO

CUBA

*Windward Passage*

HAITI

*Mona*

PORTO RICO

Port au Prince

*Occa Bay*

*Passage*

ST. KITTS

ANTIGUA

GUADELOUPE

DOMINICA

JAMAICA

Kingston

Port Royal

Fort Royal

MARTINIQUE

ST. LUCIA

*CARIBBEAN SEA*

ST. VINCENT

BARBADOS

Bridgetown

GRENADA

ARUBA

CURAÇAO

Port of Spain

TRINIDAD

La Guira

0          800 km

NORTH AMERICA
AND THE WEST INDIES

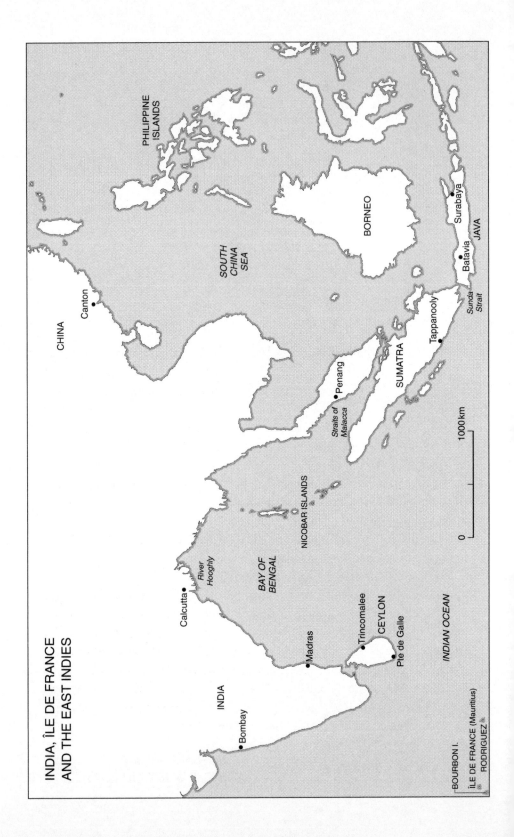

INDIA, ÎLE DE FRANCE
AND THE EAST INDIES

CHINA

Canton

PHILIPPINE
ISLANDS

SOUTH
CHINA
SEA

BORNEO

INDIA

Bombay

Calcutta

River
Hooghly

Madras

BAY OF
BENGAL

NICOBAR ISLANDS

Trincomalee

CEYLON

Pte de Galle

Penang

Straits of
Malacca

SUMATRA

Tappanooly

Surabaya

Batavia

JAVA

Sunda
Strait

INDIAN OCEAN

0          1000 km

BOURBON I.

ÎLE DE FRANCE (Mauritius)

RODRIGUEZ

# Foreword

The British Royal Navy during the Age of Nelson has proved rich in inspiration for novelists ranging from Captains Marryat and Chamier, John Davies and the mysterious 'Bill Truck', all of whom served at sea at the time, to C.S. Forester, Alexander Kent, Dudley Pope and Patrick O'Brian.

My own fascination began when, at the age of fourteen, I acquired six broken-backed volumes of William James's *The Naval History of Great Britain* from a jumble sale. They cost me my week's pocket money, the princely sum of half a crown, some twelve and a half pence. What added to my sense of excitement as I returned home with my purchase was the discovery that James's pages were uncut. I had the illusion that I was the first person to read the books.

I became fascinated by the skills and intricacies of manoeuvring ships under sail, fascinated too by the men who handled them. I also sought experience under sail myself, though I was to earn my living in more prosaically-propelled vessels. Years later, at sea in my own first command, I embarked in recording the adventures of Nathaniel Drinkwater, whose naval service is exclusively in what were then generically referred to as 'cruizers'. Notwithstanding the invention a novelist may resort to, the truth remains for me more remarkable than fiction, precisely because the pages of William James convinced me that the reality had been truly amazing.

This, then, is the story of *these* men, the real Hornblowers, Aubreys, Bolithos, Ramages and Drinkwaters. Many enjoyed lives as fantastical as their literary successors, many deserve hauling out from under the shadow of the great Nelson, while the character of most of them, one way or another, provides the answer to the question why, despite all its horrors and hardships, the British Royal Navy kept the sea and fought so magnificently for almost a quarter of a century.

Though it is set against the background of grand strategy, this book is not the history of admirals and fleets, for that would be an overview inimical to its purpose. Here the viewpoint is more intimate; here, I hope, are glimpses of men upon their own quarterdecks in pursuit of enemy men-of-war, in defence of convoys, or escaping from superior forces. Here may be found accounts of attacks on shore positions, ports, batteries and other military targets, as well as on enemy merchant shipping; in fact, on all the objectives damaging to an enemy. Nevertheless, the book only skims the surface. William James's *Naval History of Great Britain,* terse and impersonal, a mere list of incidents, requires' *six* volumes to chronicle the extraordinary extent of the Royal Navy's activities. Napoleon, exiled and reflective, was not far from the truth when he remarked that wherever there was water to float a ship, there one would find a British man-of-war. This book attempts no such global or chronological comprehensiveness; it seeks only to give the sea warriors their rightful place in history as the true exponents of naval warfare in the days of sail. Here, in short, be dragons.

Richard Woodman.

# CHAPTER 1

---

## 'Post nubila Phoebus'

On Wednesday, 2 January 1793, the small 14-gun British brig-sloop *Childers* stood into the entrance to the natural harbour of Brest on the north-west coast of France under a lowering overcast. The breeze was light and threatening to fail. Her 'master and commander', Robert Barlow, was charged with the duty of reconnoitring Brest Road to determine the state of readiness of the Atlantic squadron of the French navy based there. Upon the approach of the little *Childers*, the French batteries guarding the southern shore of Le Goulet fired a warning shot, whereupon Barlow ran up British colours, as he was bound to do. The republican tricolour was hoisted in response and two other batteries opened fire, so that shot plunged round the *Childers* as the wind died away. Barlow ordered his crew to man their sweeps, the long oars carried by small men-of-war, and by dint of effort the brig was manually pulled out of danger until a light westerly breeze filled her sails. The *Childers* then sailed past Pointe St Mathieu, out of range, as the winter night closed in.

One shot had actually hit the brig, passing through her bulwark and splitting a 4-pounder gun, but injuring no one. Recovering the ball, Barlow headed north as the wind backed and freshened. By the 3rd, the *Childers* was battling a northerly gale, tacking to windward and heading for the south coast of Cornwall. Next day she stood into Fowey, whereupon Barlow landed and, carrying the French shot, posted express

I

up to London, to make his report to the Admiralty. What until 1914 the British referred to as 'The Great War' had just begun.

Barlow's action opened the first phase of this titanic struggle with Revolutionary France, which lasted until 1802. There then followed a brief suspension of hostilities, known as the Peace of Amiens, but this ended the following year, and Britain was once more engaged in hostilities with a France transformed by the rise to imperial pretension of Napoleon Bonaparte. At best the British achievement by 1802 can only be described as a stalemate, but by the final end of the conflict in 1815 France was exhausted and in political turmoil, with her quondam emperor in exile. Britain, on the other hand, stood on the threshold of an imperial expansion which would far exceed that of Napoleonic France, while Europe and the world were to enjoy a century of relative peace under the Pax Britannica.

Although all the major European powers were involved in this long conflict, and the young United States fought Great Britain between 1812 and 1814, the outcome centred upon a direct confrontation between British sea-power and French land-power. Both the British Royal Navy and the French Grand Army produced leaders of outstanding ability. Curiously, while there are a number of English biographies of Napoleon's military commanders, there are relatively few accounts of the exploits and achievements of the British sea-officers whose abilities ultimately triumphed. Paradoxically, they are to be found instead in romanticised form, in a genre of nautical fiction popularly thought to have been established by C.S. Forester, though actually initiated by several former naval sailors. A few, like Captain Frederick Marryat, are remembered; but most, such as the able seaman known pseudonymously as Bill Truck, and Captain Chamier (who ironically enough was published in Paris), are now long forgotten. Forester's Captain Horatio Hornblower was followed by a number of sea heroes, conceived on either side of the Atlantic. Most of these novels, ancient and modern, are based on real events, for the achievements of the Royal Navy during this period provide a rich source of robust and exciting material. The novelist's hero must enjoy a succession of personal triumphs and tragedies, from which the story is fashioned, and here the novelist has the edge over the biographer in being able to cull excitement from numerous real existences, amalgamate them, and offer them to the reader as the fictional biography of his particular naval paragon. Although a real naval officer might participate in several actions, such was the size, diversity and global disposition of the British Royal Navy of the period that he was equally likely to endure decidedly un heroic *longueurs* and disappointments. But truth is stranger and often more exciting than fiction, and the neglect of the true protagonists of these exploits prompts the question why they have been supplanted by the fictional super-hero?

One possible reason is the common misperception that as far as British naval involvement was concerned, the war was as good as won when Nelson died victorious at Trafalgar in 1805. This is an oversimplified and largely erroneous view. The truth is that Trafalgar was not quite the victory of annihilation Nelson had sought; indeed, among his last remarks was an expression of regret that more enemy ships had not surrendered. The significance of Trafalgar, which can only be appreciated with the wisdom of hindsight, was that it was an empowering victory. Apart from an engagement off San Domingo in the following year, there were no further fleet actions. Thereafter, the ships of the Royal Navy fought a war of attrition against their enemies whenever and wherever they appeared, and it is in this relentless exploitation of the advantage wrested from the combined fleets of France and Spain off Cape Trafalgar that the true nature of Nelson's legacy can be found.

The men who prosecuted this long maritime campaign were generally outstanding both as seamen and as naval officers. The Royal Navy of the period was a vast and complex organisation in which brutality, disease and privation were common but, as the American naval historian Captain Mahan is so often quoted as having written, its storm-battered ships stood between the Grand Army and its domination of the world. That they were able to do so argues that the organisation behind them was superior to the populist image of a navy run on rum, sodomy and the lash.

Certainly the Royal Navy was blessed with two generations of outstanding sea warriors who collectively displayed exceptional courage.

Ruthlessly pursuing their objectives, they often found opponents worthy of their mettle, for not only the French and Spanish but the Danes, the Dutch, the Russians and the Americans learnt from the aggressive methods of their common British enemy, and many of them fought their British foe tooth and nail. If victory was what the British public came to expect, it was never a thing to put money on. British ships were occasionally fought to a standstill, and not only by the young United States Navy, although the impact upon British public opinion of the American frigate victories was profound. Several gallant enemy commanders whose fates brought them into action against the Royal Navy have their place in the story; however inevitably the British sea warriors bestride the naval history of the period.

But how did it all begin, this Great War? Why was Commander Robert Barlow, in his almost insignificant little brig-sloop, poking about in the approaches to the great French naval arsenal of Brest at the beginning of January 1793?

Barlow had been sent to Brest because of the rapidly deteriorating political situation in Europe. Despite the endeavours of William Pitt's government to remain aloof from the revolution in France so that the British economy might recover from the late wars with most of Europe over the issue of American independence, the matter was intruding into British domestic affairs. Rival factions both for and against the rising tide of revolutionary republicanism were increasingly vocal in London, and these concerned a government worrying over the failure of the harvest after a sodden summer. Still more disturbing, however, was the fact that in the winter of 1792 the French revolutionary government began to export their ideology, annexing Savoy and invading the Rhineland and the southern Netherlands, at the time an Austrian possession. The Declaration of Pillnitz a year earlier, in which the continental European monarchs had pledged themselves to the restoration of Louis XVI to his throne, had precipitated the French revolutionaries to take the offensive before a combination of their declared enemies could prevail against them. In this unstable situation, Barlow had been ordered to determine the state of the nearest and most powerful French fleet.

In January 1793 the British government was nervous, not so much about the ideological battle then breaking over the crowned heads of Europe, but because of its own state of readiness. Britain had acquired Canada and India at the end of the Seven Years' War in 1763, and the rebellion of the British colonists in North America had encouraged the retributive malice of France and Spain. In 1779 an enormous enemy fleet had entered the Channel and caused a real invasion scare. The British fleet had been hard-pressed and overstretched, trying to protect vital overseas trade and at loggerheads both with the French and Spanish and with the Dutch and the Armed Neutrality of the combined Baltic states; the saving grace had been French and Spanish ineptitude in the matter of keeping scurvy at bay.

The Royal Navy of the day was not the instrument it was to become in the greater war now looming. It was riddled with corruption and jobbery, slack in its pursuance of its objectives, and rarely had sufficient ships in commission to accomplish its objectives. But, and it is a formidable but, despite the shortcomings of its administration during and after the American War, it had learned how to maintain a fleet at sea without being immobilised by scurvy; it had coppered the bottoms of all its ships to keep out the ship-worm; and it was introducing a number of technological innovations which were to give it a considerable advantage over its opponents. Also, in enduring a period of the most profound adversity in the hopeless struggle against the independence of the United States of America, the Royal Navy had nurtured the first generation of the sea warriors it was to deploy in the far more vital struggle against France and her allies after 1793. Among them was Nelson, already a junior captain.

These young firebrands had mostly languished unemployed on half-pay during the years of peace, but at the outbreak of the French Revolution in 1789 they began to petition the Admiralty in droves for appointments to ships. Long before the politicians were willing to admit it, they sensed that another rupture with the old enemy was inevitable.

Mercifully, not only were the officers ready for war: so, unusually, was the fleet. This was in part due to a series of crises quite unconnected with France which had arisen in the previous few years. Chief of these was the 'Spanish Armament' of 1790, a partial mobilisation of the navy resulting from the territorial claims of the Spanish over the whole Pacific coast of North America. Although war had been avoided, preparations for this and two other similar 'armaments' generated by disagreements with the Dutch and Russians had ensured that the navy was in a better state than was customary at the commencement of hostilities. The scandalous naval administration during the American War had prompted some few reforming measures, and the head of the Navy Board responsible for the material state of the ships was an outstanding officer. Dedicated and innovative, Sir Charles Middleton enters our story as Comptroller of the Navy, to leave it later as Lord Barham, First Lord of the Admiralty during the campaign of Trafalgar. The speed of full mobilisation was largely due to his energetic response to the deterioration of international affairs.

A week before Their Lordships at the Admiralty (the officers and politicians charged with the political direction of the Royal Navy) sent Barlow his orders to sail from Plymouth for Brest, Middleton had had the artificers at the Royal Dockyards working 'double-tides'. Thus, in December 1792, as the government called out the militia for duty, the Royal Navy's line-of-battle ships, frigates and lesser men-of-war were readied for service, and Captain Nelson wrote jubilantly to his wife: '*Post Nubila Phoebus*... after the clouds comes sunshine... The Admiralty so smile upon me... that if I chose to take a sixty-four [gun ship] to begin with I should be appointed to one as soon as she was ready.' After Barlow's report had been received at the Admiralty, matters moved at a hotter pace. To a letter of 7 January, Nelson added three breathless sentences: 'Everything looks War. One of our ships looking into Brest has been fired into. The shot is now at the Admiralty.'

Then, on 21 January, King Louis XVI was guillotined and the French government declared war upon Great Britain, Spain and the United Provinces of the Dutch Netherlands. Paris ordered the mobilisation of thirty sail of the line and twenty frigates; in London, the French ambassador was asked to leave the country.

It was not so much the execution of King Louis that so alarmed the British as the French occupation of Brussels and Antwerp and the revoking of old guarantees about navigation on the Schelde, the river that was said to 'point a pistol at London'. The prospect of commercial strangulation, of the blockade of the Thames, up which an annual trade worth £60 millions flowed, spelled the ruin of all hopes of British economic revival. Indeed, it threatened Britain's national survival.

The British merchant marine was about three times larger than that of France, and therefore proportionately more vulnerable. The British economy relied heavily upon imports and exports of ever-increasing manufactures, and most of this trade was carried in British 'bottoms'; moreover, the British government relied upon the duties raised by this trade. The whole enterprise was exposed to the abilities of the French as commerce raiders, a form of warfare in which they excelled. Protection of trade against this *guerre de course* was just one of the duties in which the rapidly commissioning ships of the Royal Navy had to be deployed.

The war against British trade, often marginalised by historians, was to prove relentless, detached from the movements of the principal fleets. It did not in fact peak until after the strategic watershed of Trafalgar in 1805, and is one reason why the sea warriors of the Napoleonic War had perforce to maintain their exertions throughout the decade that succeeded Nelson's great victory.

Broadly the task of the Royal Navy was five-fold. First and foremost, it had to guard against invasion, and for that purpose the prime 'Western Squadron', better known to history as the Channel Fleet, was maintained in the 'Chops' of the Channel, usually off Brest or in the anchorage of Tor Bay. It thus accomplished a dual purpose, for the Royal Navy's second task was blockade: wherever an enemy fleet existed, it had to maintain at least a watching presence, to give early warning of any fleet movements so that they could be contained and, if possible, defeated. Brest was the principal naval arsenal of the French in the north, but Toulon on the Mediterranean coast was equally important, as were the lesser French naval bases on the Atlantic at La Rochelle and L'Orient. As the war escalated and the French began their domination of the Continent, other ports also required blockade.

After 1805 and the escalation of the economic war, the aim was not only to utterly deny the enemy's naval fleets access to the sea, but to strangle the maritime trade of the French Empire. The Royal Navy had to blockade almost every port between the Baltic and Constantinople, though it was the major naval ports of France and her Allies which comprised the first obligation of the blockading squadrons. These were composed of line-of-battle ships, mostly 74-gun 'third-rates', supported by frigates and lesser vessels. Overall command of a blockading squadron was vested in an admiral who might have subordinate admirals under his command or on local detachment, blockading an adjacent port. By and large we shall leave these distant, storm-battered ships to their vigil. As line-of-battle ships they were the commands of senior post-captains who had already seen many years of service and did not much object to the predictable if harsh monotony of their duty.

The British Navy's third responsibility was irksome, unpopular and tedious, but also vital: it had to provide cover, in the form of convoy escort, to literally thousands of British merchantmen and the vessels of foreign merchants carrying cargoes to and from Britain. It was irksome and tedious because it tied the hands of the young cruiser-commanders to whom it was entrusted. Unlike the senior officers commanding ships on blockade, these younger men hankered after greater freedom of action, offering the possibility of advancement, fame and fortune and it was often necessary to impress upon them the importance of convoy protection. One actually left his convoy behind, arguing that it could not keep up with his flash frigate. As an inducement, in 1803 the consortium of ship-owners, merchants and underwriters who made up Lloyd's of London established a Patriotic Fund from which *douceurs* were paid to deserving officers. Captains who defended their convoys with spirit might receive cash grants, or suitably inscribed presentation swords. But lack of opportunity was not the only drawback to trade protection. Often the independent-minded masters of the convoyed merchant ships were difficult to control, while the disparate sailing speeds of laden merchantmen usually added another dimension to the escort commander's miseries. As the convoy approached its destination, masters of fast ships would detach in the hope of reaching port first

8

and scooping the market with their cargo – and it was here, whether in the English Channel or off the mouth of the Hooghly River near Calcutta, that the French corsairs lay in wait.

If officers disliked convoy escort, they eagerly sought an independent cruise. This, the fourth function of the Royal Navy, was intended to maintain a presence wherever British influence was required, covering the trade routes and simultaneously discouraging the passage of enemy naval or merchant vessels. Whenever and wherever such ships appeared, they had to be captured or destroyed; capture, from which prize money or head money might be derived, was preferable. The importance of prize money as an incentive is a subject we shall return to, but for now it is only necessary to emphasise that an ambitious officer sent on a cruise stood to make both his fortune and his reputation if it proved successful.

Finally, the fifth principal task of the men-of-war of His Britannic Majesty's fleet was to supply ships and support to detachments of the army sent on foreign expeditions. These combined operations were real extensions of British sea-power, and upon occasion they went wrong. They did, however, greatly increase the potence of the navy, providing bases in overseas possessions. The extent to which this had become necessary is illustrated by events in South Africa. At the beginning of the war in 1793, the Cape of Good Hope was a Dutch colony. The Dutch, soon to embrace the revolutionary creed and become the Batavian Republic, denied the British the traditional staging post of Table Bay for their East Indiamen *en route* to India and China. In 1795 an operation was therefore mounted to take the Cape, but in the peace settlement of 1802 it was returned to the Dutch. When war broke out again fourteen months later, in May 1803, the British were obliged to repeat the process.

Between 1808 and 1814, with an Anglo-Portuguese army in Spain, supply and support by sea became vital. British involvement on the Peninsula began disastrously with the withdrawal from Coruña in January 1809, but this withdrawal was only achieved by sea power, and it was sea power which made it possible for the strategy to be repeated under the future Duke of Wellington and enabled him to make his final advance across Spain and into south-western France in 1814.

Trade protection and defence, independent missions and minor combined operations were largely the province of a variety of craft smaller than the line-of-battle ship, all of which were referred to indiscriminately as cruisers. This class was a broad one, comprising ship-rigged vessels mounting on their gun decks an establishment of between 28 and 44 guns. Frigates were officially the fifth and sixth rates on the naval establishment, all vessels mounting more than 50 guns being considered line-of-battle ships and comprising the first four rates. There was a smaller class of vessel included in the sixth-rate, the 20- and 24-gun ship-rigged sloop. These were known as 'post-ships' and were the smallest men-of-war that rated as a post-captain's command, more of which later. The true frigates of the fifth and sixth rates carried their main armament on a single gun deck, and accommodated their companies in a berth deck below. This not only gave their crews a marginally more comfortable life than living on the gun-decks did, but also gave the gun-deck a freeboard suitable for action in most sea-states short of strong gales and storms. Frigates were capable of extended cruises in distant waters and were largely self-sufficient for many months, even years. If the captain could lay in stocks of wood and water from natural sources, all he needed was to top up his consumable stores, powder and ball from a foreign base, or from his captures.

Below these 'rated' ships, came a whole host of smaller sloops mounting from 14 to 18 main-deck guns. These were the commands of officers known until 1794 as 'master and commander' – as was Barlow. This became plain 'commander' when they were supported by a warrant navigating officer, known as the 'second master'.

To these sloops, which were much employed upon convoy escort, must be added two other classes of vessel also used as convoy escorts. The first was the bomb-vessel, a small, very solidly built ship-rigged craft. Although designed specifically for mounting heavy mortars to bombard static targets ashore, the deployment of mortars was not common and required the shipping of gunnery specialists. Until required for such tasks, these vessels worked with convoys, usually somewhat ineffectively, for they were slow sailers and their failure to intercept privateers was notorious. The other class of purpose-built ship commonly used as an escort was the fireship.

Below the bomb vessel and fireship came yet more small vessels, usually commanded by lieutenants, most of whom were ageing men who could expect little further promotion. The small, shallow draughted gun-brig of 10 to 14 guns was the unglamorous end of the road for many a lieutenant-in-command, 'tarpaulin captains' bound on tedious convoy escort amid the tides and fogs of the North Sea and the English Channel.

The organisation of a naval ship's company was complex. Broadly, however, the command structure was the same for all men-of-war. Below the captain – a warship's commander was always her 'captain' to those on board, irrespective of his actual substantive rank – were a number of commissioned lieutenants and, except in the smallest vessels, a few Royal Marine officers. Realistically, only the lieutenants were in the running for promotion, with the aspiring young gentlemen in the midshipmen's quarters providing the next candidates.

The internal organisation of the ship required a group of specialist warrant officers and these included the master, sometimes referred to as the sailing-master, a specialist not only in navigation but in stowage and ship maintenance, skills usually deriving from service in merchant ships. Like all the warrant officers he was assisted by mates, who might be able-seamen working their way up to master, but might equally be midshipmen who had passed their lieutenant's examinations and were waiting to receive commissions. While the master might be considered respectable enough to walk the quarterdeck and qualified to remonstrate with the captain within strict limits, in the hierarchy of Georgian society he was not a gentleman. Although his responsibilities made him a highly-paid member of the ship's company, he had usually reached the end of the line. A master was only rarely commissioned lieutenant; most did not want it, enjoying both their respectable status and the better pay that went with it. There were, as we shall see, significant exceptions.

Other specialist warrant officers considered respectable enough to consort with the commissioned officers included the surgeon and the purser, the latter being the ship's store-keeper. All were appointees of the Navy Board, not the Admiralty, and had to provide qualifications or sureties against their professional conduct. The master had to produce evidence of navigational competence found by examination before the Board of Trinity House, the surgeon evidence of his skill and knowledge by certification at Surgeon's Hall, and the purser had to put up a considerable cash bond against his good book-keeping, the amount depending upon the rate of ship. The remaining warrant officers in-cluded the gunner, who acted as a sea-daddy to the midshipmen, the carpenter, the boatswain, and the cook.

Administratively, all persons on board were appointed to a division, each of which was headed by a lieutenant, and this related to where they messed and slept. Thus, beneath the captain the command and control of the vessel spread outwards and downwards, through the commissioned and warrant officers, by way of the petty officers, the yeomen, leading hands and able-seamen, to the ordinary seamen, the landsmen (the most nautically ignorant) and the boys. These last, like a few of the midshipmen, would literally be children, assigned to duties as servants. To a few of the feeblest of the men, victims of congenital disorders perhaps, would go the most menial tasks: cleaning the ship's latrines or heads, or mucking out any livestock.

There is plenty of evidence of cruelty and unpleasantness on board ship, of inhumane treatment of ordinary seamen, and of a snobbishness we should find intolerable and unacceptable today. The age, for all its superficial gentility and growing intellectual rationality, remained a brutal one. War was almost the norm for the whole of the eighteenth century, while disease was rampant in all strata of society; men and women lived close to death throughout their lives, and existence itself was a matter of hazard.

The ordinary seaman was usually picked up by the press gang. He was required solely for his brawn, and if he survived he would probably end his service with at least a rupture: more than 40,000 trusses were issued to seamen during this period. Some men, however, actually volunteered for naval service, and brought with them valuable experience. These sailors were the better-paid merchant seamen who knew that impressment would be their lot sooner or later. In time of war they preferred to accept the inevitable and take the cash bounty that went with volunteering, rather than suffer the cruel indignities of impressment.

Seamen's wages were usually month in arrears. In 1760 their Lordships at the Admiralty had been driven to the expedient of erecting the screen wall which still stands in front of the Admiralty in London, to keep at bay seamen rioting for their overdue money. Occasionally the Admiralty avoided payment of any wages at all at the conclusion of a ship's commission; the most extreme example of this is that of the *Fox*. During the Napoleonic War this frigate saw service in the Red Sea, Indian Ocean and East Indies; she was in commission for fifteen years at the conclusion of which not one penny was paid to her crew.

Stoppages were taken out of a seaman's pay for goods purchased on board from the ship, and compulsory deductions were made for medical treatment of venereal infections. Since a seaman might not be allowed shore leave for fear he would desert, whores brought on board by pimps were the only women he could resort to. It is not surprising that some men turned to their fellows for sexual comfort, even though the sentence for any detected 'detestable act' of homosexual intercourse was death.

This situation worsened as the war progressed, for these professional seamen were a finite resource and the increasing demands for manpower drove the government to desperate measures. The Quota Acts of 1795 required men to be found by every county and it was these who were usually rated as landsmen. Many were misfits and bad hats plucked by the magistrates from the county gaols, and their recruitment added nothing to the quality of life in the dank misery between decks in one of His Britannic Majesty's ships of war. During his time at sea a man would probably be affected at some time or another by scurvy. He was more likely to die of disease, probably yellow fever, or to sustain a fatal injury on board than to be killed in action. Alternatively, he might go mad, either from drink or from profound psychological disturbance; to its credit, in addition to its own hospital at Haslar the Royal Navy maintained a ward for the insane at Hoxton Hospital in London.

With such a disparate collection of humanity kept for months in the confinement of a cruising frigate, about 260 men in each ship, it is scarcely surprising that a savage discipline had to be maintained. The only means of so doing was by means of the lash, and although this was used regularly, in itself it seems not to have been greatly resented by the generality of those seamen untouched by it. This is no extenuation of the effect it had upon its victims: a man lashed was usually a man broken. What is perhaps surprising is that men so severely constrained could work and fight their ships, and do so magnificently. Perhaps the explanation is to be found in the observation of the Lord High Admiral of England responsible for the defeat of the Spanish Armada two centuries earlier: 'A portion of madness,' Lord Howard of Effingham wrote, 'is a necessary ingredient in the character of an English seaman'. Certainly action provided the effectively cathartic outlet that pent-up frustrations sought.

So much for the men; but what of the officers, who though materially and physically better off in many ways still endured privations, psychological disturbances, and all the risks attached to a life at sea? And most of all, what of the commanders in whose hands rested the responsibility for the conduct of individual ships and for the furtherance of British naval policy? Was a portion of madness necessary to them, too?

The captain who set his stamp upon this closely interlocking mass of humanity determined not only the style in which the ship was managed but the reputation she acquired. His existence was remote and often lonely, narrowly circumscribed by usage and custom, privilege and precedent. He had achieved his position by a variety of routes, chief of which was usually preferment by means of patronage or 'interest'. A full post-captain in 1793 would have entered the navy as a captain's servant, a device by which the over-generous number of servants allowed on the establishment of a man-of-war was taken up by young aspirants. After the reforms of 1794, when the number of established servants was reduced, he would enter as a volunteer before being accepted as an extra or a rated midshipman. These youngsters were usually sons, nephews or other relations of the captain, or of friends or acquaintances to whom the captain owed an obligation or from whom he expected a favour.

When a 'young gentleman' proved his worth he would be rated midshipman or sometimes, as a paper device, able-seaman, which was usually to conceal his youth. Such youngsters then had to serve six years, reach the age of twenty, (later reduced to nineteen), and pass the examination for lieutenant, which was sometimes either waived or farcical, particularly if a relative or patron was on the board of examiners. Nor was this the worst fiddle in the desperate matter of promotion. Very frequently young gentlemen in their infancy were entered on the books of a ship, to start accruing sea-time. When Lord Cochrane was still a boy, his father bought him a commission in the 104th Regiment of Foot while his uncle entered him successively on the books of the *Vesuvius, Carolina, La Sophie* and *Hind*. Such practices were common among the well-to-do. Similarly, the regulation age for promotion to lieutenant was frequently and flagrantly fudged or circumvented, though assiduously conformed with on paper. Bogus certificates attesting to age were easily come by for a shilling, and the examiners always protected themselves by affirming that a candidate *appeared* to be of the requisite age. Nelson himself was a lieutenant at the age of eighteen, a commander at twenty and a post-captain at twenty-one. While he subsequently justified this rapid promotion, his stepson, Josiah Nisbet, did not. This young man, a lieutenant at sixteen, a commander at seventeen and a post-captain at eighteen, was entirely unworthy, and an unmitigated disaster.

The world then winked at such dishonesties, regarding them as trivial; it was felt that a young gentleman of blood and mettle *should* be promoted. Moreover, although the system depended upon the opinions not only of naval officers but of politicians and others influential in the workings of government, and although it produced some poor officers, the majority carried out their duties ably enough. That said, many very able men never made the next vital step, however. The rigid workings of Georgian society were such that neither ability nor money *guaranteed* promotion, whereas social connections almost invariably did. Of course Their Lordships could, and often did, retain an incompetent officer ashore on half pay, but this did nothing to ameliorate the plight of the deserving but neglected officer who failed to rise through lack of interest. Paradoxically, money alone could not buy a career. One officer, a 'son of a man of large fortune, but obscure family' failed to rise because the large fortune had been gained in trade – an odd comment on a nation which Napoleon ridiculed as composed of shop-keepers! It is the exceptions that prove the rule, however, and there were occasional promotions based solely upon ability. A few men rose from the ranks, usually by attracting the notice of captains who had themselves acquired power and influence. Such an outsider was William Elliott, who entered the navy in 1795 as a purser's assistant and, by dint of distinguishing himself in action several times, gained a commission as lieutenant in 1802. He was made commander in 1809 and post-captain in 1810, when he was still only twenty-eight. Elliott died a Companion of the Bath and a knight of a Portuguese order.

In addition to patronage, one might therefore achieve promotion through an act of extreme gallantry in action. The first lieutenants of all the ships in a victorious fleet action could expect advancement to commander. But this was merely a half-way house. Only when an officer reached the rank of post-captain could he relax. Being 'made post' meant commanding a rated ship, a post ship or a frigate, and for three years transferring the single epaulette to the right shoulder. At the expiry of this period an officer shipped an epaulette on both shoulders, and could in due course expect command of a ship-of-the-line.

Once achieved, the rank of post-captain meant the officer had joined an inviolable queue which, if he lived long enough, would carry him up the list of post-captains until he was given his flag as a rear-admiral. But more than professional security came with this almost mystical elevation. With post-rank came a host of perquisites, and the power to dispense patronage and interest. A post-captain was a made man, an eligible parti if he was not already married, and if he was, endowing his wife with more than his mere surname. He was worth cultivating by the politicians and the squirearchy in his county, wealthy enough to acquire a small estate of his own were he not an elder son of land-owning gentry. Since a significant proportion of post-captains came from the unlanded professional classes, such a purchase was doubly significant. If he wished it, a post-captain was also a potential candidate for a seat on his local bench as a magistrate, or for political preferment.

In the eighteenth century it was perfectly possible for a serving naval officer to be a Member of Parliament. Sometimes, particularly if he supported the party in opposition, he would miss a parliamentary session by being sent to sea; on the other hand, if the government had need of him and his ship was in commission, a temporary 'job captain' would be put in his place. Such politicking had its advantages and its disadvantages. Occasionally his first lieutenant was appointed to act for him and might, if he were lucky, be able to capitalise on any opportunity which offered during his tenure.

At sea, if free of the close control of an admiral or senior captain, the port-captain was on his own, at liberty to conduct his ship according to the spirit and letter of his orders by means of his own initiative and interpretation. Sometimes that interpretation could be pretty wide, but he must always be mindful of the strictures Their Lordships laid upon him. In the small ceremony of taking command, a captain was received at the ship's side with the due pomp of a marine guard and a side-party. He was piped aboard and his officers doffed their hats. He doffed his, not in response to their salute, but to the quarterdeck above which the ensign flew, a symbol of his own subordination to the Crown and State whose commission he held, and which he now read aloud to his assembled crew. He was charged to conduct affairs in accordance with the Articles of War, and to do his utmost against the enemy. Should he fail, should he lose his nerve or lose his ship, he and his ship's company, the circumstances notwithstanding, would be called to account.

# CHAPTER 2

--------

# 'We dished her up in fifty minutes'

In June 1792, the Admiralty had ordered all frigates and guardships based in British waters to Spithead; the following month exercises had been held in the Channel under Lord Hood before the ships were dispersed to their stations again. At the outbreak of war a fleet of twenty-five ships-of-the-line and almost fifty frigates were in commission and all available vessels were sent out for a short period to 'cruise against the enemy'. Thereafer, this number steadily rose. Great Britain's first line of defence was the Southern North Sea, the Strait of Dover and the English Channel and these areas were soon 'full of frigates', with Rear-Admiral McBride commanding in The Downs having the management of them. Pending more permanent arrangements, this was a fast response to the changing situation, designed to intimidate French aggression. Orders in Council prevented any merchant ships from sailing, partly to prevent them falling into the hands of the enemy but mainly to prevent their crews escaping the hot-press that was out to man the Royal Navy's men-of-war. By March convoy escorts were available for the coasting trades and the herring fishery, while other frigates sailed to warn homeward-bound merchantmen that a state of war existed, and to emphasise the fact by poaching prime seamen out of them.

On the far side of the Channel it was a rather different story. On the military front the French Republic had capitalised on disagreements between the Allied powers, raised ragged but fervent levies, and gained her first victories. The Republic's navy was a different matter. For a start, it had formerly been officered by aristocrats, the *officiers rouges* of the upper echelons of command, and these had either emigrated or been guillotined. Lower ranks were filled with *officiers bleus*, men from the maritime community who now had to assume higher posts and strive to generate activity in the dockyards. Here they had to turn rabid ideological debate into more practical channels, flying in the face of revolutionary ideals which took republicanism to extremes. One instance of this was the abolition of a competent corps of seamen-gunners on the grounds of élitism. Every revolutionary should have the right to man artillery, it was argued, training being of no apparent account.

However, a degree of order was emerging, sufficient to despatch Contre-Amiral Sercey to the West Indies with a squadron consisting of four ships-of-the-line and frigates, while Vice-Amiral Morard de Galles assembled a major fleet of seventeen 120-, 110-, 80- and 74-gun ships and four frigates for service off the Breton coast. Other frigates, many of the fine 40-gun classes which we shall encounter later, were also preparing or were already at sea. Either singly or in small squadrons, joining the corsairs of St Malo, Nantes and Bordeaux, they went in quest of homeward-bound British merchantmen. In response the British sent out their own frigates, sometimes in small 'flying' squadrons, sometimes singly or in pairs.

It was not long before these opposing cruisers ran into one another.

As dawn broke over the coast of Devon on 18 June 1793, His Britannic Majesty's 36-gun frigate *Nymphe* hove in sight of a strange sail to the eastward. The British cruiser was a French-built ship taken in the American War. She had recently been recommissioned and was on her second cruise, having sailed the previous day from Plymouth. She was almost entirely manned by landsmen, including eighty Cornish tin-miners, though *Nymphe*'s captain had also taken the crew out of a merchant-man and placed her mate, a Mr Gaze, upon his own quarterdeck. Additional prime seamen had been pressed out of other merchantmen in the Channel during her first short cruise the month before.

Daybreak on 18 June found *Nymphe* sixteen miles south of Prawle Point. As the stars faded in the eastern sky, the strange vessel was identified as a French national frigate. *Nymphe's* captain ordered his men to make sail in chase of her.

His name was Edward Pellew.

Edward Pellew was already a distinguished sea-officer with a reputation for dash and courage. In the new war he was to acquire a name as a practical seaman far surpassing Nelson's own, and he was outstanding as a cruiser captain. Pellew had been born in Cornwall in 1757, and went to sea in the frigate *Juno* in 1770. Rated a captain's servant to Captain John Stott, he had served on an expedition to the Falkland Islands. He followed Stott to the 32-gun frigate *Alarm* in August, to be rated master's mate in November 1772. He left the *Alarm* after three years' service and in January 1776 joined the *Blonde*, 36, then on her way to Canada. The British American colonists were in revolt against the Crown.

Soon after the frigate's arrival in Canada, Pellew volunteered for detached service on Lake Champlain. He joined the schooner *Carleton,* armed with a dozen 6-pounder guns and commanded by a Lieutenant Dacres; Pellew was third in command. In October 1776 the British vessels on the lake fought a fierce action off Valcour Island against a rebel squadron under Benedict Arnold. The *Carleton* was in an advanced position and Lieutenant Dacres and his second-in-command were soon wounded. Nineteen-year-old Pellew took over, exposing himself in an attempt to set a jib and withdraw according to a signal to retire. For some minutes, as he extricated the *Carleton*, young Pellew was the conspicuous target for the combined gunfire of the enemy. He displayed a contempt for danger which was not foolhardiness but a cool detachment, and it was to form a conspicuous part of his character as a sea warrior in the years to come.

When 'Gentlemen Johnny' Burgoyne began his ill-fated expedition south from Canada in the following year, Pellew commanded a detachment of seamen acting as pioneers. As the only naval man in Burgoyne's force, it fell to Pellew to build the bridge of boats by which the British army passed over the Hudson River to meet General Gates's rebel force at Saratoga. In doing so he only narrowly avoided drowning on several occasions. It was a measure of his growing reputation that it was the obscure Edward Pellew whom Gentleman Johnny sent home the following year with news of their defeat, releasing him from the tedium of paroled restriction under open confinement in the back-country.

On Pellew's return to England he was commissioned, and appointed to the frigate *Licorne*, a captured French man-of-war, in which he cruised in the Channel until transferred into the 32-gun *Apollo* in March 1780. In June Pellew was first lieutenant of the *Apollo* when she engaged the French frigate *Stanislaus* in the southern North Sea. One finds it difficult not to believe Pellew was a darling of fate, for his captain was killed in the action as the two ships approached Ostend, and Pellew took command. As the frigates approached the port, the *Stanislaus* ran aground. Anchoring with the intention of completing the destruction of the *Stanislaus*, Pellew was warned off by shots from the shore batteries, signals of neutral protection being afforded to the distressed French vessel. Pellew was obliged to break off the action and turn for home, but the exploit earned him promotion to Master and Commander on his arrival three days later. He was made post-captain on 20 May 1782 and later given the crack frigate *Artois*, in which he saw out the war until the peace in January 1783.

In the space of a few short years Pellew had made his mark on the world, rising from an obscure nonentity involved with the most notorious British defeat of his generation, to a post-captain with a reputation as a fine seaman. Though he had no pretensions to good looks – he bore the scars of infantile smallpox – he was nevertheless physically imposing, tall and well built. Immensely popular with his crews for his unorthodoxy, he was as fearless in action as at sea and thought nothing of going aloft with the men and laying out on a yard to take in sail or, even as post-captain, of standing a four-hour trick at the wheel. Indeed, he revelled in these energetic pursuits, and such was his reputation that in later years he rarely had trouble manning his ship from his native Cornwall.

Pellew married in May 1783, as hostilities ended, and became a magistrate. He might have settled down to a life of comparative ease on his farm, but that was not Pellew's way, even in peacetime. His brother

Samuel was the Collector of Customs at the Cornish port of Falmouth, and Pellew took command of the local revenue lugger and continued his pursuit of the misguided individuals who sought to evade King George's taxes by free trading in dutiable goods. Nor did the Admiralty neglect him, appointing him to command the 32-gun *Winchelsea* in April 1786, and sending him across the Atlantic to join the squadron of Commodore Eliot at St John's, Newfoundland. Arriving in a calm, he warped his ship into port, sliding down a hawser himself to shift it from one holdfast to another. These apparent breaches of social and naval etiquette on the part of a post-captain notwithstanding, Pellew ran his ship with the strict but fair hand of a martinet. The instant obedience required of every officer and man enabled Pellew to handle his ship with the consummate skill of a master. In this, time was only to improve him.

In January 1789 *Winchelsea* was paid off and Pellew accepted an appointment in the 50-gun *Salisbury* as flag-captain to Admiral Milbanke, back on the Newfoundland station. Here he remained until the *Salisbury* returned home and paid off on 14 November 1791. Had Pitt achieved his fifteen years of peace and quiet, we might have heard nothing more of Captain Edward Pellew beyond an occasional reference to him among the justices of the Duchy of Cornwall.

It can scarcely be imagined that so active a man would have been entirely content on his farm at Treverry. 'In every undertaking by sea or land, his whole mind was in it,' an admirer wrote and as the political world beyond the Cornish sessions beckoned, this concentration was now applied to getting a new ship. His frantic petitions to the Admiralty in the winter of 1792 yielded appointment to the *Nymphe*, and he took command of her on 11 January 1793.

As he strove eagerly to get his ship fit for service and out to sea, Pellew would have heard how a British squadron on passage to the Mediterranean had chased and captured a corsair and her Spanish prize, the *San Iago*. The corsair, *Général Dumourier*, had transhipped a portion of the register ship's cargo, and the whole amounted to over £300,000. The leading frigate in the squadron was *Phaeton*, commanded by Captain Sir Andrew Snape Douglas.

Such news could only stir Pellew's cupidity.

There were strong inducements to British cruiser commanders, beyond the charge of their commissions, to exert themselves to the utmost. The acquisition of a fortune in prize-money, though not common, was by no means impossible. Occasionally truly huge sums of money were made, and this acted as a spur to many officers. A captured warship would in all likelihood be purchased into the Royal Navy, providing a goodly sum to her captor, and an even greater sum could be obtained from a merchant ship. Once 'condemned' by a Prize Court as a legitimate prize of war, her cargo, when sold on the open market, might yield a bonanza. However, this system had its drawbacks: there was a temptation to linger in search of prizes when more pressing naval matters required attention. Yet even a frustrated admiral could not be too angry with a fortune-seeking frigate captain, for if the young man were successful the admiral took one of his three one-eighth shares. Only captains sailing under Admiralty orders, free of an admiral's interference, kept all three-eighths. The remaining five-eighths were distributed among the crew on a sliding scale which benefited rank and station. These proportions were revised in 1808 to become slightly more equitable, but a ship's company might have to share its gains with another vessel in addition to a distant admiral. If one or more other ships-of-war were in sight when the prize was taken, they too were entitled to a split of the loot, even if the other warships were not in action, for it was held that their presence alone might have influenced the decision of the enemy to capitulate.

To induce captains and ship's companies to press efforts against enemy warships, irrespective of whether the ships were to be purchased into the British service or not, a bonus of 'head-money' was paid, based upon the number of crew the enemy ship had at the time of capture. An acquisitive as well as a courageous officer, Edward Pellew was well aware of all of these factors as he bore down upon the enemy frigate, *La Cléopâtre,* off Prawle Point that June morning.

*Nymphe* was not noted for her dash; nevertheless, with Pellew coaxing her, she began to gain ground on her quarry after about an hour, despite the fact that *La Cléopâtre* was also carrying a press of canvas. Seeing he was being overhauled Capitaine Mullon, an able and experienced officer who had served in the Indian Ocean under the great French admiral de Suffren, clewed up his fore course and doused his topgallants, a signal that he was prepared to accept battle under his topsails, as was customary. At about six in the morning *Nymphe* bore down towards *La Cléopâtre*, the two ships running on roughly parallel courses, the British ship coming up on the French frigate's starboard quarter. Both were cleared for action, their gun decks stripped of the furnishings and bulkheads of the captain's quarters aft, and Pellew reduced sail to match that of his enemy. He had just enough skilled seamen to manoeuvre *Nymphe*, but relied confidently upon the fighting ability of his inexperienced landsmen.

The guns of both ships remained silent as Mullon stepped up on his rail and removed his cap to hail the approaching British ship. Pellew waved his own hat and responded with a shout, whereupon his ship's company cheered. Mullon called out *'Vive la nation!'* and threw his cap of liberty to one of the seamen, who promptly ran to the mainmasthead and secured it there as the French crew bellowed their encouragement.

Half of *Nymphe*'s larboard broadside guns now bore on the enemy frigate, and Pellew replaced his hat with solemn deliberation. Waiting and watching for this signal was the captain's brother, Commander Israel Pellew. He had yet to be appointed to a ship and had volunteered to serve with Edward until such time as the Admiralty should find him one. Taking charge of the after guns as a supernumerary lieutenant, Israel immediately opened fire. *Nymphe*'s main deck broadside of eighteen 12-pounders, her one forecastle 6-pounder chase gun and her four short-range but heavy 24-pounder carronades belched fire and iron against her enemy. *La Cléopâtre*'s broadside was marginally lighter than *Nymphe*'s but her complement of 320 seasoned men was also 80 men larger than the British ship's, and they were therefore more or less evenly matched.

After about a quarter of an hour of furious cannonade at point-blank range, with shot ploughing up the decks of both ships and Israel concentrating his fire upon *La Cléopâtre*'s quarterdeck, the French frigate's mizen mast fell with a crash, the lower mast snapping off about four metres above the deck and toppling upon the gunners below. At about the same time Israel, having killed four helmsmen, shot her wheel away, and *La Cléopâtre* broached to, swinging to larboard at a right-angle to *Nymphe*.

To maintain pressure upon his opponent Pellew ordered *Nymphe*'s helm put over, and the British ship also swung to larboard as both crews continued to ply their guns. With the wind filling her forward sails, *La Cléopâtre* now swung back to starboard and Pellew followed suit until *Nymphe* was heading roughly north-east. *La Cléopâtre*, swinging much faster to starboard and out of control, crashed into *Nymphe*, her bowsprit and jib-boom running over *Nymphe*'s deck between her fore- and main-mast.

Apprehensive of being overwhelmed by boarders, Pellew shouted for those of his own men designated to grab their boarding pikes and cutlasses, to repel the expected invasion. As the men rushed to the waist it became obvious the enemy was in no fit state to board his ship, so Pellew ordered his first lieutenant to carry on and board the enemy. Lieutenant Amherst Morris led his men over *La Cléopâtre*'s upper deck while a master's mate named Ball took a second party through her gunports.

As the British boarders scrambled across to *La Cléopâtre*, she continued to swing. In spite of the weakened state of *Nymphe*'s main rigging, it was *La Cléopâtre*'s jib-boom which carried away under the strain, so that a few minutes after seven o'clock the two ships ground together. With *La Cléopâtre*'s damaged bow abreast *Nymphe*'s stern and their rigging entangled, Pellew was worried about the state of his weak mainmast, the loss of which would have rendered his ship as unmanoeuvrable as Mullon's. But a topman named Burgess lit out unbidden along the main topsail yard and, hanging down from the larboard yardarm, cut the bolt-rope sewn along the leech (edge) of *Nymphe*'s main topsail. This freed *La Cléopâtre's* main topmast studdingsail boom-iron, which had pierced the sail. Now Pellew, anxious to get his ship clear, ordered his third lieutenant Richard Pellowe forward to clear away the best bower anchor preparatory to anchoring. His intention was to let the tide carry the disabled *La*

*Cléopâtre* away from *Nymphe*, but matters were resolved before this became necessary.

Fighting their way aft in a brief hand-to-hand mêlée, the British boarding parties found the French seamen either fleeing below, calling for quarter, or throwing down their arms in token of surrender. At about ten minutes past seven the boarders reached *La Cléopâtre*'s quarterdeck and hauled down her colours. As the tricolour fluttered to the deck and the French second lieutenant surrendered his sword to Morris, the victors stumbled upon a pitiable sight.

Capitaine de Frégate Jean Mullon lay mortally wounded upon his quarterdeck, sodden in his own gore and chewing a piece of paper. A round shot had ploughed up the wretched man's back and carried away most of his left hip, yet in his agony he was attempting to prevent the secret French coasting signals from falling into the hands of the enemy by eating them, as he thought. But the signals were later found intact in his pocket: the gallant captain had been eating his own commission.

Mullon, it transpired, had ordered his men to board the British ship, but to his chagrin and despite their Republican fervour they had quailed, allowing Pellew to seize the moment.

Thus ended the first decisive frigate engagement of the war. Mullon was a worthy opponent and his ship had given a better account of herself than first appeared, as the 'butcher's bill' showed. Out of a crew of 320, 63 others besides Mullon, had been killed or wounded, among the latter 3 of her lieutenants. *Nymphe* had suffered casualties of similar severity: 23 killed and 27 wounded. Her boatswain, a master's mate, 3 midshipmen, 14 seaman and 4 marines were among the dead.

Putting a prize crew aboard *La Cléopâtre* to repair the worst of the damage and get her under command again, Pellew headed down wind for Portsmouth, arriving with his prize on 21 June. 'We dished her up in fifty minutes,' he wrote ironically to his brother Samuel at Falmouth, 'boarded and took her'. News of the action reached London in more dramatic circumstances. It was passed to King George III while he was attending the opera, whereupon he rose in his seat and jubilantly announced it to the audience.

Pellew's reputation as the doyen of British cruiser captains was now publicly established. He was sent for and, with his brother Israel, presented to the King by the then First Lord of the Admiralty, the Earl of Chatham. Edward was knighted and Israel made post, but both honours carried an element of political expediency, for Britain was in want of a substantial victory after six months of fruitless war. In the cascade of honours *Nymphe*'s first lieutenant, Amherst Morris, was made commander and, very unusually, her master, a Mr John Thomson, was given a commission as lieutenant. By way of material award *La Cléopâtre* was purchased into the British service; there already being a *Cléopâtre* she was renamed *Oiseau,* and served until she was sold out of the navy in 1816. This was not quite all. Pellew may have been an acquisitive man, but he did not neglect the widow of his late and, very gallant opponent; sending her a substantial sum of money to ease her grief.

Although Pellew's single-ship victory was made much of, inspiring a dozen print-makers and seeming to the readers of the broadsheet newspapers mere affirmation of British superiority at sea, there were soon uncomfortable reminders that war was a risky business in which nothing could be guaranteed.

Across the Atlantic that July a British frigate, the 32-gun *Boston*, commanded by Captain George Courtenay, lay off New York. Courtenay was anxious to draw the French national frigate *Embuscade* out of the neutral American port. Capitaine Jean-Baptiste Bompart was refitting after a successful cruise in which he had taken, burnt or sunk more than sixty British merchant ships. He had not been alone; such commerce raids were often made by small groups of French frigates acting in mutual support to intimidate any lone British cruisers. Indeed, in the West Indies in May Bompart's consort, the 40-gun frigate *Concorde,* had taken the British 24-gun ship-sloop *Hyena,* afterwards commissioned into the French navy as *L'Hyène. Concorde* had chased the British sloop and her captain, William Hargood, seeing the French 74s *Eole* and *América* and some more frigates in the distance, had made off. Unfortunately, because of a heavy swell then running, Hargood was unable to outrun his fleeter and more weatherly pursuer in the light breeze, so he fired a broadside and hauled down his colours.

There was no great dishonour to a commander in surrendering to superior force if he did so to 'avoid a further effusion of blood', as the stock phrase had it. To secure an acquittal at the court martial to which every naval officer had to submit if he lost his ship, it was only necessary for him to prove that he had made a creditable show of defending his flag. If the Admiralty considered he had not quite done his utmost, however, and the acquittal was more legally technical than nationally honourable, a commander could find himself languishing ashore on half pay. A gallant defence, on the other hand, though it might end in capitulation, could lead to prompt promotion into another ship, as a mark of approbation. In this case Hargood was honourably acquitted, and later commanded the *Belleisle* at Trafalgar.

On 30 July, seeing *Boston* lying offshore, Bompart sent out his first lieutenant in a boat, thinking the frigate was his consort, the *Concorde*. Bompart's lieutenant, a man named Whitynow, happened to have been born in Boston, Massachusetts and he had his suspicions about the identity of the approaching ship, so he lay on his oars until a passing pilot boat assured him the vessel in the offing was indeed French: the pilot's boat had passed close under her stern, and he said he had seen French sailors on board.

Captain Courtenay, knowing the 'communicative tendency' of the Americans, had ensured that the handful of his officers and men who knew a few words of French were hanging about the after quarters of the ship jabbering loudly when local boats were in the vicinity. Reassured, without taking the precaution of running under her stern and reading her name, Whitynow pulled directly for the ship he now took to be *Concorde*. Welcomed aboard and immediately taken prisoner, he readily agreed to write to Bompart with a challenge to come out and fight. Courtenay informed Bompart he would await his pleasure off Sandy Hook for three days. A pilot boat was signalled to come alongside and deliver the message to Bompart; after which her crew posted the news up in a New York coffee house.

That afternoon a squadron of a dozen sail appeared to seaward and Whitynow, with a sense of irony, identified them as the French squadron consisting of the two 74-gun ships *Eole* and *América,* four frigates and six corvettes which was daily expected in New York from the West Indies, the same ships that had chased Hargood's *Hyena*. Irked by this but bound to maintain his station, Courtenay stood to sea and awaited the onset of darkness, thereby avoiding direct contact with the French ships. At three o'clock next morning a sail was seen approaching *Boston* from the north and Courtenay beat to quarters, clearing his ship for action. The approaching vessel, soon recognised as a frigate, burnt flares, hoisting her colours and a blue flag bearing a white cross, the arrangements concerted in Whitynow's letter. *Embuscade* now turned to the eastward, and the two ships closed with each other on opposite courses.

The action began at dawn and was watched by a large crowd assembled some twelve miles away on the New Jersey shore. The French ship was much the heavier in build, armament and men, and ranged up on the British ship's larboard quarter to windward of *Boston*. Bompart then lay-to while Courtenay wore round, so that both ships lay hove-to, firing into each other. About fifteen minutes later, at five twenty in the morning, *Boston*'s cross-jack yard, her headsails and stays were shot away. Fifty minutes later her maintopmast was shot through and fell, hampering the gunners in her waist. As he was directing the clearing away of the raffle, Courtenay and the marine lieutenant standing beside him were killed by a single ball, and the same broadside from *Embuscade* brought down the *Boston*'s upper mizen mast. Both the other lieutenants, John Edwards and Alexander Kerr, were wounded, the first unconscious from a blow on the head and Kerr blinded.

Edwards returned to the deck to take command after having his wound dressed as Bompart sought to swing *Embuscade* across *Boston*'s stern and fire his broadside along the length of the *Boston*'s deck in a manoeuvre known as 'raking', designed to massacre the enemy crew. To be raked from astern was exceptionally dangerous and Bompart's manoeuvre would have ended the action with the loss of *Boston*. Edwards, however, avoided this ignominious fate. Using the power of the square spritsail under *Boston*'s bowsprit, he wore round and was able to frustrate Bompart. Making all the sail he could, Edwards then ran off before the wind, and though Bompart started in pursuit his own ship was so damaged that he could not risk a chase. Instead he abandoned the pursuit and headed for New York, where he spent nine weeks repairing his ship. All three lower masts had to be taken out and replaced.

As for Edwards, caught on a neutral shore he headed for the sanctuary of the Delaware River, only to learn on taking aboard a pilot that two French frigates were anchored there, one of which was the *Concorde*. Thanking the pilot, Edwards discharged him and headed for St John's, Newfoundland, where he arrived safely on 19 December. The *Boston* was afterwards sent home, and although Edwards was made a commander, he received no further advancement. He was said to have died of the effects of his old head wound, albeit thirty years later. Some accounts of the action make veiled accusations against Edwards's character and courage, but there seems to be little substance for them. Courtenay had paid with his life for a somewhat foolhardy act, though as obliged by his orders he was doing his utmost to bring the superior *Embuscade* to battle. In admiration of Courtenay the King settled a pension of £500 upon his widow and £5 per annum on their two children. Like Pellew's knighthood, such largesse was a symptom of the newness of the war; in due course such actions would be regarded as unremarkable, and widows like Mrs Courtenay merit only the meagre provisions of an indifferent state.

During 1793 a British fleet under Lord Hood supported the French royalists in Toulon with the aid of a Spanish squadron under Almirante De Langara and helped buttress the French monarchists. The siege mounted by the Republicans prevailed, however, a Corsican-born Republican artillery officer, then named Napoleone Buonaparte, was directing his batteries at Toulon with consummate skill, and making a name for himself. Amid scenes of horror Hood was obliged to withdraw in December, taking with him nineteen French men-of-war. Of the remainder of the former Bourbon fleet, fourteen were burnt by parties under the direction of Captain Sir Sidney Smith, but twenty-five fell into the hands of the Republicans. About 14,500 royalists were also carried of, the remainder being left to the bayonets and the guillotine of the revolutionaries. Thereafter Toulon was blockaded by the British navy, Hood having taken Corsica as a base, aided by a local insurrection.

31

Early in the new year Samuel Hood, aged thirty-two, was in command of the 32-gun, 12-pounder frigate *Juno* in his cousin's fleet. A tall, long-limbed man, Hood must have found life in a frigate irksome, even within the comparative luxury of the great cabin. He was 'versed in astronomy . . . navigation and geography; in ship building . . . and all branches of mechanical philosophy. He studied without exception the language, laws and customs of every country he visited in the belief that [the] . . . knowledge might one day be useful to his country.' In this he was un-typical, for naval officers were generally indifferent to the intellectual aspects of their profession. Unfortunately, despite his thirst for information Hood, as he approached the harbour late on the evening of 11 January 1794, was unaware of the evacuation of Toulon. The *Juno* was on her way back there from Malta with a number of marines from the *Romney*, 50, and some Maltese levies. The usual northerly mistral that prevailed off the French coast had frustrated Hood in getting his ship up to the entrance any sooner, and he was now anxious not to be blown to leeward again, particularly since he had so many extra mouths on board to feed and water. He therefore decided to enter the port at night, without attempting to take a pilot. Stationing two midshipmen forward by the catheads, each with a night-glass, Hood braced *Juno*'s yards sharp up and stood in to the Grande Rade under her topsails, expecting to find his cousin's squadron at anchor inside the Petite Rade.

In rounding Pointe Grand-Tour, the eastern headland of Toulon's inner anchorage, Hood found a brig anchored right ahead of him in La Petite Rade. Immediately he let fall his fore course, heaving the weather tack hard down and setting the *Juno*'s spanker to avoid collision and enable him to tack ship smartly as the wind fell away under the lee of the land. As *Juno* passed the brig a hail came from her, and after a few moments' confusion the word 'Luff!' was shouted. Fear of shoal water caused Hood to put his helm down and swing *Juno* round, but before she came head to wind he felt through the soles of his shoes the sensation every commander dreads, that of his ship being stopped in her tracks: *Juno* touched the bottom.

Immediately the best bower anchor was let go and the hands were sent aloft to take in sail. While this was in progress the wind appeared giving the ship sternway, and the spanker and mizen staysail were set and backed. With the spanker 'chappelled' in this way it was hoped to get the ship clear, but the stern remained fast and the rudder useless. Hood now ordered two of his boats to be launched, and a kedge anchor and warp were prepared. Meanwhile a French boat appeared alongside, alerted by the brig to the presence of a British frigate in the road, and some French officers came aboard. In the darkness it was some moments before their tricolour cockades were spotted by a sharp-eyed midship-man. The knowledge that *Juno* had contributed to her own capture sent a *frisson* through the ship, then Third Lieutenant Webly voiced the opinion that they might take advantage of the breeze and get out of their predicament, the bow of the ship being afloat.

Hood immediately ordered his men to their stations. The French officers protested and made to draw their sabres, but several marines confronted them and they yielded to the inevitable. Above their heads the sails were cast loose, dropped from their yards and were sheeted home while the halliards were manned and the topsail yards rose up their topmasts. As the sails caught the wind the cable was cut and, a fluke of wind filling the foresails, *Juno*'s bow swung. Gradually gaining way, the frigate dragged her stern clear of the shoal. The ship's two boats were cut adrift along with that of the French officers, and *Juno* made a bid for the open sea.

As the pale rectangles of sail reappeared in the darkness the brig's crew opened fire, and soon the guns of the forts around the harbour took up the alarm and began to fire at *Juno*. The embrasures of Fort L'Eguilette on the westernmost headland seemed to pose the greatest risk, and for a moment it appeared that *Juno* had insufficient sea-room to swing and get clear. To tack and thus remain under the hostile guns might have proved fatal but Hood, setting courses and topgallants, contrived to stand on.

His sails were pierced by shot, his rigging was damaged and there were two 36-pound shot stuck in his ship's hull, but Samuel Hood contrived to get clear to sea without the loss of a man, and finally located Lord Hood a few miles along the coast in Hyères Bay. *Juno* had been saved by Lieutenant Webly's quick initiative, but Hood's confidence in his officer played a vital part, for hesitation would have reduced their chances of escape, while the efficiency of the ship's company in so speedily reacting to their orders was equally important. Such co-ordination was the key to success: they were all, quite literally, in the same boat.

# CHAPTER 3

---

# 'Consummate professional skill'

In the new year of 1794 the British Parliament increased the naval vote from £4 millions to £5.5 millions sterling, for a fleet of 279 vessels of war actually in service manned by about two thousand commissioned officers and 85,000 seamen and marines. Apart from a rapid demobilisation in 1802, followed by an even faster reversal of the decline a few months later when hostilities resumed, all those numbers increased steadily throughout the war.

In the Atlantic theatre, Morard de Galles was removed from command of the Brest fleet. An old royalist *officier rouge* who had seen service with de Suffren and was therefore politically unreliable, he was replaced by Villaret-Joyeuse, now an admiral but formerly only a lieutenant, whose own loyalty to the Republic was monitored by a political observer and co-commander named Saint-André. The new regime's hold on the hearts and minds of the French people remained tenuous, particularly as food was short following the wet summer of 1793. A great effort was therefore made to purchase grain from the United States and carry it safely back to France: Contre-Amiral Vanstabel sailed in September to provide a close escort to the 117 loaded merchantmen awaiting a convoy back home, and the ships left Virginia on 2 April 1794.

They were expected to arrive back in France in early June, so two squadrons were sent out to support Vanstabel and provide heavy cover for the most dangerous part of the homeward passage, the approach to Brest. One under Contre-Amiral Nielly left Rochefort, the other under Contre-Amiral Villaret-Joyeuse sailed from Brest and both succeeded in evading Lord Howe's Channel Fleet.

This had itself lately escorted a mass of outward-bound British merchant shipping clear of the coast, but now went in quest of the French convoy. Encountering Villaret-Joyeuse, Howe's fleet fought a battle far out in the Atlantic on what was to become known as 'the Glorious First of June'. As a British tactical victory it was impressive: Howe's twenty-five of the line took six and sank one of Villaret-Joyeuse's twenty-six-strong fleet without loss to itself. Much was made of this first fleet-action of the war, but unfortunately it must be regarded as a strategic failure. Howe, an old man who had spent the greater part of the day sitting in a chair on the *Queen Charlotte*'s quarterdeck, did not order a pursuit to destroy the convoy. So the opportunity was lost and the French government was saved.

The new generation of sea warriors who would supersede that of Howe and Hood as flag-officers, the paradigm of which was Horatio Nelson, were to prosecute the naval war with a greater vigour, seeking annihilation of the enemy even at the expense of prize money. But their stars were only just rising, and the evidence of a change of pace in naval warfare had been demonstrated rather by the *French* commanders during the action of 1 June 1794. The *Vengeur*, battered into a sinking condition, did not strike her colours until she was actually foundering. In defiance of custom, several other captains who had struck their colours actually rehoisted them when they were not immediately boarded by the British. No doubt the ever-looming shadow of the guillotine worked on their minds to prompt this resurgence of valour, or perhaps it was simply republican contempt for a mode of warfare that smacked of the affectations of the *Ancien Régime*. Whatever the cause, it gave a signal that war with the French Republic was no longer to conform to the elegant conventions of the eighteenth century.

The slow manoeuvrings of these two fleets in the misty Atlantic on the last day of May and that first day of June were in contrast to the activity in the English Channel, where the encounters between British and French frigates became increasingly frequent as more vessels were commissioned and the war against trade concentrated cruisers of both sides in the Chops of the Channel. In general the large French 40-gun cruisers were superior in design, weight of metal and sea-keeping qualities to their British counterparts. They also benefited from the skills of the seafaring population of France's maritime provinces, as the line-of-battle ships of France's main fleets on the whole did not, manned as they were largely from *levées en masse,* as and when required. The advantages of joining a 'flash-frigate' were exactly the same for the common seamen of France as for their enemies and most of the French cruiser commanders were competent officers, so experienced little difficulty in mustering large crews of volunteers.

The French, determined to prosecute the war against trade with more vigour than Lord Howe, sent out flying squadrons of three or four frigates intent on commerce raiding. Too powerful for the limited escorts often provided by the British Admiralty, they had been markedly successful, so much so indeed that six large new frigates were under completion at Le Havre solely for the purpose. The French were developing a new form of cruiser, a heavier and more effective frigate than their predecessors and more than a match for the standard frigates of the Royal Navy. These heavy frigates were either new purpose-built ships or converted 74- or 64-gun line-of-battle ships. The latter were 'razed', that is, cut down to a single gun deck, their longer waterline length giving them an automatic advantage of speed. These 'razées' and new super-frigates had one thing in common: their main armament was of 24-pounder guns. The British responded with razées of their own, taking in hand three fast-sailing 64-gun sister ships, the *Indefatigable, Anson* and *Magnanime,* and also augmented their fleet by captures from the French.

To annihilate these serious threats to trade and before their own new razées were available, the British Admiralty organised all frigates not assigned to convoy duty into squadrons based mainly on Falmouth. Among these flying squadrons the pre-eminent was commanded by Captain Sir John Borlase Warren, hoisting a commodore's broad pendant in his frigate, the 36-gun *Flora.* Warren was given a free hand, charged with protecting British trade between Cape Finisterre and Cherbourg, a remit wide enough to become a poisoned chalice had he not had subordinate commanders of merit. First, there was Sir Edward Pellew. He and his ship's company were transferred lock, stock and barrel into the *Arethusa* by Admiralty order. Built at Bristol in 1778, *Arethusa* was a superior vessel to *Nymphe,* her main armament consisting of thirty-eight 18-pounder guns: a 'crack-ship', in short, she became known throughout the Royal Navy and to the British public at large as 'the saucy *Arethusa*', after a song of that name composed in her honour. They were joined by three other 36-gun ships, *Melampus*, Captain Thomas Wells, like *Flora* armed with 18-pounders; *Concorde,* Captain Sir (John) Richard Strachan; and Pellew's old *Nymphe,* now commanded by Captain George Murray, both of which were 12-pounder ships. As was common practice, all these ships carried additional guns on their upper decks, increasing their broadsides above the notional establishment of their ratings.

All the captains of Warren's ships stood high in the Admiralty's esteem, and it was no coincidence that they had been brought together under Warren. New frigates armed with 18-pounders had been coming into service, and such was the importance attached to these squadrons that only tried and tested commanders were posted into them. Among the officers appointed into other cruisers assigned to the same duties were Sir James Saumarez of the *Crescent,* Sir Sidney Smith of *Diamond,* Sir Andrew Snape Douglas of *Phaeton,* Edmund Nagle of the *Artois* and Richard Goodwin Keats of *Galatea.* Although these men eventually advanced to flag-rank by virtue of their seniority, they formed a core of competent cruiser specialists known for their aggression, initiative and superb seamanship. It was this last attribute that made them outstanding. Contemporary opinion held that Keats was the finest seaman of his age, with Pellew a close second, but in truth there was little to chose between them; they were distinguished only by the opportunities offered each of them by fate. Saumarez was another highly competent seaman, and Douglas was known for his luck with prizes. Their reputations enabled them to attract the best of such volunteers as came forward for naval service and, running tight but efficient ships with competent subordinate officers and petty officers, they commanded instruments of great potency.

In April 1794 Warren's squadron was cruising 24 miles south-west of Guernsey and about 14 miles west of Roches Douvres, intent on suppressing the Breton coastal trade as well as ensnaring enemy cruisers. Before dawn on the morning of the 23rd, St George's Day, the wind was from the south-south-west. Warren had just turned the squadron, which was heading south-east on the starboard tack in line ahead, when four sails were seen ahead on a reciprocal course and the opposite tack.

This was a fine squadron of four cruisers under Commodore Desgarceaux in the 36-gun *Engageante*, with the *Résolue* of 36 guns under Capitaine Villéon, the 44-gun *Pomone*, Capitaine Pévrieux, and the 20-gun ship-corvette *Babet*, Lieutenant Belhomme. Desgarceaux formed line ahead as the day dawned.

At daylight Warren hoisted the signal for a chase and led Pellew, Wells, Strachan and Murray towards the enemy. As the bigger frigates crowded on sail, Murray's slower *Nymphe* fell astern. The squadrons passed one another and then Warren tacked his advanced frigates in succession, coming round into the enemy squadron's wake. Fortuitously, the wind now backed two points to the south, giving Warren the weather gage as *Flora*, *Arethusa*, *Melampus* and *Concorde* slowly began to overhaul the French squadron, coming up on the *Babet* 's weather quarter.

At half-past six *Flora* exchanged gunfire with the *Babet* and gradually drew past her to engage *Pomone* and *Résolue* as well. *Babet* and the much heavier *Pomone,* armed with 18-pounder guns, now inflicted considerable damage on *Flora*. After an hour *Flora*'s main topmast had been shot away, her main top was wrecked, her foremast and all her yards were battered, and her rigging was cut up. So badly was her rig damaged that Warren was compelled to drop astern as both squadrons set more sail, and Pellew eagerly took his place. The *Arethusa*, *Melampus* and *Concorde* were less injured in their rigging than *Babet* and *Pomone*, and in two hours the unfortunate *Babet* had lost her fore topmast and been so battered that Lieutenant Belhomme hauled down his colours.

Pellew left Warren to take possession of *Babet* and with Strachan in close support concentrated upon the *Pomone*. Had the French commodore doubled back and fallen upon his tormentors he might have achieved a coup, but Desgarceaux stood on in *Engageante* with *Résolue* in his wake.

The *Pomone*, already damaged by Warren, was now assailed by Pellew and Wells, and it was not long before Capitaine Pévrieux's frigate had lost her main and mizen masts. The wreckage encumbering *Pomone's* waist then caught fire, and Pévrieux capitulated to Pellew at half-past nine. But *Arethusa* had been damaged aloft and was in no condition to chase; so Warren sent Wells and Strachan, with *Nymphe* endeavouring to catch up, in pursuit of *Engageante* and *Résolue*. Strachan, commanding the faster ship, crowded on sail, succeeded in catching up with the two fleeing enemy vessels, and engaged them. His intention was to cripple *Résolue* and leave her to his colleagues, then press on and nail the *Engageante;* but then Desgarceaux belatedly did what he should have done earlier, and put about to the assistance of Villéon in *Résolue. Engageante* tacked and ranged up on the *Concorde's* larboard bow, shooting high to disable Strachan's rig. In this Desgarceaux was partially successful, for *Concorde's* main topmast was hit, though it did not fall.

It was now clear to Strachan that *Melampus* was unlikely to catch him up, and *Nymphe* certainly could not. Giving up on *Résolue*, Strachan transferred his gun-crews to the larboard batteries and engaged Desgarceaux as *Engageante* loomed through the gunsmoke. As *Résolue* fled, to end up in Morlaix, *Engageante* and *Concorde* were locked in a spirited action from noon until a quarter to two in the afternoon, when the French guns fell silent and her people called for quarter. Shortly afterwards all *Engageante's* masts fell overboard.

The loss to the British had been trifling, about ten men dead and two dozen wounded, while the French had about a hundred and twenty killed and disabled. Patching up his own ships, Warren led them and his three prizes in triumph past Pendennis Castle and the Black Rocks into Falmouth Harbour, anchoring in Carrick Roads with colours flying, the British ensign superior to the French on the captured ships. *Engageante*, too damaged for active service, was hulked as a hospital ship and not broken up until 1811. *Babet* was also put into commission in the Royal Navy, and eventually went missing in the West Indies in October 1801. *Pomone* was a fine ship and a fast sailer, but had suffered to her detriment and, although she saw service as a cruiser, was prematurely broken up in 1802.

The ebb and flow of events in these early years of war is exemplified by one sharp action fought in mid Atlantic in defence of a convoy. The merchant ships had assembled in Cork Harbour on the south coast of Ireland, and on the morning of 5 May 1794 were three days into their outward passage under the escort of two ships-of-the-line, *Swiftsure*, 74, and *St Albans*, 64.

In spite of this heavy escort, Capitaine Charles Linois in the crack French 36-gun frigate *Atalante*, in company with the corvette *Levrette*, pounced upon the convoy. Linois was to become well-known to British sea warriors, and this first encounter with him was dramatic. The two British ships could not completely cover the sprawling mass of the convoy, but Captain Boyles of *Swiftsure* immediately headed for the enemy, followed by Captain Vashon in *St Albans*. It was almost six o'clock in the evening before the two British ships closed the French raiders sufficiently to hoist their colours and fire warning shots after them. *Atalante* and *Levrette* each ran up the tricolour, Linois firing his stern chasers. The *Levrette* then bore up, and with *St Albans* still in chase disappeared into the darkness, ultimately to escape her pursuer.

Boyles clung on to Linois during the night, and at four the next morning, with the wind in the north east quarter, the *Atalante* was only three miles ahead to the westward. All day the chase went on, and as evening approached Boyles began to fire after Linois, hoping to inflict sufficient damage to halt his retreat and bring him to action. By seven o'clock, however, *Atalante* had again increased her distance to two miles, and Boyles ceased firing. The two vessels sped on into the darkness of a second night.

At midnight Linois abruptly put his helm over and turned *Atalante* south, hoping to throw off his pursuer, but Boyles had seen the ruse and followed suit. At two o'clock in the morning of the 7th Linois hauled his yards hard round, trying to beat to windward and gain ground

41

thereby, but Boyles again swung *Swiftsure* after his quarry, and now renewed the engagement at long range. For an hour the *Swiftsure*'s shot tore at the French frigate's rigging, finally wreaking so much damage that, with ten men killed and thirty-two wounded out of an exhausted crew who had been at quarters for forty-eight hours, Linois hauled down his colours.

A British prize crew was put aboard the *Atalante* and during the next few hours the rigging of both ships was made serviceable. At ten o'clock three 74-gun ships were seen approaching. These were from Nielly's squadron (which, it will be recalled, had been sent to sea from Rochefort as cover for the much-needed grain convoy), and immediately the tables were turned. *Swiftsure* and *Atalante* now made sail on diverging courses to divide their pursuers. Filled with anxiety for his prize and her prize crew Boyles remained in sight of his pursuers until ten o'clock, but then outran them in the darkness – as, luckily, did *Atalante,* though not without hazard. Her prize-master, finding himself with a shot-torn and largely ineffective main topsail, enrolled some help from the French sailors to cut away the old sail, haul up a new one, stretch it yard-arm to yard-arm and stop it off along the yard, setting it in due course to considerable advantage and bringing his prize in safely to a British port. As there was already a sloop-of-war named *Atalante*, on her purchase into the Royal Navy Linois's ship was renamed *Espion*, a fine, fast 36-gun 12 pounder frigate. Linois himself was duly exchanged, and he too will reappear in the story.

Although frustrated on this occasion, Nielly's squadron had already enjoyed considerable success. Earlier that month of May, the British 32-gun frigate *Castor* was the sole escort of a British convoy on passage to Newfoundland when she ran foul of Nielly's Rochefort squadron, which took the greater part of the convoy together with its escort. The *Castor*'s captain was Thomas Troubridge, a man of unusually humble origins, the son of a London baker; despite a later period as one of Nelson's 'band of brothers', he was a man destined for disappointment. His encounter with Nielly was sadly typical of a man unable to make his own luck. Overwhelmed by the French squadron, he surrendered his ship without dishonour to the 74-gun *Patriote* and in due course became a prisoner of war in the *Sans Pareil*. He was released when the *Sans Pareil* was captured during Howe's victory on 1 June and later joined his old shipmate and friend Nelson.

So much for her captain. The *Castor*'s fate was not yet sealed, however, for just as Nielly had run into a British convoy, Villaret-Joyeuse ran into a Dutch one. The Netherlands had not yet been subjugated into republicanism, so he attacked it, and in due course one of the Dutch prizes, a merchant brig, was taken in tow by the captured *Castor* and sent eastwards. The *Castor* had been placed under the command of a French officer named L'Huillier and manned by 200 men drawn from the combined French fleets. Nineteen days after her capture *Castor* fell in with the small 28-gun British frigate *Carysfort*. Captain Francis Laforey immediately gave chase, L'Huillier cast off his tow, and for an hour and a quarter without a break the two ships hammered away at each other. Badly hulled, with his main topgallant shot away, *Castor*'s mainmast badly damaged and sixteen officers and men killed, L'Huillier had to strike his colours: *Castor* and the twenty of her original crew remaining aboard her fell back into the hands of the Royal Navy.

The recapture of the *Castor* was one of those cases which tested the prize law. Both Admiralty and Navy Board claimed that, as she had not been in to an enemy port and was not therefore a 'complete prize', they were only bound to pay Laforey and his crew salvage money. This Laforey challenged, and in a test case in the High Court of Admiralty the judge, Sir James Marriot, ruled that since, according to L'Huillier's deposition, Contre-Amiral Nielly was empowered by his commission to arm and fit out those prizes of war he thought suitable to enter the service of the French Republic, the *Castor* had become a French ship-of-war and, having been duly engaged and overcome in that capacity, subsequently fell a legitimate prize to His Britannic Majesty's frigate *Carysfort*. Their Lordships seem not to have regarded this challenge as insubordinate, and were sufficiently impressed with Laforey's achievement to promote his first lieutenant, Richard Worsley, to the rank of commander. Laforey was well connected and soon afterwards inherited a baronetcy; he later commanded the 74-gun *Spartiate* at Trafalgar and went on to flag-rank.

Occasionally, however, convoy escort could yield its own rewards, as Captain The Honourable William Paget discovered in the Mediterranean. His ship, the 50-gun *Romney*, was escort to a small convoy of British and Dutch merchantmen on passage from Naples to Smyrna in the Levant. On 17 June Paget and his charges were passing clear of the Cyclades between Tinos and Mikonos. Three British frigates with which the *Romney* had shortly before been in company were in the offing when Paget's lookouts spotted a French frigate at anchor off Mikonos with three merchant vessels. Immediately Paget signalled his own convoy to join the *Inconstant*, *Leda* and *Tartar*, and hauled round to close Mikonos Road.

Bearing down upon the enemy vessel, the 40-gun frigate *Sybille*, flying the broad pendant of Commodore Jacques Rondeau, Paget cleared his own ship for action and anchored her close to the French frigate, sending an officer in a boat to demand her surrender to prevent unnecessary bloodshed. Rondeau rejected the summons and hove in on his cable, placing *Sybille* directly between *Romney* and the town. To avoid hitting the innocent Greek islanders, Paget sent out his boats with a second anchor and warped ahead, clapping springs on his cables so that he might veer his ship and traverse his broadside. Having a vacant gunport in his engaged side, Paget also shifted one of his 24-pounder guns from the opposite broadside. All this activity went on unmolested by Rondeau, who took no advantage of the British being thus dispersed and preoccupied. Pager's ship now utterly over-awed Rondeau's broadside of 18-pounders.

Once the town was clear of his field of fire Paget sent his men to their guns, and at one o'clock in the afternoon opened fire. Rondeau responded, and for the following seventy minutes the two ships cannonaded each other at short range. Sadly for Rondeau, many of *Sybille*'s crew fled ashore, and with 46 men killed and 112 wounded he was forced to strike his colours. The *Sybille*, built at Toulon only three years earlier and a fine frigate, was purchased into the Royal Navy where she remained until 1833. Paget's losses amounted to 10 men killed and 28 wounded; his first lieutenant, William Brisbane, was promoted to commander.

The impact of the loss of such French frigates was more than just material: the drain of experienced seamen into the appalling British prison hulks anchored in Portsmouth and elsewhere had an effect on morale, besides reducing the pool of available seamen. British frigates continued to hunt down French cruisers whenever and wherever they could be found in home waters, but were sometimes themselves taken at a disadvantage.

Sir James Saumarez was commodore of a flying squadron which comprised his own *Crescent*, 36, the *Druid*, 32, Captain Joseph Ellison, the 24-gun ship-sloop *Eurydice*, Captain Francis Cole, and a lugger commanded by Lieutenant Barker. This was a relatively weak squadron to be cruising close to the French coast, and was additionally hampered by the notoriously poor sailing qualities of the 24-gun post ship *Eurydice*.

In these dangerous waters in the autumn of their first year of war Saumarez had succeeded in taking the French frigate *Réunion* without suffering a single casualty from enemy fire, though one seaman had had a leg broken from the recoil of the gun he was manning. Such was the sanguinary nature of the public of the day that bloodless victories were less admired than those in which the bill in killed and wounded was heavy on both sides. Nevertheless, Saumarez was knighted, and the City of London showed their appreciation of the disposal of a notorious commerce raider by making him a gift of plate.

Saumarez, a Channel Islander, was back in his own home waters off Jersey at dawn on 8 June when daylight revealed a powerful French squadron to windward. There were two large French razées, *Scévola* and *Brutus*, both cut down 74-gun ships now mounting 50 guns; two 32-gun frigates, *Danaë* and *Félicité*; a 14-gun brig-corvette; and some smaller *chasse-marées*, which fired upon Barker's lugger. Caught in this perilous position, Saumarez ordered *Eurydice* and the lugger to make for Jersey while *Crescent* and *Druid* followed them under easy sail. The four British vessels slowly approached the north coast of Jersey with the French squadron overhauling them. Saumarez now realised that he would lose *Eurydice*, and possibly *Druid*, unless he seized the initiative. *Crescent* therefore boldly bore up and stood along the enemy line, exchanging fire and giving *Druid*, *Eurydice* and the lugger an opportunity to escape.

This caused the French to believe the *Crescent* would be the more easily secured by their superior force, and they concentrated their combined fire upon her – just as Saumarez had anticipated. He ordered a press of sail hoisted and *Crescent*, running the studding sail booms out, spread her wings on course for Sark and Guernsey. As the closely following French ships chased him to the north-west, Ellison and the others were able to slip along the north coast of Jersey under the protection of batteries at Bouley Bay.

Heading for the narrow and almost impassable strait between Sark and Guernsey, Saumarez now took his second bold decision of the day: since the wind permitted it, he elected to try that dangerous passage between the two islands, known as the Russell, never before made by a ship-of-war and requiring the use of transits and leads to avoid the rocks and reefs that littered the winding channel. Only local knowledge could save Saumarez, and with the assistance of a local pilot he carried *Crescent* into the safety of St Peter's Port anchorage, to the frustration of the French commodore, who dared not follow. The Lieutenant-Governor of Guernsey, observing *Crescent* as she made her way through the Russell, described Saumarez's manoeuvres as 'masterly' and his conduct as exhibiting 'consummate professional skill'.

Later that August Saumarez attracted attention of a rather different kind when his squadron were sighted from Weymouth Bay, where lay the *Trusty*, 50. She was anchored as guardship to the Royal Family, then holidaying in the town, for it was feared George III's fondness for 'sea-bathing' might have reached the ears of the more obsessive regicides in Paris. Saumarez's four frigates failed to answer *Trusty's* private signal and were judged hostile, possibly a special French expedition fitted out to kill or carry off the King! This would have been a bold coup indeed, but the reaction perhaps owed more to the popular reputation of enemy flying squadrons than to any definite intelligence information. The *Trusty's* marine drummer was ordered to beat to quarters, an alarm gun was fired and the battery ashore on The Nothe was hurriedly manned. Meanwhile the King and his household were warned, the horses put-to and the royal party's carriages prepared. That evening, anchoring in Weymouth Bay, Saumarez revealed his identity, to the general relief of all concerned.

Like Saumarez, Warren had been busy since his action in April, though the composition of his squadron had altered somewhat. On 7 August he sailed from Falmouth in *Flora* with Pellew's *Arethusa*, Nagle's *Artois*, Sir Sidney Smith's *Diamond*, Jonathan Faulknor's *Diana* and Eliab Harvey's *Santa Margarita*. All except the last were 38-gun frigates, Harvey's frigate was a former Spaniard taken off Ferrol in 1779 during the American War and now mounting thirty-six 12-pounders as her main armament. Warren was in quest of a French flying squadron reported to be operating west of the Scillies. Finding nothing in the area he stood across the Channel towards Ushant, hoping to locate them closer to their home waters, for the French were known not to remain as long at sea as the British. His instinct proved correct, and as he closed the entrance to Brest harbour on the 23rd, several ships were sighted. While *Flora* and *Arethusa* went in chase of two ship-corvettes, the other four British frigates closed on another ship, the French frigate *Volontaire* of 36 guns. Driven close inshore, she was forced to anchor off a reef known as the Penmarcks, south of the entrance to Brest, where she was so savagely attacked that Capitaine Papin cut his cable, intending to seek a better position. Before he could make sail *Volontaire* was driven aground, and took such a pounding on the rocks that her pumps were quite inadequate to the task of keeping her afloat. Papin was obliged to abandon her, whereupon the British frigates drew off.

Meanwhile Warren and Pellew drove the two ship-corvettes round the Pointe du Raz and into Audierne Bay, where they anchored. *Flora* and *Arethusa* stood after them, however, and the two corvettes weighed again and moved closer inshore to seek the protection of three shore-batteries, whereupon they both took the bottom. The British captains engaged the batteries and the corvettes until after six o'clock in the evening, by which time they had shot away the corvettes' masts. Men could be seen struggling through the breakers as the tide ebbed, so Warren sent Pellew close in with the boats from both frigates. Pellew discovered the corvettes to be the *Alerte*, 12, and *Espion*, 18, captured former British sloops. He and his seamen took more than fifty prisoners, but since the two corvettes were full of wounded he forbore to set them on fire, content that they were badly bilged and therefore total losses. Having inflicted this damage on the very threshold of the French navy's main Atlantic base, Warren recalled all his frigates and stood offshore.

That autumn Pellew temporarily relieved Warren as commodore of the flying squadron and was again off Ushant on 21 October. *Arethusa*, *Diamond* and *Artois* were now accompanied by *Galatea*, a brand new 32-gun frigate mounting 18-pounders and commanded by Captain Richard Keats. At daybreak the squadron sighted a strange sail and gave chase. Nagle's *Artois* was by far the fastest of the British frigates, and as they were to windward they were able to cut the stranger off from the refuge of Brest Harbour. She was the *Révolutionnaire* (Capitaine Henri-Alexandre Thévenard), one of the 40-gun, 18-pounder frigates newly built at Le Havre, whence she had recently sailed with a freshly drafted crew whose morale was not of the most fervent. Coming up with the *Révolutionnaire* Nagle opened fire and for forty minutes the two ships exchanged broadsides, *Artois's* guns gradually taking effect on the *Révolutionnaire's* rig and reducing her speed. Sir Sidney Smith now ranged up on Thévenard's unengaged quarter and, with a typical eccentric courtesy, unwilling to steal Nagle's thunder, fired two guns only as a warning of what was to come if Thévenard persisted in his gallant but useless resistance. Beyond *Diamond* Thévenard could see the hand-over-fist approach of *Arethusa* and *Galatea*, soon obvious also to his ship's company, which now showed a marked reluctance to continue the fight. Thereupon Thévenard, who was slightly wounded himself and had lost eight seamen killed and four wounded out of a crew of 351, struck his colours. Of her crew of 281, *Artois* had lost one marine officer and two seamen killed, with five seamen wounded.

As a result of his part in the action Nagle became Sir Edmund, while his first lieutenant, Robert Oliver, became a commander. *Révolution-naire* was purchased into the Royal Navy (she was in better condition than the *Pomone*), and her name was simply anglicised. Pellew, reputedly piqued by Nagle's honour, was certainly galled by not having got into action, and complained of *Arethusa's* disappointing lack of speed. Unworthy though it was, this petulance was later to have significant consequences.

During 1794 there was action too in foreign waters. In the West Indies a force under Vice-Admiral Sir John Jervis conveyed troops under Lieutenant-General Sir Charles Grey which succeeded in taking the French colonies of Martinique and St Lucia. It was in the waters east of the Cape of Good Hope, however, that the cruiser war was to flare up intermittently over the next twenty years. The French maintained a strong base for their men-of-war at Île de France, better known to the British as Mauritius, largest of a small archipelago lying to the east of Madagascar, an ideal place from which to assault East Indiamen on passage between India and China and the Cape of Good Hope. The importance to the French of damaging the British economy by interdicting this trade cannot be over-emphasised.

The presence of French national ships-of-war and private corsairs at Île de France meant that British cruisers had to be stationed off the islands to prevent attacks on their trade. In late 1794 these cruisers were the 50-gun *Centurion* and the small, obsolete, two-decked 44-gun *Diomede*, and on 22 October the two were lying to the east of the island when a squadron of French ships was sighted to the west. These were under the orders of Commodore Jean-Marie Renaud with his pendant in the 36-gun *Prudente*. Renaud had sailed from Port Louis on the Île de France with the express purpose of destroying the British cruisers, and was followed by the *Cybèle* of 40 guns, Capitaine Tréhouart, the 20-gun ship-corvette *Jean Bart*, and the brig-corvette *Courier* of 14 guns.

The British ships closed the enemy line, Captain Samuel Osborne leading in the *Centurion*, with Captain Matthew Smith astern in *Diomede*. Osborne took station abreast the interval between the *Prudente*, upon which he concentrated most of his guns, and the *Cybèle*, while Smith was to engage *Cybèle* and *Jean Bart*. At half-past three in the afternoon, with colours hoisted and the ships at close range of 'half musket-shot', a general cannonade opened. The French gunners aimed high and Osborne's ship took considerable punishment, dropping astern with Smith hanging back behind him. Renaud then inexplicably ran off to leeward, out of range, followed by *Jean Bart* and *Courier*, leaving *Centurion*'s gunners to ply their fire on *Cybèle*. Capitaine Tréhouart shot away *Centurion*'s mizen and fore topgallant masts but then, the wind falling light, received a considerable bruising from *Centurion*'s guns before the wind freshened again at five o'clock. Though *Cybèle*'s main topgallant mast went by the board, Tréhouart was able to draw away after his consorts. Osborne tried to pursue but *Centurion* was incapable, and he was unable to prevent Renaud taking Tréhouart's ship in tow and returning to Port Louis. *Centurion*'s masts and rigging were so cut up that Osborne was obliged to quit his station, thereby raising the blockade of Île de France and permitting French corsairs to enter port with their prizes and leave again for the rich pickings in the Bay of Bengal. For all his pusillanimity in breaking off the action, Renaud ironically achieved his objective.

Osborne did not feel that Smith had supported him, while Smith fell back on the old argument that preservation of the line was paramount. Apparently the two officers did not get on well, and Osborne made his complaint formally. The captain of the *Diomede* was therefore court-martialled for not doing his utmost. The court decided the charge was proved, and Smith was dismissed the sea-service. The sentence was later quashed on appeal when Smith returned home in 1798, but although he was restored to his rank he was retired on half pay soon afterwards and never employed at sea again.

French cruiser squadrons also carried out wide-ranging offensive operations, and the British had to exert themselves to achieve mastery of the seas. To demonstrate this, and in justice to the best French naval commander of his generation, the exploits of Zacharie Allemand's force during 1795 must be touched upon.

A portion of the British press has always dwelt in the gutter, from where it has fostered the notion that one sturdy Briton is worth half a dozen frog-eating Frenchmen. Throughout the course of the French Revolutionary War, however, no serving British naval officer could ever assume superiority, moral or material. True, an almost unbroken string of victories was to crown *major* British naval operations, but matters were otherwise on the margins. And while it is true that an unworthy assumption of superiority infected elements of the officer corps later in the war, this was by no means typical, and was firmly rejected by more senior officers who had been blooded in the first round.

Zacharie-Jacques-Théodore Allemand, a French officer quite capable of waging war as relentlessly as his best British counterparts, sailed from Brest in the late summer in one of the large 50-gun razées, the *Expériment*, formerly a 74-gun ship-of-the-line. His squadron consisted of the frigates *Vengeance* and *Félicité*, the brig-corvettes *Mutine* and *Épervier*. His objective was to attack the British slave-trade on the coast of West Africa, and on 28 September his ships, with two captured Guineamen (slavers), appeared off Sierra Leone flying British colours. Allemand anchored before the miserable town, known to generations of British sailors for its sweat, squalor and syphilis. The British ashore largely slave-dealers, duly hoisted the Union flag in token of welcome. There were no men-of-war in the anchorage, so Allemand ran up the tricolour and began a bombardment.

Defenceless, the inhabitants hauled down the British flag to signal submission, but Allemand's gunfire continued for two hours. Balls ploughed up the dirt tracks and demolished the skimpily constructed buildings. The French then landed, leaving unmolested any of the native population they encountered, though most had long ago deserted the town. Everything British was burnt, and for a month Allemand raided British posts up and down the coast, until sickness infected his ships. He then withdrew; he had destroyed ten Guineamen on charter to the Royal African Company and taken the *Harpy* of London, a 400-ton slaver mounting 12 guns. Allemand next sailed for Senegal, where he continued his depredations, taking in all more than two hundred slavers and merchantmen belonging to British, Spanish and Portuguese owners. He landed their crews and any slaves found on board, but retained their masters as captives.

This was a punishing raid by any standards. As an attack upon British trade it was highly successful, for the slave trade, reprehensible though it was, constituted a highly lucrative element in the British economy at this time. Moreover, the quality of ships built for the so-called Guinea trade was high: the vessels were fast and weatherly, equally good as privateers. The fates of the merchant seamen abandoned ashore are uncertain; they were clearly a loss to the Royal Navy's impressment service. As for their captive masters, there was no exchange system to relieve them of the tedium of confinement and, since they had usually sunk their capital into their ships, they were ruined men in all senses of the word.

# CHAPTER 4

---

# 'A very heavy gale'

The Lords Commissioners for Executing the Office of Lord High Admiral at the British Admiralty in London were now headed by Lord Spencer, a Whig who had just joined Pitt's government to replace the indifferent Chatham. At the conclusion of 1794 Spencer and his board were far from complacent about the naval war. The French had almost completed their invasion of The Netherlands and consequent acquisition of the Dutch fleet, much of it ignominiously captured by French cavalry riding over the frozen Zuider Zee.

In anticipation of events, early in the new year of 1795 the Admiralty issued orders that all Dutch ships in British ports were to be seized, and two convoys of merchantmen then sheltering in Plymouth Sound and several Dutch men-of-war, fell immediately into British hands. By May the newly constituted Batavian Republic had declared war on Great Britain, placing fifteen battleships plus frigates and lesser vessels at the disposal of Paris: Their Lordships had now to order the Navy Board to fit out another fleet to watch the Dutch coast. A tall Scot named Adam Duncan hoisted his vice-admiral's flag to the 74-gun *Venerable*'s foremasthead and took command of the North Sea squadron. Here he was joined in August by twelve Russian sail-of-the-line and seven frigates under Vitse-admiral Piotr Hanikov.

Before the end of the year Duncan's fleet had taken two corvettes from the Texel, the *Suffisante* and the *Victorieuse,* heading north to attack British whalers off Greenland, and his cruisers had ranged as far afield as the Norwegian coast after Dutch frigates, capturing the *Alliantie*, 36, off Egerö.

Meanwhile the land war in Europe was fizzling out for the time being. On 30 April the French concluded a treaty with Prussia and soon afterwards Spain, Hesse-Cessel and George III's patrimony, Hanover, made peace. On the Continent, only Austria's provinces in northern Italy remained a battleground. The legitimacy and the future of the French Republic now seemed assured, although there was a lingering but persistent opposition of royalists in north-west France, in due course savagely repressed. There was fighting in the West Indies, but it was to the southern tip of Africa the principal British overseas expedition was sent. A fleet under Vice-Admiral Sir George Elphinstone landed troops under Major-General Craig in August, and the Cape of Good Hope was taken from the Dutch. On completion of this operation Commodore John Blankett of the 64-gun *America* was sent on with a small squadron to the Red Sea. Here he was joined by the frigate *Fox*, on her notoriously long commission, sent from the East Indies squadron.

What now seemed groundless to Their Lordships at the beginning of 1795 was any fear of a cross-Channel infection of republicanism. This was a legitimate concern, for the dissenting republican tradition dating from the Levellers of the English Civil War had been resuscitated during the American War of Independence. There has been considerable support for the American colonists, thought by many to be fighting the Englishman's battle for liberty by proxy and though the influential liberal intellectual Tom Paine was compelled to seek refuge abroad his ideas were firmly rooted in the English countryside and enjoyed wide popularity.

Their Lordships were well aware, however, that while a spirit of disaffection was currently widespread in British men-of-war, it was not republicanism and, more to the point, it did not affect the fighting spirit of the ships' companies. In general, as long as they were not tyrannised over, seamen accepted the social inequities of the age with a pragmatic tolerance. Certainly the regime was harsh, savagely so at times; and certainly the generality of captains regarded their companies as mere muscle-power, which in fact is what they were; but there *were* captains, like Cuthbert Collingwood, who never used the lash. His compassion was untypical, however, and a captain was regarded as humane if he flogged only sparingly. In theory the maximum sentence was limited to three dozen lashes, but most captains exceeded this, and a seaman of the frigate *Macedonian*, Samuel Leech, records that Captain Lord William Fitzroy frequently handed out fifty lashes for relatively trivial offences. Not that savagery was a prerogative of aristocracy, for Fitzroy's successors were no less heartless. Paradoxically and perversely, however, the very savagery considered necessary to instil discipline actually motivated the men to fight like devils: it was a potent form of cartharsis.

Upon occasion, trouble of the worst kind erupted. In December 1794 there was a very ugly incident when the crew of the *Culloden*, then lying at anchor in Spithead, suddenly mutinied on the forenoon of the 3rd. The ship was under orders to sail and the hands had been called to begin the lengthy process of unmooring. The order, given by the first lieutenant, was refused. The officers called the marines to arms. The marines were under oath to uphold discipline, but six of them were among the mutineers barricading themselves below decks. Summoned from shore where he was attending the port-admiral, *Culloden's* captain rushed aboard, impetuously threatening to 'swab out' the mutineers with bayonets from behind their barricade below – a reaction perhaps only to be expected from no less a person than the fiery Sir Thomas Troubridge. This had little effect, but in the course of the next few days the loyal warrant and petty officers together with a fair number of seamen, most of whom had been held hostage, were released by the mutineers.

The ship was visited by Admirals Lord Bridport (another of the ubiquitous Hoods, this time Alexander, first Viscount Bridport), Cornwallis and Colpoys in an attempt to recall the men to their duty, but to no avail. It was the 11th before Captain The Honourable Thomas ('Mad-Pack') Pakenham, an eccentric Anglo-Irishman with decidedly complex views on egalitarianism (in the *Invincible* he dressed his entire

crew alike, both officers and men) persuaded the remaining 250 mutineers to desist. Fatally, however, the matter concluded with promises
of pardons all round.

In the event, ten of the ringleaders were court-martialled, two
acquitted, and the remainder sentenced to hang. Although three received
a royal pardon, the other five were swung aloft by their own shipmates
on 13 January 1795. Grim though this was, for the British Admiralty
of the day it was clemency of a high order. But it was not what had
been 'promised', and the memory of those five corpses swinging in the
wind at the yardarms, as *Culloden* lay surrounded by boats bearing
'representative' witnesses to the punishment, lingered long in the
collective memory of the fleet's seamen.

Although a row over pay had long been brewing, it was neither pay
nor the imminent and unpopular departure of the ship that had sparked
the trouble; it was the cranky and leaking state of the *Culloden*. The
men were presumptuous enough to deem her unseaworthy. The mutineers had sent Bridport a reasonable note asking that *Culloden* should
be dry-docked, or that they should all be drafted into seaworthy ships;
but the signature was that of 'A Delegate', a noun with sinister republican connotations which stiffened authoritarian resolve. After
Pakenham pacified Troubridge's crew, it was Troubridge who arrested
the ten ringleaders. Asked afterwards if he could pick out a potential
mutineer, he replied, 'Whenever I see a fellow look as if he was thinking,
I say that is mutiny.'

It was the questioning of authority by the *Culloden*'s crew that
provoked the crack-down, not the weakness of their case. They knew
better than anyone, how much pumping was necessary to keep the
*Culloden* afloat; but the imperatives of war as much as the well-known
venality of the dockyard commissioners and their professional experts,
quite capable of pronouncing a ship serviceable if leaned on by higher
powers, over-rode the instincts of simple sailors. Real or imagined, the
fears of the mutineers were not without precedent. The circumstances
of the loss of the *Royal George* in August 1782, from which Philip
Durham escaped when she sank dramatically in the same waters of
Spithead, were suppressed not only at the time but for more than two

centuries: a contributing factor was the ripe state of the great ship's hull. The *Culloden* was docked, in due course, then went on to fight with Nelson at the Nile and later to serve as flagship to both Pellew and Collingwood, before being broken up in 1813. For the time being, the whiff of mutiny had evaporated.

Six months later, in May 1795, the *Boyne*, another ship-of-the-line at anchor in Spithead, caught fire. It took a firm hold, and though all but eleven of her crew escaped, her loaded guns were sparked off and killed three men in other ships. The *Boyne* burnt through her cable and drifted on to the Horse Sand, only to blow up shortly afterwards when the fire reached her magazine. The cause of the disaster was never discovered, but rumours of sabotage lingered long after the pall of smoke lying over the shattered wreckage had dispersed. The *Boyne* had lately been in the West Indies and was still flying the flag of Vice-Admiral Sir John Jervis, a punctilio known to history as Earl of St Vincent who was no Cuthbert Collingwood when it came to the lash.

The state of French morale worried Their Lordships not at all, but they were much preoccupied by the strength of the French fleet. Despite the losses inflicted by the Royal Navy, this remained impressive in terms of ships-of-the-line, the fleet units or capital ships which were capable, *en masse*, of inflicting real change upon the world. At the end of 1794 there were thirty-five ships-of-the-time at Brest, fitted and ready for sea, and a further five building or in dockyard hands. Further along the coast at L'Orient one 80 and two 74-gun ships were under construction, while at Rochefort three battleships mounting 110, 80 and 74 guns were being built. Forty-six battleships were therefore available to the French on the Atlantic coast.

However, the naval authorities at Brest were hard-pressed to feed the crews of these ships, and as the Toulon squadron was under strength it was decided to sail the whole Brest fleet to cover the shifting of six of the line thither under Contre-Amiral Renaudin. Two other expeditions to reinforce Île de France and San Domingo were cancelled from lack of stores, while only sufficient for a fortnight was available for the covering ships of Villaret-Joyeuse. He sailed at Christmas with the Brest fleet and Renaudin's six sail-of-the-line, accompanied by thirteen frigates and a cloud of small craft. Heavy weather destroyed the cohesion of the plan, and the 110-gun *Républicain* was lost amid the confusion of getting out of Brest.

Hearing rumours of this disaster, the Admiralty ordered Sir John Warren's frigate squadron to reconnoitre in force, and on 2 January 1795 Warren sailed from Falmouth with *Arethusa* and *Diamond* in company. Arriving off the Goulet the next day, he ordered Sir Sidney Smith to beat up against the easterly wind and take a look into Brest Road. Tacking to windward in cold weather, Smith headed *Diamond* towards the Goulet, and at two in the afternoon saw three French ships-of-war also beating inwards. Smith stood boldly on and at five o'clock, as the tide turned against him, *Diamond* was anchored a mile off Pointe St Mathieu. In the winter darkness the French ships could be seen at anchor a short distance away.

At eleven that night *Diamond* weighed and stood in again under full sail, the young flood tide under her keel assisting her progress. Slowly *Diamond* passed the anchored ships, and as the tide turned against him, Smith remained tacking under all sail to avoid rousing suspicion. Entering the narrow Goulet at daylight, Smith observed fifteen coasters anchored in Camaret Road to the southward, and was intrigued to see the wrecked *Républicain* lying off Petit-Menou Point to the north. But there were no men-of-war abreast the ramparts of the arsenal ahead of him: the Brest fleet was still at large. Smith put up his helm and stood out to sea.

To see a frigate beating into the anchorage was one thing, to see her suddenly turn and head to sea was another. Alarmed and suspicious, the authorities hoisted signals from Bertheaume castle, but Smith merely ran up French colours and continued his leisurely outward passage, sailing parallel to a corvette running along the north shore beneath the batteries there. This vessel hoisted the French naval recognition signal, to which Smith could not respond.

Instead, *Diamond* was headed towards the line-of-battle ship near which she had previously been anchored, and which the knot of British officers on *Diamond*'s quarterdeck could see was under jury topmasts.

Running close alongside and hailing her in his excellent French, Smith offered assistance, which was declined. In the few moments' conversation possible as *Diamond* swept past, Smith learnt from her commander that she was the *Nestor* and had been with Villaret-Joyeuse, but had sustained heavy weather damage and been compelled to put back three days earlier. Expressing commiseration, Smith stood on, observing the new French frigate *Virginie* and the 74-gun *Fougueux*, recently fitted out at Rochefort and acting as escort to the convoy in Camaret Bay. This completed the identification of the trio of vessels he had entered the Goulet with the previous afternoon.

Having in this bold reconnaissance gleaned exactly what was required, by mid-morning *Diamond* had rejoined *Arethusa* offshore, where Pellew was waiting in the offing to come to Smith's aid if necessary. Both frigates then rejoined Warren, who was lying well to the westward. This incident demonstrates a number of qualities inherent in the Royal Navy of the day. Warren's first attribute as senior officer was that he was prepared to delegate; the second was that he assigned to his subordinates the tasks most appropriate to the individuals concerned. Smith not only spoke French but was a cool (if highly opinionated) officer, exactly suited to the ruse he undertook. As for Sir Edward Pellew, cool restraint was not his forte, but he was precisely the right man to have waiting in readiness, like a hawk on the leash. Had Smith got into trouble, there is no doubt but that Pellew would have sped full tilt to his aid.

Of Villaret-Joyeuse's sally a little more must be related, for it was not entirely a disaster. Three more ships foundered in a succession of gales, and another ran aground, but he took more than a hundred merchant ships and one sloop-of-war, the *Daphne*, before returning with the bulk of his fleet to Brest. A few ships ended up in other French ports; Renaudin did not detach for Toulon but sailed again on 22 February and eventually reached the Mediterranean.

Various subsequent movements of large French squadrons, often in support of convoys, engaged the attentions of detachments of Howe's Channel Fleet, the best-known of which, 'Cornwallis's Retreat', occurred off Belle-Isle in June. Vice-Admiral The Honourable William Cornwallis was flying his flag in the 100-gun *Royal Sovereign,* in company with four 74s. He had with him two frigates, the *Phaeton*, now commanded by Captain The Honourable Robert Stopford, and the *Pallas*, Captain The Honourable Henry Curzon.

On 17 June Cornwallis was confronted with a powerful French fleet under Villaret-Joyeuse comprising one 120-gun ship, eleven 74s, eleven frigates, five corvettes and two cutters. Cornwallis made sail and withdrew to the south, but one of his 74s, the *Mars*, fell astern and was in danger of being captured by the French ships, which closed round her and opened fire. An enemy success seemed certain until Cornwallis turned the *Royal Sovereign* round and 'bore up' to cover the escape of the *Mars*. The effect of her broadside was intimidating enough to halt the *Mars*'s tormentors. Stopford's *Phaeton*, meanwhile, the advanced lookout frigate well to the southward, came in sight of some distant merchant ships and made signals as if to a friendly fleet, causing Villaret-Joyeuse to break off the chase and allow Cornwallis to escape.

Cornwallis's account of the *Royal Sovereign*'s part in the affair was self-deprecatingly and typically brief, but later, as Commander-in-Chief in sole charge of the blockade of Ushant, he prosecuted a far closer watch on the port than his predecessors, no doubt mindful of the risks run by allowing the French to escape in force.

A few days after 'Cornwallis's Retreat' another action was fought in almost the same waters, as a consequence of an ill-fated expedition sent to Quiberon Bay in support of the royalists still fighting in north-west France. Sir John Warren had transferred into *Pomone* and commanded a force which included two 74s, a 64 (the *Standard*, Captain Joseph Ellison) and the frigates *Anson* (Captain Philip Durham), Nagle's *Artois*, Keats's *Galatea* and the *Concorde* and *Arethusa*, both now under new captains.

Philip Durham came from an ancient Scots family. He had been appointed commander of the *Spitfire*, an under-armed fireship, in February 1793, and had the good fortune to capture the French corsair *L'Afrique* the following day, the first French vessel to be taken in the war. For his energetic action in the *Spitfire* Durham was made post-captain. He had been put in command of the 44-gun frigate *Anson* as a reward for bringing a convoy of 157 laden merchantmen home safely from the Mediterranean. He had only been a post-captain for sixteen months and was to remain in Anson for six years.

The expedition's purpose was to land a force of *émigré* royalist troops to assist the local peasantry loyal to the Bourbons. Though they occupied the Île de Yeu and were subsequently reinforced by 4,000 British soldiers under Major-General Doyle convoyed by *Jason*, 32, the military operation was a disaster. The Royal Navy did its job, however: they had landed the troops, and afterwards they re-embarked them.

Meanwhile Lord Bridport, had relieved Howe, who was sick, of command of the Channel Fleet.

On 22 June 1795 Bridport, covering Warren's operation, encountered Villaret-Joyeuse, who had been sent out to wreck it. Villaret-Joyeuse, with an inferior fleet, fell back towards L'Orient with Bridport in pursuit. Early the next morning Bridport's van overtook the French rear and three 74-gun ships, *Alexandre*, *Tigre* and *Formidable,* surrendered. Content to draw off with his prizes, Bridport failed to force a fleet action on Villaret-Joyeuse, who escaped into L'Orient.

Two similarly unsatisfactory actions between British and French squadrons were fought in the Mediterranean, where Vice-Admiral William Hotham had relieved Lord Hood. Off Genoa in March Hotham took a French 80 and a 74, and in an action off Hyères in July one French 74 struck her colours before catching fire and blowing up. Far more successful was the dislodging of the Dutch (now allied with the French) from Trincomalee by Rear-Admiral Peter Rainier. By the following February all the Dutch forts in Ceylon (modern Sri Lanka) and India had fallen to the British.

The first frigate action of 1795 took place off the French island of Guadeloupe in the West Indies on 5 January. The island had been briefly in British hands the previous year and was thereafter invested. The 32-gun frigate *Blanche*, was assigned to cruise in the vicinity, and her captain, Robert Faulknor, had set about making a nuisance of himself. In late December, after a bold action, *Blanche*'s boats had cut out an armed French national schooner from the small off-lying island of Désirade where she lay under the guns of a fort.

Faulknor then set sail for the port of Pointe-à-Pitre on Guadeloupe, where he knew a French frigate lay at anchor. On the way and under the noses of the French he took an American schooner bound for Pointe-à-Pitre. On the afternoon of 4 January Capitaine Conseil was sent out in the 36-gun frigate *Pique* to put an end to the *Blanche*. In a brief encounter that afternoon there was an exchange of shots, whereupon Faulknor shortened sail and lay-to, an act of provocation which Conseil ignored – understandably as a few hours earlier the frigate *Quebec* had been seen in the offing and Conseil was anxious lest she would intervene.

As *Blanche* withdrew towing her prize *Pique* therefore followed at a distance. Under cover of darkness Faulknor cast off his tow and put about, and shortly after midnight on 5 January the *Blanche* passed to leeward of *Pique* on the starboard tack and exchanged broadsides. Faulknor immediately put about to come up in his opponent's wake, and *Blanche* ranged up on *Pique*'s starboard quarter. But Conseil was to windward, and just before one o'clock in the morning he wore his ship, with the intention of getting athwart *Blanche*'s hawse and raking her. Faulknor was equal to this and put his own helm up, wearing inside *Pique* so that the two frigates were parallel, running before the wind and pouring broadside after broadside into one another with a thunderous roar, the gunfire throwing flashes which briefly illuminated the opposing ships like lightning. This phase of the engagement lasted for an hour and a half until Faulknor, having drawn slightly ahead, ordered *Blanche* swung to larboard across *Pique*'s bow to rake her. At this critical moment *Blanche*'s shot-damaged main and mizen masts came crashing down across her quarterdeck, causing a confused disruption to her handling.

With his enemy suddenly immobilised under his bow, Conseil could not avoid running *Pique* into *Blanche*'s larboard quarter, and as the two ships collided with a jarring thump, he ordered his men to board the enemy. As they mustered, the French were met by a fierce resistance. *Blanche*'s quarterdeck guns and those few of her main deck guns that would bear poured a heavy fire into *Pique*'s bow. The men aboard *Pique* in her fore and maintop retaliated with a vicious small-arms fire, and a couple of her quarterdeck guns were run inboard, swung round and trained on the waist of the British frigate.

Faulknor now ordered a hawser roused out from below, intending to lash the two ships together, as he and his second lieutenant, David Milne, and some seamen passed ropes round the *Pique*'s bowsprit and took them to *Blanche*'s main capstan. At this moment Faulknor was shot through the heart. *Blanche*'s fore sails were still full of wind, and as her captain fell dead she swung round, so that the extemporised lashing parted and the *Pique* tore free. Unmanageable, having lost most of her sails from the collapse of her fore and mizen masts, she slowly crossed the *Blanche*'s stern before crashing back alongside, her larboard bow against *Blanche*'s starboard quarter. Under the direction of *Blanche*'s first lieutenant, Frederick Watkins, the seamen who had by now hove the hawser on deck, passed it immediately round *Pique*'s bowsprit. *Blanche* now began to tow her opponent downwind, and although Watkins' marines were able to prevent Conseil's men from cutting their ship free, a stinging hail of small-arms fire from *Pique*'s maintop continued to scour *Blanche*'s quarterdeck.

Frigates of *Blanche*'s vintage and class had no stern gun-ports, and only a pair of quarterdeck 6-pounders could be brought to bear on the enemy astern. Parties were therefore mustered to drag the after 12-pounders on the gun-deck inboard and swing them aft. The stern window of the *Blanche* was blown out, the resulting fires quickly extinguished and then the two guns opened fire on the enemy hull exposed by the breach in *Blanche*'s transom.

At this point, about a quarter past three in the morning, *Pique*'s mainmast fell. She now lay dead astern of *Blanche* on a short scope of cable, without a single gun capable of responding to the raking fire of the two 12-pounders belching fire and iron from *Blanche*'s shattered stern, as her marines continued to pick off anyone attempting to cast off the tow. *Pique*'s situation was hopeless, and two hours later a few voices were heard crying out for quarter.

Lieutenant Milne and about ten seamen then attempted to crawl along the cable, which dipped in the water and swept them off, so that they were obliged to swim to the *Pique;* scrambling aboard, they received the surrender of the ship. The action had lasted five hours. Besides her captain, *Blanche* had lost 7 killed and 21 wounded out of a crew of 198 (the crew number were somewhat reduced, from the provision and dispersal of prize-crews), whereas out of a crew of 279 *Pique* had suffered the prodigious loss of 76 killed and 110 injured. Conseil himself was mortally wounded.

The shattered *Blanche* and her prize limped into the British anchorage at Les Saintes. In due course *Pique* was refitted and added to the British fleet. In April both Watkins and Milne were promoted, Watkins to post-captain and Milne to commander – he had been only twelve months a lieutenant. Both men subsequenty rose to flag-rank, Milne with great distinction.

French losses were by now considerable. The corvettes *Espérance*, *Jean Bart*, *Coureuse*, *Courier National* and *Prompte* and the frigates *Tourterelle*, *Gloire* and *Gentille* were taken by British cruisers in the first five months of 1795, while the *Liberté* was attacked and sunk. That the balance was thus tipped in favour of the British was a direct consequence of the increasing number of British frigates and sloops at sea and the intelligent allocation of their cruising stations. Ships taken by frigates or ships-of-the-line attached to fleet operations weighed little in the balance: the frigate squadrons were fast becoming the most potent weapon in this war for domination of the trade routes.

Sir Richard Strachan in *Melampus* was now in command of one such hunting group, supported in early May by Smith's *Diamond*, *Hebe* (Captain Paul Minchin), *Niger* (Captain Edward Foote), and *Syren* (Captain Graham Moore). Lying at anchor off the coast of Jersey, Strachan's lookouts spotted a convoy moving along the French coast. The order being given to weigh, Strachan's frigates chased the convoy into Carteret Bay, on the west side of the Cherbourg Peninsula. Here all but one were destroyed or captured, despite the protection of two gun-vessels and a small battery on the beach. The importance of acts such as this lay not so much in the loss of shipping inflicted on the enemy, though all in this particular convoy were substantial vessels, the largest almost 400 tons, but in the inconvenience caused to the

French navy because these merchant men were loaded with ship-timber, gun powder, guns, cordage and shot. Nor were these actions bloodless: Strachan's squadron suffered two men killed and seventeen wounded. A couple of months later *Melampus* and *Hebe* fell upon another military convoy escorted by a ship-corvette of 26 guns, two brig-corvettes and a *chasse-marée*. Out of the thirteen merchantmen, six were taken, along with one of the brigs, the *Vésuve*.

Having peevishly complained of *Arethusa*'s sluggishness, Sir Edward Pellew had been subject to a second Admiralty transfer. Captain and crew had been ordered into the razée *Indefatigable* and Pellew had, moreover, been made commodore of his own flying squadron. He ought to have been in his element, but 1795 was to be a frustrating year for him.

*Indefatigable* had been launched at Buckler's Hard on the beautiful River Beaulieu in 1784 as a 64-gun ship, a sister to Nelson's *Agamemnon*. By early 1795 work had been completed in cutting her down and converting her to a powerful fifth-rate frigate of 38 guns, similar to Durham's *Anson*. Her main gun-deck mounted twenty-six 24-pounders; her quarterdeck eight 12-pounders and four 42-pounder carronades; her forecastle bore a further four 42-pounder carronades and four long 12-pounder chase guns.

Captain and crew joined her in February and Pellew, living up to his new ship's name, set about the dockyard commissioners, demanding alterations to her rig until they complied with his exacting requirements. Pellew hoisted his broad pendant and sailed in March with *Concorde*, 36 (Captain Anthony Hunt), and *Jason*, 38 (Captain Charles Stirling). Having destroyed a convoy near Brest, Pellew was reinforced by the 16-gun brig-sloop *Fortune* and the hired lugger *Duke of York*, and sent to cruise off Cape Finisterre. Here, running close inshore at an estimated 10 knots, *Indefatigable* struck an uncharted rock. Despite its world-wide commitments, the Royal Navy had at this time no proper hydro-graphic department producing accurate charts. For its first hydrographer the Admiralty had had to turn to an experienced surveyor of the East India Company, Alexander Dalrymple, who took up his new duties that very year. With a tiny staff of four he was mainly employed collating the charts produced by private surveyors for mercantile purposes. It was 1801 before the British Admiralty published its first chart, eighty years after the French navy.

Having fallen a victim to this neglect Pellew, with typical resource, got the ship off and headed south for Lisbon, where he careened *Indefatigable* to effect repairs by heaving her down alongside the sheer-hulk. Pellew himself dived beneath *Indefatigable*'s injured hull to assess the extent of the damage; he patched his ship up and returned to Plymouth, where she was made good in dry-dock. Once *Indefatigable* was back in commission Pellew's squadron was reconstituted and he was joined by *Revolutionaire*, *Quebec* and *Crescent*. They saw frustratingly little action that autumn, thanks to a series of severe westerly gales, and were back in Plymouth by the end of December.

It was a curiosity of Pellew's life that January was invariably a significant month for him; his otherwise frustrating sojourn in Plymouth added another jewel to his crown. On 9 December 1795 a large force of military transports and storeships had departed from Spithead for the West Indies. The naval escort was commanded by Rear-Admiral Cloberry Christian, and once arrived in the Antilles he was to reinforce the British garrisons there and put an end to French successes in the area. In the Western Approaches Christian's ships ran into a storm so tremendous that the entire force was scattered, and every captain and commander was compelled to save his own ship.

Among the scattered ships was the chartered East Indiaman *Dutton*, whose commander made for the shelter of Plymouth. Plymouth Sound is open to southerly winds and exposed to a heavy swell, and though Lord Howe had long since warned the Admiralty that it was the potential 'graveyard of the fleet', not until 1818 was the building of a breakwater begun. In January 1796, therefore, it was not the haven of refuge so desperately sought by Commander Sampson of the *Dutton* for his battered vessel. Because of the low tide he could not get the deeply-laden *Dutton* up into the Cattewater, so on the afternoon of 25 January he moored the large Indiaman to two anchors as the wind and swell drove round Rame Head, over the Draystone, and up into the Sound. The *Dutton's* crew struck her upper spars, but that night the wind backed into the south. It 'blew a very heavy gale with a tremendous sea', and during the following forenoon the anchors began to drag. The *Dutton* was drawing perilously close to the rock at Mount Batten, so in desperation Sampson cut the cables, set a scrap of sail forward and tried to work his ship into the Cattewater. News of the *Dutton's* plight had by now spread rapidly through Plymouth and Docktown, and a crowd had assembled on Plymouth Hoe. All might have been well had not the buoy on Cobbler's Reef also been driven from its station by the severity of the weather: in rounding it in good faith, *Dutton* passed over the rocks and lost her rudder. Now unmanageable, she drove ashore beneath the Citadel on the Hoe.

Sampson immediately ordered her masts cut away, hoping to provide a bridge to the shore, and two men were killed in the operation. A few active fellows struggled ashore, but the masts proved inadequate for the general evacuation of the ship. Among the watchers on the Hoe, was Captain Sir Edward Pellew, and with a handful of his Indefatigables he was soon directing the rescue operations. As ever, Pellew's 'supervision' included an active and conspicuous part played by himself. A rope was run between ship and shore and all the fit officers and men, including Sampson, got ashore; then Pellew and the exhausted captain discussed the best means of rescuing the remainder and concluded that a form of breeches-buoy could be rigged. It was two hours after noon when both captains hauled themselves out to the ship whereupon many of the sea-sick soldiers were transferred ashore. An hour later the gale began to abate, and boats sent out from the dockyard could get close enough to the offshore side of the *Dutton* to evacuate about three hundred soldiers, eighty sick, and some women and children. Pellew was rewarded with a baronetcy for his decisive intervention, which undoubtedly saved most of the unfortunates left aboard the ship. It also brought to his attention one of the ship's young officers, Jeremiah Coghlan, who took up Pellew's offer of a place as midshipman. As for the *Dutton* herself, she broke up, and it was six years before her remains were removed entirely.

Admiral Christian's fleet had reassembled by March and eventually reached the West Indies where the troops under Lieutenant-General Sir Ralph Abercromby took Grenada and St Vincent. Other combined operations were carried out by various forces operating under the several British flag-officers in the Caribbean, but despite this considerable naval presence the British blockade was weak and two French frigate squadrons were able to reinforce the French islands. Both expeditions, one under Thévenard, the other under Capitaine Guillaume Thomas, escaped and returned to Brest unmolested.

# CHAPTER 5

---

# 'Broadside uppermost'

In the crisis that would beset British fortunes during 1796 and 1797 Britain's cruising frigates deserve as much credit as the fleets of Sir John Jervis and Adam Duncan for retaining a tenuous advantage at sea when for a while all seemed lost elsewhere. Not that the beginning of 1796 seemed much different to its predecessor; the manpower of the fleet was increased to 110,000 men for 376 men-of-war in commission, and costs rose in proportion. At sea the struggle continued: on 10 March *Phaeton* took the 20-gun *Bonne Citoyenne* in the Bay of Biscay and prevented her joining Sercey in the Indian Ocean; the French cutter *Aspic* was captured off The Smalls by *Quebec,* and a brig was later also taken by the British frigates cruising in the Bay of Biscay.

British operations were carried out during 1796 against the Dutch in the East Indies. The Commander-in-Chief, Rear-Admiral Peter Rainier, was busy making a fortune for himself in prize money (the capture of the islands of Amboyna and Banda was said to have yielded £15,000 to the captains of the squadron), but Contre-Amiral de Sercey was still based at Île de France, and as long as that island was in French hands, British eastern trade remained vulnerable. The Dutch made an attempt to retake the Cape of Good Hope, a squadron evading Duncan's blockade and reached Saldanha Bay. Here, however, it was summoned to surrender by a large British squadron under Elphinstone, and Vice-Admiral Engelbertus Lucas bowed to superior force.

Meanwhile, interference with the French coastal traffic so vital to a large country with poor roads was prosecuted vigorously. On 18 March Sir Sidney Smith in *Diamond* had been joined by the 14-gun brig-sloop *Liberty*, Lieutenant George M'Kinley, and the hired cutter *Aristocrat*, Lieutenant Abraham Gosset. Smith had chased a convoy into the north Breton port of Erqui west of Cape Fréhel, and after sending in his boats to sound the depth in the narrow entrance he decided to attack. Undeterred by four 24-pounders in commanding positions on the cliffs above the port, Smith stood boldly inshore, leading his smaller consorts. Having silenced one gun, he rounded the point and came under the fire of three others. Unable to elevate his own broadside sufficiently, he sent ashore a party of marines and seamen under the *Diamond*'s first lieutenant, Horace Pine. As the boats approached the beach, a detachment of French infantry sent down from the battery, subjected them to so galling a fire that Pine withdrew.

Undeterred, Smith spotted a landing-place at the foot of the cliff below the guns and hailed Pine to make for this spot. Acting promptly, Pine and his men scrambled up the steep cliff before the French soldiers had regained their post; they spiked the guns, then returned to the boats and *Diamond*. Pine's party had suffered only a single casualty, Lieutenant Carter of the marines, who was mortally wounded. The three vessels then moved towards the convoy and its escort, the 16-gun corvette *Étourdie*, which defended themselves with the support of the troops ashore. The action ended with the burning of *Étourdie* and seven merchant vessels, but Pine and five other men were wounded and a further two seamen were killed in the fighting.

Smith subsequently shifted his cruising ground to the Baie de la Seine and anchored *Diamond* off Le Havre on the morning of 17 April 1796. A few days earlier he had retaken a British merchantman which had been captured by a fast privateer-lugger, the *chasse-marée Vengeur*. The corsair had escaped Smith's pursuit on several previous occasions and she was now known to be anchored off Le Havre: Smith went after her. *Diamond* was on her own but Smith had adequate resources at his disposal. *Vengeur* was anchored in water too shallow for *Diamond*, so he set about cutting her out with his boats. The frigate's heavy launch was swung out from the waist and armed with an 18-pounder carronade while four other boats were prepared.

Smith was faced with a dilemma however: he was desperate for officers. Pine had been sent home wounded in *Aristocrat* with news of the action at Erqui (which found its way onto the stage at Covent Garden as a hastily composed operetta) and his second and third lieutenants were ill, leaving him only a French royalist officer who had lingered on with him after the débâcle at Quiberon. In the event he left his sailing master on board, for he valued the man's knowledge of the French coast, and led the cutting-out party himself. Lieutenant Pearson, second of the ship and sick in his cot, was left in command.

The cutting-out party consisted of fifty-two men led in detail under Smith by three junior officers, including the Frenchman, and six midshipmen aged between twelve and sixteen. Smith himself boarded a small two-oared boat, filled with loaded muskets, and with him went his so-called secretary, a protégé named John Wesley Wright, then rated midshipman.

At ten o'clock in the evening the boats pulled inshore. Making a wide sweep so that they might be taken for local craft rowing out from the shore, they ran alongside *Vengeur* and seized her after a short struggle. While Smith was below interrogating her officers and checking her papers, word was sent down that someone in the *chasse-marée's* crew had cut her cable, and she was drifting inshore on the tide. The light breeze had now dropped and there was no anchor on board heavy enough to hold *Vengeur*, so the boats were manned and an attempt was made to tow the lugger offshore. The flood tide was too strong for them, so a small kedge anchor was let go which slowed the drift, but it did not prevent *Vengeur* dragging slowly east into the Seine estuary until they were brought up close to Harfleur, opposite Le Havre.

It was now almost daylight. Smith pushed off in his boat to return to *Diamond*, but some small craft, including a second *chasse-marée*, were seen approaching from Le Havre and he returned to his men as they prepared for a fight. He sent off the corsair's crew to Harfleur on parole not to interfere, got *Vengeur* under weigh and prepared to engage the approaching enemy. The *chasse-marée* and several other boats had now surrounded *Vengeur,* and after a vicious fire-fight Smith was obliged to surrender.

Pearson waiting Offshore, could do nothing in the prevailing calm. He sent in a boat under a flag of truce and was informed, as he afterwards reported to Lord Spencer at the Admiralty, that Smith, his officers and men had been imprisoned. It was soon learned that Smith, Wright and the royalist officer had been taken to Rouen, on their way to Paris. Smith's exploits on the French coast had earned him the flattering soubriquet of *Le lion de la mer,* but he had also a more sinister nickname, given him by General Bonaparte as a result of his activities in burning the French fleet at Toulon: *Capitaine de Brûlot,* Captain of Arson.

Smith's rather boastful and vainglorious character contributed to the popular French image of him as a diabolical incendiary. To him was attributed responsibility for all manner of deeds, which included among other things the planting of inflammable materials then being found beneath the building slipways of French ship-yards. He was known to be friendly with a wide circle of émigrés in England, and his attacks on coastal shipping were notorious. Smith's reputation at this time exceeded that of any other British naval officer; had Nelson not eclipsed all others of his generation, it would be Smith who was best known to history as the personification of British naval genius.

Smith was truly a remarkable, if eccentric, man. Well-born in Westminster in 1764, he had joined the Royal Navy at eleven and gained rapid promotion thanks to a fearless disposition and an impressive self-conceit. After action in the American War, he was a post-captain in command of the frigate *Alcmene.* Peace did not suit him, and he spent some time as a guest of the Duc d'Harcourt near Caen, becoming fluent in French. He later travelled to Morocco, a sort of self-appointed spy, sending unsolicited reports back to the Admiralty. When war broke out in 1788 between Sweden and Russia, he proceeded to Karlskrona and accepted a commission in the Swedish navy. Here he acted as a adviser at the highest level, to the further elevation of his own self-esteem and the hatred of his Swedish brothers-in-arms.

Smith returned home with a Swedish knighthood, but Their Lordships were not impressed and he was only rescued from official displeasure by the Foreign Secretary, Lord Grenville, who sent him to Constantinople on a secret diplomatic mission. Here he is thought to have acted as adviser to the Turkish navy against the Russians, for the outbreak of war with revolutionary France found him in Smyrna, where he promptly rounded up a small band of unemployed British seamen. Buying a small vessel which he christened the *Swallow Tender* he sailed for Toulon where, though he was officially unemployed and on half-pay, he volunteered. He still had his seniority on the vital list of post-captains, however, and acting on Lord Hood's written orders he became *Capitaine de Brûlot*.

His past activities as an arsonist now precluded the exchange Pearson had hoped to arrange, and Smith and his companions, were taken to Paris as political prisoners.

A few days before Smith was taken prisoner in the Seine, Pellew was off Ushant with his frigates. *Indefatigable* was accompanied by the 44-gun *Argo* (Captain Richard Burgess), Francis Cole's *Revolutionaire*, 38, the 36-gun *Amazon* (Captain Robert Reynolds), and Hunt's *Concorde*. Pellew also had with him the lugger *Duke of York*, commanded by a master's mate named Benjamin Sparrow, and three captured *chasse-marées*. A sail was sighted upwind to the south-west and Pellew hoisted *Revolutionaire*'s number with the signal to chase, she being the most windward of the British frigates. Determined, if she proved to be French, to cut the stranger off from Brest, Pellew made sail with the rest of his vessels.

*Revolutionaire* bore away on a course to intercept the stranger, but the weather was misty and at the onset of darkness Cole lost sight of his quarry. He pressed on, however, and at nine o'clock was rewarded by another sighting. The speed of the French-built *Revolutionaire* under a press of sail was sufficient to enable Cole to overhaul the French frigate. He ordered the marine drummer to beat to quarters, and his crew cleared *Revolutionaire* for action. With the two frigates running close alongside one another at ten knots in the darkness, Cole invited his opponent to surrender. '*Non!*' bellowed the French captain, whereupon Cole called out 'Open fire!'

The speed of the engaged ships was carrying them rapidly towards the coast at Penmarch and Cole, to starboard of his enemy, decided to force the issue before it was too late. He boldly put his helm over and yawed to larboard, intending to run aboard the Frenchman. As the *Revolutionaire* closed the distance, cries for quarter were heard. A few moments later the French tricolour fluttered down to the deck in token of submission, and Cole found himself in possession of the *Unité*. A humiliated Capitaine de Vaisseau Linois had been compelled to strike because his crew refused to do anything more. They had lost nine killed and eleven wounded, but disaffection was the greater agent of capitulation, for the majority were conscripted landsmen; thirty had fled below pretending to be wounded, and eighteen royalist Vendéeans had simply refused to fight. Cole's ship suffered no casualties, and triumphantly he brought his prize up under the guns of the other British frigates.

Pellew had the wife and family of the governor of Rochefort (including Madame Le Large's domestic servants) removed from the *Unité* and sent them into Brest in one of his captured *chasse-marées*. He then rounded Ushant and headed north. Detaching *Revolutionaire* to escort the prizes into Plymouth, where in due course *Unité* was purchased into the Royal Navy, Pellew lay off the Lizard on the morning of 20 April. Cole and his charges were still in sight, weathering the cape in a south easterly breeze, while *Indefatigable*, *Argo*, *Amazon* and *Concorde* lay hove-to. A suspicious sail came in sight to the westward and Pellew ran up the recognition signal, upon which the strange sail tacked away to the south. Sending *Argo* after Cole to cover his prizes, Pellew hoisted No. 7, the signal to the rest of his squadron for a general chase.

Now the sailing qualities of *Indefatigable* came into their own, in particular the speed she was capable of from the combination of her long hull with the spread of sails and the span of spars which Pellew had refused to allow the master-rigger to shorten when the ship was cut down. Driven mercilessly by Pellew, who hoisted his royal yards aloft, the big razée left her consorts astern as the hunt ran off to the west. With the wind at south-east the French frigate could not make Brest, and instead attempted to outrun her pursuers by sailing directly downwind. The day drew on as the frigates reeled off the distance, reaching speeds of 11 and 12 knots. The enemy set every scrap of canvas his spars could take, and for fifteen hours and 168 miles Pellew pressed his ship. Darkness fell; Pellew hoisted a lantern, to illuminate his colours and to show his position to *Concorde* and *Amazon* astern of him. The enemy responded by hoisting a lantern in his turn, to highlight his own flying colours, and his continued defiance. Still the chase ran on, with *Indefatigable* slowly reducing the distance between them. By midnight, as a full moon rose, Pellew was close enough to engage. In the moonlight *Indefatigable* loomed up on the larboard and windward quarter of the enemy. She was the 44-gun *Virginie*, commanded by Capitaine Jacques Bergeret, and quickly responded to *Indefatigable*'s gunfire. A running fight started, both frigates still carrying a press of sail.

For almost two hours broadside was met by broadside in a thunderous exchange. The discharge of the cannon lit up the night, and the ships ran so close together at times that burning wadding from the guns of either vessel struck the other. On the upper and main decks men toiled: swabbing, loading and ramming, then hauling the trucks with their brute weight of artillery back through the gun-ports. The gun captains bent and sighted along their barrels, motioning to their crews for a slight traverse or the insertion of another quoin – but by and large aiming was crude, and speed of discharge all-important. Satisfied, they stood back and applied their linstocks; in the chamber of the gun, the charge exploded and drove the shot and charge of langridge out of the muzzle. As the gun recoiled the process began again, in a seemingly endless succession of frantic labour. The noise was tremendous, the men's ears rang until they heard very little, responding to gestures and carrying out the mindless routines they had been drilled to execute. Along the decks, the lieutenants and their subordinate midshipmen hopped and ducked, exhorting their men and seeking any advantage obtainable at the enemy's expense.

And all the while the enemy muzzles vomited iron in response. Shot hit the ships' sides and beat them in. Here huge splinters struck from the timbers exploded into the crowded spaces, there a ball took off a man's head, his arm or his leg. A slow-moving gunner had his foot crushed as his gun, becoming almost sentient as it heated up in its bloody business, leapt back in recoil, while the gun captain shouted for more shot from the garlands and more paper cartridges from the magazine far below.

On the upper decks it was no better. Along the bulwarks men served the carronades while the knot of quarterdeck officers gathered about their commander watched every move of the enemy; the sailing master supervised the actual sailing of the ship, the midshipmen ran messages, and the master's mates at their stations were ready to brace the yards, to make or shorten sail at an instant's warning, to cut free sails and spars shot away by the enemy or to make quick, temporary repairs. And all the while each commander sought to divine the intentions of his opponent, watching for a shift of wind, howsoever slight, that might give him the chance to rake.

Pellew indisputably held the advantage. The eighteen big 42-pounder carronades on his upper deck fired their heavy balls into *Virginie* while the *Indefatigable*'s main armament of 24-pounders on the main gun deck pounded her. Bergeret's gunners succeeded in shooting away *Indefatigable*'s mizen topmast and breaking her spanker gaff. Pellew had also lost the use of his main topsail; balls from *Virginie* having cut the bolt-ropes which ran down the vertical leeches of this important sail.

But *Virginie* suffered more. Her mizen having already gone by the board, at two in the morning of the 21st her maintopmast fell, immediately followed by her fore topgallant. As a result of this loss of power she slowed, and *Indefatigable* shot ahead of her. With *Virginie* swinging under the drag of the wreckage over her starboard side, Bergeret almost succeeded in raking *Indefatigable*'s suddenly vulnerable stern, but Pellew foiled this manoeuvre by putting over his own helm. As the two combatants drew apart the guns fell silent. Pellew sent his topmen aloft to reeve new braces so that he could work back up to windward, but by now Hunt was coming up fast, intending to place *Concorde* athwart *Virginie*'s stern, and *Amazon* was also approaching. Poor Bergeret had run out of luck. *Virginie* had lost fifteen men killed and twenty-seven wounded, ten seriously; she also had one and a half metres of water in her hold. Bergeret ordered a gun fired to leeward, and lowered his lantern in surrender.

This celebrated action and *Virginie's* gallant fight inspired the London print-makers and the artist Nicholas Pocock. Almost new, having been built at Brest in 1794, she was purchased into the Royal Navy. Bergeret was paroled and became both a guest and a friend of Pellew; the two corresponded for years afterwards. At first Bergeret was offered to M. Otto, the French commissioner for prisoners then resident in London, as an exchange for Sir Sidney Smith; this was refused, but in due course he was exchanged for another British captain in French custody.

The Admiralty now increased the number of frigates patrolling the Irish coast, where the numerous fine but remote natural anchorages, strategically positioned to windward of mainland Britain, were useful for enemy corsairs. The important trade into Liverpool from Africa, the West Indies and North America which passed through St George's Channel was a rich source of plunder, for which French privateers lay in wait off the Pembrokeshire coast. The great harbour of Cork on the south coast of Ireland, was a principal rendezvous for the assembly of convoys, and it was here that Vice-Admiral Kingsmill, the flag-officer responsible for the organisation of convoys and for the frigates known as the Irish Guard, had his static flagship.

The cruisers of the Irish Guard generally took their stations in the Celtic Sea south of the entrance to St George's Channel, hunting for corsairs or predatory enemy frigate squadrons. One of the latter sailed from Brest on 4 June under Commodore Moulston, an adventurous American citizen in the French service and a seaman of considerable ability. Moulston, in *Tribune,* ran into fog and lost touch with one of his ships, the *Proserpine.* In the small hours of 8 June, fifty miles to the west-north-west of the Isles of Scilly, he found two British frigates running down towards him in the darkness. These were the 32-gun, 18-pounder *Unicorn,* Captain Thomas Williams, and the ex-Spanish 36-gun, 12-pounder *Santa Margarita,* Captain Thomas Byam Martin. Martin was a graduate of the academy at Portsmouth which was a belated and only partially successful attempt by the Royal Navy to produce officers whose technological accomplishments were equal to their social advantages.

The two British frigates overhauled Moulston, who was obliged to carry easy sail to cover his weakest unit, the 18-gun corvette *Légère*. His third ship was Fradin's *Tamise*, formerly the British *Thames*. Allowing *Légère* to make her escape, Moulston and Fradin accepted battle. Martin went after Fradin, and Williams chased the French commodore. The French stern chasers aimed high and cut up the rigging of *Santa Margarita* and *Unicorn* as they approached, but as the *Unicorn* drew past the *Tamise* in pursuit of *Tribune* she fired into Fradin's ship. He bore up to avoid this, at the same time raking *Santa Margarita* from ahead; Martin quickly swung *Santa Margarita* away, and the two ships began a short cannonade. At about twenty minutes past four o'clock in the afternoon, the *Tamise* surrendered. She was heavily damaged and had suffered badly in both her hull and her people, losing thirty-two dead and nineteen wounded. Martin, on the other hand, lost two killed and three wounded. *Tamise* was taken back into the Royal Navy under her original name. Not only was honour restored, but the recapture of *Thames* put an end to her depredations: she had captured more than twenty prizes during her time as a French man-of-war.

While Martin secured his prize, *Unicorn* continued in pursuit of *Tribune*. Moulston crowded on sail, and held Williams at bay for hours in a running fight. Aiming high to disable his pursuer, Moulston's gunners shot away *Unicorn*'s main topsail. After dark the wind dropped; *Unicorn* set her studding sails and, creeping up on *Tribune*, Williams managed to place his ship directly to windward of *Tribune* to steal her breeze. Thus, an hour and a half before midnight and after a chase of 210 miles, *Unicorn* finally ranged up on the weather side of *Tribune*. Cheering, the British gunners opened fire. The French responded, and the two ships traded broadsides for thirty-five minutes. In the smoke and noise, *Tribune* dropped slightly astern, and Moulston put his helm over to cross *Unicorn*'s stern and rake. But Williams, advised of this, hauled *Unicorn*'s yards round and caught the wind aback, driving his ship astern, so that she took up a position on *Tribune*'s weather bow from which she was able to shoot away the French ship's fore and main masts, and her mizen topmast. With thirty-seven – more than ten per cent – of his men killed and fourteen badly wounded, Moulston lowered his colours. Williams had suffered not one casualty, evidence of the French gunners' folly in firing high. There was no bloody butcher's bill, but despite this, and probably because he was the senior officer of a pair of frigates which took two of the enemy, Williams was knighted, and his first lieutenant, Thomas Palmer, was made commander. *Tribune* was taken into the Royal Navy, but did not last long, being wrecked off Halifax, Nova Scotia in November 1797.

The lost member of Moulston's squadron now fell foul of another frigate of the Irish Guard, the 36-gun, 12-pounder frigate *Dryad*, cruising off Cape Clear on 13 June under the command of Captain Lord Amelius Beauclerk. An hour after midnight, as *Dryad* was close hauled on the starboard tack, heading south-west with the wind in the north-west quarter, a sail was seen right ahead – the *Proserpine*. Sighting the *Dryad* bearing determinedly down, and realising she was not the mislaid consorts he was in search of, Capitaine Etienne Pévrieux ordered *Proserpine* put about to escape.

It was about eight in the forenoon before the pursuing *Dryad* could open fire, which she did just as Pévrieux ordered *Prosperpine*'s colours hoisted. The chase continued for an hour by which time Beauclerk had worked *Dryad* up under *Proserpine*'s lee quarter. A close action began. The weather station of the French ship prevented her from doing any serious damage to *Dryad*'s spars, though her rigging was badly cut about and her ensign was shot away. Beauclerk ran his colours aloft again on the mizen mast, while his gunners extorted a terrible toll of thirty killed and forty-five wounded in the three-quarters of an hour the engagement lasted. With the whole larboard side of his frigate badly battered, Pévrieux hauled his ensign down. In due course, and with due deference to her aristocratic captor, *Proserpine* was added to the British fleet as *Amelia*. A week later the unfortunate *Légère* was caught by the *Apollo*, 38, and *Doris*, 36, as she tried to return to Brest. Captured, she too was added to the Royal Navy and the annihilation of Moulston's force was complete.

British cruisers were also successful elsewhere. Jervis's ships took a number of French prizes in the Mediterranean, and in October, when hostilities with Spain began, Richard Bowen in *Terpsichore* took the Spanish *Mahonesa,* which was added to the British fleet. He was less fortunate in December, when he fought and took the French frigate *Vestale.* The weather was bad, with a heavy sea running, and only a small prize-crew got aboard the captured frigate. Later, when *Terpsichore* was out of sight, they were overwhelmed by a rising of the *Vestale*'s crew, and the ship was carried into Cadiz. No less a person than Nelson, now a commodore caught up in the British withdrawal from the Mediterranean, also lost his prizes: his small squadron had taken two ships when a vastly superior Spanish squadron came up with him and he was compelled to relinquish them.

Duncan's ships in the North Sea secured several prizes, and Captain Henry Trollope of the *Glatton* fought off a squadron of seven French frigates. *Glatton* was a hybrid man-of-war, a former East Indiaman armed solely with carronades, twenty-eight 68-pounders on her lower deck and the same number of 32-pounders on her upper deck. In the action she was said to have so mauled her enemies that one sank after being chased into Vlissingen. The value of the carronade at short range was demonstrated by Commander John Searle in the sloop *Pelican* in the West Indies, where he beat off the frigate *Médée* and several other engagements were fought and captures made. In the East Indies, Contre-Amiral Sercey drove off an attempt by two British 74s to engage his five-strong frigate squadron and continued his attacks on British and Indian ships in the Bay of Bengal and Sunda Strait.

The war was now approaching the first of its two climacterics. In Paris, the Republican government had overcome most of its internal problems. General Lazare Hoche had broken the power of the revolt in the Vendée, the resources of the Batavian Republic were now at France's disposal, and in Italy the French were doing rather well against the Austrians under a general who had altered his name since his early artillery days and now signed himself Napoleon Bonaparte.

In fact, the French did very well during 1796. By October they had signed the Treaty of San Ildefonso with Spain, the principal effect of which was to amalgamate the French Mediterranean fleet with the

Spanish. Before the end of the year, therefore, the Royal Navy was compelled to abandon the Mediterranean (and its base of Corsica) and withdraw its fleet to Gibraltar, from where it exchanged Cadiz for Toulon as a blockade station. By this time the British ex-Mediterranean fleet was under Sir John Jervis, a decisive admiral of whom Nelson (who was then serving under him) remarked, 'Where I would take a pen-knife . . . [he] takes a hatchet.' Hostilities between Great Britain and Spain were declared in October.

The union of the French and Spanish fleets was a grave matter for Their Lordships, quite different from that of the French and Dutch navies. Whereas the Dutch, superb seafarers though they were, were limited in the size of their best men-of-war by the shallowness of their native waters, the Spanish were subject to no such restrictions. Spanish naval ship-building was of a very high order, both at home and abroad, especially in the dockyard of Havana where the largest warships of the day, great *navios* of 110 and 120 guns, were produced from Honduran mahogany. Nor were the Spanish incompetent at sea. A combined Franco-Spanish battle-fleet was therefore greatly to be feared.

This fear had been preceded by a deeper worry: word had reached London that spring of 1796 that Paris was meditating a major expedition against Great Britain. Full-scale invasion seemed a remote possibility, but in its disaffected state Ireland was clearly a fruit ripe for the picking. A secret organisation called The United Irishmen, led by Lord Edward Fitzgerald and Wolfe Tone, was busy fomenting rebellion, but had been infiltrated by Pitt's agents. The government therefore knew where – but not when – the enemy were likely to attack. The Channel Fleet was reorganised to take into account this additional contingency, and Command-in-Chief was vested in Lord Bridport, with a number of subordinate admirals commanding subsidiary squadrons. Early warning of any attempt to sail by the French squadron in Brest was of vital importance, and British cruiser captains were instructed accordingly.

During this period, an uncertain one for British fortunes, a number of important procedures were being established. Misconduct on the part of one rear-admiral notwithstanding, (Man, who returned to Britain in defiance of Jervis's instructions), the old ways were being superseded as adversity improved the Royal Navy's collective proficiency in two important ways, one practical, the other psychological.

The first improvement was a product of experience and slow but certain progress in logistics. The ability of ships to 'keep the sea', personally unpleasant though it was, improved steadily, particularly in the smaller vessels-of-war. Thus The Admiralty, linked with its principal fleet anchorages and bases in Britain by a remarkably efficient telegraph system, could transmit orders to its port admirals on the home coast. From the coastal termini, these instructions could be quickly sent to the squadron commanders and detached cruisers at sea in the growing number of cutters, luggers and sloops which acted as 'advice-boats'. It became common to attach these despatch vessels to all fleets and even to frigate squadrons, so that senior officers could transmit intelligence back to London without weakening their main force.

The concomitant improvement was to the psychological dynamic, for this constant sea-keeping encouraged a state of mind common to all commanding officers. Now, while they undoubtedly still sought personal enrichment and advancement, increasingly this self-serving became generally subordinate to the greater naval objectives in the thinking of all but the most intellectually obdurate. The sense of common purpose that began to imbue all captains, but in particular cruiser-commanders, not only eased some of the difficulties of decision-making, but united them in their joint conduct when in company and in mutual support of one another.

These qualities were hard bought during that year of adversity. While Jervis was losing several of his ships-of-the-line to bad weather and grounding, the French were on the offensive. In addition to the frigates of Thévenard and Thomas, Contre-Amiral de Richery had slipped out of Toulon and reached Cádiz. From there, even before the Treaty of San Ildefonso had been signed, the Spanish were persuaded to sail a large fleet to cover the further departure of de Richery: Don Juan de Langara, Lord Hood's former ally at Toulon, obliged. De Richery crossed the Atlantic with seven of the line and three frigates, and in September raided the British Canadian fishing communities along the coasts of Nova Scotia and Newfoundland. De Richery then detached Commodore Allemand, who scoured the coat of Labrador, with the

*Censeur* and *Duquesne*, 74s, and the frigate *Friponne*. Altogether these attacks destroyed about a hundred fishing and merchant vessels, though their crews were landed at Halifax in a cartel. Returning to France, de Richery reached Rochefort on 5 November and Allemand put in to L'Orient on the 15th.

De Richery's homeward passage had in fact been planned to integrate with the proposed descent upon Ireland, concerted with the insurgent Irish leadership when Lord Edward Fitzgerald and Arthur O'Connor met Général Hoche at Basle. The French Minister of Marine, Vice-Amiral Laurent Truguet, duly passed instructions to his admirals. Morard de Galles (who had replaced Villaret-Joyeuse at Hoche's instigation) was to sail from Brest with a battle-squadron of twenty-six of the line and a large troop convoy. To add to the fifteen of the line then in Brest, de Richery was to bring seven sail-of-the-line from L'Orient, and Villeneuve the remaining six from Toulon. De Richery was not able to make L'Orient on his return from Newfoundland, however, frustrated by the presence offshore of a British squadron. When he finally picked up the L'Orient ships, he then had to evade a second British squadron off Brest, under Vice Admiral Sir John Colpoys. By the time de Richery got into port on 11 December, most of the ships he had brought with him were declared unfit for sea. Moreover, Villeneuve had not arrived, nor would he, for it eventually transpired that he had been driven into L'Orient by Colpoys on 23 December.

Nevertheless, taking advantage of an easterly wind, between 15 and 16 December, de Galles left Brest, bound for Mizen Head and the west coast of Ireland. Though smaller than planned, De Galles's fleet was formidable: seventeen sail-of-the-line, thirteen frigates, six corvettes, a powder vessel, and seven transports with about 18,000 soldiers on board under Général Lazare Hoche. But the expedition was doomed from the start.

As the fleet emerged to gain an offing, de Galles decided to change the orders and direct his ships through the open Iroise, rather than the narrower Passage du Raz. It was already growing dark, and only a few of his consorts saw the admiral's signal. The fleet began to divide. De Galles fired guns and burned flares to call attention to his own progress in his flagship, and also directed the brig-corvette *Atalante* to chase and bring back that part of the fleet heading for the Passage du Raz. The *Atalante*'s guns and flares only added to a confusion which, bad enough already, was about to be gleefully exacerbated by the singular exertions of Sir Edward Pellew, ever observant, cruising offshore in the darkness.

Humiliating though the evacuation from the Mediterranean was, and notwithstanding the importance of trade from the East and West Indies, it was mastery of her home waters which was critical to Britain's self-preservation. The threatened invasion and potential occupation and annexation of Ireland was thus a major crisis of the war.

Pellew's task during the greater part of the year had been to maintain the advanced observation post outside Brest on behalf of the blockading squadron of ships-of-the-line lying 20 miles west of Ushant under Vice-Admiral Sir John Colpoys. From time to time his frigates had pounced on enemy vessels, but for the most part his continuing presence was merely intimidating.

Besides *Indefatigable*, Pellew's squadron was composed of Francis Cole's *Revolutionaire*, Robert Reynolds' *Amazon*, Robert Barlow's *Phoebe*, and Benjamin Sparrow's lugger *Duke of York*. On 11 December Pellew had sent *Phoebe* out to Admiral Colpoys and *Amazon* to England with news of de Richery's arrival at Brest with the men-of-war from L'Orient. On the 15th, when the first outward movement of the expedition was observed, Pellew sent *Phoebe* back out to Colpoys with the information, and closed up towards the Bec du Raz with Cole and Sparrow in company. On the next afternoon, as the huge fleet was coming out of the Goulet, Pellew sent Cole's *Revolutionaire* to update Colpoys, and remained on station in *Indefatigable* with the intention of making a thorough nuisance of himself.

In the closing hours of daylight on the 16th the flares and guns fired by de Galles and the *Atalante* to restore order to the French fleet were added to by Pellew, who had spent the afternoon playing cat-and-mouse with a line-of-battle ship and five frigates. Further confusion was caused by the distress rockets sent up from the 74-gun *Séduisant*, which had run aground and during the night became a total wreck, costing the lives of seven hundred men. While this disaster was occurring, *Inde-*

*fatigable*, with the lugger *Duke of York* hanging on like a shadow, sailed within gunshot of the emerging enemy ships. Just before dawn Pellew finally stood offshore, clear of the French and in search of Colpoys, sending Sparrow off to Falmouth with his despatches.

Meanwhile, Captain Barlow in *Phoebe* had been unable to find Colpoys who had shifted his station to the north-west of Ushant, and it was the 19th before he joined the admiral with news that was already out of date. Colpoys pressed south-west in deteriorating weather, intending to catch the French ships emerging through the Passage du Raz. Not surprisingly, he missed the main body; but he did see Villeneuve's Toulon squadron attempting a late arrival at Brest, and promptly chased them in to L'Orient. During this period the first of what proved to be a series of gales was in progress and Colpoys, sustaining damage throughout his squadron, withdrew towards Spithead.

Pellew in the meantime, having failed to find Colpoys's squadron, had reached Falmouth on the 20th. In response to his news the Admiralty ordered Lord Bridport to sea, and the main body of the Channel Fleet weighed from Spithead on Christmas Day to intercept the French. A series of collisions between the very unhandy first- and second-rates manoeuvring in close proximity in the strong wind caused a series of delays which postponed Bridport's departure until 3 January: no unit of the Channel Fleet was therefore in a position to prevent an enemy descent upon Ireland. The Channel Fleet was maintained for precisely this task, and now it had failed.

Everything therefore depended upon the frigates then at sea.

Meanwhile the French fleet, that part of it standing through the Passage du Raz under Contre-Amiral Bouvet, had turned west once clear of the dangers. Having lost sight of de Galles, Bouvet opened his secret orders, and on the forenoon of the 19th turned north-west for Mizen Head, to cruise in the vicinity for five days as instructed. In the succeeding hours he picked up most of the rest of the ships, so that by noon only nine were missing. Fatally, one of these, the *Fraternité,* bore de Galles.

Bouvet assumed command of the expedition himself, and in poor weather made for the rendezvous off Mizen Head, afterwards giving orders for the fleet to enter the long inlet of Bantry Bay where he picked up pilots, who thought the ships were British. The nearest British ships were in fact Kingsmill's frigates of the Irish Guard at Cork, so matters appeared propitious as Bouvet's fleet began to beat up Bantry Bay against an easterly headwind. A few ships managed to anchor off Bere Island, but in the following days the French were confronted by a succession of easterly storms which threw the entire enterprise into total confusion.

De Galles's flagship, the *Fraternité*, finally reached the Irish coast, only to be chased far to the west by *Unicorn* and *Doris* of the Irish Guard, which had been alerted to the presence of the French expedition. Of the other French men-of-war and transports, some escaped total destruction, some were captured and others wrecked when they dragged their anchors in the bad weather. Though there were no British troops to oppose a landing, no French troops were put ashore; instead, they were subject to the continuing miseries of sea-sickness, confinement and bad food. In those first dull and stormy days of the new year, the whole expedition disintegrated. Most ships still capable of the passage made for home, their only triumph a hollow pursuit of the outnumbered British frigates *Doris* and *Unicorn*. Some returned safely to Brest, others were chased by Bridport's Channel Fleet, which had finally put to sea, but the weather was so bad and the visibility so poor in the short winter days, that they escaped, some running as far south as Rochefort.

A few French ships had proceeded further north along the Irish coast to the mouth of the Shannon, one of them the *Droits de l'Homme* of 74 guns, Commodore La Crosse. On 5 January 1797 La Crosse captured a British ship, the *Cumberland* (Captain Peter Inglis) a deeply-laden West Indiaman carrying a letter-of-marque and thus, technically, a privateer. La Crosse quitted the Irish coast on 9 January and stood south, intending to make a landfall on Belle Isle. Unfortunately, on the 13th he found the weather so thick that he dared not approach the coast, so *Droits de l'Homme* was headed south under easy sail until the visibility cleared, having the westerly wind on her starboard beam.

In the early afternoon La Crosse saw two ships to the westward, and squared away for fear they were British. It seems probable however that they were the *Fraternité*, still flying de Galles's flag, and the *Révolution,* returning from Ireland and heading for the Île de Ré. *Droits de l'Homme* sped south-east before a rising gale, only to discover, at half past three, two other ships on her *lee* bow, heading to cut her off from the land. These proved to be the *Indefatigable* and *Amazon.* Despite the severity of the weather, it was business as usual for Pellew's frigate squadron, cruising on its station.

Still fearful that the ships astern were British, La Crosse cleared for action, but could not open his lower deck gun-ports in the heavy sea. Moreover, his main topsail braces parted, and soon afterwards the fore and main topmasts carried away, leaving him under courses and mizen topsail; the lack of upper sail caused *Droits de l'Homme* to roll heavily as she ran to leeward. It was now about half-past four, and growing dark. The British ships coming up on the lee bow had drawn apart, with the larger *Indefatigable* several miles ahead of *Amazon.* An hour later La Crosse's men had cleared their ship of the fallen spars, and by the time *Indefatigable* was within close range they were ready to fight her.

The lack of lower-deck guns due to the rolling of the ship, and of steadying sail aloft, robbed the *Droits de l'Homme* of any superiority inherent in her status as a 74-gun ship. La Crosse was, moreover, matching himself and his demoralised crew against one of the best ships his enemy possessed. The only slight edge the *Droits de l'Homme* might have been said to have was the presence on board of Général Humbert and a considerable detachment of troops who were beginning by now to acquire their sea-legs.

As Pellew approached, the sky cleared a little and a fitful moonlight gleamed on the turbulent sea through which the partially dismasted French line-of-battle ship wallowed. The British frigate was overhauling her at almost twice her speed. As the wind rose Pellew double-reefed *Indefatigable*'s topsails and hauled up to rake *Droits de l'Homme,* but La Crosse, helped by the upper after-canvas of the mizen topsail, followed round. The ships exchanged broadsides and Humbert's troops loosed a storm of musketry at *Indefatigable,* then both vessels paid off before the wind again. Having the advantage of speed, Pellew next sought to overtake his opponent and swing across La Crosse's bow to rake, but La Crosse boldly turned *towards* Pellew, intending to board *Indefatigable* and use his advantage of manpower to good effect. Although he missed *Indefatigable's* larboard quarter, La Crosse drove *Droits de l'Homme* across her stern, the prime position to rake. But the high sea-state, the rolling of his ship and his lack of heavy lower-deck guns deprived La Crosse of this master-stroke, and his broadside was largely ineffective. The two ships then again ran on, exchanging fire, and aboard *Droits de l'Homme* an 18-pounder gun burst, with horrid consequences.

By now *Amazon* was coming up fast, and Reynolds tried in turn to rake by crossing *Droits de l'Homme's* stern. He too was frustrated, in this case by La Crosse's steadiness of manoeuvre, and the sail they were carrying in comparison with the *Droits de l'Homme* caused both British frigates to shoot ahead. There now occurred an hiatus during which all three ships' companies made hurried repairs, knotting and splicing the braces, sheets, lift and halliards that had been shot away and without which their vessels were unmanageable. The wind had backed a little and the weather had become somewhat hazy in the intermittent moonlight.

Hampered by his loss of forward upper sails, east-south-east was the best course La Crosse could make as, at half-past eight, the two British ships approached for the *coup de grâce*. Taking station on either bow, Reynolds and Pellew now yawed in succession, raking the *Droits de l'Homme,* while La Crosse also yawed and raked but to far less effect. Guessing correctly that the British frigates would be undermanned, he constantly sought an opportunity to run aboard his tormentors and use Humbert's troops to carry them. But Pellew and Reynolds, fully appreciating their danger, almost danced out of the way of the leviathan in their wake. It was a dazzling display of seamanship by all concerned in the alternating darkness and moonlight of a boisterous night in which the three ships were swept by intermittent snow squalls; and it was destined to end in a climax quite as desperate and dramatic as the long running action.

By half past ten the mizen mast of the French line-of-battle ship was so badly damaged that La Crosse ordered it cut away, to ensure it should not fall and interfere with his gunnery. Seeing this, Pellew and Reynolds promptly dropped astern and engaged from opposite quarters as La Crosse, down to his last fifty round-shot, began to fire hollow shells. At some time after midnight the British frigates drew off again to secure their own damaged rigging, an operation in which the Indefatigables exhausted all their spare cordage. They were also busy securing a number of guns, some of which had broken their breechings as many as four times. The sea was driving in through the open gunports aboard both British frigates. The gun-crews had been up to their waists in water, and had had to draw the sodden charges from their weapons and reload them with dry cartridges before they could use them. The three ships continued meanwhile to run to leeward, and the British soon resumed their attack, until twenty past four in the morning of the 14th when the moon suddenly emerged from the clouds. Lieutenant George Bell on the *Indefatigable*'s forecastle saw breakers ahead. The cry went up – land was in sight, dead to leeward!

On the *Droits de l'Homme*'s starboard quarter, Pellew hauled round to the south, hove down his tacks, braced sharp up and clawed his way offshore; Reynolds on the larboard quarter wore ship and stood north. La Crosse, superb seaman that he was, also swung to starboard, but the *Droits de l'Homme* could not stand the strain and as he hauled to the wind the battered foremast went overboard, tearing out the bowsprit. In desperation he let go an anchor, but the great ship struck the bottom. As she was pounded in the heavy, breaking sea, her mainmast went over the side. Throughout 14th, 15th and 16 January the wreck was swept by the sea. Some of the crew escaped, but many of the seamen and soldiers drowned as they tried to struggle ashore. A handful of survivors was taken off by corvettes sent out from Brest on the 17th but about a thousand Frenchmen perished in the disaster, killed in action, drowned in the wreck, or dying of exposure.

Nor did the British escape unscathed. While Pellew clawed *Indefatigable*'s water-logged hull with its wounded spars offshore, *Amazon* followed *Droits de l'Homme* onto the Breton coast. Reynolds had fatally lost ground by wearing round and was then unable to beat offshore partly because of the battered state of *Amazon*'s rigging. Instead he fell slowly but inexorably to leeward during the next half-hour, then ran aground under the north shore of Audierne Bay. All except six men escaped onto the land in the succeeding hours; surrendering themselves to a detachment of troops later in the morning, they were imprisoned at Quimper. Later in the year Reynolds himself was exchanged, and honourably acquitted of the loss of his ship.

Pellew, his crew reduced by nineteen men wounded, spent several hours manoeuvring *Indefatigable* out of danger, unaware of his precise location until daylight revealed it as Audierne Bay. Exhausted after the night's action, both captain and crew nevertheless lived up to the name of their ship as they fought to save her. At ten minutes past seven, as they regained deep water with the wind blowing dead on shore, they passed one mile clear of the *Droits de l'Homme*, lying 'broadside uppermost, with a tremendous surf beating over her'.

Despite the disruption of the British blockade by the storms, in addition to being wrecked through the extremity of the weather several vessels belonging to the Irish expedition were captured by British cruisers. On 30 December Captain George Lumsden in the *Polyphemus* took the troop-ship *Justine* off the Irish coast, and few days later, on 5 January, *Polyphemus* engaged the *Tartu* in a running fight. At the end of four hours the French frigate struck and was added to the British navy under an anglicisation of her original name, *Urania*. Some storeships and the corvette *Mutine* were taken, and on the 10th *Phoebe* captured de Galles' messenger, the corvette *Atalante*.

The unmitigated disaster of the Irish expedition rocked the Directory in Paris. The United Irishmen were abandoned to their own devices and their hopes eventually perished on the slopes of Vinegar Hill on 21 June 1798.

# CHAPTER 6

---

# 'The Devil in harbour'

The British public saw the dramatic destruction of the *Droits de l'Homme* as evidence that French ambitions in Ireland had been frustrated by the Royal Navy. Nor were the government anxious to dispel this misconception: the weather might have been largely responsible for putting an end to the Directory's expedition, but this was no reason why the ministry should not take the credit. They were soon afterwards to pay for this hubris.

Bridport was off Brest a few days after Pellew had left the scene of horror. Having satisfied himself that the French were back at their moorings licking their wounds, he sent some of his fleet to Jervis at Gibraltar and returned to Spithead. He made another sally to Ushant in March, and in early April a squadron of nine sail-of-the-line under Rear-Admiral Roger Curtis was stationed off Brest. Due to leave Spithead again, on 15 April 1797 Bridport passed word to unmoor. The ships' companies of the Channel Fleet refused. They would maintain the ships in perfect order and discipline, they said, but they would not proceed to sea in accordance with the Commander-in-Chief's orders.

The causes of the mutiny at Spithead were simple. Prior to the fleet's departure for the March cruise, the ships' crews had jointly petitioned Lord Howe with a list of grievances which they desired him to forward to the Admiralty, in the expectation that redress would be forthcoming from

Their Lordships by the time the fleet returned to Spithead. Nothing was done, however, so when the order was given to go to sea again, the seamen of the fleet demurred. The most unpopular officers were landed but the majority, treated with assiduous courtesy, were confined to their quarters. Ironically, the greatest aggression was exhibited by one of the admirals sent to treat with the representatives' delegates in the great cabin of the *Queen Charlotte*. As the authorities entrenched themselves, Sir Alan Gardner lost his temper in exasperation and threatened the delegates.

In fact the seamen's behaviour at Spithead was on the whole exemplary; moreover their grievances, chiefly concerning pay and conditions, were very real. Pay was unchanged since the reign of Charles II, more than a century before. While the cost of living, in particular the necessaries of life purchased on board ship, known as 'slops', had increased thirty per cent over this period. The seamen simply wanted parity with the army, where pay had risen in step with this inflation. As to conditions, food, or rather the lack of it, was the primary complaint. The notorious short measure of the purser's fourteen- ounce pound, the inedible salted meat which had often been *decades* in the cask, the staleness of cheese (from which it was common to carve little boxes: one frigate's main truck was made from an uncut wheel of cheese, into which flag halliards had been fitted) and the lack of fresh vegetables even when at anchor in sight of shore, were all adduced. As to other matters, the treatment of the sick was complained of, and there were accusations of embezzlement of the comforts supplied for their easement. That men wounded in action were deprived of their wages until they returned to duty or were discharged was considered cruel, and it was pointed out that the curtailment of liberty while in port only led to increased venereal infection and desertions.

Already there had been evidence of disaffection, in addition to the *Culloden* incident; there were the mutterings about sabotage after the *Boyne* blew up, and the incident of the previous autumn when the frigate *Amphion* exploded while alongside the sheer-hulk in Plymouth. Moored on the opposite side of the sheer-hulk lay the Plymouth Receiving Ship *Yarmouth*, full of unhappy, pressed seamen. The cause of *Amphion*'s loss was never established, and it is possible that some angry souls took action. She too had been under orders to sail on a cruise and her captain, Israel Pellew, was dining aboard with a colleague. About a hundred wives, children and sweethearts were thronging below decks, saying farewell on the eve of departure. The explosion killed more than three hundred people aboard *Amphion,* plus a number in *Yarmouth* and the sheer-hulk. Israel Pellew's guest was among the dead but the blast threw Pellew himself out through a shattered stern window, and he survived. Most of the other survivors were either on deck or aloft, hurled high into the air before falling into the water. No one troubled to investigate whether sabotage was involved.

The Channel Fleet's grievances were both wholly justifiable and moderate. Only the ships-of-the-line were involved: the delegates insisted that the frigate squadrons and independent cruisers take no part. They pledged that if an enemy invasion fleet appeared in the Channel, they would go to sea; significantly, there were no complaints about the press – clear evidence that this was not revolt, but an orderly and partial withdrawal of labour. The leaders were careful to maintain a unified front, and no one man emerged or took upon himself the role of conspicuous leader. At the end of tortuous negotiations, Lord Howe, though old and infirm, successfully treated with the men on behalf of the government. 'Black Dick' was trusted not only by the seamen but by the king, who regarded the Channel Fleet as 'Earl Richard's' personal fiefdom. In due course the grievances were met without reprisal.

As the Admiralty met the demands of the Channel Fleet, trouble broke out at the Nore, in the Thames estuary, almost certainly formented to some extent by infiltrated french agents. The Nore mutiny was a less temperate affair which met with no such tolerant accommodation as that at Spithead, and ended in the hanging of its identifiable leaders. The ships involved were largely from Duncan's fleet, though the bulk of his force remained in Yarmouth Roads, and discipline did not break down entirely. The mood among them was ugly, however: one of Duncan's ships was commanded by 'Bounty' Bligh. Meanwhile the handful of Duncan's frigates, cutters and luggers maintained a fictional blockade, signalling to imaginary ships over the horizon.

Elsewhere too violent mutinies were violently suppressed, not least in Britain's finest squadrons, those under Jervis based on Lisbon. Jervis insisted on imposing the death sentence, but his iron hand prevented a general and concerted mutiny from breaking out in his fleet. His aphorism that 'without order and discipline, nothing is achieved' was apt, but his assertion that he would flog a man who did not respect a midshipman's coat was telling. Other outbreaks occurred at the Cape and elsewhere, usually when ships from Britain arrived on station, but all were put down. The severity of the punishments tended to discourage further trouble, but as late as 1801 seditious pamphleteering earned a seaman named King from the frigate *Active* a 500-lash flogging round the fleet.

At this time, however, there was also a rise in the number of courts martial sitting in judgement upon officers accused of ill-treatment, a sign that the authorities were beginning to recognise the importance of improving the regime aboard ships-of-war. Occasionally a crew rose against the tyranny, real or imagined, of their commander. At the Cape of Good Hope in October 1797 the crew of the 74-gun *Tremendous* mutinied, albeit futilely, against Captain Stephens. Off Ushant in March 1800 the crew of the frigate *Danaë* rose against Captain Lord Proby and took their ship into Brest, which they had been blockading. Expecting a sympathetic reception from the republicans, enhanced by their surrender of an aristocrat, they found themselves imprisoned. To their fury, the unpleasant Proby was kindly treated.

The worst of these personal revolts, one justifiable in its inception by the cruelty of Captain Hugh Pigot but then carried to unforgivable excess, occurred in the West Indies. At night on 22 September 1797 the crew of the *Hermione* rose and murdered Pigot and several of his officers. The ship was surrendered to the Spanish authorities at La Guayra, on the north coast of South America, and commissioned into the Spanish navy.

But such intermittent and disparate trouble was relatively un-important: mutiny in a single cruiser could not affect the course of the war, whatever its local propaganda value. Mutiny in a fleet on service was a real threat to British security; and in a fleet such as Jervis's, in particular, mutiny was an indication of something seriously amiss. Only months before his ships had had something to celebrate, and were in expectation of prize- and head-money. On 14 February 1797, outnumbered two to one, they had smashed a large Spanish fleet off Cape St Vincent and earned Jervis his subsequent eponymous earldom.

In this action the British line-of-battle was led by Troubridge in *Culloden* as it passed between the two Spanish lines. With perfect precision Jervis tacked to set upon Almirante De Cordova's weather division, but it was Nelson in the 74-gun *Captain* who unconventionally broke the British line and frustrated De Cordova's escape. Nelson was followed by Collingwood in *Excellent,* and these two ships promptly engaged the Spanish van, the *Santissima Trinidad,* the largest warship in the world, bearing 136 guns, the 110-gun *San Joseph* and the 112-gun *Salvador del Mundo.* In the confusion caused by the attack of *Captain* and *Excellent* the Spanish formation disintegrated, allowing Jervis to come up in the *Victory* with the bulk of the fleet and destroy De Cordova's ships in detail. On the deck of *Captain* Nelson drew his sword and led the boarders who took two first-rates, the *San Josef* and the 80-gun *San Nicholás,* the second over the deck of the first.

Insurrection in a fleet such as had fought on St Valentine's Day 1797 had to be a matter of grave concern, but hindsight shows that in spite of the flood of mutinies that occurred in 1797 and intermittently afterwards, and in spite of a continuing savage repression of the civil liberties of seamen up to the end of the war in 1815, the Royal Navy remained generally loyal. There were indications that this was so as early as October 1797, when Duncan's disaffected North Sea fleet defeated the Dutch under Vice-Admiraal De Winter at Camperdown. The victories of Cape St Vincent and Camperdown spelt ruin to the first of a series of grand plans to invade mainland Britain. Both De Winter and De Cordova had been intending to unite with de Galles at Brest in preparation for a descent upon the English coast in the following year. Both had been destroyed.

Notwithstanding the failure of the Irish venture, which was put down to extremities of weather, and the setbacks at St Vincent and Camperdown, French plans for an invasion of England continued. Flotillas of *bateaux* were constructed all along the French Channel coast, one of the inspectors-general charged with the project being La Crosse, now a contre-amiral. This ambitious enterprise was not immediately within the compass of the French Directory and its allies, however. An odd little incursion they made meanwhile, in February 1797, was as disastrous in its way as the expedition to Ireland.

A force of 1,500 desperate French criminals induced to volunteer as soldiers had formed themselves into what was known as the Black Legion. Led by a volunteer American, William Tate, they embarked aboard a frigate squadron with the intention of raiding and harrying the English coast, as Captain John Paul Jones had done so successfully in 1778, during the American War. Designed to strike at the heart of Britain's commercial wealth, their first descent was to be on Bristol; they were then to attack Liverpool. In fact they landed at the small north Devon town of Ilfracombe, then re-embarked to cross the Bristol Channel and land at Fishguard in West Wales. There, without achieving anything, the Black Legion ignominiously surrendered on 22 February to Welsh yeomanry, fencibles and militia commanded by Lord Cawdor. As they did so, the ships that had conveyed them to the Pembroke coast ran home. Capitaine Jean-Baptiste Laroque, aboard the *Résistance* of 40 guns, not only abandoned the Black Legion at Fishguard but then lost touch with the frigate *Vengeance* and *chasse-marée Vautour*. In company with only the 22-gun corvette *Constance,* Laroque was approaching Brest on 9 March when he was spotted by two British frigates returning from a reconnaissance of the French port to report to Bridport, then lying west of Ushant with the Channel Fleet.

It was early in the forenoon as Captain Sir Harry Neale of the 36-gun *San Fiorenzo* and Captain John Cooke of the *Nymphe* ran out of the Iroise. The French fleet was anchored astern in Brest, and in the easterly wind, intervention by some of the anchored ships was a possibility. Neale and Cooke worked to windward as Laroque attempted to dash past them into the Goulet. Pointe St Mathieu was only 9 miles away, but the *San Fiorenzo* and *Nymphe* bore down on Laroque. After an unequal engagement of twenty minutes the *Résistance* struck her colours, Laroque afterwards claiming that a damaged rudder had made his ship difficult to handle. Neale and Cooke swiftly took possession of their prize, then fell upon her consort coming up from the rear. Despite the overwhelming force of his opponents, Capitaine Purchet in *Constance* put up a stouter fight than his commodore, striking only after suffering casualties and with the British 74-gun *Robust* and 28-gun frigate *Triton* in sight to seaward; the corvette's mainmast and foretopmast fell a few moments later. Nevertheless, *Constance* was purchased into the Royal Navy under her own name; *Résistance* was renamed *Fisgard*, the contemporary spelling of the Welsh seaport she had lately visited.

The mutiny at Spithead caused the frigate squadrons to be drawn home to patrol the Channel during April, May and June, and the French took the opportunity of this respite on the Biscay coast to convey quantities of naval stores into Brest, L'Orient and Rochefort. But by July Warren's squadron was back on the Breton coast. Shortly after midnight on the 16th they ran across a convoy of fourteen ships to seaward of Audierne Bay, escorted by the frigate *Calliope* and two corvettes. As Warren bore down, the corvettes made off to the southward round Penmarch Point. Unable to follow, the *Calliope* was run ashore and reduced to a wreck. Meanwhile the prizes from the convoy were sent home: a transport, three brigs and four *chasse-marées*. A vessel laden with ship-timbers and a brig had been run ashore and lost, and only four vessels had escaped.

The constitution the frigate squadrons was constantly changing. The escort of prizes home, the transmission of despatches and intelligence to England and to the heavy squadron offshore put a constant demand on these ships. On 11 August Warren was off La Vendée with a reorganised squadron. Early in the forenoon a convoy was seen leaving the Basque Road through the channel known as the Pertuis d'Antioche, between the Île de Ré and the Île d'Oléron. Sighting the British ships offshore, the convoy's escort commander in a 20-gun ship-corvette ordered his charges to run for Les Sables d'Olonne, where there were heavy shore batteries and a river estuary to afford them shelter. Warren withdrew, leaving the corvette *Réolaise* damaged but with her convoy intact, a detail Warren fudged in his report.

Warren's cruisers then moved south to the mouth of the Gironde, where at sunset on 27 August they caught sight of another French convoy. Chasing to the south-west for the whole night, the two windward ships, *Jason* and *Triton*, captured five merchantmen. Warren then worked back inshore and the following day a 12-gun cutter creeping along the shore near Arcachon was spotted from *Pomone*. Warren sent his boats after her, but the cutter refused to surrender until *Pomone* loomed up and shot away her mast. The cutter, named *Le Petit-Diable*, was run ashore to prevent her becoming a prize. These events prompted Warren to pen one of his notoriously embroidered letters which, as he had confidently expected, was published in the *London Gazette*, enhancing his public image.

Sir Edward Pellew was out of action during the greater part of 1797 while *Indefatigable* was repaired. On recommissioning the big frigate returned to sea, and under Bridport's direct command as Commander-in-Chief Pellew took her out into the Atlantic to cruise in protection of trade. In mid October *Indefatigable* took a French corsair, the 12-gun *Ranger*, off the Canaries. A few days later, on the 25th, Pellew hove in sight of another sail, the *Hyène*, which as the British frigate *Hyaena* had been captured by the then French frigate *Concorde* (herself now in the Royal Navy) in May 1793. The *Hyène* had been sold to a Bordeaux *armateur*, an owner and operator of privateers, an enterprising gentleman who had improved the qualities of a notoriously bad sailer by cutting away her raised forecastle and quarterdeck. Thus reduced to a flush-decked ship, she had been sent to sea as a corsair.

Approaching *Indefatigable* under the assumption that she was a Portuguese East Indiaman, the *Hyène* was surprised when Pellew gave chase, revealing his vessel as a British man-of-war. Conditions favoured the modified *Hyène*, and Pellew pressed her hard for eight hours without gaining on her. Then *Hyène* lost her foretopmast, fell under *Indefatigable*'s guns and struck her colours. She was afterwards restored in her modified form to the British navy under her old name, and Pellew and Bridport shared the profits.

War with Spain introduced one bright and significant consideration into the minds of British cruiser captains: treasure. The mines of Potosí, in what is now south-west Bolivia but was then part of Spanish South America, yielded quantities of silver and gold, much of it taken back to the Spanish exchequer in 'register-ships', usually fast and well-armed men-of-war sailing in pairs. From time to time throughout the wars of the eighteenth century some of these were captured by British cruisers. Fortunes were made by the lucky captains concerned, and even a common seaman might receive sufficient money to buy himself out of the service. On one occasion the seamen's individual shares amounted to £485 apiece. In the celebratory binge which followed, several of the sailors are said to have bought gold watches for the sole purpose of *frying* them, as evidence of their wealth!

No commanding officer who cruised off the Spanish coast ever closed his eyes in his cot without dreaming of a Spanish prize, and cupidity was perhaps a mild enough vice in men deprived of a normal life. Notwithstanding the significant privileges attaching to the rank of captain, life in a ship was far from physically comfortable. Such was the status of a post-captain, moreover, that his existence was lonely in the extreme: his opportunities to enjoy the society of others were constrained by convention, and unless a man was in the company of his peers he could not unbend without compromising his dignity. Aspiration for a treasure ship had become a favourite wardroom toast, and in April 1796 two such laden frigates were approaching Cádiz. Informed by some fishing boats that they had fallen between the main British blockading fleet offshore and the smaller inshore squadron and seeing hostile ships approaching, the Spanish commanders promptly transferred their silver specie into the fishing boats, thus divesting themselves of the wealth sparkling in the imaginations of Captains Martin and Berkeley even as they bore down in the 74-gun *Irresistible* and the 36-gun frigate *Emerald*. The Spanish frigates, the *Ninfa* and the *Santa Elena*, were chased into a bay between Cádiz and Cape Trafalgar, where they were attacked and taken. When they discovered how they had lost the treasure, Martin and Berkeley perhaps reflected ruefully on the many slips 'twixt cup and lip.

Elsewhere in the world there were encounters between French and British warships. There was inshore fighting along the Channel coast and Straits of Dover; de Sercey was still active in the Indian Ocean; Trinidad had been taken from the Spaniards, but they had defended Tenerife against an ill-advised attack by Nelson in which he lost his right arm. Yet for all its successes, the Royal Navy remained on the defensive. It had prevented a combination of the French, Dutch and Spanish fleets, but had also been made aware of the deficiencies of a lax blockade of Brest.

This was the key to command of the Channel, and it posed Their Lordships of the Admiralty a problem. It was all very well for intrepid frigate commanders like Pellew and his colleagues to keep the sea in all weathers and in all seasons, but the retention of a battle fleet on station all year round was an impossibility at this time. Instead a compromise had been reached, the withdrawal of the blockading line-of-battle ships to the English coast when conditions off Ushart became untenable. The only safe anchorage to which the Channel Fleet could retire was Tor Bay, but in the prevailing south-westerly winds, Tor Bay was to leeward of Brest. If the fleet could not maintain a constant presence off Ushant, was there a more weatherly, westerly alternative?

In the winter of 1797 Pellew sailed to the Isles of Scilly to investigate the possibility of using St Mary's Road as a fleet anchorage. He thought it was suitable, but he was wrong: it was too small, and the holding ground was later discovered to deteriorate rapidly in its northern part. Moreover, although there were alternative approaches suitable for use in varying wind conditions, a fact while recommended it to Pellew, their navigation was intricate. Pellew was misled by his own abilities. Mercifully the Admiralty decided against acting on his advice, so the spectacle of Bridport's cumbersome three-deckers lumbering into one another as they tried to pick their way through the islands' several navigable Sounds remained the stuff of nightmare.

By 1798 it was clear that defence of the realm rested upon maintaining as close a blockade as was possible upon the port of Brest. Moreover, the widespread outbreak of mutiny had persuaded Their Lordships of an old truth, that seamen were better governed at sea than in port. As 'Mad Charlie' Napier, afterwards an admiral but a midshipman at this time, succinctly remarked, the men were 'the devil in harbour'. Accordingly, a dozen sail-of-the-line and three frigates sailed to cruise in the Bay of Biscay at the end of January and a second detachment of the Channel Fleet left Plymouth to cruise off Ireland in early April, followed a few days later by Bridport with ten of the line bound for Ushant.

At about midday on April 21st the wind was in the north-east quarter, blowing out of Brest, and Bridport's fleet was heading roughly south across the outer Iroise. Inshore to windward were three flanking British ships 'on the lookout', and these observed two sails about twelve miles to the east, close to the land. The three British men-of-war were the 74-gun *Mars* and *Ramillies*, with the 38-gun frigate *Jason*, which gave chase. The fresh wind favoured the heavier 74s, which soon caught up with the strange sails, whereupon a third was seen trying to get in to Brest from the south-east. Having the appearance of an enemy line-of-battle ship, this vessel swiftly attracted the unwelcome attention of the three British ships, which sought to cut her off from Brest. At about half-past six in the evening the *Ramillies* lost her fore topmast and fell out of the chase; *Jason*, unable to keep up with the *Mars*, fell astern. It was now dusk. The *Mars* (commanded by Alexander Hood, brother to Samuel whose earlier escape from Toulon will be recalled) stood on and Hood observed the enemy trying to pass into Brest by the Passage du Raz, against the tide. Failing to make good her escape, however, the enemy ship anchored south of the Bec du Raz in the entrance to the channel and her captain ordered a spring clapped to her cable, to allow him to swing his ship broadside-on to the approaching *Mars*.

Hood clewed up his courses and approached the enemy line-of-battle ship, which opened fire on *Mars*. Hood's gunners responded as shot struck the bowsprit and foremast. The tide frustrated Hood in his attempt to hold his position under sail, so he ranged ahead, let go his starboard bower and veered cable, intending to bring up parallel at pistol-shot from the French vessel. But *Mars*'s anchor fouled that of the Frenchman and the two ships crashed together, broadside to broadside, so that they poured gunfire into one another, gun muzzles close together. The noise and carnage were frightful. Naval cannon were crude weapons, with little science in their operation: they functioned best when fired fast at short range, becoming machines for battering oak or human flesh into submission.

The action began about a quarter past nine and continued until half-past ten, a dreadful cannonade, hull to hull, in which the lower-deck guns could not be hauled out through the ports but were fired within the gun-decks. The enemy ship was the 74-gun *Hercule*, newly built at L'Orient and on her way to join the Brest fleet. Her commander, Capitaine Louis L'Héritier, twice ordered his crew to board, and twice they were repelled. The vessels were almost equally matched in terms of their complements, the *Hercule* with a crew of 680 against the *Mars*'s 634; but the rate of British gunfire was telling, and the starboard side of the *Hercule* was appallingly beaten in, riddled with shot and blackened by the flaming discharge of the British guns. About forty per cent of *Hercule*'s crew were killed and several guns in her batteries were dismounted or damaged. *Mars* lost some gun-ports in the collision, her hammock nettings, boats and spare spars were wrecked and she took several shots in the hull, but because of the French gunners' significantly slower rate of firing she had suffered far less. Among her 30 killed and 60 wounded, was her captain, Alexander Hood, who had a femoral artery severed and quickly bled to death on his own quarterdeck. The *Mars*'s first lieutenant, William Butterfield, took command and the prize was secured with the aid of the *Jason*, arriving opportunity on the lurid scene. A spell of fine weather enabled the British to get *Hercule* back to Portsmouth, where she required extensive repairs before joining the fleet under her own name. Butterfield was promoted commander after the action.

It now became an objective of the British to bedevil and frustrate the French preparations for invasion, and endeavours in this respect occupied enormous resources on both sides until the crisis finally passed about 1810. In particular it was an objective of the Royal Navy to be remorseless in their attacks upon coastal shipping carrying naval stores to the French ship-building ports.

Three years earlier, in July 1795, Sir Sidney Smith had landed and captured two low islands off the east coast of the Cotentin peninsula in the Baie de la Seine near St Vaast la Hogue, the Îles St Marcouf. The islands had been fortified – ships' guns were man-handled ashore – and garrisoned ever since by a small Royal Naval party of about five hundred seamen and marines under the command of Lieutenant Charles Price, supported by another lieutenant and a marine officer. Price had a tender, a 4-gun captured Dutch hoy renamed the *Badger*, of which he was the nominal commander. On her frequent trips to Portsmouth *Badger* brought back provisions and bags of earth, and other small cruisers operating in the Baie de la Seine were also instructed to take sacks of earth and land them at St Marcouf. By this means a garden was made which provided the garrison and the sloops and gun brigs in the area with fresh vegetables. By 1798 an additional tender, the *Sandfly*, commanded by Lieutenant Richard Bourne, had also been assigned to Price, and Bourne was quartered on the smaller island. Price, commissioned lieutenant in 1778, was an officer without interest, a coarse man who made the most of his unusual billet by bringing out his mistress, a Portsmouth whore, and keeping her openly on the island.

It was an affront to French honour that these islands remained in British hands, supporting the blockade of the French Channel ports from La Hogue to Le Havre. A M. Muskein had been commissioned into the French navy to design some special flat-boats to be used in the projected invasion of England. In April 1798, determined to prove his craft, Muskein had himself appointed to lead an invasion force against St Marcouf.

The principal British presence in the Baie de la Seine that spring was under Sir Richard Strachan in Smith's old frigate, the *Diamond*, and with him was Sir Francis Laforey in *Hydra*. On 8 April these two 38-gun frigates observed Muskein's flotilla of flat-boats anchored off Caen on their way from Le Havre to St Marcouf. Strachan worked *Diamond* inshore and opened fire, but ran into shoaling water and was unable to bring his frigate within range of the enemy. Muskein continued along the shore to the west, until the appearance of the 50-gun *Adamant*, in addition to the British frigates in the offing, persuaded him to retire east again. Taking refuge in the Orne estuary, he lay low until the coast was clear, meanwhile receiving reinforcements, and was able to reach La Hogue, where he awaited suitable tides and calm weather for his projected assault on St Marcouf.

By early May the British ships nearby consisted of *Adamant* (Captain William Hotham), the 24-gun *Eurydice* (Captain William Haggit), and the 18-gun sloop *Orestes*, but on the windless night of 6 May Hotham's ships were unable to interfere with Muskein's attack. About five thousand soldiers under Général Point had embarked in fifty flat-boats, supported by brig-corvettes which anchored offshore and provided covering fire as the flat-boats pulled in at daylight towards the landing places. Counting the heavy guns in the leading barges and the broadsides mounted in the brig-corvettes, the enemy were able to bring about eighty guns to bear on the defences. The British garrison immediately responded with their own artillery. On the western and larger island, Price's six 24-pounder, two 6-pounder and four 4-pounder long guns, with two 32-pounder and three 24-pounder carronades, opened up. The lesser island, under Bourne, mounted a similar number of small long guns and two heavy 68-pounder carronades, but these did not come into action until the end of the attack.

As the French rowed boldly inshore the British guns sank half a dozen flat-boats before they made the beach, which deterred the others, while British marines kept up a galling fire from the shore. The French losses were never admitted, but were estimated at upwards of a thousand men shot, drowned or missing. Price, by contrast, lost one man killed and four wounded. As the French retreated, light airs enabled Hotham's three men-of-war to get closer and fire a few shots after them. Price was promoted commander for this action (and later was made post,) but although Bourne was recommended, it does not appear that he was confirmed in a new rank.

During that same month of May the war was taken into the enemy camp, though with little success. A large force of small ships commanded by Captain Sir Home Riggs Popham, having a detachment of troops embarked, raided the locks at Ostend with the intention of disrupting the invasion plans. The expedition was a disaster, however, and some of the troops and seamen ashore were obliged to surrender to superior forces.

After these exchanges, the blockaded Brest fleet was largely quiescent during the summer of 1798. Not that the French naval authorities were idle: on the contrary, building of ships-of-the-line, frigates and corvettes went on under the urging of General Bonaparte who, in this as in the strategic summaries he prepared for the government, was laying the foundations for that great challenge of economic warfare he was himself to prosecute a few years later, as Emperor of the French.

# CHAPTER 7

## 'I shall return'

In May 1798 the rebellion of the United Irishmen broke out again when insurgents rose and took the city of Wexford. Support had again been promised from France, where Wolf Tone had been sent to negotiate, but in the event French help was too little, too late; the rebels were defeated by Crown forces at Vinegar Hill in June, long before the French had bestirred themselves.

Having actively encouraged the unfortunate Irishmen, the French were unable to despatch their two new expeditions on time because they could not pay their own troops! One squadron did leave Rochefort on 6 August, however, unobserved by the blockaders, and four frigates under Commodore Savary with 1,200 soldiers under Général Humbert reached Killalla Bay in County Mayo on the 22nd. These were the *Concorde*, 40 (Capitaine Papin), *Franchise*, 36 (Capitaine Guillotin), *Médée*, 36 (Capitaine Coudin), and the 28-gun *Vénus* (Capitaine Senez). Besides the soldiers, all were laden with arms and ammunition for 3,000 United Irishmen. These armaments and Humbert's troops were disembarked that evening and disappeared inland, brushing aside a small detachment of fencibles and yeomanry. Humbert thereafter marched halfway across Ireland, gaining some support from the rebels but far less than had been anticipated, and on 8 September was confronted by Lieutenant General Lake, to whom he surrendered at Ballinamuck.

Savary meanwhile returned to France, as undetected as on his departure. A by-blow of this sortie was the cruise of the *Anacréon*, a letter-of-marque from Dunkirk bearing, in addition to arms, ammunition and clothing, Général Rey and the Irish patriot Napper Tandy. She reached the coast of Donegal, where she learned of Humbert's fate, then made off northwards, took two British privateers and returned to her home port safely.

The Brest component was the more important of the two French expeditionary forces, consisting of 3,000 men and a vast quantity of arms, ammunition, stores, field and siege artillery. The troops were commanded by Général Ménage and Général Hardy, the ships by Commodore Bompart. Bompart flew his broad pendant in the 74-gun *Hoche* (Capitaine Maistral). The *Hoche* was accompanied by the 40-gun frigates *Romaine*, *Loire* and *Immortalité*, and the 36-gun frigates *Coquille*, *Bellone*, *Résolue*, *Embuscade*, *Sémillante* and *Biche*. Having paid the troops Bompart's squadron slipped its moorings on the night of 16 September and sought to evade the vigilant British by stealing out through the Passage du Raz. Unfortunately his ships were seen by the inshore squadron under Richard Keats, who now commanded the 38-gun *Boadicea*. With Keats were *Ethalion*, 38 (Captain George Countess), and Commander John White's *Sylph*. Leaving his two juniors to maintain contact, Keats ran out to the north-west to inform Bridport, who sent him home with this intelligence. Meanwhile, early next morning Countess and White were joined by Captain The Honourable Charles Herbert in *Amelia*, 44, as they followed Bompart to the south-east. Intending to mislead the British into thinking they were on passage to L'Orient, Bompart eventually turned away from the coast and sent *Loire* and *Immortalité* in chase of the British frigates. These fell back as Bompart next set a course as though for the West Indies, and the *Loire* and *Immortalité* soon broke off the chase. Later Bompart encountered a large homeward-bound British convoy from India but did not engage, on the grounds that his mission was more important. He had also had trouble aboard *Hoche*, where a sprung topmast had had to be replaced.

The British frigates hung on to the French squadron and on 20 September were joined by Captain Durham in *Anson*. By noon on the

22nd Countess could see the distant French topsails heading more to the west and, convinced he knew their destination, sent White in *Sylph* directly to Cork to inform Kingsmill.

*Ethalion*, *Anson* and *Amelia* kept company with Bompart, who was now heading north, until on 4 October a south-easterly gale closed the visibility and caused *Amelia* to separate and *Anson* to lose her main topmast and mizen topgallantmast. Despite this Durham pressed on towards Ireland. In the meantime, Their Lordships' response to the information brought by Keats had been to order Commodore Sir John Warren out from Plymouth on the assumption that Ireland was the French destination, and off the south coast of Ireland Warren fell in with the brig-corvette *Kangaroo* sent out by Kingsmill. Commander Brace told Warren of the likelihood of a French force being near Black Sod Bay, and Warren then made directly for Achill Head, off the north-west coast of Ireland, assuming that Bompart would disembark near Savary's landing-place.

Warren, no longer in a frigate, now commanded the 74-gun *Canada* and had under his orders the 80-gun *Foudroyant* (Captain Thomas Byard), the 74-gun *Robust* (Captain Edward Thornbrough), and the 44-gun *Magnanime* (Captain The Honourable Michael de Courcy). On 10 October Warren was joined by the two 36-gun frigates *Melampus* (Captain Graham Moore), and *Doris* (Captain Lord Ranelagh), which, being part of the Irish Guard stationed in Lough Swilly near Derry, had been sent by Kingsmill to cruise off Donegal and Mayo. Warren sent *Doris* to raise the alarm along the coast and the next day, the 11th, he was joined by *Anson, Ethalion* and the *Amelia*. This speedy concentration of force was a fine example of what could be achieved by wind-driven ships in the pre-radio age.

Although Bompart had been intending to land at Killalla Bay, the delay in his departure persuaded him that, assuming that the French troops had advanced northward he could better assist Humbert, whose surrender was unknown to Bompart, by landing in Lough Swilly, so in a stiff north-westerly wind he headed for the Donegal coast. At midday Bompart's leeward frigate, *Immortalité,* signalled enemy ships in sight at the same moment that *Amelia*, scouting for Warren, sighted the

French to windward. Warren immediately ordered a general chase and the ensuing pursuit ran all through the night, during which the wind freshened to a north-north-westerly gale. Stress of weather caused *Anson* to carry away her main yard, main topsail yard and mizen mast, resulting in her being left behind the next day. The *Hoche* also suffered, losing both her fore and mizen topmasts and (again) her repaired maintopmast; but at daylight on the 12th both squadrons were still in sight of one another, and the wind had dropped with the dawn.

Bompart now headed south-west, the wind on his starboard quarter and his ships extended in a rough line: *Sémillante, Romaine, Bellone, Immortalité, Loire, Hoche, Coquille* and *Embuscade. Résolue* was leaking and had been sent inshore with *Biche* as escort, and for the moment they went unmolested. The British ships were in no formation, so Warren hoisted *Robust*'s numbers with the signal to form line astern of her. *Magnanime* quickly joined Thornbrough, and they both came under fire from *Embuscade* and *Coquille* shortly after seven o'clock in the morning. Captain Thornbrough brailed up *Robust*'s spanker and clewed up her mainsail as she bore down to engage *Hoche* broadside to broadside. Astern of Thornbrough, Captain de Courcy engaged *Coquille* and *Embuscade,* but *Magnanime* overshot *Robust.* Seeing the near collision of the British ships, *Bellone, Immortalité* and *Loire* hauled out of their line to try to rake *Magnanime,* but the approach of the *Foudroyant, Ethalion* and *Amelia,* as the other British ships also caught up, persuaded their commanders to resume their course to the south-west. Captain Moore in *Melampus,* not having seen Warren's signal to form line, bought his guns to bear on the *Hoche,* as did *Canada* herself a little later. At ten minutes to eleven Maistral hauled down his colours and he and Bompart, as well as Wolfe Tone, fell into British hands. The *Embuscade* surrendered forty minutes later, having been mauled first by *Magnanime* and then by the overwhelming 80-gun *Foudroyant.*

Seeing the surrender of their commodore, the remaining French ships fled, with the majority of the British in chase. *Robust* had been disabled and *Anson* was still approaching from the south-east, but the rest forced *Coquille* to strike; then *Bellone,* having been mauled by *Foudroyant* and *Melampus*, was compelled to capitulate, Capitaine Jacob finally striking to Countess as the *Ethalion* came up to engage him.

The five fleeing French men-of-war shot at *Anson* as they passed her, inflicting further damage on Durham's ship, but *Canada*, *Foudroyant* and *Melampus* were in pursuit, and just before midnight *Melampus* came in sight of *Immortalité* and *Résolue*. Falling upon the latter, Captain Moore opened fire with his 24-pounders. Capitaine Bergeau had troubles enough. His leaking ship had been making more than a metre of water an hour, and was not properly cleared for action. Bergeau fired a few of his 12-pounders to defend the honour of France, then hauled down his ensign, allowing *Immortalité* to slip away in the darkness.

Having sent Warren north, Admiral Kingsmill had despatched *Révolutionaire*, *Mermaid* and *Kangaroo* after him from Cork. On the forenoon of 15 October these ships sighted *Sémillante* and *Loire* off Achill Head. Sighting the British in their turn, the two French frigates separated. Captain Thomas Twysden followed *Sémillante* in *Révolutionaire*, leaving Captain Newman and Commander Brace to chase *Loire* in *Mermaid* and *Kangaroo*.

By that evening Twysden and Newman had both lost their quarry, but *Loire* was seen again next morning and at three in the afternoon of the 16th, Brace caught up with the French frigate. The British brig carried sixteen 32-pounder carronades, but Capitaine Ségond shot away Brace's foretopmast, disabling *Kangaroo*, so she failed to get close enough to use them. The pursuit ran on through the evening and night and at about six on the morning of the 17th Ségond decided to give battle, having only *Mermaid* in sight astern. The *Loire* therefore shortened sail and engaged *Mermaid* as she came alongside, both frigates running before the wind as they fought it out. *Mermaid* was a 32-gun frigate armed with standard 12-pounder guns, whereas *Loire* mounted forty 18-pounders.

Despite this inequity the fire-fight lasted for two and a half hours, until *Mermaid* lost her mizen mast, which fell across some after guns and overboard. Deprived of his manoeuvrability, his ship badly battered, Newman pulled away from the *Loire*. Ségond swiftly made off, but he was not to escape: shortly afterwards he lost his main and foretopmast, then he ran into the half-rigged *Anson*, still labouring along with the *Kangaroo*, which appeared to windward on the morning of 18 October. Neither Durham's ship nor Ségond's were in a fit state to manoeuvre, but Brace's crew had rigged a new fore topmast. The *Loire* and *Anson* engaged at half past-ten o'clock, and seventy-five minutes later had battered one another to a standstill. At this juncture Brace joined in, and Ségond was compelled to strike his ensign.

By the 20 October the *Immortalité*, having abandoned *Résolue* in the small hours of the 14th, had reached Ushant, only to encounter Captain Byam Martin in the former French *Résistance*, now His Britannic Majesty's 38-gun frigate *Fisgard*. Martin engaged at half-past noon and the two ships hammered at each other in a fierce action. *Fisgard* lost ten killed and twenty-six wounded, but *Immortalité* lost 115, including Capitaine Legrand, and his colours were lowered at three o'clock.

There remained the *Sémillante*, *Romaine* and *Biche*. The first reached L'Orient safely, while Capitaine Mathieu Bergevin took *Romaine* close to the Irish coast to find out what had happened to the squadron. Learning that the rebellion had been put down he set sail for Brest, meeting *Biche* on her way, and both ships were back in Brest Road on 23 October.

Bergevin was not alone in his concern about Humbert's fate. On orders from the French authorities Commodore Savary sailed again on 12 October in *Concorde* with *Médée*, *Franchise* and *Vénus*. The squadron reached Sligo Bay on the 27th without mishap, learnt of the failure of the expedition, and headed back to France. On the homeward passage Savary was chased for three days by a powerful squadron consisting of the 80-gun *Caesar*, the 70-gun *Terrible* and the 38-gun frigate *Melpomène*.

It was an ill-timed and hopelessly disjointed enterprise, and the results were almost as disastrous as those of the previous year. The chief beneficiary was, of course, the Royal Navy, which gained several ships. Warren had ordered *Robust* to tow the wrecked *Hoche* into Lough Swilly, a difficult task for a damaged ship; fortunately, Lord Ranelagh's

*Doris* was able to assist and the *Hoche*'s own crew laboured to save her for her enemy, though they were not obliged to do so once they had surrendered. In due course the 74-gun ship was repaired and refitted as *Donegal*. She was assigned to Nelson's fleet in 1805, but missed the battle of Trafalgar because she was at Gibraltar, taking on provisions. *Embuscade* and *Bellone* were added to the Royal Navy, the latter changing her name to *Proserpine*. The following March *Proserpine* was sent to the Elbe, carrying the Foreign Secretary's brother, Tom Grenville, on a mission to Berlin to bring Prussia back into the Second Coalition as an ally. In terrible weather the frigate struck the Scharhörn Reef off the island of Neuwerk, in the Elbe estuary. The sea then froze, and *Proserpine* was first beset and then lost; a few of her people struggled over the ice and the half-frozen river to the safety of Cuxhaven. The fate of the *Coquille* was little better: she was under repair at Plymouth in December when she caught fire and was also lost. *Loire* and *Immortalité* were refitted as cruisers while *Résolue* was used as a hulk at Portsmouth and finally broken up in 1811.

Several first lieutenants involved in the encounter were promoted. David Colby of the *Robust*, George Sayer of the *Ethalion*, John Carden of *Fisguard* and William Turquand of *Canada* were all made commanders. Carden we shall meet again, but Turquand was drowned when his sloop *Hound* was lost with all hands off the Shetland Isles in September 1800.

Warren's pell-mell action and its subsidiary engagements were a further blow both to the French government and to the United Irishmen, whose founder Wolfe Tone, taken in the *Hoche*, was tried for treason and condemned to death. The Irish patriot died in prison by his own hand. As for the French government, the Directory postponed their invasion plans for both England and Ireland, already embarked upon a greater enterprise initiated by their shrewd Minister for Foreign Affairs, Charles de Talleyrand. Egypt, nominally a Turkish possession, was to be siezed, annexed, and developed as a French colony, opening up a route to the Red Sea by which an attack was to be launched on India using Sercey's frigates and dhows hired from the Sherif of Mecca. This was by no means an impossible scheme, for they had a man available – a man, too, much better employed *outside* France – who was ambitious enough to attempt it. Général Bonaparte, always hyperactive, readily jumped upon Talleyrand's band-wagon and produced his own memorandum. Postpone the invasion of England, he argued: he would go to Egypt, he said, 'to establish myself there and found a French colony, [which] will take some months. But as soon as I have made England tremble for the safety of India, I shall return to Paris and give the enemy its death blow'.

News of French activity at Toulon caused the Admiralty to send a British naval squadron back into the Mediterranean. St Vincent was ordered to detach Rear-Admiral Nelson (over the heads of two rear-admirals senior to him) to blockade Toulon. Nelson's investment was laxly conducted, with the idea of inducing the French to sail and thereby bringing them to battle, a dangerous stratagem which resulted in the escape of the entire expedition. Nelson's anxiety thereafter to locate the French was extreme; he beat up and down the Mediterranean, passing within a few miles of the lumbering French armada, but only located Brueys' fleet at anchor after Bonaparte's army had disembarked. The French ships lay in Aboukir Bay on the Nile Delta and here, on the evening of 1 August 1798 and the following night, Nelson's fleet almost entirely annihilated the French. Only two line-of-battle ships and two frigates escaped.

Nelson's ships were commanded by a group of captains who became known to history as the 'Band of Brothers'. They included James Saumarez, Samuel Hood, Thomas Troubridge and Thomas Hardy, sea warriors whose seniority (except that of the last, who was not made post until October) had elevated them into Nelson's line-of-battle. All subsequently followed their chief to flag-rank, and as commanders-in-chief some will reappear in our story; but in the closing years of the War of the French Revolution a new generation of cruiser commanders was also emerging in their wake.

There was one irony in the aftermath of the British victory at Aboukir Bay, in the capture of the British 50-gun ship *Leander*. Commanded by Captain Thomas Thompson, *Leander* was on her way to England with Nelson's despatches, in the charge of Edward Berry, his flag-captain in *Vanguard*. Off Candia *Leander* ran in with the 74-gun *Généreux*, one of the only two line-of-battle ships to have escaped destruction at Nelson's hands. The wind was light and the *Généreux* carried a breeze up to *Leander* which was unable to escape. Although short of men in consequence of the fighting at Aboukir Bay, Thompson accepted battle, and, after a furious action lasting six and a half hours, reluctantly surrendered. During the action *Leander* lost all her masts, yet Thompson was able to rake *Généreux* before being raked in return.

The *Leander* was completely shattered, but so was *Généreux*; having no boats serviceable, the two French officers accepting the surrender were obliged to swim across to their prize. Despite the heavier metal and stronger construction of *Généreux*, she seems to have suffered more in her hull than the *Leander*, and her casualties were much higher, about a hundred killed and 188 wounded, against British losses of 35 killed and 57 wounded. Among the latter were Thompson, who received three severe wounds, and Berry, who had part of a man's skull driven into his arm. The French plundered *Leander* and robbed her officers. Her surgeon had his case of instruments taken, so could not attend to Thompson. To make matters worse Capitaine Lejoille exaggerated the *Leander*'s force in his despatches. More importantly, though she was in sight of the French ship, Lejoille failed to capture the little brig *Mutine*, unaware that she was carrying Nelson's duplicate despatches which duly reached London. Thompson and Berry both survived to be knighted and reach flag rank. Thompson later served as Comptroller of the Navy and Member of Parliament for Rochester; Berry was with Nelson again at Trafalgar.

Meanwhile the French military expedition to Egypt had its impact in the Indian seas, where Sercey's cruisers, *Vertu* and *Régénérée* among them, had already caused Rear-Admiral Rainier's East Indies squadron a number of problems. Sercey was fortunate in being able to use the Dutch dockyard at Batavia (modern Djakarta), where he had refitted his ships at the end of 1797 and from where he had sailed in the new year with quantities of rice, cordage and canvas. In January 1798 Sercey and his frigates *Forte*, *Seine*, *Vertu*, *Cybèle*, *Prudente* and *Régénérée* were off the eastern end of Java, passing back into the Indian Ocean by way of the Strait of Bali, when they encountered what was thought to be a British squadron of large frigates and ships-of-the-line: in fact they were five deep-laden East Indiamen, homeward bound from Canton. With commendable presence of mind the senior commander, Charles Lennox, adopted a bold stratagem, hoisting a blue ensign aboard his own ship, the *Woodford*, which was duly copied aboard the *Ocean*, *Taunton Castle*, *Canton* and *Boddam*. As the Royal Navy was then still organised under the 'three-squadron' system of red, white and blue introduced in the reign of Charles II, to perfect his subterfuge Lennox had only to hoist a plain blue flag at *Woodford*'s mizen masthead to impersonate Rainier, a rear-admiral of the blue. Giving the impression of being a naval squadron, the Indiamen boldly headed towards Sercey, who took alarm and veered away.

In truth Rainier's resources were slim enough. In July 1798 he had inexplicably lost one frigate, the 44-gun *Resistance*, anchored in the Banka Strait on station to interdict Dutch trade. For some unknown reason *Resistance* exploded, killing 332 men instantly, including her captain, Edward Pakenham. Thirteen people who survived by clinging to wreckage eventually landed and constructed a raft, by which means they attempted to reach the Sumatran coast. Alas, in a strong wind the survivors were further reduced and but five managed to land, only to be imprisoned by the Sumatrans. Only one man, Thomas Scott, lived to regain his freedom and in due course tell his incredible tale, a solitary testament to the cost of sea-power in terms of human life.

Rainier's responsibilities were as wide as his resources were slender, extending from the Red Sea to the China Sea, whither he had sent two frigates in January 1798 in quest of the Spanish treasure ship that arrived annually from the Pacific coast of Spanish South America. Laden with silver and gold from Potosí destined for the treasury in Madrid this was a tempting prize, but on this occasion the *Sibylle* and *Fox* missed their objective, merely attacking some Spanish forts in the Philippine Islands with no very glorious outcome.

The East Indies station may have been *the* command for prize money, but the news that the French Directory were mounting an expedition against India by way of Egypt only added to Rainier's problems. After destroying the French fleet in Aboukir Bay Nelson had sent Lieutenant

Duval of the *Zealous* to Aleppo; from there, in Arab costume and with a string of camels, Duval had slogged overland to Baghdad, where he paid his respects to the Bashaw. He then went on to Bussorah (modern Basra), and by way of the Bombay Marine packet *Fly* reached Bombay on 21 October. Thus were the Governor-General in India and the naval Commander-in-Chief appraised of the presence in Egypt of an hostile army, and of Nelson's victory.

The French had a powerful ally in Tipu Sultan of Mysore, who was opposed to British incursions in India, and the threat posed by the Directory's plans alarmed the authorities. On land as well as at sea the British already had their hands full. Tipu Sultan was in revolt, and in March 1798 had co-operated with Capitaine Jean L'Hermite, whose 36-gun frigate *Preneuse* had taken two British East Indiamen, *Woodcot* and *Raymond,* from Tellicherry Road on the Malabar Coast.

In expectation of increased French naval activity, which the lucky escape of the China ships under Lennox only emphasised, Rainier now decided to augment his force in the South China Sea. In January of 1799 he sent to Macao the *Arrogant*, 74, the 64-gun *Intrepid*, whose captain William Hargood was the senior officer, and Pellew's old prize, the *Virginie*, 38. It was just as well, for Sercey, furious once he learned how he had been deceived by Lennox, took a powerful Franco-Spanish squadron to the mouth of the Pearl River to ambush homeward-bound Indiamen coming downstream from Canton.

Sercey flew his flag in the corvette *Brûle-Gueule* and had with him L'Hermite's *Preneuse* and the Spanish 74s *Europa* and *Montanes* from Manila. As the enemy ships hove into sight Hargood immediately slipped his cables, followed by *Arrogant* and *Virginie*, which soon took up the leading station. Astonishingly, the Franco-Spanish squadron fled: 'their running away from a force so much inferior to their own is [not] . . . to be accounted for, but from their dread of a conflict . . .' Thus Sercey proved himself incompetent, throwing away at a stroke the chance not merely of seizing a valuable convoy, but of establishing Franco-Spanish dominance in Indo-Chinese waters. The allied squadron broke up (Sercey sent some of his ships home, as we have seen), and in May 1799 British land forces in southern India defeated Tipu Sultan at Seringapatam.

Although further naval operations were carried out against the Dutch in Java, for a while the enemy threat in the East Indies faded.

For Rainier there remained the problem of the French in Egypt: it was possible that Sercey's self-preservation tactics resulted from a need to save his ships to escort Bonaparte's army from a Red Sea port to India. French troops did in fact reach Kosseir, where they were contained by Royal Naval and East India Company ships sent by Rainier. These were joined by a small squadron under Rear-Admiral Blankett who, it will be recalled, had been sent on to the Red Sea from the Cape of Good Hope. Kosseir was shelled by *Daedalus* and *Fox* in August 1799, and during British operations in Egypt in 1800 troops from India were landed there and advanced on Alexandria. But by then Bonaparte, having lost his fleet to Nelson at the Nile and had his attempt to extricate himself thwarted by Sir Sidney Smith, as we shall see, had long since thrown up the Egyptian expedition. The war in the Indian Ocean and the China Seas temporarily died down, and the critical cockpit of the struggle for supremacy at sea in the closing years of the century remained in the Western Approaches to the English Channel.

Meanwhile, the frigate squadrons which had frustrated Savary and Bompart in their attempts to raise rebellion in Ireland had not been idle. This almost incessant activity wore out men and ships, and it is perhaps unsurprising that the year 1798 ended with a major setback for the Royal Navy, one made much of by the propagandists in Paris.

The 32-gun frigate *Ambuscade* was on station off the Gironde and in daily expectation of being joined by the 32-gun *Stag*. She had taken some prizes and had sent off prize-crews under the second lieutenant, replacing these men with thirty-odd French prisoners willing to work the British frigate. On the morning of 14 December a sail was seen approaching, running before the wind directly for *Ambuscade*; no recognition signals were exchanged, but the crew were sent to breakfast on the assumption that the other ship was the *Stag*. As the stranger drew near, she suddenly hauled round and began to stand offshore, whereupon Captain Henry Jenkins, realising she was a French ship, made sail in chase. By noon Jenkins was close enough to open fire, at which the enemy ship clewed up and accepted action.

The French vessel was a large corvette, the 24-gun *Bayonnaise*, commanded by Lieutenant de Vaisseau Jean-Baptiste-Edmond Richer and homeward bound from Cayenne. In addition to her complement *Bayonnaise* had a detachment of troops on board, and these were to have a significant impact on the outcome. The engagement was hot and the ships were cannonading one another when suddenly a midships 12-pounder aboard *Ambuscade* exploded, blowing a hole in her side, destroying the boats on the booms and killing eleven men. Hard-pressed, for up to this point his ship had had the worst of the encounter and both he and his first lieutenant were wounded, Richer took the opportunity to make sail. After a few minutes Jenkins renewed the chase and overtook the *Bayonnaise*, this time attacking from leeward and using his undamaged broadside.

With the British attack renewed, the state of *Bayonnaise* was now desperate. With her commander and his second wounded, her rigging badly cut up and her chances of escape minimal, the officer commanding the troops on board suggested to the remaining naval officer that they should try to counter-attack by boarding, using his soldiers to advantage. The helm of the *Bayonnaise* was accordingly put over and she was deliberately crashed into the *Ambuscade*, damaging her whole starboard quarter before finally dropping astern, still foul of the British frigate.

The *Bayonnaise*'s forecastle now overhung the *Ambuscade*'s quarterdeck and, though aboard *Ambuscade* a gun was swung round and fired through the cabin windows into the *Bayonnaise*'s bow, the French troops above opened a brisk musketry fire. Jenkins was shot through the thigh-bone, his first lieutenant Dawson Main was mortally wounded in the groin, Lieutenant Sinclair of the marines was hit in the thigh and shoulder, Mr Brown the master had his brains blown out, and the only remaining lieutenant, Joseph Briggs, who had been confined ill in his cot, came on deck to be shot in the head for his pains. *Ambuscade*'s quarterdeck was now covered in the dead and dying, some cartridges had blown up, damaging the frigate's stern, which was already on fire, and her after part was being evacuated for fear of further explosion. The only senior officer, the purser, Mr William Murray, failed to rally the remaining men, who showed signs of lack of spirit. By now the French soldiers and the *Bayonnaise*'s crew were pouring over her broken bowsprit and aboard the *Ambuscade*.

The outcome was inevitable: *Ambuscade* fell into French hands. British losses were ten killed and three dozen wounded, against sixty casualties in the *Bayonnaise*. Captain Jenkins, though personally courageous, was not an efficient officer and did not run an efficient ship. His mistaken and perverse conviction that it was amusing to praise some men while holding others up to ridicule, yet nevertheless require them still to do their duty willingly, had created an atmosphere of fiction on board. The consequent fatal disloyalty, coupled with a lax regime, combined with the demoralising effect of the exploding 12-pounder to so shake his crew that *in extremis* the greater part of them lost heart. Furthermore, compounding his moral ineptitude, in his eagerness to chase the ship that had surprised him and then beat off to windward, Jenkins had reduced *Ambuscade*'s resistance to the wind by having the crew take the hammocks below. During daylight they were usually stowed along a man-of-war's rail both to air them and to provide a protective breastwork in action – rolled up, they were quite capable of stopping a musket ball. Without this protection and under a galling fire from the soldiers of the Alsace Regiment, the morale of already dispirited men was swiftly worn down.

The capture of a British frigate by a French corvette delighted the Directory. Handsome bounties were paid to the *Bayonnaise*'s crew and the wounded Richer was promoted directly to *capitaine de vaisseau*, although the troop commander whose initiative had secured the little victory had been killed. *Ambuscade* was commissioned into the French naval service as *Embuscade*, a replacement for the ship of that name lost earlier off Ireland. Captain Jenkins survived and was repatriated the following autumn, to be court-martialled aboard *Gladiator* in Portsmouth. The court acquitted both captain and crew, but not without qualifying their judgement; the fact that Jenkins was still so ill of his wound undoubtedly persuaded the court to leniency. Though he lived on for twelve more years Jenkins was never promoted, nor does he appear to have gone to sea again. Slack and inept he had been, defeated he had been; nevertheless, he had persisted in his attempt to defeat Richer; and he had paid the price for being found wanting in the exacting profession he had chosen.

# CHAPTER 8

---

## 'I will lead you myself'

The re-entry of the Royal Navy into the Mediterranean was a major gain for the strategists in London. Not only had Nelson destroyed the Toulon fleet in Aboukir Bay, but in November 1798 Commodore Sir John Duckworth and General Charles Stuart captured Minorca, giving Britain another Mediterranean base. Moreover, although the Neapolitan Kingdom of the Two Sicilies later fell to the Republicans, Sicily itself remained an ally, giving Britain access to her ports and resources, and during 1799 Austria renewed her hostility to France.

But the French Republic was over her birth-pangs, and appeared to thrive on this augmentation of her enemies. The personnel of the French navy had suffered great losses, but they were at last paid, and new ships were laid down. With the direct intervention of the Minister of Marine, Eustache Bruix, a wind of change blew through the great naval arsenal of Brest, helped by British failures to stop incoming convoys laden with supplies and *matériel*, several of which successfully ran the gauntlet of the Royal Navy's blockade.

In late April 1799 Bruix assembled command of the French Atlantic squadrons, broke out of Brest and sailed south, deceiving Bridport, who assumed his objective was another attempt on Ireland. Bruix was to have picked up reinforcements from the Spanish at Ferrol and Cádiz, but although the Ferrol ships sailed to join him they missed the rendezvous and ended up at Rochefort, while contrary winds kept the Spanish in Cádiz. Avoiding the dispersed units of St Vincent's wide command, Bruix reached Toulon safely. The Spanish finally sailed from Cádiz meanwhile, but took such a battering from heavy weather that they struggled to reach Cartagena. It was now clear that Bruix and the Spanish, under Almirante Massaredo, were attempting to reassert their joint power in the Mediterranean, intending to go to the support of Bonaparte in Egypt. St Vincent, having fallen ill, handed over his squadrons (which included Nelson's at Palermo) to Lord Keith. By the end of June, having first succoured Genoa which was then under siege by the Austrians, Bruix effected his juncture with Massaredo off Cartagena. From here, however, instead of destroying Keith's fleet and making for Egypt, the forty-strong Franco-Spanish fleet headed west again. In passing Gibraltar Bruix took a British cutter commanded by a certain Lieutenant Frederick Lewis: sixteen years later, the Emperor Napoleon was to surrender to him. Keith followed three weeks later with thirty-one sail-of-the-line but Bruix meanwhile put in to Cádiz, so that Keith had almost caught up with the Franco-Spanish fleet before it reached Brest. As he approached Ushant Keith was reinforced with ships sent by Bridport, among which was Pellew in *Impetueux*. Much against his will Pellew had left his beloved *Indefatigable* and transferred into this seventy-four, taken from the French at the Glorious First of June. When Keith sent Pellew ahead to reconnoitre, Sir Edward discovered the enemy had regained Brest the previous day.

Pellew had been with Bridport in April when he learned of Bruix's escape from Brest and had made for Bantry Bay to lie in wait for the expected invasion of Ireland. Here he had had the unpleasant experience of mutiny, which he and his officers quickly quelled. Meanwhile Bridport and the remainder of the Channel Fleet had made for Rochefort, where they found the Spanish ships from Ferrol. These had been kept under constant observation by the *Indefatigable*, now commanded by Pellew's successor, The Honourable Henry Curzon. The blockading force left by Bridport off the Basque Road made an abortive attack on the moored Spanish ships, but the defences were too strong and they withdrew. In September the Spanish squadron escaped and made for Brest, but returned to Ferrol when they found the British in the offing. From this time the British blockade was enforced with slowly increasing rigour, and this immense enemy armament lay idle for the remainder of 1799. During Bruix's absence, the yards at Brest had completed five ships-of-the-line however, so that upon his return the Franco-Spanish fleet there numbered forty-seven sail-of-the-line.

Quite apart from his own fruitless incursion into the Mediterranean, the dispersed squadrons which came under Keith as Commander-in-Chief of 'Lisbon and the Mediterranean' had been active. The French army had swept down the Italian peninsula, the hereditary princes had fled, and the Pope had been captured; Nelson himself had conveyed King Ferdinand from the turbulence of Naples to the safety of Palermo. The Russians, however, had taken the Ionian Islands – and finding there the captured *Leander*, had on the express orders of the Tsar returned her to Britain. Nelson had mustered his ships to counter Bruix, but after the crisis and Bruix's retreat, he operated on the Italian coast, enjoying the charms of Lady Hamilton.

Bonaparte meanwhile had made Egypt a French possession, in name at least. He then tried to open negotiations with Constantinople, only for the Pasha at Acre in Syria to send sent troops south to oppose him. A French army 13,000 strong accordingly began a coastal march towards El Arish, Jaffa and Acre. Nelson had left a small squadron to blockade the few French cruisers still in Alexandria, under the command first of Samuel Hood and then of Troubridge. In early March 1799 Sir Sidney Smith arrived to take over.

In May 1798 Smith and his protégé John Wesley Wright had escaped from their imprisonment in Paris. A bold and ingenious plan successfully carried out by a group of royalist Frenchmen had deceived Smith's gaolers and he had slipped out of the country at Le Havre to join a British cruiser lying offshore. His appearance in the Levant ten months later was unpopular, particularly with Nelson, who deeply resented Smith's appointment within his own command. Smith's coolly haughty manner was not endearing, but the trouble arose chiefly from the dual nature of his assignment. In the 80-gun *Tigre*, of which he was captain, Smith was subordinate to Nelson; but he was also accredited as Joint Minister Plenipotentiary to the Sublime Porte at Constantinople, whither he had gone to consult with Sultan Selim III and his Vizier before joining Nelson's command. In other words, Smith's brief was wide: he was free to exploit his diplomatic status to exert every effort to help the Turks and, if this happened to run contrary to Nelson's wishes, to cock a snook at his commanding admiral. In complaining of this, Nelson referred sarcastically to Smith as 'the Swedish knight', on account of his foreign honour – fine irony from the Sicilian Duke of Brontë! For a man like Smith, as wayward in his own fashion as Nelson and as determined to seek the bubble reputation at the cannon's mouth, exploitation of such a situation was limited only by the opportunities Fate offered. With Bonaparte and his army marching on Syria, Fate was about to oblige Smith in full.

Relieving Troubridge at Alexandria, Smith sent Wright off to Acre to concert a plan of defence with the Pasha, Achmed Djezzar, a cruel elderly Bosnian Francophobe. Learning that Bonaparte had taken Jaffa by storm, Smith sailed to Acre in *Tigre* with the *Theseus*, 74, the *Alliance*, 22, and two sloops, and immediately set about harrying the French advance, thwarting them at every opportunity. They captured the entire siege train, which was moving along the coast in small craft, and the guns thus acquired were used to augment the defences of Acre. The French frigates under Contre-Amiral Perrée at Alexandria brought up more artillery, but the city's defences, originally built by the Crusaders, had been cunningly strengthened by a royalist engineer, Colonel Antoine de Phélippeaux, a former classmate of Bonaparte's at the military academy of Brienne. To the defence Smith added the resources of himself, Wright and the ships' companies of his small squadron, and they proved critical to the defence of the ancient city. Acre was besieged by Bonaparte from 19 March until 20 May, during which time eight assaults were repulsed. Smith, constantly conspicuous on the ramparts, survived several assassination attempts.

A large Turkish relieving force sent by the Pasha of Damascus was defeated by Général Kléber at Mount Tabor, but an attempt by Perrée's ships to aid Bonaparte was thwarted by Captain Ralph Miller in

*Theseus.* During the chase an explosion of shells aboard *Theseus* killed forty-four men including Miller, a veteran of Cape St Vincent and the Nile, but Perrée failed to interfere. Finding Acre impregnable, and with bubonic plague in his own camp, Bonaparte threw up the siege and retreated to Egypt. During their retreat across the desert his soldiers endured terrible privations, and abandoned their sick and wounded. To his infinite relief, at Alexandria Bonaparte found instructions from Paris ordering him to return home: his conquests in Italy having in his absence been reversed by Austro-Russian forces, he was required to repeat them. After fighting off an attempt by the Turks supported by *Tigre* and *Theseus* to land at Aboukir, Bonaparte in effect deserted his army in Egypt, leaving the command to Kléber.

Smith meanwhile returned to Constantinople and then, with a Turkish army embarked in a large Turkish fleet, attempted a second landing in Egypt. At Damietta between 29 October and 1 November, in a bloody series of actions, Kléber threw back the invading forces. Another attempt was made in March 1800 to dislodge the French from Egypt, but Kléber defeated the Turks at Heliopolis, only to fall to an assassin's knife in June. After a remarkable campaign in Upper Egypt, his successor Desaix negotiated a truce with Smith later that year.

Months earlier Bonaparte had left Egypt in the *Muiron,* bearing the flag of Contre-Amiral Ganteaume, with a small squadron of frigates which managed to evade British cruisers and reach Fréjus on 9 October 1799. Soon he was in action in Italy again. During 1798, while carrying out his duties as a general officer of the French Republic, Bonaparte had privately meditated setting himself up as a Middle Eastern potentate. Long afterwards, in exile on St Helena, the quondam Emperor acknowledged that between himself and his destiny had stood the sea warrior Captain Sir Sidney Smith.

In Europe, the British were on the offensive themselves. Persuaded that the republican spirit in The Netherlands was waning, they sent a major expeditionary force comprising British and Russian troops across the North Sea. The fleet of Admiral Duncan was closely involved with this operation and seized several Dutch men-of-war, but the military expedition, commanded by the Duke of York, proved a disaster. Badly supplied and with terrible weather to compound the misery of the soldiers, the campaign was first thwarted and then fizzled out, having achieved nothing noteworthy, and required withdrawal. The captured Dutch ships were of little value, and the leeward coast off which the British men-of-war were operating cost the Royal Navy dear. The *Nassau*, a partly armed 64-gun ship, the frigates *Blanche* and *Lutine* and the 12-gun brig *Contest* were all wrecked. The loss of the 32-gun *Lutine* was a sad and serious blow, for all but two of her complement were drowned, and pay for the troops amounting to £140,000 went down with her.

In the age of wind-driven ships, the greatest risk to the cruisers of the Royal Navy lay in the sea itself, rather than the malice of the enemy. Losses such as those off the Dutch coast were attributable to foundering in heavy weather, but the risks were many. Other extreme weather conditions, such as beset the *Proserpine* in the frozen Elbe; or striking rocks, because of faulty navigation or imperfect charts; or running aground, as occurred to Nagle's *Artois* on the French coast in July 1797: all these dangers far outweighed that of capture by the enemy. As an admiral, Cuthbert Collingwood warned his captains to be vigilant: 'Rocks and tides', he wrote, 'have more of danger in them than a battle once a week.' Sir George Murray, promoted from a frigate into the 74-gun *Colossus*, lost her when in a gale she drove from her anchorage in St Mary's Road in the Isles of Scilly, and Philip Durham's worn-out *Anson* was eventually wrecked in Mount's Bay on the Cornish coast in 1807. Bad weather could disable a ship, sometimes so seriously that she became ungovernable and was rendered temporarily useless. Before the Battle of the Nile, Nelson's flagship *Vanguard* had been so severely battered by heavy weather in the Gulf of Lyons that she had to be taken in tow. Fortunately, for the Mediterranean fleet at least, the tall Corsican pines furnished a ready supply of mast timber.

But stress of weather was no excuse if duty demanded action. On the afternoon of 6 February 1799 a raging westerly gale was blowing over the Balearic Islands where, off the eastern end of Majorca, the 74-gun *Leviathan* (Captain John Buchanan) and the 44-gun *Argo* (Captain

James Bowen), were working their way along the coast under storm staysails. Opening the Bahia de Acude, on the southern promontory of which stood a fortified tower, they discovered two prudent Spanish ships-of-war lying quietly at anchor in the lee of the island. The two Spaniards, the *Proserpina* and *Santa Teresa*, immediately cut their cables and made off to the north-north-east.

Bowen and Buchanan set all the sail their ships could stand and went in pursuit, but the maintopsail of the *Leviathan* soon carried away and she dropped astern. Night was coming on and the Spanish frigates, seeing one of their pursuers disabled, first ran alongside one another and then, having decided to diverge, separated, the *Proserpina* hauling sharp up to the north, the *Santa Teresa* setting her topgallants and running off before the wind. Bowen, undaunted, signalled Buchanan; but the *Leviathan* lost contact in the dusk, leaving Bowen to press on alone.

James Bowen was an interesting man. A native of Ilfracombe in north Devon, he had gone to sea in the merchant service, and by 1776 had risen to command. During the American War of Independence he joined the Royal Navy and was sailing master successively of the *Artois*, the *Druid* and the 74-gun *Cumberland*. During the peace which followed he commanded the revenue cutter *Wasp*. At the outbreak of war with France in 1793 Lord Howe requested him as master of his flagship of the Channel Fleet, the *Queen Charlotte*, and soon Bowen was proving the wisdom of that choice.

Cruising to the westward of the Channel, Howe was anxious to get the fleet into the anchorage of Tor Bay, but the weather was thick. The ships had been navigating on dead-reckoning for days, and no one had any real idea of their whereabouts. Bowen volunteered to get them into Tor Bay and Howe agreed, against the advice of his flag-captain and chief-of-staff. They remonstrated with Bowen that making the Channel was notoriously difficult in such conditions: a century earlier Admiral Shovell had lost his whole fleet on the rocks of the Isles of Scilly, while more recently the line-of-battle ship *Ramillies* had wrecked herself just north of Bolt Head, giving her name to Ramillies Cove. If they struck the land, the officers argued, the whole fleet might be lost. 'The fleet won't be lost,' was Bowen's curt reply.

With the *Queen Charlotte* leading the fleet, Bowen laid a course for Start Point. He then directed that the frigate *Phaeton* should take station ahead on the flagship's lee bow, with the fleet despatch vessel, the lugger *Black Joke*, on *her* lee bow. These two vessels were thus ahead of the *Queen Charlotte*, and their commanders had been told to keep a sharp lookout: *Black Joke* was to watch for land, *Phaeton* was to watch *Black Joke*. This was the clever key to Bowen's stratagem: the remainder of the fleet were stretched astern *en echelon* on *Queen Charlotte*'s windward quarter and each was watching her next ship ahead, so that the whole could be made to tack if and when the *Black Joke* tacked, giving the first alarm. She would be followed by *Phaeton*, then the flagship, and so on. By this clever device the Channel Fleet, under a press of canvas, was duly brought into Tor Bay.

As master of the fleet Bowen had the conduct of *Queen Charlotte* through the days leading up to and during the battle of the Glorious First of June. Afterwards, as a measure of the esteem felt for him by the officers of the British ships, he was made prize-agent, a lucrative favour, and Howe promised him anything which lay within his gift. To Howe's surprise, Bowen asked for a lieutenant's commission. Howe argued that Bowen stood high in his profession, that he was no longer a young man, and that by accepting a commission he would become the most junior lieutenant on the list. But Bowen knew that if he wished to be regarded as a gentleman, as society then understood the term, he must hold the King's commission, not a warrant of technical expertise, and his insistence was such that Howe acquiesced.

Bowen was acutely conscious of his social inferiority as a warrant officer and former merchant master. Invited to visit the studio of Mather Brown and pose for his portrait in the great painting of *Queen Charlotte*'s quarterdeck at the height of the battle on 1 June 1794, he saw that Brown had painted in a well-connected midshipman. He enquired the reason for the midshipman's presence in the painting, and Brown explained the social desirability of including him. Bowen expostulated – the brat had been below during the whole of the battle, and if he was to be included, then Bowen would not be – and he stalked from the studio in dudgeon. So it is that no likeness of James Bowen appears on Brown's otherwise magnificent canvas.

Within a year of the battle, Bowen was first lieutenant of the *Queen Charlotte*, appointed (as was not uncommon in a flagship) over the heads of senior lieutenants. From here the step to commander was easy, and he achieved it after 'Bridport's Action' of 23 June 1795. He was made post-captain a few months later and placed in temporary command of *Prince George*, 98, then *Thunderer*, 74, before his appointment to *Argo*. Such was the man now in pursuit of the 34-gun *Santa Teresa* in a westerly gale off Majorca.

During the dark evening of 6 February *Argo* slowly drew up with the Spanish frigate until her bow-chasers came within range, whereupon Bowen opened fire. The running fight went on for some hours until, just after midnight, *Argo* ranged up alongside the *Santa Teresa* and emptied her broadside into the fleeing Spaniard. Without replying, Capitán Pablo Perez surrendered his ship, with her crew of 280 men and 250 soldiers embarked, victualled for four months. She was added to the British fleet, thereby enriching *Argo*'s captain and crew.

After taking the *Santa Teresa*, Bowen was sent to Algiers and succeeded in freeing a number of Christian slaves; by the time of the Peace of Amiens he was commodore on the African coast. When hostilities were renewed in 1803 he was appointed a Commissioner of the Transport Board, and as Transport Agent and Commodore commanded the transports that rescued Sir John Moore's shattered army from Coruña in 1809 in the teeth of Marécha Soult's attack. For this important service Bowen received the thanks of both Houses of Parliament. In 1816 he was appointed a Commissioner for the Navy and sat on the Navy Board until his retirement in 1825, when he became a superannuated rear-admiral and died in 1835. He had brothers and sons in the service, his brother Richard, captain of the *Terpsichore*, being during Nelson's ill-fated attack on Tenerife in 1797.

The principal station for action remained the Chops of the Channel and the approaches to Brest. Here the immense concentration of British naval force was largely responsible for the quiescence of the Franco-

Spanish fleet during the second half of 1799. Both the French and Spanish had nevertheless to maintain contact with their overseas possessions in South America and the West Indies, and with Sercey in the Indian seas, so the prospect of catching an incoming or outgoing frigate was ever in the minds of British cruiser captains. For weeks or months their ships thrashed their way up and down their assigned stations, through heavy weather and calms, through days of overcast skies and misty rain and through idyllic days of brilliant sunshine and sparkling blue seas. The men laboured at taking in or setting sail, at scouring their ships' decks, slushing down spars, overhauling rigging, stitching miles of sail seams, pumping bilges, rousing casks of salt horse from the tiers in the hold, until monotony was broken by the cry of 'Sail ho!'

Then a flurry of activity would ensue. A midshipman would be sent aloft with a telescope to identify the stranger. Perhaps the recognition signal would be hoisted, to reveal a friendly British cruiser or a despatch vessel coming south with orders, newspapers, even mail and some vegetables; perhaps a British merchant ship would pass, a straggler from a convoy; or a neutral, in which case a boat was prepared to board and examine the vessel for contraband destined for France. But perhaps the recognition signal would be ignored, the strange sail appear suspicious. Then the anxious captain, surrounded by the master, the first lieutenant, and the third with his signal-party, would stare intently at the approaching ship through his Dollond glass. Perhaps he would lower it decisively and, closing it with a clearly audible snap, order the ship cleared for action.

The ship's course would be altered to intercept, the yards would be trimmed and perhaps a reef shaken out. On deck the marine drummer would hammer his snare-drum insistently, beating out the order that sent the men to their quarters, while the bosun's pipes shrieked at the companionways, turning up the entire ship's company. The bulkheads separating the commander's cabin from the rest of the main deck would be folded up to the deckhead and the domestic air of the upper length of the ship would be transformed, revealing the brutish 12- or 18-pounders on their painted trucks, each surrounded by its kneeling gun-crew. At every companionway would stand a marine sentry, to prevent any but those approved from leaving their battle-stations to seek safety in the bowels of the ship, while below the surgeon and his mates would drag the midshipmen's chests together to make a rough operating table and lay out their instruments, the saws, forceps, probes, catlings and curettage knives of their grisly trade.

Such were the circumstances aboard His Britannic Majesty's 38-gun frigate *Clyde* at half past eight o'clock on the morning of 20 August 1799. The *Clyde,* cruising between the Gironde and the Île d'Oléron, lay 20 miles west by north of the Cordouan lighthouse. Captain Charles Cunningham had been commissioned lieutenant in 1782 and made commander in October 1790; three years later he was made post, so that by 1799 he was already a senior captain, in line for a larger ship. He had reconnoitred Rochefort the previous day and *Clyde* was running south before a northerly wind when the cry came from the fore topgallant that sails were visible to the south-west. *Clyde* immediately altered course to intercept, and by eleven was within sight of two enemy cruisers which held steadily to their course, standing towards her.

At half past twelve, when the three ships were within two miles of one another, the strange frigates turned and ran off before the wind on diverging courses. Cunningham determined to make after the larger of the two, leaving the other, a 20-gun corvette, to herself. The *Clyde* rapidly overhauled her quarry, which turned out to be the *Vestale* of 32 guns, and coming up alongside her Cunningham hoisted his colours and fired a gun. Cunningham's opponent, Capitaine Mayor-Michel-Pierre Gaspard, ran up the tricolour and answered with a broadside.

Capitaine Gaspard and his consort, the corvette *Sagesse*, were homeward bound from the West Indies, where more than thirty of *Vestale*'s crew had died of yellow fever. Many of the men with him were ill of the fever, which explains his conduct in running rather than engaging the solitary British frigate. In the action which followed Gaspard handled his ship with commendable skill, but he could not outmanoeuvre the experienced Cunningham. Ranging up on her larboard side, Cunningham fell back after exchanging broadsides with *Vestale*, veered across her stern, raked her, and then ran up her starboard side. He repeated this manoeuvre and *Clyde*'s guns battered the enemy until Gaspard, at twenty minutes past three, could do no more than strike his colours.

The *Vestale* had been in action with *Terpsichore* in 1797, when she surrendered to James Bowen's brother Richard. She had subsequently been retaken but not apparently been much repaired, which contributed in part at least for her weakened state when she met *Clyde*, and resulted in her not being purchased into the Royal Navy. Cunningham also lost her consort *Sagesse*, which escaped into the Gironde, although she was eventually captured in the West Indies in September 1803 by the *Theseus* and hulked at Portsmouth, to end as a convict hospital ship. Cunningham himself went on to become a Knight of Hanover, and served as a Commissioner of the Victualling Board and at Deptford Dockyard.

Strong winds often forced small and otherwise fast French cruisers to submit to larger enemies when they could not out-run them. Many 74-gun ships were relatively fast in a stiff breeze, conditions which forced a small corvette to shorten sail, and thus was the 18-gun brig-corvette *Aréthuse* taken off L'Orient by the 74-gun *Excellent*, commanded by that former frigate captain, The Honourable Robert Stopford.

Stopford was born in 1768, third son of the second Earl of Courtown. He joined the Royal Navy at twelve and was serving under Rodney at The Saintes in April 1792 when the French under de Grasse were defeated. He was commissioned lieutenant in 1785 and four years later made commander, appointed to the 14-gun *Ferret* in the Mediterranean. Made post in 1790, he commanded the 32-gun frigate *Aquilon* and was with Howe on the Glorious First of June. Lieutenant de Vaisseau Emmanuel Halgan, faced with so formidable a foe commanded by so experienced an officer, had little option but to submit, and *Aréthuse* was commissioned into the Royal Navy as the *Raven*, later to be wrecked off Sicily. Of Robert Stopford we shall hear more.

British frigates did not always have it their own way. Cruising in the entrance of a French port they could be caught at a disadvantage, by a sudden shift of the wind, a calm, or the aggression of the enemy. Occasionally, like the *San Fiorenzo* and *Amelia* off Belle Île in April 1799, they had to fight superior odds. These two British ships, having taken a peep into L'Orient, were running down the coast to reconnoitre the anchorage behind Belle Île; here, among numerous merchant ships, lay three French frigates, the *Cornélie* and *Vengeance*, both of 40 guns, and the 38-gun *Sémillante*. A sudden north-westerly squall carried away the *Amelia*'s main topmast and her fore and mizen topgallants, which wrecked her mainsail in their fall. Captain The Honourable Charles Herbert was thus rendered temporarily *hors de combat* and the French squadron, observing this, let fall their topsails, slipped their cables and stood out to sea, accompanied by a gun-boat. Ashore the gunners in the batteries on the island of Hoëdic manned their artillery pieces and prepared to open fire. Undaunted by the approach of the French, *San Fiorenzo*'s captain, Sir Harry Neale, hoisted the signal for action and stood in towards the emerging enemy under easy sail. Herbert had cleared away the raffle in his waist, and under fore and mizen topsails stood in after Neale.

As the two groups closed, Neale and Herbert hauled round in close line ahead and fired at the approaching ships, which were constrained to haul round to larboard and to leeward of the British to return fire. The gunnery of the two British ships was so fierce that the French, thinking them razées, edged away and in due course broke off the action and made for the Loire estuary, leaving the gun-boat to return to the anchorage. In addition to the damage sustained from the squall, the *Amelia* and *San Fiorenzo* had had their rigging badly cut up, but Neale was not so immobilised that he could not take a French merchant brig that same evening.

The perennial desire to take a Spanish ship occasioned by the possibility of thereby acquiring a fortune, led Captain James Macnamara of the 32-gun *Cerberus* to attack a large Spanish convoy off Cape Ortegal on the evening of 20 October. The convoy consisted of about eighty vessels escorted by the frigates *Ceres* of 40 guns, the 34-gun *Diana*, *Esmeralda* and *Mercedes*, one unidentified frigate and two brigs. Macnamara engaged one frigate, placing *Cerberus* to leeward of her to prevent her escape, and fighting her until her guns were silent. The other Spanish men-of-war were now approaching, however, and Macnamara broke off the action, taking and burning a merchant brig as he withdrew into the night.

Though Macnamara's gamble had almost paid off, he had in fact already missed the jackpot, for it had fallen to an extraordinarily lucky group of British frigates only five days earlier. At eight o'clock on the evening of 15 October 1799 the 38-gun *Naiad* was cruising in the Atlantic out to the west-north-west of Cape Finisterre. *Naiad*'s lookouts reported two sails, which turned out to be the Spanish frigates *Santa Brigida* and *Thetis*. Captain William Pierrepont immediately gave chase. The wind was from the north-west and the ships were running free to the south-east; at half-past three the next morning another ship was seen to the south-west, and an exchange of night signals revealed her to be the 38-gun *Ethalion* (Captain James Young), which promptly joined in the chase. Daylight brought into sight two other British frigates, the *Alcmène*, 32, in the west and the *Triton*, 32, astern, and these too made sail after the fleeing Spaniards.

This coincidental appearance of four frigates in the vast Atlantic testifies to the immense resources the British put into the prosecution of the war. That the four frigate captains proceeded to act in such perfect concert is further evidence, if it were needed, of the shared standards of mutual help and assistance. The promise of a Spanish capture was of course a spicy condiment.

It was now about seven in the morning, and the Spanish commanders divided their force to escape on diverging courses. Observing this, Pierrepoint hoisted *Ethalion*'s number. Young's frigate was closest of the British ships to the Spanish, and he was instructed to pass the *Santa Brigida* and press on after the *Thetis* to prevent her escape. At nine o'clock *Ethalion* drew past the *Santa Brigida*, firing a few guns at her as she did so. Young continued after his quarry, and by at half-past eleven *Ethalion* was so obviously overhauling *Thetis* that Capitán Don Juan de Mendoza suddenly bore up and boldly prepared to rake *Ethalion* from ahead. Young promptly wore round, firing two broadsides; both ships ran on for a further hour, aiming high to cripple one another's rigging, until Mendoza gave up and struck his colours.

Meanwhile, at the point of divergence the *Santa Brigida,* proving the faster ship, headed for Cape Finisterre. At dawn next morning she drew near the coast and, using local knowledge, ran very close inshore. She was followed by *Triton*, commanded by John Gore, and *Alcmène*, making 7 knots in her wake. By ill-fortune *Triton* struck a reef, but rode off it quickly enough not to be left behind, and with *Naiad* coming up astern, both Gore and Henry Digby of the *Alcmène* opened fire on the *Santa Brigida* as hunters and hunted approached Muros. Here the navigation became intricate. The coast was deeply indented with re-entrant 'rias' running back into surrounding high ground which cut off the wind. Capitán Don Antonio Pillon, becalmed, outmanoeuvred and outnumbered, his ship over shallow reefs and the prospect of grounding imminent, struck his colours under the cliffs of his native land.

On 21 October the four British frigates entered Plymouth with their prizes. Neither of the 34-gun frigates was considered of interest to the British navy, but their cargoes were, not least to those ships' companies in sight of one another during the chase. *Santa Brigida* had on board indigo, cochineal, cocoa and sugar to the value of about £5,000. Pillon's frigate also bore 446 chests, each containing 3,000 silver dollars, together with bags and kegs also containing cash.

On the 28th and 29th more than sixty artillery wagons, escorted by armed troops and military bands and watched by curious and envious crowds, moved this treasure to the citadel high on Plymouth Hoe. A month later, similarly escorted, it was moved to London, where it was deposited in the Bank of England. Those fortunate enough to share this prize-money were gratified by substantial sums: seamen received £182 each, midshipmen £792, warrant officers £2,468, and lieutenants £5,091; Pierrepont, Young, Digby and Gore each benefited to the tune of a cool £40,731. This was the richest prize of the entire war, and they were made men.

Several actions were fought in the West Indies during 1799, but the bloodiest was an almost private affair which approached its crisis on the same day that Pierrepont entered Plymouth in triumph, 21 October 1799.

A month earlier the Commander-in-Chief at Jamaica, Admiral Sir Hyde Parker, received word that the Spanish frigate *Hermione* (Capitán de Fregata Don Raimondo de Chalas) lay under the guns of the Spanish fort at Puerto Cabello on the Spanish Main in what is now Venezuela.

It will be recalled that the crew of this former British ship had mutinied and given her up to the Spanish in 1797, unable to tolerate the abuse of their commander, Captain Hugh Pigot. There are few instances of a mutiny being more justified (the notorious case aboard the insignificant armed transport *Bounty* was weak by comparison), but the mutineers' action was extreme, doubtless a reflection of the extreme cruelty of their commander.

Pigot was not merely a brutal officer; he was a sadist. He was a man whose measure of his own competence was the smartness of his ship, and his ship was one in which men were treated as mere automata. While such slick manoeuvres such as taking in a reef as a ship tacked through the wind were often a matter of pride for a whole ship's company, they relied upon a perfect understanding between officers and men, and were rarely achieved by bullying. Aboard *Hermione* Pigot flogged men daily. He lashed one man eight times in ten months, and killed at least two with the cat-of-nine-tails, one of whom took eighteen weeks to die. These manifold cruelties and humiliations came to a head when the hands were reefing sail in a squall. Pigot shrieked his usual promise to flog the last man off the yards when the job was done, and in their fearful hurry to get back on deck three young seamen fell from the mizen yard at his feet. Looking at the three twitching bodies on his quarterdeck, Pigot ordered them thrown overboard, and then, as the watching crew groaned collectively, ordered the rest all 'started', or beaten by the boatswain and his mates.

That night the marine sentry at Pigot's cabin door was knocked unconscious, the door was kicked down and Pigot was attacked. He defended himself with a short-sword until, finally overcome, he was flung, still living, through his own cabin window, into the *Hermione*'s wake. In a frenzy of blood-lust the infuriated mutineers then killed the first lieutenant and several other officers and midshipmen, and thereby passed beyond the pale of any remote possibility of clemency.

Pigot had been a protégé of Sir Hyde Parker, who therefore had a personal interest in the recovery of *Hermione*. Learning of her whereabouts, Parker sent for Captain Edward Hamilton of the 28-gun *Surprise* (the former French *Unité*), who volunteered to cut the *Hermione* out from Puerto Cabello. Considering this too dangerous, Parker gave Hamilton sealed orders, sending him to cruise off Aruba in the knowledge that *Hermione* was bound for Havana and must pass that way. Hamilton accordingly lay off the coast for some weeks, taking prizes but without any sight of *Hermione*. With his provisions running low, he decided to reconnoitre Puerto Cabello before he returned to Jamaica, to ensure that he had not missed the Spanish frigate. On the evening of 21 October, therefore, *Surprise* stood in towards Puerto Cabello. The *Hermione*, with her sails bent and masts aloft, could still be seen moored head and stern under some two hundred guns in the embrasures of the fortifications. *Surprise* stood on and off the coast for three days; then, on the afternoon of the 24th, Hamilton invited his officers to dine with him, and put his plan to them. They acquiesced and, dinner over, captain and officers appeared on deck after mustering the hands in the waist.

Hamilton, himself a strict and severe officer, addressed his assembled crew: 'I find it useless to wait any longer; we shall soon be obliged to leave the station, and that frigate will become the prize of some more fortunate ship than the *Surprise*; our only prospect of success is by cutting her out this night.' It is said his men cheered as Hamilton proclaimed, 'I will lead you myself.'

Hamilton and his officers and men made meticulous preparations. Weapons were readied; blue clothes were to be worn and no white was to be seen anywhere; passwords were arranged; boat crews were nominated, divided into boarders and oarsmen, with reliefs detailed off. At half-past seven in the evening the boats were hoisted out; Hamilton took the pinnace which, with the launch and jolly-boat, was to board *Hermione*'s starboard side; the second division, consisting of the gig and both cutters, was to board on the larboard. The approaching British boats were spotted by one of two Spanish guard-boats being pulled across the anchorage, whereupon the alarm was raised. Hamilton nevertheless pressed on directly for his objective, though several of his boats were distracted into attacking the guard-boats.

The *Hermione*'s crew were called to general quarters as Hamilton's pinnace drew close. A shot passed over the pinnace, which became foul of the frigate's mooring and dropped alongside under *Hermione*'s starboard bow. Hamilton ordered his boarders to clamber up the frigate's side; the first men were to continue up the shrouds to loosen the foresail, so that it made a screen behind which the rest of the pinnace's crew could gain the deck. Hamilton and his party next cleared the forecastle, then advanced down the gangway; the Spanish seaman in the gun deck below seemed oblivious of the scuffling struggle now going on above their heads.

As more British boarders scrambled over the side a desperate and savage fight for possession of the *Hermione*'s quarterdeck took place. In the mêlée Hamilton received a serious head-wound from the butt of a musket, but shortly thereafter the marine officer arrived on deck with his soldiers who fired a volley and stormed down onto the main-deck with bayonets fixed. In this way about sixty Spaniards were confined in the cabin, by which time the *Surprise*'s carpenter had cut the after cable, allowing *Hermione* to swing to the wind. Aloft, a handful of British seamen were loosening the topsails, and in a few moments more the bow cable was severed and the ship was under tow of the boats, all of which had been left with a sufficiency of oarsmen and hook-ropes to lodge in *Hermione*'s overside ironwork. Then the fore and mizen topsail were sheeted home, their yards braced round and the sails allowed to draw. *Hermione* gathered way, steered by three men, all of whom were wounded.

As *Hermione* drew out of the bay the guns of Puerto Cabello opened fire, and several shots struck home. Resistance was petering out below and an hour after boarding, *Hermione* was back in British hands. A dozen of the Surprises were wounded, Mr Maxwell the gunner very seriously, but no one had been killed. They had however dealt the Spaniards a cruel blow. Of 365 men aboard *Hermiore*, 119 were killed and 97 wounded. All the survivors were afterwards put aboard a schooner which had been taken by *Surprise* off Aruba, and sent back in to Puerto Cabello. Hamilton returned to Port Royal in Jamaica, with his prize. In due course he was knighted, but he was troubled by his head-wound for the remainder of his long life.

As for the mutineers, over a period of nine years, twenty-seven fell into the hands of the naval authorities. Ironically enough, William Bligh, then captain of the *Director*, sat on the court martial that judged the surviving officers for the loss of the ship, while Pellew was a member of a court which condemned several seamen to death. Naval justice was harsh, but not always indiscriminate, for Sir Hyde complained bitterly when one court acquitted three youths, one of whom was all of twelve years old.

*Hermione* was duly returned to the Royal Navy – but not as *Hermione*, that name having been disgraced. Sir Hyde Parker vindictively renamed her *Retaliation* but the Admiralty, wisely considering this provocatively tactless, substituted *Retribution*. With a number of other frigates she was used in a cordon of armed blockships moored in the Thames between 1803 and 1805 under the management and ensign of Trinity House. After Trafalgar and the end of the invasion scare of 1805, she was broken up.

# CHAPTER 9

---

# 'So daring an enterprise'

At the end of 1799 peace overtures were made from Paris, where the Directory had given way to the Consulate, a triumvirate soon reduced to a single figure of influence. Though he had been thwarted in Syria by Rear-Admiral Nelson, Achmed Djezzar Pasha and Captain Sir Sidney Smith, the new head of the French state was the First Consul: Napoleon Bonaparte. The Consulate offered no concessions; the British government rightly judged that the French were only looking for a temporary suspension of hostilities, to gain time to consolidate their position. The proposals were therefore rejected.

A division of the Channel Fleet therefore maintained the blockade of Brest during the spring of 1800, losing the 64-gun *Repulse*, which struck rocks off the Breton coast near Quimper. All her people were taken prisoner, except twelve who reached Guernsey in one of the ship's boats. In late March Bridport joined Vice-Admiral Sir Alan Gardner and took over command, his flag flying in the 100-gun *Royal George;* thirty-eight sail-of-the-line now cruised off Ushant.

A month later Bridport was relieved by Earl St Vincent in the 100-gun *Namur*. Apart from investing Brest more closely than his predecessor, in June despatched Sir Edward Pellew in *Impétueux* with a large detachment of ships and transports to assist a French royalist uprising in southern Brittany. Among those sea warriors involved, besides Pellew, were de Courcy in the *Canada*, 74, Sir Richard Strachan in *Captain*, 74, Thomas Byam Martin in *Fisgard*, Charles Herbert in *Amelia* and Viscount Ranelagh in *Doris*. Several other frigates also took part, among them *Amethyst, Diamond* and *Thames*. Five battalions of infantry with artillery were embarked and the ships carried out raids, but the objective of the operation, Belle Île, proved impervious to assault, and after languishing for some time on the island of Houat the troops were sent on to the Mediterranean.

Some time after this abortive expedition, while the seventy-fours *Captain* and *Marlborough* were cruising off Quiberon, the *Marlborough* struck a rock. The position of the rock was said to be 'uncertain', from which one deduces that it was inaccurately charted, or that the *Marlborough* was indifferently navigated. The ship was refloated but sank soon afterwards, though without loss of life.

In the Mediterreanean, Lord Keith continued the blockade of Toulon and Cartagena, with a squadron watching Cádiz, assisting the Austrians in their fight against the French in northern Italy. Keith was ashore at Livorno on diplomatic business when his flagship *Queen Charlotte* caught fire and burned to the waterline before sinking. Of the 829 people on board only 156 were saved, some by American ships in the vicinity which lost a few of their own men in the rescue.

In due course Keith concentrated on Genoa, into which city the French had been driven and where Général André Masséna held out stubbornly against his Austrian and British besiegers. The same day that Masséna evacuated Genoa, Bonaparte entered Milan after crossing the Alps and, in a series of victories culminating at Marengo on 14 June (where Bonaparte was saved from disaster by the timely intervention of Desaix, who had followed him home from Egypt), broke the power of Austria. Genoa fell back into French hands so suddenly that the *Minotaur*, then in the port, only narrowly escaped being blown to pieces by the French-manned guns of the fortresses by hurriedly warping out of the harbour.

The island of Malta was now important to the course of the war. On his way to Egypt in 1798 Bonaparte had landed at Valletta, dislodged the ruling knights, and established French rule in the island under Général Vaubois. This duly became highly unpopular with the inhabitants, who solicited help from passing British warships. The Royal Navy supplied the Maltese with French small arms captured at Aboukir, landing seamen and marines under Captain Alexander Ball of the 74-gun *Alexander*. They helped in attacking the French garrison, driving them into the fortifications of Valletta and the surrounding cities.

In February 1800 the French tried to succour this beleaguered force, sending out Contre-Amiral Perrée with a squadron of frigates, corvettes and storeships. The only ship-of-the-line with Perrée was his flagship, the *Généreux*, one of the two French ships to have escaped destruction at Aboukir Bay. On 18 February Perrée's ships were sighted and chased by a division of Keith's fleet under Nelson. In the action which followed Nelson's flagship, the *Foudroyant*, with the *Northumberland* in company, slowly overhauled *Généreux*, but the escape of the French ship was prevented by Captain Shuldam Peard of the 32-gun frigate *Success*. Peard boldly hove-to athwart the *Généreux*'s hawse and raked her as she approached, then immediately wore round and loosed his starboard broadside as the French ship thrashed past his frigate under a press of sail. The great ship's fire brought down some of *Success*'s spars, but Peard filled his sails and joined the chase until Nelson signalled him to come under the *Foudroyant*'s lee. By the time *Foudroyant* and *Northumberland* caught up with *Généreux*, Perrée had been wounded in the eye and had both his legs shot off at the thigh. His outgunned flagship surrendered after discharging a broadside at the British battleships ranging up on either quarter. Perrée was considered to have broken his parole and the uncompromising British officers aboard *Foudroyant* declared him 'lucky in having redeemed his honour by dying in battle'.

The officer sent to take *Généreux* to Port Mahon was a certain Lieutenant Lord Cochrane, and on her way to Minorca the *Généreux* ran into heavy weather. Badly hulled in the action, the ship leaked and required nursing into her refuge, seamanship which earned Cochrane a recommendation from his squadron commander, Nelson.

Perrée's failure to relieve Vaubois' garrison at Malta worsened the situation in Valletta. Rats and rabbits were selling for exorbitant prices and the French governor determined to send word to Toulon that unless he received supplies he would be compelled to capitulate. Accordingly he sent Contre-Amiral Denis Decrès to sea in the sole remaining survivor of the Nile, Capitaine de Vaisseau Saulnier's 80-gun *Guillaume Tell*.

Nelson meanwhile had gone home overland, by way of Vienna and Hamburg, in the lubricious company of Emma Hamilton and her compliant husband Sir William. Local command of the British ships around Malta fell to Captain Manley Dixon in *Lion*, 64, who had with him *Foudroyant* (Captain Sir Edward Berry) *Alexander*, 74, commanded in Ball's absence at Malta by her first lieutenant, the frigate *Penelope* under Captain The Honourable Henry Blackwood, and the 16-gun sloop *Minorca*.

The *Guillaume Tell* slipped out of Grand Harbour an hour before midnight on 30 March. It was a dark night with a strong southerly gale blowing up from the coast of Tripolitania, but within an hour she had been seen from *Penelope*, lying hove-to just off the island. Blackwood sent *Minorca* to warn Dixon at anchor a few miles away and then, setting as much sail as *Penelope*'s spars would stand, went in chase of the big line-of-battle ship. Half an hour later he came up under *Guillaume Tell*'s stern and luffing his frigate, discharged his larboard broadside. Tacking, Blackwood again caught up and, ranging up on *Guillaume Tell*'s larboard quarter, fired his starboard 18-pounders into her. Decrès and Saulnier fired back but could not linger to destroy their insolent tormentor, for they could see other sails pale against the darkness astern. Blackwood continued to harry the much larger ship, raking her repeatedly until *Penelope*'s guns had shot away *Guillaume Tell*'s main and mizen topmasts, and her mainyard.

Dawn was lightening the eastern sky as *Lion* came up and Dixon, taking over from Blackwood, fired a triple-shotted broadside into the French ship as he passed her. Once ahead of *Guillaume Tell*, Dixon luffed up and raked the enemy's bow, carrying away her bowsprit but receiving considerable damage in return. By six o'clock *Lion* was so badly impaired as to be unmanageable, and dropped out of the action, but *Foudroyant* was now rapidly approaching and ran past, also firing a triple-shotted broadside. The French responded in kind, and refused to strike when Berry hailed. He now over-shot his quarry, and it was seven or eight minutes before the *Foudroyant* engaged yardarm to yardarm. In a few minutes her foretopmast, main topsail yard and jib-boom went by the board, and she fell away.

Dixon and Blackwood had meanwhile set their damaged rigging to rights, and now worked their ships up on *Guillaume Tell*'s larboard side. By half-past six they had shot away the *Guillaume Tell*'s main and mizen masts, just as Berry, having freed himself of the wreckage of his own masts and rigging, renewed the action. At eight o'clock the *Guillaume Tell*'s tottering foremast crashed down. She was now quite surrounded, the *Foudroyant* on her starboard side, the *Lion* to port, and *Penelope* lying across her bow; Decrès and Saulnier had gallantly defended their ship for eight exhausting hours, but at twenty past eight they struck her colours. Blackwood took possession of her and towed her to Syracuse where, renamed *Malta*, she became one of the two largest two-deckers in the Royal Navy. Out of more than 1,200 men engaged the British lost 17 killed and 110 wounded; the French losses are uncertain but are known to have been heavy, estimated at more than two hundred. Saulnier's defence of the *Guillaume Tell* was a most gallant action. He inflicted sufficient disabling damage on his successive tormentors that he might have escaped, had not British ships been smartly handled and quickly refitted.

Vaubois, another very determined man, maintained his presence in Valletta, finally capitulating only on 5 September. He had attempted to save the remaining French frigates in Grand Harbour by sending them to sea in late August. One, the *Diane*, was taken and renamed *Niobe*; the other, the *Justice*, succeeded in reaching Toulon. Her captain was Jean Villeneuve, an aristocrat of republican tendencies for whom was reserved a far worse fate than that of Decrès, whom Napoleon appointed a member of the order that afterwards became the Légion d'honneur, and maritime prefect at L'Orient. He later rose to become Minister of Marine.

After the débâcle at Belle Île it was clear that while little could be expected of royalist uprisings, the potential of Royal Naval ships to 'annoy the enemy' was considerable. Hit-and-run raids, the taking of batteries and the cutting-out of merchantmen anchored under their protection had long been part of a cruiser captain's repertoire of tactical options, but larger forces properly concerted might, it was hoped, achieve far more.

It will be recalled that a Spanish squadron from Ferrol had tried to reach Brest the previous year but had been forced to return to its base. A portion of the ships which had been sent to Belle Île under Pellew now joined a squadron under Sir John Warren to deal with those Spaniards. Warren was currently a rear-admiral flying his flag in the 74-gun *Renown,* and with him were the 98-gun *London,* Pellew's *Impétueux,* the *Courageux* commanded by Samuel Hood, Strachan's *Captain,* and the frigates *Indefatigable* (Captain The Honourable Henry Curzon), *Amelia* (Captain The Honourable Charles Herbert), *Amethyst, Stag* and *Brilliant,* with the sloop *Cynthia*. Troops were conveyed in some transports and there were a few gun-boats involved.

The Spanish ships in Ferrol were the 112-gun *San Hermenegildo* and *Real Carlos,* the 96-gun *San Fernando,* the 80-gun *Argonauta* and the 74s *San Antonio* and *San Agustín*. Warren landed troops, guns and seamen under the direction of Pellew, who acted as beach-master, and they fought two engagements with the defenders, gaining the heights over the town. But the following day Lieutenant-General Sir James Pulteney pusillanimously decided that the cost of taking Ferrol would be too great, and re-embarked. Disgusted, Warren sailed south to join Keith; the naval officers, especially Pellew, were scarcely able to conceal their contempt for the army commander. In due course the Spanish ships were able to move to Cádiz, but only once the British Mediterranean fleet were elsewhere.

Keith, with Warren, was to have made a raid on Cádiz, but decided against it on learning that bubonic plague raged in the city. The whole combined force returned to Gibraltar in October, but did not languish long at the Rock: before the end of the year the troops had embarked again, minus Pulteney. Keith sailed eastwards the length of the Mediterranean, to Aboukir Bay, where 16,000 troops under General Sir Ralph Abercromby were landed.

The French army still in Egypt under Général Menou had received some small reinforcements since Nelson's destruction of their fleet. The

'Black Dick', Admiral Lord Howe

Vice Admiral Lord Collingwood        'Dismal Jimmy', Admiral Lord Gambier

The Board Room at the Admiralty

Rear Admiral Sir James Saumarez

Admiral Sir William Cornwallis

Rear Admiral Sir John Borlase Warren

Admiral Sir Edward Pellew, later first Viscount Exmouth

The French frigate *L'Incorruptible*

A typical British frigate

The young Captain Horatio Nelson

Captain Sir Sidney Smith

Rear Admiral Sir Richard Goodwin Keats

H.M. 38 gun. Frigate. PHAETON. Captain Sir Andrew Snape Douglas.
. ONE YEARS CAPTURES.

PROMPTE - 28 gun frigate - 180 MEN

LA BLANCHE - CORVETTE - 22 GUNS

To the victor the spoils
HM Frigate *Phaeton* and her prizes in 1793

Destruction of *Droits de l'Homme* by *Indefatigable* and *Amazon*, January 1797

*Loire*, engaged by *Anson* and raked by *Kangaroo*, off the Irish Coast, October 1798

frigates *Égyptienne* and *Justice* and the corvette *Lodi* had slipped past the British blockade off Toulon and the *Régénérée* had escaped from Rochefort, but these were trifling when set against Menou's wants. Abercromby's landing was contested nevertheless, carried out through a heavy surf in the teeth of fierce opposition. A battalion of a thousand seamen went ashore with the soldiers, under the command of Sir Sidney Smith. Abercromby was mortally wounded, but this joint operation between the British services succeeded in destroying French ambitions in Egypt. As the main force advanced up the Nile from the Delta towards Cairo, two detachments of troops from India were landed from the Red Sea. One came ashore at Suez, the other at Kosseir, convoyed thither by Rear-Admiral Blankett and Captain Sir Home Popham respectively.

The capitulation terms provided that the remnants of the French army should in due course be conveyed to France by the Royal Navy, but meanwhile several French ships fell into British hands. Three, including the *Justice*, were handed over to the Turks (who by the British action recovered the pashalik of Egypt), while the *Régénérée* and *Égyptienne* were added to the British fleet. The former, renamed *Alexandria*, had been laid down as a 74 and then converted to a heavy frigate in 1799; she made a fine 48-gun cruiser and, her consort *Égyptienne*, a 36-gun, 12-pounder frigate, proved a very fast ship.

There were successes too, against Great Britain's other enemies. The war against the Dutch was carried on largely in the North Sea and resulted in a number of captures. The extensive Dutch East Indies were not threatened by the Royal Navy to any great extent for the time being. In the Dutch West Indies, however, the interdiction of trade and consequent economic effects of isolation from the mother-country, created widespread disaffection. In 1798 Surinam surrendered to Britain on favourable terms, and in September 1800 Captain Frederick Watkins of the 36-gun frigate *Néréide* took the surrender of Curaçao.

Relations were meanwhile deteriorating between Britain and the Scandinavian countries, whose ships were of course subjected to search by the Royal Navy on the high seas. In 1798 an entire Swedish convoy laden with contraband cargoes to the value of £600,000 was apprehended, condemned as a legitimate prize, and seized. Stockholm protested vigorously. In the December 1799 following, a Danish frigate which resisted attempts by British cruisers to search her convoy was compelled to accompany them to Gibraltar, from where she was shortly afterwards released. No neutral nation enjoyed what it considered interference in her freedom to trade, particularly as the British blockade increased prices in Europe generally and in France in particular. Of the two principal belligerents it was Britain, therefore, which came in for the obloquy expressed in neutral capital cities.

Nevertheless, the policy of blockade and the annoyance and destruction of French coastal commerce remained absolute priorities for Britain's navy, prosecuted with vigour by its smaller cruisers off the Channel Islands on 5 February 1800, the two British sloops *Harpy* and *Fairy* were on the lookout for a French frigate which had chased the brig-sloop *Seaflower* the previous day. They sighted their quarry off St Malo, making her way westwards along the Breton coast towards Brest. Capitaine de Frégate Jaques Epron aboard the 38-gun *Pallas,* took the bait and engaged the two sloops during the early afternoon. Commander Joshua Horton of *Fairy* succeeded in raking *Pallas* before Epron broke off the action as the wind freshened from the south-west, leaving the *Fairy* and *Harpy* to splice their rigging before they could follow. *Harpy* led the chase when suddenly *Pallas* was seen to alter course to north-north-west, Epron having seen two strange sails ahead of his ship. Horton hoisted the signal for *Harpy* to work to windward of *Pallas* as they in turn caught sight of the strange ships, which were now joined by a third and appeared to be holding a fair wind from the south-east. Horton was confident they were British, so both *Fairy* and *Harpy* flew the signals for an enemy in sight, firing guns every five minutes to attract attention.

Equally convinced that the approaching vessels were British, Epron hoisted a British ensign and fired guns too; but he failed to deceive them, for the three had left Plymouth specifically to locate *Pallas* before she reached Brest, and were on the lookout for her. They were the *Loire*, Captain James Newman, the *Danaë*, Captain Lord Proby (yet to be subject to mutiny), and *Railleur*, Commander William Turquand. Confronted by this trap, Epron ran off before the wind with all sail set in what had now become a light south-easterly breeze. By nightfall, however, the *Railleur* was cutting her off and at a quarter to eight the *Pallas* had to tack offshore, passing *Loire* and exchanging fire. The *Loire* now closed with *Pallas*, which began a fierce action, receiving some support from shore batteries on Les Sept Îles. She was quickly engaged by *Railleur*, *Harpy* and *Fairy* as all stood on in a running fight. At half past one in the morning of the 6th, after a brilliant defence in which he had been hindered by about a hundred 'volunteer' ex-convicts on their way to join the Brest fleet, Epron struck his colours. *Pallas* was commissioned into the Royal Navy as *Pique*, replacing the British frigate of that name lost the previous year. At the other end of the English Channel, on 7 July 1800, a raiding party attacked a squadron of four French frigates lying in Dunkirk Road. The raid was led by Commander Patrick Campbell of the sloop *Dart*, one of a pair of experimental vessels with revolutionary hull forms mounting thirty-eight 32-pounder carronades. *Dart* was supported by two gun-brigs, *Biter* and *Boxer*, and four fireships, *Wasp*, *Comet*, *Rosario* and *Falcon*, plus boats from the frigates *Andromeda* and *Nemesis*. The *Dart* fired a double-shotted broadside into one of the French frigates before running alongside the *Désirée* and, after a desperate fight, boarded and carried her. The other French frigates cut their cables and avoided the fireships, but the *Désirée* was brought offshore and later commissioned into the British service. The French and Dutch coasts were constantly the scene of such desperate skirmishes, often carried on in poor weather and always subject to the strong tides of the English Channel and North Sea.

In similar circumstances Warren's squadron, now the *Renown*, *Defence*, *Fisgard* and *Unicorn*, harried the south coast of Brittany from Brest to the Loire estuary, destroying merchant ships and coastal batteries. On one occasion in July the boats of the squadron were engaged in a raid on the anchorage behind Noirmoutier Island. The *Thérèse*, a 20-gun corvette, two other armed vessels and fifteen merchantmen were destroyed but on returning to their ships offshore the British boats ran aground on a shoal. French troops waded out to attack them and 92 officers and men were captured, while the remaining hundred or so escaped.

Pellew was in the same area later that month. One of his smaller vessels was the 14-gun cutter *Viper*, commanded by his protégé Jeremiah Coghlan, who had been reconnoitring L'Orient, where a 74 and two frigates then lay at anchor. Coghlan had observed a number of vessels in Port Louis, on the opposite river bank to L'Orient, and decided to try to cut out a small gun-brig lying there. He withdrew to consult Pellew and ask for a cutter and a dozen volunteers. Pellew agreed, so Coghlan, a midshipman and six seamen from *Viper* manned the cutter and another boat from their own vessel, and *Amethyst* sent a third.

The other boats could not keep up with Coghlan's as the party pulled inshore. Seeing that the gun-brig, *Cerbère,* lay athwart their passage, a spring on her cable and her crew at quarters, Coghlan ran his boat directly at the brig's stern and jumped aboard. Here he stumbled into a trawl net, and thus entrapped, received a pike-thrust in his thigh. Repulsed by the eighty-odd men in the gun-brig, his fellow boarders were soon forced back into their cutter. A second attempt to board was also defeated, and several British seamen were thrown into the water. Incredibly, Coghlan went at the enemy a third time, gained the deck, killed six of the defenders, wounded twenty more and finally captured the gun-brig.

The British losses were one man killed and eight wounded – Coghlan himself had taken two wounds, and Midshipman Paddon six. The two other boats arrived in time to tow the 7-gun *Cerbère* out to sea, but only Coghlan and the cutter's crew profited from the sale of the gun-brig: the rest of the fleet remitted their share, in honour of what Pellew in his report to the Commander-in-Chief called 'so daring an enterprise'. Indeed, Earl St Vincent was so delighted that he confirmed Coghlan's acting commission with immediate effect, and presented him with a sword. Coghlan was exactly the sort of officer St Vincent approved of: unpretentious, determined, and wedded to his profession.

These aggressive actions were in marked contrast to the duty of convoy escort which fell to such officers as the splendidly-named Captain Rowley Bulteel. Bulteel's 64-gun *Belliqueux* was escorting six outward-bound East Indiamen towards St Helena when shortly after dawn on 4 August 1800, off the coast of Brazil, a squadron of French frigates was seen bearing down towards the convoy. These ships were the *Concorde*, 40 (Commodore Jean-François Landolphe), *Franchise* (Capitaine Pierre Jurien), *Medée* (Capitaine Jean-Daniel Coudin), and a prize-schooner acting as tender. Landolphe's ships, escaping from Rochefort in March 1799, had proceeded to raid British shipping, particularly on the coast of Africa. Bulteel made for the largest enemy vessel, the *Concorde,* and signalled the convoy to make sail in pursuit, a bold front which induced the French to bear away. *Belliqueux* fired into *Concorde* for ten minutes, whereupon Landolphe surrendered.

The schooner and the *Franchise*, throwing overboard all encumbrances, successfully escaped, but in the meantime the Indiamen *Exeter* and *Bombay Castle* had gone in chase of the *Medée*. Commander Henry Meriton, master of the *Exeter,* overhauled the *Medée* and, gesturing to the *Bombay Castle* approaching astern, invited Coudin to strike to superior force. Coudin agreed and Meriton quickly sent a boat with an officer to receive his sword. When he boarded *Exeter* Coudin, dismayed by the small size of the quarterdeck guns, asked to what ship he had surrendered. 'To a merchant ship,' Meriton drily replied, to the mortification of the French captain.

This was yet one more of several instances of British East Indiamen fooling French officers into thinking they were two-decked men-of-war, but not all enemy commanders were so gullible. One of the most remarkable French sea-officers was the corsair commander Robert Surcouf. A native of St Malo, Surcouf was born in 1773 and went to sea in a merchant ship in 1789, just as the Revolution broke out. Despite the egalitarian French government's prohibition of slave trading in 1794, many traders off France's west coast persisted in defying the law, and Surcouf served in slave ships. Arrested, he escaped to become a privateer commander of tremendous skill and daring. His successes in the East Indies aboard the *Émilie,* the *Clarisse* and later the 26-gun *Confiance* made him the scourge of the British East India Company, as well as of British and Parsee trading houses in Bombay and Calcutta and their 'Country' ships. Operating from the Île de France he appeared in the Bay of Bengal in 1796, and took two 'Country' ships and a pilot brig off the Sandheads, using the brig as a decoy to seize more prizes. Eluding capture he then struck elsewhere after seeing his prizes safe in to Port Louis. In 1798 he took the East Indiaman *Triton,* captured several more 'Country' ships, and at one time blockaded the Hooghly single-handed. In October 1800 he captured the East Indiaman *Kent* in the Bay of Bengal, killing her master, Commander Robert Rivington. Surcouf's success gained him an appointment as *enseigne* in the French navy, a somewhat paltry reward for a sea warrior of such skill and daring.

Several more enemy cruisers fell into British hands before the war was briefly suspended. *Vengeance* was taken on 20 August 1800 off Puerto Rico by the *Seine,* following a running fight of nine hours. Three times she shot away the British frigate's rigging, and three times Captain David Milne's crew refitted fast enough to bring their ship into action again – clear evidence that the tactic of immobilising an enemy by destroying her rig was generally futile.

It was a tactic which also failed the French 40-gun frigate *Africaine.* She had escaped the British blockade off Rochefort with the *Régénérée* and was on her way to Egypt with guns and stores and 400 soldiers when on 19 February 1801 she ran into the *Phoebe,* 36 (Captain Robert Barlow), just east of Gibraltar. An engagement lasting two hours ensued, during which *Africaine*'s gunners fired high and wrecked *Phoebe*'s rigging. But the British guns wrought a terrible havoc aboard the crowded *Africaine,* battering her hull and inflicting such execution that she capitulated. Commodore Saulnier (late of the *Guillaume Tell* and subsequently exchanged) and 199 officers, seamen and soldiers were killed, including three surgeons who lost their lives tending the wounded in the orlop. *Africaine*'s senior officer after Saulnier was Capitaine Jean-Jacques Magendie, and he was among the 143 casualties, many of whose wounds were mortal. Barlow acknowledged the carnage in his report, considering those figures an under-estimate. He had difficulties securing his prize, for neither ship was in a fit condition to beat to windward in the strong westerly that blew up that evening. In the end Barlow managed to struggle into Port Mahon with her, and in due course Africaine was taken into the Royal Navy under her own name. Barlow was knighted and his first lieutenant, John Holland, was made commander.

Although Sercey had now ceased to command in the Indian Ocean, a last attempt was made by the French navy to attack trade in the east; at the same time they hoped to colonise the Seychelles, landing political prisoners there who had been banished from France. On the British side, Vice-Admiral Rainier was particularly concerned that his own operations then in train in the Red Sea might prove vulnerable to attack. The 36-gun *Chiffone* and the 18-gun corvette *Flèche* were both located in the Seychelles, and Rainier sent the *Sybille* to smoke them out. The British frigate negotiated the reef-strewn passage into Mahé and anchored with springs on her cable to attack the *Chiffone*. In an action lasting seventeen minutes during which *Sybille* was raked by a French battery ashore, Captain Charles Adam pounded his quarry. Capitaine Pierre Guieysse cut his cable, drifted ashore and then struck his flag. Adam sent a boat to take possession, meanwhile turning his guns on the battery and silencing it.

*Chiffone* was added to the British navy, but her consort *Flèche* suffered a different fate when the 18-gun ship-sloop *Victor* brought her to battle off the islands on 2 September 1801. The two vessels fought for an hour and a half, the *Flèche* cutting up *Victor*'s rigging. Having immobilised his foe, Lieutenant de Vaisseau Jean Bonavie made sail, leaving Commander George Collier to his refitting. Collier chased *Flèche* and briefly lost sight of her, but then saw her entering Mahé on the afternoon of the 5th. Heaving-to overnight Collier sent his boats in to sound the channel, and the next day repeated Adam's feat. Collier entered the passage, enduring a raking fire, and so battered the corvette in the following two and a half hours that her crew cut their cable. When she drifted ashore they set fire to her and she was burned to a cinder.

The operation of 'cutting-out' was always dangerous and desperate. One of the most fiercely contested such episodes occurred on 21 July 1801 when the boats of two British frigates attempted to seize the French corvette *Chevrette* from Camaret Road, near Brest.

In February 1801, upon a change of government, St Vincent had hauled down his flag as Commander-in-Chief to take up the post of First Lord of the Admiralty. Admiral Sir William Cornwallis succeeded him and at once began to set the relentless standard for the investment of Brest that was to be the ideal until 1814. A crucial element was the close watching of the inner Iroise, and for this three frigates, the *Uranie, Beaulieu* and *Doris,* had been assigned the inshore station. In July they lay at anchor off Pointe St Mathieu, in full view of the Franco-Spanish fleet then moored in Brest Road, observing the approach of *Chevette,* a large, deeply laden corvette which was in fact outward bound for Senegal and then Guadeloupe.

The *Uranie* was not actually present when Captain Stephen Poyntz and Captain Charles Brisbane were joined by Lieutenant Woodley Losack, first lieutenant of Cornwallis's flagship, the *Ville de Paris.* *
Losack's orders were to take command of the boats of the two frigates *Beaulieu* and *Doris,* which were to be manned by volunteers for the cutting-out of the *Chevrette*. The boats began the hard pull towards Camaret Bay after dark on 20th July, but they failed to keep together. They became separated, some turning back as dawn broke, others lying on their oars within sight of their objective and thus betraying their intentions.

All eventually returned to their ships, but the alarmed French moved the *Chevrette* higher up the bay under some shore batteries, and reinforced her crew with troops. The boarding nettings were rigged and the corvette's guns were crammed to the muzzles with grape-shot in anticipation of a renewed attack. Ashore, some temporary redoubts were thrown up and a gun-vessel with two long 36-pounders was sent out from the dockyard to maintain a guard. Loaded with military stores, the *Chevrette* was of more importance than her size suggested. Having thus secured his ship, in a calculated and provocative insult her commander hoisted a large French tricolour above a British ensign, plainly visible from *Beaulieu* and *Doris,* now rejoined by *Uranie* and the barge and pinnace of *Robust*. Altogether there were fifteen boats and 280

---

* This extraordinary name for a British flag-ship arose from the capture of De Grasse's flagship *Ville de Paris* by Rodney at the Battle of the Saintes in 1782. This vessel foundered on her way to England, but a new vessel of the same name was launched in 1795.

men mustered for this very difficult service, and at half-past nine in the evening of the 21st they set off.

Detaching six boats, Losack made after a French craft which was rowing guard, leaving the others to await his return. The time passed, and the next senior lieutenant, Keith Maxwell of the *Beaulieu,* decided that unless they made a move without further delay another night would be lost. With six miles to row, Maxwell led about 180 men into Camaret Bay, having revised their orders: the topmen of his own frigate, once aboard the French vessel, were detailed to ascend the masts and cut loose the enemy's topsails, while Quartermaster Wallis took the *Chevrette*'s helm.

At about one o'clock in the morning of the 22nd Maxwell's nine boats pulled directly for the *Chevrette,* to be met by a hail of grape-shot and musketry followed by a fusillade from troops ashore. Maxwell led *Beaulieu*'s boats to the corvette's starboard bow while the *Uranie*'s boat under Lieutenant Martin Neville, *Robust*'s under Midshipman Robert Warren and *Doris*'s under Lieutenant Walter Burke made for the larboard.

There followed a frightful hand-to-hand fight, the French resisting with musketry, swords, tomahawks and pikes. Some scrambled down into the very boats as the British tried to clamber up the *Chevrette*'s side. Having lost their fire-arms, the British relied upon cold steel in a desperate struggle for mastery of the situation. Gradually they prevailed. The *Beaulieu*'s topmen, some badly wounded, reached the yards only to find the footropes lashed up; undaunted, they ran out along the yards, slashing at the gaskets, so that while the contest for the deck raged beneath them, the topsails and courses fell from their yards. Below, under the bow, the cable had been sawn through: with a light breeze coming off the land, the *Chevrette* began to drift to seawards, helped by the tide.

As the French realised their ship was under weigh, some dived over-board to avoid the horrors of a British prison ship, others ran below to the waist and galled the British boarders gaining control of the upper deck with musket-fire. This was soon silenced, but the wind dropped and the ensuing calm threatened the British escape as the shore guns now opened fire. Then the fluky wind strengthened again and *Chevrette* drew out of the bay, steered by the wounded Wallis. At this point she ran into the missing boats, and Losack climbed aboard.

The losses inflicted on the French were savage, 92 killed and 62 wounded, including her commander. The British losses were 11 killed, including Warren, and 57 wounded, including Neville and Burke, the latter mortally. Losack was promoted to commander, but word that he had not taken part in the action itself soon reached Cornwallis. The admiral instituted an enquiry, the upshot of which was that Maxwell received immediate promotion.

If the cutting-out of the *Chevrette* was a bloody and courageous frontal assault carried out against superior numbers, no less courage and a good deal of guile attended the taking of the Spanish xebec-frigate *Gamo*. This vessel was a 32-gun frigate, ship-rigged on a xebec hull built in the Mediterranean fashion. In early April 1801 she had appeared off southern Spain, masquerading as a merchantmen. Taking her for such, the British brig-sloop *Speedy* was decoyed close under her guns. *Speedy* was herself not what she seemed, for she was wearing a Danish ensign and her hull was painted in the manner of Danish merchantmen. As soon as her commander realised that he had caught a tartar, he ordered one of his lieutenants who spoke Danish to play the part of master. As a Spanish boat came alongside the supposed Dane told the officer in it that the brig had just come from a Barbary port in which the plague was raging. First boat and then the *Gamo* sheered away, leaving *Speedy* to resume her cruise.

The *Speedy*, built in 1781, was commanded by a succession of up-wardly mobile young officers on their way to captain's rank. In April 1801 her commander was Thomas, Lord Cochrane, a tall, red-haired Scot, scion of the ancient but impoverished aristocratic house of Dundonald. Born in Scotland in 1775, he was heir to the ninth Earl of Dundonald, an eccentric inventor and egalitarian from whom his son inherited outspokenness, a strong sense of justice, and the application of logic to all circumstances in life.

Proud, fiery, resourceful, courageous and opinioned to a fault, Cochrane excited jealousy and hatred among both his contemporaries and his seniors. He did not go to sea until he was seventeen; a lieutenant by 1796, he promptly quarrelled seriously with the first lieutenant of his ship, for which he was reprimanded by a court martial. Typically, he always claimed that he was never insubordinate, but only reasonable. His commendation by Nelson for bringing *Généreux* safely into Port Mahon earned him promotion from the Commander-in-Chief, his fellow Scot Lord Keith: Cochrane was sent to *Speedy*.

Captain Lord Cochrane was too tall for his cabin. Every morning he set his shaving mirror on the quarterdeck beside his cabin skylight, through which his head and shoulders emerged, and in this wise completed his toilet. He made *Speedy* the bane of Spanish coastal shipping despite the fact that she was inadequately armed, having only fourteen 4-pounders unaugmented by carronades. He claimed he could carry his ship's broadside in the tail-pockets of his coat.

As a commander and captain Cochrane was to show himself unfashionably careful with his men's lives, never needlessly exposing them to danger and taking the greatest pride in achievements that cost no casualties. Since this was contrary to the blood-thirsty appetites of the times his exploits were often disregarded, but his men appreciated his concern and his care.

As Pellew reached flag-rank, the unorthodox Cochrane succeeded him as the quintessential cruiser-captain. But Pellew, for all his raw courage, was an establishment man, a shameless nepotist, a man seduced by political faction. Cochrane was of an altogether different stamp: a dangerous, outspoken maverick against whom the establishment conspired and whom, in due time it brought low. But all this lay in the future:

After his brush with *Gamo* Cochrane determined to take her, suspecting her to have been sent out with the sole purpose of destroying the pestilential *Speedy*. As *Speedy* lay off Barcelona at daylight on 6 May 1801 a sail was seen. The winds were light, and it was nine o'clock in the forenoon when the two vessels approached one another. Cochrane ordered *Speedy* to wear American colours – a wise precaution, for it was not long before his opponent proved, to his satisfaction, to be the *Gamo*. The Spanish man-of-war, besides her twenty-two 12-pounders, eight 8-pounders and two heavy carronades, had a complement of 319, including 45 marines. Against this overwhelming force, Cochrane brought to bear his fourteen 4-pounders, 54 men and boys and a cool and resourceful courage.

The *Gamo* held the weather gage as the two ships approached one another on opposite courses. Cochrane tacked *Speedy* under his opponent's lee and, as the British ensign was substituted for the American, a running fight began, broadside to broadside. This lasted for forty-five minutes, as the Spanish commander, Capitán Don Francisco de Torris, constantly tried to edge down, run alongside and overwhelm *Speedy* by boarding her. Cochrane foiled these manoeuvres, losing three seamen killed and five wounded. He was equally determined to board, despite his manifest weakness in numbers.

Cochrane briefed his men. Ensuring that his broadside guns were double-shotted, the quoins removed for maximum elevation and all hands armed for boarding, he ordered his surgeon, James Guthrie, to take the wheel. He then ran in under *Gamo*'s larboard side, and as the two hulls bumped together he ordered his starboard broadside fired. His brig was so small that at close range the enemy's round-shot flew over *Speedy*'s deck, but her own 4-pound round-shot and langridge smashed upwards through *Gamo*'s bulwarks and into the clustered Spanish seamen and marines lining the rail in anticipation of a swift victory. The effect was horrible, and in the brief hiatus of shock Cochrane led his entire crew (with the exception of Guthrie at *Speedy*'s helm) up and over the enemy frigate's rail. There followed a sanguine struggle; the Spanish first retired, then rallied and began to drive the insolent British backwards. Sensible of this, Cochrane detached himself, stepped back to the shattered rail and leaned over. 'Send up another fifty men, Mr Guthrie!' he allegedly bellowed, in stentorian tones.

The solitary surgeon, no slouch in the uptake, is said to have roared his assent. At this Cochrane turned and resumed the fight, but the Spanish had heard the order and, so Cochrane afterwards claimed, the heart went out of them. With De Torris already dead, as were fourteen others, and more than forty wounded, the Spanish ship was surrendered.

Because of her xebec hull, *Gamo* was not bought into the Royal Navy but sold instead to the Algerines – which infuriated Cochrane, who lost money on the sale. Furthermore, he did not receive the immediate promotion to post-captain as he expected, and when he did, he had lost his little brig. On 9 June he was off the Castilian coast in company with the 18-gun brig-sloop *Kangaroo*. Here the two small cruisers destroyed a 20-gun xebec and three gunboats, capturing three brig-rigged merchantmen under the guns of a battery. On 3 July, while patrolling in the Strait of Gibraltar, Cochrane encountered a French squadron of three sail-of-the-line and a frigate, on their way from Toulon to Cádiz under Contre-Amiral Charles Linois.

Despite Cochrane's skilful manoeuvres, two of Linois' 74s trapped *Speedy* against the African coast, and he was obliged to capitulate. Capitaine Jean Christi-Pallière of the 74-gun *Desaix* courteously refused his sword, but confined him aboard the French ship until after the battle of Algeçiras. Quite extraordinarily, his little brig, renamed *Le Saint Pierre*, was presented by First Consul Napoleon Bonaparte to the Pope, himself a prisoner of France.

As a prisoner aboard *Desaix* Cochrane found himself in a unique position, as we shall see, and Linois's squadron was to have more dramatic impact in the Gut of Gibraltar than merely taking a small cruiser like the *Speedy*.

The failure of French efforts to succour their army isolated in Egypt prompted First Consul Bonaparte to make a greater effort during 1801. The successful concentration of the Franco-Spanish fleet at Brest was now to be undone, in pursuance of a different objective at the far end of the Mediterranean. Putting out word that an expedition was to leave for San Domingo – Haiti – where the black republic of Toussaint L'Overture, having embraced the Rights of Man, was a paradoxical affront to France, Bonaparte gave Contre-Amiral Honoré Ganteaume secret orders: he was to embark 5,000 troops and proceed to Egypt. To facilitate his escape, orders also went to every French man-of-war along the Biscay and Channel coasts to make conspicuous preparations for sea, with the intention of distracting and dividing British resources.

On 8 January 1801 Ganteaume stood out to sea by way of the Passage du Raz with seven sail-of-the-line, two frigates and a corvette, but was observed by a division of the blockading British Channel fleet and obliged to return. Then on the 23rd, a strong northerly gale drove the British from his doorstep and Ganteaume again blundered out to sea. Several of his ships were damaged or separated, and some were seen on the 27th by Captain Robert Barton, then cruising off Cape Finisterre, in the *Concorde*, which fought a brief engagement with the 40-gun *Bravoure*. Ganteaume gathered his ships off Cape Spartel in Morocco and, capturing a small British sloop, the *Incendiary*, passed through the Strait of Gibraltar on 9 February. Some time previously Keith's fleet had also sailed for Egypt, as already related, and only the frigate *Success* was at The Rock. Her captain, Shuldham Peard, weighed his anchor with the intention of warning Lord Keith. In the following days *Success* overtook the French, but in light winds could not out-run them and was captured by superior numbers. Peard did not lose his wits, but capitalised on his misfortune, informing Ganteaume that Keith was already off the Egyptian coast while Warren, in *Renown* and with his accompanying frigates, could not be far away. This intelligence so dismayed Ganteaume that he abandoned his enterprise and headed for Toulon, where he arrived on 19 February 1801.

Barton had raced to Plymouth meanwhile, and by 3 February the news that a major French fleet was at sea had been telegraphed to the Admiralty. To the strategists in London the obvious destination of such a fleet was the West Indies, and thither accordingly was sent Rear-Admiral Sir Robert Calder with seven of the line and three cruisers. Finding nothing in the West Indies, Calder came home. Warren for his part was off Cádiz, where he heard news of the French. Going on to Gibraltar, he then spent the next weeks seeking information as to their destination in the western Mediterranean, a task complicated by diplomatic issues arising from Sicilian politics. On 25 March he learned that Ganteaume had left Toulon again, galvanised into action by the First Consul, who ordered him to land the troops somewhere on the coast so that they might march to Egypt, by-passing the British anchored off the Nile Delta.

Warren and Ganteaume had a brush with one another off Sardinia and the French ships returned once more to Toulon, only to be kicked out yet again by an infuriated Bonaparte. Additional orders to take Elba on his way east gave Ganteaume an easier objective: he sailed on

27 April and blockaded that island. In the following weeks Warren's ships interfered with these operations, retaking the *Success* and reinforcing the Tuscan garrison on Elba with a detachment of 690 seamen and marines who were led by Captain John Chambers White, now Warren's flag-captain in *Renown*. White suffered two men killed and three injured when *Renown* was struck by lightning during this period, and the operations ashore earned him his patron Warren's 'warmest thanks', evidence of great goodwill from a man usually chary of praising others.

Thanks to the British presence the French failed to take Elba. Ganteaume, having sent several ships back to Toulon, continued south, passing the Strait of Messina on 25 May. On 5 June his ships chased the *Pique*, but Captain James Young escaped to warn Keith, a warning reinforced when a French reconnoitring corvette was taken by the *Kent* and *Hector*, 74s. Ganteaume went no further east than Benghazi, where he had to abandon his attempt to land his troops when British men-of-war arrived to capture several of his transports. Heading west on 24 June he next ran into *Swiftsure*, 74. Captain Benjamin Hallowell tried to reach Malta to warn Warren, but was captured by five of Ganteaume's ships, all of which now returned to Toulon bearing their prize in triumph, as justification for the failure of their mission. They had been defeated by British strategy and the co-operation of her sea warriors. (*Swiftsure* was later retaken at Trafalgar.)

The ships sent back to Toulon by Ganteaume from Elba were in their turn ordered to sea on 13 April under Linois. Linois had embarked 1,500 troops under Brigadier-General Devaux for proposed operations against Portugal which, hitherto neutral, was now under Franco-Spanish attack. This was the squadron that took Cochrane's *Speedy* on their way to Cádiz. Here Linois was to join forces with six ships-of-the-line sold by Spain to France which lay ready for sea at Cádiz under Contre-Amiral Dumanoir Le Pelley, and six Spanish ships under Vice-Almirante Don Juan de Moreno.

Word that a French squadron had passed the Straits had been sent from Gibraltar to Sir James Saumarez, now the rear-admiral in command of the blockade of Cádiz, and Linois in his turn learned from Cochrane of Saumarez's presence off his destination. Linois decided to turn back, reaching Algeçiras on the afternoon of 4th July in full view of the British at Gibraltar on the other side of the bay. Saumarez himself actually received the news of Linois's passage of the Strait early the next morning, brought to him by Lieutenant Janvrin in a small sailing boat. Quitting his station with six line-of-battle ships Saumarez headed for the Strait, his plans based on information that Linois was anchored off Algeçiras with three sail-of-the-line and a frigate. Saumarez's squadron bore straight into the bay at seven in the morning of 6 July, led by Samuel Hood in *Venerable,* and engaged the French as they were warping inshore under the batteries of the Spanish town. The battle was furious, and an hour before noon the British 74-gun *Hannibal* ran aground. Despite the efforts of her company and of boats from the other ships she could not be refloated, and after a desperate defence Captain Solomon Ferris was compelled to surrender. By this time the French ships had cut their cables to order to lengthen the range, and the better to shelter beneath the Spanish batteries, and they too were aground.

The winds and unpredictable current combined with the damage to his ships forced Saumarez to break off the action. Most of the British squadron were badly battered, so he retired to Gibraltar to refit.

By 12 July Linois had refloated his ships and been reinforced by Moreno from Cádiz. The Spanish admiral had swept Saumarez's frigates from their station off Cádiz and these, with a Portuguese frigate commanded by a British officer in the Portuguese service, successfully joined Saumarez at Gibraltar. One of the British ships, the *Pompée,* was too badly damaged to refit quickly, so Saumarez decided to abandon her temporarily. Her crew were transferred into the other ships, where strenuous efforts were being made to ready the squadron for further action. The combined Franco-Spanish force now consisted of two 112-gun ships, one of 94 guns, three of 80, three of 74, three heavy frigates and one corvette. Against these, Saumarez had his flagship, the 80-gun *Caesar,* four 74, two frigates, and two smaller vessels.

At noon on 12 July Linois and Moreno sailed from Algeçiras, heading west. Three hours later Saumarez was after them like a terrier. By nightfall his enemy was out of sight, however, and in desperation Saumarez ordered Captain Richard Keats to press on ahead and try to make contact. Under every stitch of canvas Keats could hoist, the fast *Superb* disappeared into the night, followed in a straggling line by the rest of the British squadron, each ship making her best speed in pursuit of Moreno and Linois. During the night a running fight took place in a rising gale which then died away as the protagonists cleared the Strait. Keats ran through the enemy ships, causing confusion as he fired into them in passing, and behind him came the other British ships, each doing the same, in an attempt to cut the enemy off from their refuge in Cádiz. The operation was not wholly successful, for by morning Hood's *Venerable* had been badly mauled, but the enemy was savaged appallingly. In the night the 74-gun *Saint Antoine* had been captured, and both the 112-gun ships, the *San Hermenegildo* and *Real Carlos,* had caught fire after tangling and mistaking one another for the enemy. The rest of the Franco-Spanish squadron had been driven back into Cádiz, where Saumarez blockaded them with three of his ships, while the remainder helped the crippled *Venerable* back to Gibraltar.

Although it was not a fleet battle, Saumarez's action, following as it did the apparent disaster which had overtaken his ships in Algeçiras Bay, was a brilliant example of the extent to which British sea-power could achieve results in apparently adverse circumstances. As a culmination to the succession of events set in train when the First Consul of France order Ganteaume to sea, it provided a fitting climax, a triumph of cruiser warfare.

The unmolested prosecution of British policy by means of sea-power had also manifested itself earlier that same year. We have already seen how the ire of the Scandinavian powers was provoked by Britain's insistence on her right to search neutral merchant ships for cargoes of value to the enemy. The climax came in the summer of 1800 when a Danish frigate, the *Freja*, resisted the attempts of a British frigate squadron to interfere with her convoy in the southern North Sea. Ignobly forced to strike her ensign, *Freja* and her merchantmen were brought into the Downs, where her colours were ordered rehoisted until the incident had been laid before the Government. In due course a diplomatic embassy led by Lord Whitworth was sent to Copenhagen, backed by a powerful naval force, and the matter appeared to have been resolved. Russia, however, remained unhappy. Her Tsar was a mentally unstable character and had his own designs upon Malta, however he not unreasonably protested against the right of search, then sequestered all British property and embargoed all British merchant ships in Russia, reviving the coalition of northern states known as the Armed Neutrality which had operated against Britain during the American War. Russia, Sweden and Prussia induced Denmark (of which Norway was then a part) to join, and the direct result of this combination was to inhibit vital supplies of 'naval stores' to the Royal Navy.

To abandon the right of search would have been to empower France by default. Britain responded in a number of ways. The small West Indian colonies belonging to Sweden and Denmark were captured that spring, and a huge fleet under Vice-Admiral Sir Hyde Parker was sent to the Baltic, with Nelson as his second-in-command. On 2 April 1801 Nelson engaged the Danish fleet moored off Copenhagen, and the city's defences as well. In the course of a furious battle Nelson famously ignored the signal to break off the action sent him by his pusillanimous chief. In the ensuing armistice, negotiations persuaded the Danes that resistance was pointless and they gave way. Amid the subsequent collapse of the Armed Neutrality, Great Britains' right of search was asserted.

Elsewhere, other overseas possessions were taken. Portugal had become an enemy, having made peace with France and Spain, and Madeira, Goa and all her Far East posts except Macao near Canton were taken by British forces. The Dutch too lost their colonies: Ternate, for instance, was taken by East India Company troops after a resistance of fifty-two days. But such triumphs were illusory; it was on the European continent that the matter would be settled.

# CHAPTER 10

## 'The peace which passeth all understanding'

After their defeat by Bonaparte at Marengo the Austrians had signed a treaty at Lunéville, and now peace overtures were in the air between Paris and London, the preliminaries of which began to be aired in October 1801. The negotiations were troubled, and few in diplomatic circles thought that any agreement, if and when reached, would last long. But on 27 March 1802 France, Spain and the Batavian Republic (The Netherlands) signed an agreement with Great Britain at Amiens, though it was a month before the peace was proclaimed in London.

The elder Lord Palmerston wittily described it as 'the peace which passeth all understanding', and the French were prompt to take advantage of it. The feint of the previous year became reality, and the First Consul sent his brother-in-law Général Leclerc to put down the revolt of the black republicans in Haiti. Any sense that Britain had achieved a peace with honour must be set against the consideration that although apparently she enjoyed the spoils of war, this was a chimera. It was true that Britain had acquired colonies. It was true, too, that she had ousted the French from Egypt, but this was a defensive measure to secure India and her eastern trade, without which she would lack the means to wage war. It was also true that she had destroyed the Armed Neutrality, but this was yet another defensive measure, to maintain her vital right of search *and* preserve her Baltic sources of naval stores. Moreover, although French attempts to invade Ireland, as well as the south coast of England, had indeed been defeated, these actions too were obviously and necessarily defensive. *Not one* of these 'successes' had been the purpose of the war: in fact, the French still controlled the Schelde, the French royalists were defeated, and French republicanism seemed secure.

The French triumphed in breaking up Britain's Continental alliance, in holding on to the Schelde, in having restored to their 'owners' by negotiation most of the captured colonies, and most notably the Cape of Good Hope. Only Trinidad and Ceylon were retained by Britain, who lost her base at Port Mahon in the Balearic Islands and gave up her forts on the Îles St Marcouf in the process. She also promised to relinquish Malta, returning it to the corrupt rule of the Knights, whose absentee Grand Master was the unstable Tsar Paul of Russia.

The French negotiators were led by the cunning and dissembling Talleyrand; he who made much of France 'relinquishing' Egypt, which in point of fact had already fallen to British arms, unaware of this though Lord Cornwallis's delegation were at the time. Of more than mere symbolic importance too was the fact that the government under Addington agreed that King George III should relinquish all British claims to the throne of France, expressed since 1415 by the inclusion of the lilies of France in the Royal coat-of-arms. The importance of this concession lies in what was exchanged for it: precisely nothing. Bonaparte made the most pertinent comment on the pragmatic value of the end of the war: 'Peace is necessary to restore a [French] navy, peace to fill our arsenals, empty of material, and peace because only then is the one drill-ground for fleets, the sea, open.'

This was not a British victory, and there was another facet to it. Although Great Britain had almost entirely destroyed the overseas trade of France, in so doing she had herself lost 3,466 British merchant ships, along with about three per cent of her own trade. As for France, compared with her shaky status in 1793 she was now immensely strong, her new institutions were secure, and she dominated Europe. Moreover, as Bonaparte pointed out, the sea was open for her fleets to exercise in.

In the Royal Navy, the peace was greeted with mixed feelings. Sixty out of the 102 line-of-battle ships were laid-up 'in ordinary', their masts and yards sent ashore, their guns and stores taken out of them, and all hands but their 'standing warrant officers' and the skeleton crews left to look after them at their moorings in the Medway, in the Hamoaze at Plymouth and at Portsmouth dispensed with. A large number of frigates and sloops remained in commission, but these were gradually laid up over the following months. All but the most enthusiastic and devoted seamen rejoiced. Peace meant the freedom to return to their families, the resumption of their normal lives as shoe makers, tailors, cowhands, blacksmiths, wheelwrights, fishermen, or merchant seamen with regular watches and pay. About 40,000 were discharged but ominously, not all of them could get work immediately. For the officers, peace meant a return to half pay and to social uncertainties, and it meant a lack of opportunity. A few had made sufficient money to look forward to a quiet retirement, while those who had succeeded in being made post could at least relax. For officers and men of both sides held in captivity, whether under parole or imprisonment, peace meant a restoration of liberty.

Curiously, Sir Edward Pellew, in command of the inshore squadron off Rochefort, heard the news from the enemy. One of his frigates ran aground and a French cruiser was sent out to assist in the refloating, as she did so informing the British of the cessation of hostilities. Pellew went home to take his seat in the House of Commons as the member for Barnstaple.

Cochrane too came home. He had been breakfasting aboard *Desaix* with his captor as Saumarez attacked Linois's ships in Algeciras Bay, and Capitaine Jean Christi-Pallière was insisting they would finish their breakfast when a round-shot came in through the cabin window and showered the table with broken glass. The arrival of Moreno's squadron had made an exchange possible, and Cochrane had reached Gibraltar just before the celebrated action in the Straits. On 18 July, aboard the *Pompée*, he was court-martialled for the loss of *Speedy*, and honourably acquitted. When his acquittal became known in London, his enemy St Vincent reluctantly allowed his promotion to post-captain; but there was no ship for him, and he returned to Scotland to bide his time on half pay.

For the rest of the world, peace provided in opportunity for international trade to resume, and the Americans were not slow to take advantage of it. Partly as a consequence of her British origins, the new republic had extensive maritime commercial interests which had already brought her into an ambiguous relationship with France.

In 1801 the Barbary states of North Africa, some of which were semi-independent pashaliks of Constantinople, customarily demanded a form of protection money from governments whose merchant ships entered their ports or coastal waters. The United States were already paying the Dey of Algiers $21,600 a year, and in 1801 Yusuf Karamanli, Pasha of Tripoli, demanded parity. The Americans refused, and on 14 May Karamanli declared war. In June a small frigate squadron consisting of the United States' ships *President,* 44, *Philadelphia,* 36, *Essex,* 32, and the schooner *Enterprise* of 12 guns sailed for the Mediterranean, ignorant of the Pasha's latest move. Commodore Richard Dale (who was first lieutenant of John Paul Jones's *Bonhomme Richard* during the American Revolution) arrived off Tripoli on 24 July to blockade the port and the *Enterprise* captured a small Tripolitanian vessel, from which Dale learned of the Pasha's declaration of war. He returned to Norfolk, Virginia, with the news, but resigned when Congress not only took a dim view of his course of action in leaving his station, but also refused to make him an admiral, a rank not then in the United States Navy.

The arguments continued, but eventually Commodore Richard Morris left Hampton Roads in the *Chesapeake* on 27 April 1802 to take over the Mediterranean squadron. Quite incredibly, it was *more than a year* before Morris reached his ships. He happily socialised with the British at Gibraltar between 31 May and 17 August, then swanned amiably round the south coasts of Spain, France and Italy before putting in to Malta. When at last he set off to join his ships off Tripoli he was blown back to Grand Harbour, whereupon he decided to sail instead to Tunis, to confer with the American minister there. But here, much to his astonishment, he was taken hostage by the Bey for alleged discourtesy and had to be ransomed before he finally arrived off Tripoli in May 1803 to take command of the United States' ships and vessels of war lying off the port. Morris proceeded to compound his previous follies by treating incompetently with Karamanli, who utterly outclassed him in cunning; when word of his negotiations reached home, he was recalled. President Jefferson dismissed him, refusing his request for a court martial on his conduct, and appointed the hot-tempered and anglophobic Edward Preble in his stead.

In the 44-gun *Constitution* Preble reached Tripoli and took command of the little squadron, which now consisted of *Philadelphia*, two 16-gun brigs, *Argus* and *Siren,* and three schooners, *Enterprise, Vixen* and *Nautilus.* On 31 October 1803 the *Philadelphia* ran aground in chase of two Tripolitan ships and her captain, William Bainbridge, was compelled to surrender. The Pasha thereby acquired three hundred hostages, and the Tripolitans captured and refloated the *Philadelphia,* taking her in to Tripoli where her guns were added to the city's defences. It was a humiliating disaster for Preble. In due course he sent for Lieutenant Stephen Decatur, the proud, handsome and ambitious commander of the *Argus.* On the moonless night of 16 February 1804 Decatur led a raiding party of seventy-five men into Tripoli harbour; they succeeded in setting fire to the *Philadelphia,* which blew up under the ramparts of Karamanli's citadel.

Preble next borrowed six gunboats from the odious King Ferdinand of the Two Sicilies, and on 3 August attacked the Pasha's shipping in Tripoli, supporting the gun-boats and small American vessels with broadsides from *Constitution* lying just offshore. Preble bombarded the city again on 7 and 25 August, and on 3 and 4 September, when he sent in a prize stuffed with explosives and manned by volunteers. It blew up with spectacular effect but did little damage and may indeed have been ignited prematurely by red-hot shot from the gunfire of the Pasha's batteries. Alas, there were no survivors to tell the tale. Karamanli would not relinquish the *Philadelphia*'s crew, and Bainbridge was made to view the grisly remains of a dozen of his fellow countrymen. This failure was Preble's last action, for Commodore Barron now arrived in the *President* in company with *Congress, Constellation* and *Essex* to supersede him. Refusing to serve under Barron, Preble returned to the United States and an honoured retirement.

Barron maintained a blockade for three months, and, after patient negotiation, an accommodation was eventually reached. Bainbridge and his crew were ransomed for $60,000, and the American Mediterranean squadron sailed for the Chesapeake. Decatur arrived home to find that he had been voted a Sword of Honour by Congress and promoted captain over the heads of seven senior officers: he was just twenty-five.

In this overseas campaign, a mixture of comedy, heroism and tragedy, the United States Navy was blooded. Its cocky young sea warriors, proud as peacocks, touchy as to their own and their republic's honour, had acquired a thirst for glory. It is said that Nelson, watching as the *Constitution* left Gibraltar, commented that in her lay 'a nucleus of trouble for the navy of Britain'.

Meanwhile, even in peacetime the Royal Navy was storing up troubles of its own devising; for it was not only Napoleon Bonaparte who had a navy to restore: so did Earl St Vincent. Unfortunately, this bluff, unimaginative sea-officer, unlike the sophisticated British politicians, could not see the fragility of the peace. Rightly believing the infrastructure that supported the Royal Navy to be riddled with corruption, jobbery and peculation, he seized the opportunity to reform it.

He began with the dockyards, 'those foul sinks of iniquity', with which he had had difficulties when preparing the immense armament sent to the Baltic in 1801. At this critical time the dockyard artificers had struck for double pay, and St Vincent had threatened them with dismissal – a risk, given the urgency of their work. The incident only sharpened his appetite for reform, once peace gave him the chance, and he did the same with the bakers of the victualling office, remarking that 'compromises . . . [did] infinite mischief'. Harsh, unbending and punctilious he may have been, but he had a point. The practice of bribing the receiving clerks to accept rancid provisions was well established and gendered an entirely justifiable and seemingly eternal sense of grievance among the seamen of the fleet.

There were even worse corrupt practices which struck at the very fabric of the fleet. Perhaps the most iniquitous, described by a contemporary authority as a 'foul and hellish fraud', was that of simulating the copper bolts fundamental to the very structure of the hulls of men-of-war: many such bolts were several feet long, passing through the keels, stem and stern-timbers. Wooden trenails were often substituted at these crucial locations, their ends finished off with copper heads a few inches long (the copper thus saved was of course sold). It was suspected that the foundering of several ships – including the *Blenheim*, which took Thomas Troubridge to his untimely death – was due to the use of these 'devil-bolts'. One ship at least survived to tell the scandalous tale and prove how she had been compromised by them.

St Vincent forced a bill through Parliament appointing a Commission to enquire into 'irregularities, frauds and abuse in the navy departments and in the . . . prize agency'. Its work went on even after war had been renewed and old St Vincent had gone back to sea, and it finally reported to Parliament in 1809. Among its findings was evidence to impeach the Pittite Henry Dundas, Viscount Melville, First Lord of the Admiralty between May 1804 to May 1805.

St Vincent's reforms were castigated during the peace by Pitt and his party, then in opposition while Addington's lack-lustre ministry ploughed its unpopular furrow. It fell in the spring of 1804, but it survived Pitt's motion of censure in 1802. This was opposed for the Government by the Member for Barnstaple: Sir Edward Pellew was no public speaker, but his opinion as a sea-officer was respected, and Pitt's motion was defeated by 201 votes to 130.

The tragedy of St Vincent's reforms was that they were long overdue, and did not go far enough; the resumption of war overtook them, and in the event not a lot changed until the final peace in 1815. What effect they did have at the time was disastrous, and exacerbated the problems caused by a shortage of ship-building timber. This worsened in any case during the years after Trafalgar, intensified by the closure of the Baltic states to British trade as a result of Napoleon's 'Continental System' embargo. But all this lay in the future.

During the hiatus in hostilities during 1802 and early 1803 Napoleon continued to meddle in Europe, intervening in Switzerland and northern Italy, failing to withdraw troops from The Netherlands, and building up the naval arsenal of Antwerp. The Addington ministry, which had been elected to make peace, then refused to relinquish Malta. As a consequence Lord

Whitworth, the British minister in Paris, was subjected to a humiliating tirade from Bonaparte at a reception at the Tuileries. In response to his accusations of perfidy, Addington reluctantly declared war on 16 May 1803.

In a plebiscite held in France in 1804 the people elected their First Consul Emperor. In Notre Dame on 2 December 1804 Napoleon took the imperial crown from the Pope's hands and placed it upon his own head. He had found it, he afterwards claimed, in the gutter. This elevation of the extraordinary and perverse genius of Napoleon Bonaparte brought about the great crisis of what afterwards became known as the Napoleonic War.

For the next nine years the outcome remained uncertain. In 1803 Britain was still on the defensive, and for her defence she relied upon her navy. Then as always, her only hope of totally defeating a Continental land-power lay in the cultivation of allies with military strength, and to this end successive ministries laboured to construct and maintain a European Coalition. This cost money, and the availability of that money depended upon the conservation of Britain's trade. Until 1812, therefore, Britain waged her naval war and slowly secured her economic base, gradually destroying the economic resources of her implacable principal enemy.

For Napoleon, approaching the height of his power and now aspiring to far more than a middle eastern kingdom, Great Britain was the only obstacle. The long-moribund Directory had begun the construction of a huge invasion flotilla, and Napoleon immediately resurrected it. At the end of 1803 these invasion craft numbered some 1,273 vessels, and in the next two years frequent embarkation drills were held as Napoleon began to mass 'the Army of England' in a great arc along the littoral from Antwerp to Le Havre. It soon became evident, however, that most of these craft would have difficulty carrying troops across the Channel, and that the operation would take longer than was originally thought. There is no doubt that, if the French had been able to concert their naval operations so as to gain control of 'Le Manche' for two weeks of good weather, they *might* have attempted an invasion; but disillusionment began to set in for Napoleon on 20 July 1804, when a grand rehearsal was held. A gale was blowing, and Amiral Bruix tried to postpone the exercise. Napoleon insisted it should go ahead, and a furious Bruix had to be restrained from drawing his sword upon his imperial master. The result was a disaster, augmented by the guns of four small British cruisers, *Harpy*, *Autumn*, *Bloodhound* and *Archer*.

Several other similar incidents notwithstanding, Napoleon never entirely gave up the notion of or the preparations for invasion. But he was soon making other plans – indeed, the invasion plans had been laid aside in 1805 *before* Nelson destroyed the Franco-Spanish fleet at Trafalgar. The Army of England was transformed into the Grand Army and Napoleon marched it deep into Moravia to annihilate the Austro-Russian armies at Austerlitz on the first anniversary of his coronation, 2 December 1805. Thus, at the end of 1805 the land-power of Imperial France was arrayed against the sea-power of Great Britain.

In the ensuing decade a new and subtly changing situation confronted the sea warriors of the Royal Navy, as the war became one of attrition.

Despite the timber shortage, St Vincent's intrusive investigations and the lack of commissioned men-of-war, at the resumption of war, in May 1803 the dockyards were busy and a hot-press was soon out rounding up seamen. Challenged in the House of Lords as to the safety of the realm, the elderly St Vincent rose stiffly to his feet and raked the chamber with his formidable glare. 'I do not say the enemy will not come, my Lords,' he pointed out; 'I only say they will not come by sea.' He sat down again to cheers, confident in the dispositions he had made and the rigour with which his orders would be carried out.

Lord Keith commanded the North Sea from The Nore in the Thames estuary, with three detached squadrons in The Downs, at Great Yarmouth and in the Thames estuary itself, the last under Sir Sidney Smith. All were charged with the defence of the English coast, the defence of trade, and the annoyance of the enemy.

The Mediterranean Fleet was now under Lord Nelson, whose chief task was to bottle up the French in Toulon; after 1804 he had the additional responsibility of watching the Spanish naval ports of Cádiz and Cartagena. The Channel Fleet was under that great exponent of the close blockade, Admiral The Honourable William Cornwallis, brother to Lord Cornwallis who surrendered to George Washington at Yorktown in 1781, and who had been the chief negotiator at Amiens. Sir William's detached junior squadrons under Collingwood and Pellew blockaded Rochefort and Ferrol. There were also, of course, reflecting Britain's wide commercial interests, the overseas commands at Halifax in North America; in the West Indies, where Rear-Admiral Sir John Duckworth flew his flag at Jamaica; and in the Leeward Islands, where Sir Samuel Hood now flew his broad pendant as a commodore. Vice-Admiral Peter Rainier remained Commander-in-Chief in the East Indies.

Already France had sent reinforcements out to Île de France. In March 1803 General Decaen had sailed as governor with Contre-Amiral Linois in the 74-gun *Marengo*, accompanied by the frigates *Atalante*, *Sémillante* and *Belle-Poule* and the transports *Marie-Françoise* and *Côte d'Or*. As the war became increasingly one of economic attrition, so Britain's Indian and China trades remained vital to her economy, and thus the Indian Ocean became a critically important theatre – a fact generally ignored by naval historians grown euphoric in the post-Trafalgar glow.

The expedition to Haiti and the restoration of France's West Indian colonies by the Peace of Amiens resulted in a considerable French naval presence in the Caribbean Sea. After the resumption of the British blockade the French made great efforts to maintain communications, send reinforcements, and generally sustain all these overseas posts. Small groups of powerful frigates, usually with a corvette, conveyed stores and mail before carrying out predatory cruises against British merchant shipping. To these were added the exertions of their corsairs bound upon the *guerre de course* at which French seamen excelled. In the Bay of Bengal, Surcouf's *Revenant* was to acquire a reputation for almost supernatural properties, from her ability to strike, disappear, then strike again in a different quarter.

The situation as it thus evolved left the main fleets of ships-of-the-line on blockade duty, with some 74-gun ships acting as detached cruisers alongside a vast number of frigates and sloops. Many of the latter were engaged on convoy work, which in time became highly organised though it remained ploddingly dull, but others were to fight some spectacular actions in the years ahead. As the older sea warriors rose from senior captains to admirals a new generation emerged, and if St Vincent regarded many of them with a jaundiced eye, largely they proved their worth.

However, until the Franco-Spanish fleet encountered its nemesis at Trafalgar on 21 October 1805, it and the spectre of invasion continued to dominate the war at sea insofar as the Admiralty and the main battle-fleets were concerned.

Napoleon had made an elaborate plan to gain control of the Channel and pass his so-called Army of England across the Strait of Dover, and it was sent to the Minister of Marine, Vice-Amiral Denis Dècres, for implementation. As Lord Keith's small cruisers battered, bombarded and raided the Channel coast of France, preparations for this grand design were put in hand. The Franco-Spanish fleet in Brest was now commanded by Ganteaume, who was to embark 35,000 troops, sail, and land this corps in either Ireland or Scotland. The fleet was then to double Scotland and sail south into the North Sea to release the Franco-Dutch squadron blockaded in the Schelde, thus controlling the Thames Estuary and closing the Strait of Dover from the north-east. The French Toulon fleet was also to sail, join with Spanish squadrons from Cartagena and Cádiz, then cross the Atlantic in such force as to raise the British blockade in the Caribbean. Here they were to pick up isolated French men-of-war from the West Indian islands before returning across the Atlantic headed for the Western Approaches to the Channel; once in Le Manche they would seal off the Strait of Dover from the south-west.

The plan was not quite impossible of execution, and embodied a worrying precedent for the British: in 1779, during the American War of Independence, a Franco-Spanish fleet *had* achieved domination in the Channel when it was left defenceless by the Channel Fleet under the incompetent Admiral Hardy. Panic and alarm had seized English coastal ports and towns, and only scurvy and dissension had ruined the enemy's enterprise. The memory of this alarm lingered in the imaginations of many people in England.

But although Napoleon could impose a ruthlessly enforced timetable for the Grand Army's marches from Boulogne to Austerlitz, he could not so order the movements of wind-driven ships. The ocean was not the 'drill-ground' he assumed it to be, and his plan took little account of the difficulties of evading the blockading British.

Like the previous war with France, the Napoleonic War began off Ushant, where on 18 May 1803 a French *chasse-marée*, the 14-gun lugger *Affronteur,* went in chase of a British 'West Indiaman'. It was an error Lieutenant de Vaisseau Morce Duthoya was to pay for with his life: his prey was in fact the frigate *Doris*, reconnoitring ahead of Cornwallis, who had left Torbay the previous day. Realising his mistake, Duthoya put about as Captain Richard Pearson sent a shot wide of the lugger to bring her to. Duthoya decided to run, and *Doris*'s bow chasers then opened a regular fire until the two were running alongside each other. Duthoya put up a stiff resistance, but he and eleven of his crew were killed and a further fourteen wounded, upon which the *Affronteur*'s ensign was hauled down.

In the succeeding weeks several more French ships fell into the hands of the waiting British. The inward-bound were ignorant of the renewal of war, the outward-bound desperate to inform distant colonies of it.

But success came at a price, for risk-taking often led to disaster. The 38-gun frigate *Minerve*, one of Saumarez's Channel Island squadron, lay off Cherbourg on the night of 2 July, blockading the port in the strong Channel tides and a dense fog that together were to prove dangerous. Cherbourg was then undergoing major construction works, with two huge, outreaching breakwaters at an early stage: *Minerve* ran aground on one of the submerged stone piles accumulating on the seabed. At this fatal moment the fog lifted, revealing the embrasures of Fort Liberté a mile away and the batteries on the Île Pélée at a little more than half that distance. The French guns opened fire while two enemy gun-brigs, *Chiffon* and *Terrible*, began pulling out towards *Minerve*.

In the course of his brief year as a commander the *Minerve*'s captain, Jahleel Brenton, had preceded Cochrane in *Speedy*. He was now in a situation that would have challenged even that resourceful sea warrior. Brenton lowered his boats and sent them inshore to cut out a lugger with which to carry out his best bower anchor, and to cover this sortie despatched his launch with its carronade to drive off the French gunboats. Lieutenant The Honourable William Walpole captured the lugger and brought her alongside as the *Chiffon* and *Terrible* took up positions on *Minerve*'s bow. This was a dangerous situation for Brenton, for while his own guns could not bear, the enemies' could rake *Minerve*. As the now moonlit *Minerve* lay under fire from three sources, her crew laboured to empty the captured lugger of her cargo of stones while her carpenters tried to stop the leaks that appeared in her hull. Aboard the frigate the upper deck guns ineffectually returned the gunfire from the shore battery; the main armament on the frigate's gun-deck had been unlashed and pushed aft to lighten the bow. The boats now carried out a smaller kedge anchor, by which means the lugger was to haul herself off and drop the main bower and at about midnight the men on the lugger began hauling in on the rope run out to the kedge.

As they drew the lugger off *Minerve*'s side, the ship's heavy cable dragged behind them. At this critical moment the rope to the kedge was shot away, and the lugger drifted backwards until the ship's boats took her in tow, and got her out to the correct position for the bower to be let go. Brenton was in a lather to get his ship off: the tide was rising, but so was the sun. Then, as he was on the verge of success, the wind dropped. Brenton gave up all hope. Ordering the wounded lowered into the lugger, and combustibles made ready to burn *Minerve*, he went below to destroy his papers. Perversely, the moment this had been done, the wind freshened; Brenton ordered the wounded back into the cockpit and the capstan manned – although all the ship's masts were badly damaged. Round shot ploughed through the circling hands as they began to draw *Minerve* off the obstruction and into deep water. Brenton heaved a sigh of relief – whereupon the wind dropped again and the rising flood tide set the frigate into the harbour, where she stuck upon a second heap of stones.

It was now six in the morning, the tide was turning, and began to fall. *Minerve*'s crew were exhausted, with eleven dead and sixteen wounded. Brenton's situation was now hopeless. He struck his ensign, handing his sword to the commanding officer of the *Chiffon*. Napoleon was informed of these events while at the theatre in Brussels, and announced to the audience that the war had begun in happily auspicious circumstances with the capture of a superb enemy frigate. It was an irony perhaps past Napoleon's comprehension that he had merely regained what had formerly belonged to France.

Another British frigate was lost off the Cotentin peninsula on the filthy, gale-swept night of 10 December, when the brand-new 36-gun *Shannon* grounded on the island of Tatihow. She was later burnt by the crew of the 16-gun sloop *Merlin*, but her crew were taken prisoner.

An almost identical wreck occurred on the last day of the year, when the gun-brig *Grappler*, another of Saumarez's cruisers, was cast ashore in bad weather on the Îles Chausey.

But these incidents, painful though they were for their captains and crews, were the exception. In material terms they were far offset by the successes of British cruisers in that first year of the war. In July, in defiance of the strong tides that run the length of the Breton coast, off the Passage du Raz *Doris*'s boats cut out a small schooner named *Providence* which yielded a valuable cargo of armaments. That same month, off L'Orient, Captain William Bedford in the 74-gun *Thunderer* took possession of the Bordeaux privateer *Vénus* of 16 guns. Also off L'Orient, the following day, the fast former French frigate *Égyptienne*, 40, took the *Épervier*, bound inwards from Guadeloupe with despatches. She had left France under the command of Jérôme Bonaparte, who had gone to the United States to marry an American beauty. Though he later repudiated her in favour of a Württemburg princess and the Kingdom of Westphalia, his great-grandson became secretary of the United States Navy in 1905. A second Bordeaux corsair, the *Atalante*, was taken that day after a chase by the *Plantagenet*, 74, and the 10-gun ship-sloop *Rosario*.

In November the 38-gun frigate *Boadicea* captured the *chasse-marée* *Vautour* off Finisterre; the lugger bore despatches from San Domingo. Also off Finisterre four days later, on the 28th, the French frigate *Bayonnaise*, being used as a transport from Havana to Ferrol, was chased by the *Ardent*, 64, one of Pellew's cruisers. Rather than submit to capture, Capitaine Leblond-Plassan ran his ship hard aground, set her on fire, and left her to blow up.

Although British cruisers had caught a number of French privateers before they could get away from their home coasts, soon both privateers and French national ships began to attack British commercial shipping. Two instances which occurred on the same August day in 1803 but had very different outcomes will suffice to show the delicate balance of power that still tended to characterise the war at sea. The 44-gun French frigate *Poursuivante*, commanded by Capitaine Jean Baptiste Willaumez, was homeward bound from the West Indies when, on August 14, 200 miles east of the American coast, she encountered the *Juno*, a Liverpool-registered merchant ship of 18 guns. Although he was under-manned and out-gunned, her master, Lutwidge Affleck, was reluctant to submit. Commanding 'a set of the bravest fellows that ever swam salt-water', he fought an action for two hours against vastly superior odds. Anxious to secure a valuable laden merchant ship, Willaumez's gunners aimed high and wrecked the *Juno*'s rigging. With *Juno* unmanageable, two men killed and his mate badly wounded, Affleck struck his ensign. He was received courteously by Willaumez who refused to accept his sword but took his prize into Charleston, South Carolina, intending to refit her. The American authorities refused him clearance, however, and to his chagrin, Willaumez was obliged to burn the *Juno*.

Far to the east of America, though well to the west of Ushant, the homeward-bound and heavily-laden East Indiaman *Lord Nelson* was making up for the English Channel. Her master was Commander Robert Spottiswoode and she had a crew of 102 men, some passengers and an armament of 26 guns, twenty long 18-pounders and six long 12s. Lying in wait for just such a prize was the ship-rigged privateer *Bellone* of St Malo, Capitaine Jacques Perraud. In 1801 Perraud and *Bellone* had enjoyed a successful cruise in the Indian Ocean, taking three lucrative prizes; sent out again by the Malouin *armateur* Conte, they now sought riches in the Atlantic. With an eager crew of 260 men, Perraud chased the *Lord Nelson* and brought her to action. Spottiswoode fought for an hour and a half as Perraud tried to close and board, but though he evaded this tactic once he could not avoid the second attempt, and the French swarmed aboard after bringing down the *Lord Nelson*'s mizen mast. In the hand-to-hand fighting Spottiswoode and four men were killed, a total of about thirty were wounded, and the Indiaman was captured. A forty-strong prize crew was put aboard and, escorted by *Bellone*, the *Lord Nelson* headed for Coruña, since the British blockade made a return to France too risky for Perraud, but Spain was then a neutral state. On 20 August a British frigate hove in sight but was drawn off by the *Bellone*. The superior sailing qualities of the corsair ensured her escape, but three days later the *Lord Nelson* encountered a small British privateer, the cutter *Thomas and John* of fourteen 6-pounders from Plymouth. The cutter engaged her, but was fought off after an hour's engagement.

The next day an unidentified naval cutter dogged the *Lord Nelson* during daylight, but did not close with her. Then, at about noon on the 25th a British vessel approached from upwind. She proved to be the 18-gun brig-sloop *Seagull* (Commander Henry Burke), and gave chase. When she came up with the captured Indiaman at five in the afternoon the *Lord Nelson* hoisted French colours and fired a defiant gun. Burke continued to slowly overhaul her, and at seven opened fire. There followed a running fight which lasted throughout the night until six the next morning. The privateersmen knew their work; they hulled the British sloop, cut up her rigging and shot her foreyard in the slings. At half-past eight Burke disengaged to refit his rigging; within minutes, more sails were in sight ahead of the fleeing *Lord Nelson*.

It was Commodore Sir Edward Pellew, his broad pendant flying in the largest two-decker in the navy, a prize of the Nile, the 80-gun *Tonnant*. With him were three other sail-of-the-line, the most advanced of which, the *Colossus*, came up with the *Lord Nelson* just as Burke reapproached her. Perraud's prize-master had little alternative but to strike to Burke, for with *Spartiate* and *Mars* in the offing the game was up. Perraud himself reached Puerto Passages in north-west Spain, recruited crew and sailed for the Indian Ocean, where he was eventually captured off Ceylon.

During the months of peace the French had succeeded in taking prisoner the negro leader of the republic of Haiti, Toussaint L'Overture. He was most dishonourably treated, carried to France and incarcerated in the

Juran fortress of Joux, an *oubliette* where he soon died of privation. Toussaint's deputy, a fearsome and fearless black soldier named Jean Jacques Dessalines, renewed the war against the French and drove them into the coastal town of Cape François, off which British warships lay maintaining a blockade. To these the desperate French proposed terms, but Commodore Loring refused them, compelling Général Rochambeau to treat with Dessalines who agreed that the French should evacuate Cape François using their own vessels lying in the port. Unfortunately for the fugitives. Loring's close blockade prevented the French from leaving by the agreed day, 30 November, and Dessalines's troops prepared to open fire on the French ships with red-hot shot. This was precisely the impasse that Loring desired. He now sent in a flag of truce, and arranged that the French ships should sail, discharge a broadside to defend their honour, and then strike to the besieging British when a shot was fired across the bows of the French men-of-war. Under this convention some merchant vessels emerged, escorted by the 40-gun frigate *Surveillante*. A second French frigate, the *Clorinde*, carrying 900 people including numbers of women and children, ran aground under the guns of Fort St Joseph. The stiff onshore wind which was now blowing sent in a swell upon which the ship lifted, dropping on the reef with sickening and frightening shudders until her rudder was torn off. Her situation looked hopeless, and panic rapidly spread through the wretched civilians on board.

Rescue was at first considered too risky, but Acting Lieutenant Nisbet Willoughby, in charge of one of the boats taking possession of the prizes as they came out, decided not to abandon the *Clorinde*. Avoiding the terrified people swarming down into his boat, Willoughby scrambled up the side of the *Clorinde* and managed to persuade the French officers that they should dispense with the formality of a shot across the bow, and strike their colours immediately. Once he had hoisted the British ensign, Willoughby hailed the commandant in Fort St Joseph and sought an interview with Dessalines. This was granted, and Willoughby pulled ashore to point out to Dessalines that although the *Clorinde* remained within the port limits, she was now British. Dessalines agreed and Willoughby, with some assistance from the shore, returned on board to signal to Loring that he required the assistance of the squadron's seamen. In due course the frigate was lightened of her passengers and some of her freight, and hauled off to deep water. She was eventually commissioned into the British fleet.

Willoughby was one of the most extraordinary characters in the Royal Navy. Born into the minor aristocracy in 1777, his ancestors had fought at Crécy, Poitiers and Agincourt. All his brothers served in the army, but Willoughby joined the navy as a volunteer in 1790 and served in a succession of cruisers, distinguishing himself in the cutting-out of five French vessels in April 1793 and being appointed prize-master of one. His ship, the *Orpheus*, went on to the Indian Ocean, where Willoughby took part in the capture of a French ship off the Île de France and in the taking of Malacca, Amboyna and Banda from the Dutch, serving in several ships under Rainier until promoted into a vacant lieutenancy aboard the *Victorious*, 74, in January 1798.

From here he was granted acting command of a Dutch prize, the sloop *Amboyna*, though he fell sick and was invalided to the Cape of Good Hope. He was not incapacitated for long, however, and soon afterwards joined the *Sceptre* (Captain Valentine Edwards); he took her boats through the surf of the island of Rodriguez in the Indian Ocean to capture the French corsair *L'Éclair*. Later Willoughby further enhanced his reputation for daring by jumping overboard in an unsuccessful attempt to rescue a seaman who had fallen into the sea. When heavy weather drove the *Sceptre* ashore to her destruction in Table Bay, Willoughby returned home, and in April 1800 he joined the *Russell*. In this 74-gun ship he fought at Copenhagen, boarding the Danish blockship *Provesteen*, in which he fought ferociously; he was a vicious hand-to-hand warrior, whose contempt for danger was beginning to earn him the nickname of 'The Immortal'.

He was also, however, a man much given to a natural cantankerousness, and this led to his dismissal from the Navy in 1801. But on the renewal of war he volunteered again, and joined Sir John Duckworth's flagship *Leviathan* in the West Indies. Here, in a small boat manned by two midshipmen and seven seamen, he chased and took the French armed vessel *L'Athénaïse*, surprising the lieutenant in command with the news that the peace of Amiens was at an end. As a result he was reinstated in October 1803 in an acting capacity, and joined Loring's squadron, an offshoot of Duckworth's overall command.

Willoughby was to be wounded more times than any other Royal Naval officer surviving the Napoleonic War. A brutal and ruthless man, his reckless courage was none the less widely admired, as much by the lower deck as by his seniors, though he continually rubbed his colleagues up the wrong way. During his service in the West Indies under his patron Sir John Duckworth he distinguished himself by being in the fiercest fire at Curaçao during 1804, saving his ship during a terrible hurricane off the Florida Keys, and manning a merchant prize as an auxiliary man-of-war. We shall encounter him again.

The British blockade of San Domingo produced one highly discreditable occurence which, among so many successes, emphasises how few such incidents arose from an innately corrupt system of 'interest' and preferment. On 3 November the 36-gun British frigate *Blanche* attempted to cut out a French cutter lying in Mancenille Bay from under the guns of a French-held battery at Monte Christi on the north coast of San Domingo. The cutter, *Albion,* was carrying bullocks for the besieged garrison of Cape François: its destruction was deemed necessary. In an onshore wind Captain Zachary Mudge sent an inadequate force, which was driven off in broad daylight.

Mudge stood away along the coast, and the following day, after 'an obstinate conflict', a boat from *Blanche* commanded by a master's mate named Smith took a French schooner coming out of the Caracol Passage. Mudge decided to return, and renew the attack on the *Albion* that night. Lieutenant Nicolls of the Marines (which had been made 'Royal' the previous year) volunteered to lead it. He left the ship just before midnight on the 4th with a dozen men in the *Blanche*'s cutter. Hardly had he left *Blanche* than Mudge, reflecting that this too was an inadequate force and that the French would be on the *qui vive*, sent his first lieutenant, The Honourable Warwick Lake, after Nicolls with reinforcements and orders to supersede him.

Lake, catching up with Nicolls, refused to believe the anchored vessel they were approaching was the *Albion,* and rowed off in search of her.

Angrily, Nicolls went ahead with his attack on the *Albion,* and after a fierce struggle carried her deck, taking a pistol ball in his stomach which traversed his rib-cage before lodging in his arm. So that the shore battery should not open up on them, Nicolls ordered his marines to go on firing their muskets and thus simulate a continuing struggle while the seamen were cutting the cable and hoisting sail. This was a wise precaution, because the enemy battery was a mere musket-shot away. But at this point Lake rowed up, ordered the marines to desist and clambered aboard to take command. The instant the artillerymen in the battery realised the *Albion* was in British hands, they opened fire. Fortunately the *Albion* was out of range before the enemy guns had been laid on her.

A few days later Mudge sent a boat ashore to obtain sand for scouring the decks and filling fire-buckets, in the charge of Midshipman Edward a'Court. Although the party was not formally armed, the sailors themselves had laid half a dozen muskets in the boat in order to prevent either the seamen or their young officers from rashness. Having loaded the sand, a'Court was pulling leisurely back towards the distant *Blanche* at twilight when, upon rounding a headland, he sighted a schooner and decided to attack her. Thinking she might be a privateer, and to conceal his approach, he pulled up in her wake and had almost gained her stern before he was seen. She was a French vessel, on her way to Cape François with two score soldiers on board under the command of a colonel. These men succeeded in mortally wounding one of a'Court's seven seamen, but a'Court's boat pulled alongside, and with the remaining six seamen and one marine he jumped aboard. Astonishingly, he rapidly overcame all resistance, and carried his prize back to *Blanche.* The colonel claimed that sea-sickness had afflicted his demoralised men, who were in any case escaping Dessalines's troops. A silver plate over half the colonel's skull covered a hideous wound whose origin was engraved upon it as a battle-honour: *Arcola,* it read.

In reporting these events, Mudge made no mention of a'Court's exploit, ungenerously arguing, no doubt, that the impulsive boy had acted with a foolhardy disregard of orders (although the example of Willoughby might have been adduced to the youth's credit). In the matter of Smith's cutting-out he gave the master's mate little credit but heaped it upon the youthful Midshipman The Honourable Frederick Berkeley, who 'behaved nobly, and was much to be envied'. As for the cutting-out of the *Albion*, Mudge gave all the honour to his protégé Lake, denying Nicolls even the mention of his three wounds.

Mudge was of course, a purblind snob who had his favourites, whom he advanced for personal reasons. Both Berkeley and Lake were not merely aristocrats, but well-connected. What benefits Mudge derived from this unkind and unjust partiality can only be guessed at, but the consequences for the Royal Navy were most unhappy. Given all the credit, Lake was marked for preferment, and three years later was promoted to commander. Like Willoughby he was brutal man, but he had none of Willoughby's counter-balancing merits.

In 1807 Lake was in command of the brig-sloop *Recruit,* lying in the Cornish port of Falmouth. His officers pressed a seaman out of a privateer, a Cornish blacksmith, named Robert Jeffrey. The *Recruit* then sailed for the West Indies and there, in November, her crew were put on short allowance of water. At this time Jeffrey was alleged to have stolen some rum from the gunners' cabin, and a few days later was observed to draw off two quarts of spruce beer from a cask. These were undeniably punishable offences, but Lake decided to exceed even his draconian powers under Admiralty regulations, and put Jeffrey ashore on the uninhabited island of Sombrero with neither food nor water. The man was barefoot, and had only the clothes upon his back. Landing him, Lieutenant Richard Mould took pity on Jeffery to the extent of begging a pair of shoes from one of the seamen in the boat's crew; he also generously donated his own and his accompanying midshipman's handkerchiefs, for making signals. As a final indignity, Jeffrey's absence from the *Recruit* was explained in the brig's books by the letter 'R': officially, Jeffrey had deserted, or 'run'.

Word leaked out, however, and the scuttlebutt in due course reached the ears of the Commander-in-Chief at the Leeward Islands. When Sir Alexander Cochrane (an uncle of Lord Cochrane) learned of this outrage, he sent Lake back to rescue his wretched victim. On 11 February 1808 *Recruit* anchored off Sombrero and lowered a boat.

The landing-party could find no trace of Jeffery, alive or dead. Lake was made post in September 1808 despite this scandal, but the news spread beyond the Caribbean and brought the Admiralty into disrepute.

The popular and radical press, then clamouring for reform in British institutions, made much of this unlawful deprivation of liberty. The tyrannical behaviour of Captain The Honourable Warwick Lake became a *cause célèbre*, and word of it spread across the Atlantic to the United States to exacerbate the anti-British feeling already running high over the right to search. Lake personified the very worst of British naval arrogance, not to mention that of the British aristocracy and its view of the established order of things. At this point rumours reached London that Robert Jeffrey was living in Marblehead, south of Salem in Massachusetts, having resummed his life as a blacksmith. The British Government sent for him, first to Halifax, Nova Scotia, and then by way of the 10-gun schooner *Thistle* to Portsmouth. Here the world learned his story.

On Sombrero Jeffrey had subsisted for eight days on limpets and rainwater caught in the fissures of his rocky prison. He saw several vessels in the distance but could not attract their attention, and grew daily weaker. But on the ninth day the schooner *Adams* of Marblehead appeared off the island and her master, John Dennis, took Jeffrey aboard, and back to his home port, where he had settled.

Upon the conclusion of Jeffrey's examination at the Admiralty on 22 September 1810 he was given all his back-pay, and the infamous 'R' was removed from his name. With an additional and substantial sum of money subscribed by embarrassed friends of The Honourable Warwick Lake, Jeffrey returned to his Cornish home at Polperro. Nemesis had caught up with Lake himself some months earlier. As soon as news that Jeffrey was alive had reached London, a court martial was assembled aboard *Gladiator* in Portsmouth. On 5 and 6 February 1810 it heard the evidence, largely from Lake's own officers; Lake pleaded that he thought Sombrero was inhabited, though it emerged that he had been informed by both his lieutenants and his sailing master that it was not; indeed, this contemptible and worthless officer had had to ask the master the name of the island on which he was proposing to maroon Jeffrey. The court found the charge against Lake proved, and he was dismissed the King's service.

It was true that many captains and commanders in the Royal Navy were harsh, not to say brutal in their treatment of common seamen. However, even in the savage temper and the rigid social hierarchy of the times, men who abused their authority with breathtaking arrogance, like Pigot and Lake, were not as common as popular legend suggests. The Admiralty, having vigorously prosecuted Pigot's murderers precisely because they were murderers, made amends to Jeffrey, at least to the extent of restoring him his honour with his back-pay. Of course, they would not go so far as to mete out a suitably condign punishment to The Honourable Warwick Lake. The view was held that disgrace and obloquy would work their own corrosion upon the odious man. Perhaps they were right; one certainly hopes so.

# CHAPTER 11

---

# 'England expects'

Upon the renewal of war in May 1803, Vice-Admiral Lord Nelson sailed for the Mediterranean in *Victory*, 100, but then left her off Ushant in case she was wanted by Cornwallis and proceeded onwards in the 32-gun *Amphion*, whose captain was Thomas Masterman Hardy. Cornwallis sent *Victory* after Nelson, and on 28 May the first-rate ran into the French frigate *Embuscade*, formerly the disgraced British *Ambuscade*, taken by the *Bayonnaise* in 1798. The *Victory*, almost uniquely for a first-rate, sailed as well as a fast 74 and soon ran down the French ship. *Embuscade,* only partially armed on her homeward voyage from San Domingo, could not escape and surrendered to the *Victory*, to be recommissioned into the Royal Navy under her original name.

On *Victory*'s arrival off Toulon Nelson rehoisted his flag in her, taking Hardy with him as flag-captain. Among the captains in Nelson's fleet were Sir George Murray, aboard *Victory* as Captain-of-the-Fleet or chief-of-staff to Nelson; Sir Robert Barlow in *Triumph,* and Richard Keats in *Superb*. And here in the Gulf of Lyons, as Nelson kept watch and ward during the tedious months of blockade, 'invasion fever' gripped the southern counties of England.

Throughout 1803 fencibles, yeomanry and militia were mustered and drilled, coastal defences were beefed up, and across the River Thames at the Lower Hope a cordon of frigates was moored. Unable to man all of them when hostilities were renewed, the Admiralty turned ten over to the management of Trinity House, which manned them with the Royal Trinity House Volunteer Artillery at its own expense. The ten were *Retribution* (former *Hermione*), *Daedalus* (back from the Indian Ocean), *L'Unité, Modeste, Resource, Vestal, Iris* and *Heroine*, and the Royal Yachts *Princess Augusta* and *Royal Charlotte*, the latter commanded by Sir Harry Neale. Many of these ships were so worn out that they were broken up when the cordon was dismantled at the end of the scare, but others were recommissioned after having their hulls doubled, evidence of the Admiralty's desperation for cruisers in the years after Trafalgar.

Professional naval officers were sceptical about the likelihood of a French appearance on the English shore, but the smaller cruisers struck ceaselessly at their preparations. One such was the under-manned 18-gun brig-sloop *Vencejo,* which in May 1804 was raiding the south coast of Brittany. Her commander was John Wesley Wright, Sir Sidney Smith's protégé who had escaped with him from the Temple prison in Paris.

Wright had spent three months causing a deal of trouble in the Morbihan area, wrecking the coastal trade. Such was his daring that he had beached and repaired *Vencejo* on an island only four miles from the mainland, despite having a crew of only fifty men and twenty-four boys – this disproportion a clear manifestation of the difficulties of manning the fleet so hurriedly. Dawn on 4th May found him in difficulties: *Venejo* lay becalmed, and Wright was compelled to anchor lest she be set on rocks by the strong tide. He laid out an anchor and was sweeping his sloop clear of danger when he observed the approach of six brigs and a number of luggers and gun-boats, totalling thirty-five craft in all. Under Lieutenant de Vaisseau Laurent Tourneur these opened fire on *Vencejo* at half-past eight in the morning, and Wright prepared to defend his ship. Over the next two hours the *Vencejo* was subjected to a bombardment at close range from some heavy cannon mounted in her assailants, fire equivalent to that of a heavy frigate. *Vencejo*'s hull was battered, her rigging demolished, three guns were dismounted by shot, and two men were killed and a dozen wounded,

Wright among them. When his top-hamper crashed down and prevented his men from working their guns, Wright ordered his colours struck.

Wright was returned to the Temple and there, according to the *Gazette de France*, he took his own life a week after Trafalgar. There is ample circumstantial evidence that he was in fact murdered on Napoleon's orders, though in exile the former Emperor always denied this. Wright's death remains an enigma, but his abilities speak for themselves. He was one of a remarkably able and intrepid group of naval officers who remain, in the curious contemporary term, 'ornaments to their profession'.

Meanwhile Wright's former patron, Sir Sidney Smith, was in the 50-gun *Antelope* with his squadron, attacking Dutch elements of the invasion force in the Ostend area; and all along the Pas de Calais Captain Edward Owen in the 36-gun *Immortalité* led another division of Keith's extended command as the ceaseless harrying of the invasion preparations continued. By the late summer Owen had been joined by a considerable squadron of a score of ships under Rear-Admiral Thomas Louis, and in December an unsuccessful attempt was made by Captain Sir Home Popham to blow up Fort Rouge in Calais using a primitive form of proto-torpedo.

While Cornwallis maintained a rigid blockade of Brest, Nelson's grip on Toulon was more subtle. It was also riskier, considered positively lax by some of his contemporaries in light of the experience of 1798. Nelson kept the Mediterranean Fleet well offshore, sometimes in Sardinian waters, with only a small detachment watching Toulon itself. The Gulf of Lyons was of course subject to the strong northerly mistral, and the consequent heavy weather was wearing on both men and ships – but Nelson's intention was to induce a battle, and he was confident of winning it. But, 1804 passed with no major encounter, though there were some brushes with French ships, one of which was claimed as a French victory. By the new year, however, the Mediterranean Fleet had acquired additional responsibilities: Spain was once more at war with Britain, and Cartagena also again required blockading.

Spain's re-entry into hostilities was brought on by a deliberate British act of provocation. The treaty of San Ildefonso of 1796, had bound

Spain to a continuing obligation to supply troops and ships-of-war to France, or to remit the obligation by payment of a huge subsidy. The British view was that Spain was less dangerous as a declared puppet state enemy than as a supposedly neutral power which was in effect a vassal state of France. The British Government therefore determined upon a *coup de main*: the Royal Navy would prevent the annual topping-up of Spanish coffers.

Cornwallis and Nelson were both ordered to contribute frigates to make up a scratch squadron bound 'upon a secret service'. To put the matter beyond peradventure, Nelson added the 74 *Donegal* to his two frigates, but she did not join the little force assembling off Cádiz in time, and the consequence was a terrible loss of life among the unfortunate Spanish involved.

The frigates selected for the job of provoking war were the *Indefatigable* (Captain Graham Moore) and the *Lively*, 38 (Captain Graham Hamond), both from Cornwallis's fleet; with the *Medusa*, 32 (Captain John Gore) and *Amphion*, 32 (Captain Samuel Sutton), from Nelson's. On 3 October 1804 these four cruisers made their rendezvous off Cádiz, whither Sir Robert Barlow, captain of the *Triumph*, 74, had also been sent to convoy home all British merchantmen in the port.

The purpose of Moore's frigates was to intercept a Spanish squadron, under Contra-Almirante Don Josef Bustamente, known to be bound to Cádiz laden with the annual treasure from all over the Spanish colonies of South America. Moore was to detain the Spaniards 'by force or otherwise' and he did not have long to wait. On the 5th he sighted Bustamente off Cabo de Santa Maria, near Faro, midway between Cape St Vincent and Cádiz. Seeing the British squadron Bustamente, formed line, uncertain of their purpose but suspecting the worst. His own ship, the *Medea* of 40 guns, lay astern of the *Fama* and was followed by the *Mercedes* and *Clara*, all of 34 guns. The *Medusa* came in on the weather beam of *Fama*, *Indefatigable* and *Amphion* fell in astern of her, each abeam of a Spanish frigate, and *Lively* drew up on the lee side of *Clara*.

Moore now hailed *Medea*, demanding that Bustamente shorten sail; receiving no reply, he fired a shot across the bow of the Spanish admiral.

Followed by the other frigates, *Medea*, then shortened sail and Moore lowered a boat with an officer to plead with Bustamente to submit without bloodshed, but the Spanish admiral refused. Although the British ships were superior in force they were equal in number, and Don Josef could not bring himself to compromise his honour as a Spanish hidalgo. Had *Donegal* been present, as Nelson intended, Bustamente could have immediately struck to overwhelming force.

Moore now fired a second shot across *Medea*'s bow and edged closer. *Mercedes* immediately fired into *Amphion* and the *Medea* into *Indefatigable*, whereupon Moore promptly broke out signal number 16, for close action. After a ten-minute cannonade the *Mercedes* suddenly exploded with an awesome roar, sending flames and debris high into the air and killing, among many others, Doña Alvear, her four daughters and five of her sons. The hapless father, Capitán Alvear, and his heir happened to have transferred to the *Medea* that morning to breakfast with the admiral, and watched as fortune and family disappeared when the tremendous detonation of the magazine disintegrated the *Mercedes*. Within thirty minutes *Clara* and *Medea* struck their colours, but *Fama* made sail and began to haul past *Medusa*. Moore signalled *Lively*, his fastest ship, to give chase with *Medusa*, and that afternoon they compelled the remaining Spanish frigate to submit.

Despite the loss of the laden *Mercedes*, the haul was enormous. The three surviving frigates were freighted with vicuna wool, cascarilla, ratinia, seal skins and oil, ingots of tin, copper and gold, besides quantities of silver dollars. The value of the coin alone was well in excess of a million sterling, and some authorities put it much higher. A few men stationed on her forecastle providentially escaped from the *Mercedes*, but otherwise the loss of life was heavy; of the 1,120 people embarked in the Spanish squadron, no fewer than 257 were killed, and 80 were wounded. British losses were two killed and seven wounded, one by splinters from the *Mercedes*. The only mitigating factor in this deplorable tale was the restitution of Capitán Alvear's fortune: £30,000 compensation was paid to him by the British Government.

Captain Graham Moore was brother to General Sir John Moore,

then training the Light Brigade at Shorncliffe and destined to die at Coruña in January 1809. As war had not been formally declared, the value of the prizes acquired in this reprehensible incident were judged a Droit of the Crown, but payments were made to the participating ships sufficient to permit Moore to buy himself a country estate. He had done all that convention required of him, as had Bustamente, and no one could have predicted the fate of the *Mercedes*; but the fact that she exploded, killing women and children among her passengers, attracted opprobrium both at home and abroad. As for the three Spanish frigates, all were bought into the Royal Navy.

The restoration of West Indian colonies to their former owners under the provisions of the Peace of Amiens now presented the Royal Navy with a number of problems. The countless seamen and marines whose lives had been lost acquiring them in the first place were set at nought, and the work was now to be done all over again. Curaçao, for instance, which had eagerly submitted to Captain Watkins of the *Néréide,* now resisted attempts to make it renounce Dutch sovereignty a second time. In January 1804 an attempt to take it by a naval force failed. The ships consisted of two 74s, *Theseus* and *Hercule*, Zachary Mudge's *Blanche*, the *Pique,* and the 10-gun schooner *Gipsy*, Acting Lieutenant Michael Fitton. Among the officers involved was the redoubtable Lieutenant Nisbet Willoughby. The fighting was fierce and bloody, but the Dutch, who held strongly fortified positions, received reinforcements while the British suffered from sickness (a common problem when seamen used to the open ocean air spent several weeks in a tropical environment) and a spectacular desertion *en masse* of some marines the *Hercule* had recruited from among the French forces at San Domingo. Expatriate Poles, these men doubtless discovered soon enough that transfer from French to British service was far worse than leaping from the frying pan into the fire. At least in the French service each man could believe he bore a marshal's baton in his knapsack; in the British army they merely 'conquered in the cold shadow of aristocracy', as General Napier remarked of the British infantry.

Commodore Samuel Hood had better luck at Surinam in April, but his greatest success had been achieved in January, at Martinique. The French could not be immediately dispossessed of the island and its port, Fort-de-France, was difficult to bar to French and neutral American shipping. Hood therefore conceived the idea of acquiring a 'stone-frigate', from which a watch could be kept and a battery operated, by taking possession of a small island off Fort-de-France, the Diamond Rock. The precipitous nature of the rock, the persistent heavy swell and the paucity of landing places would have discouraged lesser men than Hood and the ship's company of the 74-gun *Centaur*. A party was landed, and after extraordinary exertions and some fine seamanship – which included the rigging of an aerial runway between *Centaur* at anchor offshore and the adjacent cliff-top – two 24-pounders, each weighing two tons, were hoisted ashore. The work owed much to the rock-climbing skills of Hood's first lieutenant, James Maurice. Made acting commander, with 120 men, fifteen tons of water and four months' provisions, Maurice manned what was officially commissioned as HM Sloop-of-War *Fort Diamond*.

In late February Hood returned with two long 18-pounders from English Harbour at Antigua. By stupendous labours these too were hauled up to the thousand-foot summit. From here they commanded the approaches to Fort de France, and constituted a considerable annoyance to the French for the following fifteen months. During this time Maurice's men constructed a sophisticated defensive system and signal station, in addition to their gun emplacements. As well as fortifying *Fort Diamond*, Hood had also sent Lieutenant Robert Carthew Reynolds to cut out the brig-corvette *Curieux* from Fort-de-France. This the French were anticipating, and the fight was extremely bloody; Reynolds was incapacitated by five wounds, and prevented from commanding his prize.

Before briefly relating the events culminating in the action of Trafalgar it is necessary to note two of significance in the Indian Ocean, whither Linois had sailed from France in March 1803. The contre-amiral had as his flagship the 74-gun *Marengo* (Capitaine Joseph Vrignault), which was accompanied by the 40-gun frigate *Belle-Poule* (Capitaine Alain

Bruilhac), the 36-gun *Sémillante* (Capitaine Léonard Motard), the 22-gun corvette *Berceau* and the Dutch brig *Avontourier*, which joined him at Batavia. Linois, described as a man 'with a reputation but no ability', cruised at the eastern end of the Malacca Straits off Pulo Aur, awaiting the 'China fleet', the convoy of British merchant ships which left Canton and the Pearl River at the end of January. This was usually escorted by men-of-war, but in 1804 the two warships assigned to the duty were late joining. The 'fleet' had therefore to rely upon its own resources for defence, and these were largely vested in the East Indiamen. These vessels of about 1,000 tons each bore thirty to thirty-six 18-pounder 'cannonades', cheap guns made for the defensive arming of merchantmen, plus some carronades. There were sixteen Indiamen in the 'fleet', led by Commodore Nathaniel Dance in the *Earl Camden* and including Commander Henry Meriton's *Exeter*, the ship which had taken the French frigate *Medée*. With the East Indiamen were twelve large armed 'Country' ships, two other merchantmen and the East India Company's cruiser *Ganges*, a brig of the Bombay Marine. The value of the Indiamen alone was estimated at about £8 millions sterling.

The Company possessed a reasonable signals system, and an officer corps of considerable *esprit*. Dance himself, fifty-six, at this time, had been in the company's service since the age of eleven and had risen to commander by 1787. Oddly enough, he also had aboard his ships part of the crew of the surveying tender *Porpoise*, an offshoot of Commander Matthew Flinders's surveying expedition to Australia in the *Investigator*. The *Porpoise* had been ship-wrecked, and these men had made their way to Canton, in the hope of returning home in an Indiaman. The two lieutenants and a midshipman were aboard *Earl Camden;* the last, John Franklin, who acted as signal midshipman, was later to die in the search for the North-west passage.

On sighting Linois's squadron on the afternoon of 14 February 1804, Dance first detached the *Ganges* with the Indiamen *Alfred, Royal George* and *Hope,* to stand towards the French in the light wind and ascertain their nationality. Once this had been signalled as hostile Dance formed line, with the Indiamen to windward of the individual 'Country' ships. The size of the 'fleet' was larger than Linois had expected, and he imagined he saw three two-decked men-of-war in the line of Indiamen. In these circumstances, Linois signalled to his ships that he would withdraw and attack the next day, on the premise that if the British ships were only merchantmen they would scatter under cover of darkness, each seeking her own safety.

Dance, the better psychologist, held the 'fleet' united through the tropic night, hove-to with some 'battle-lanterns' hoisted, and sent a boat down the line with further instructions. As the sun rose at six o'clock *Ganges, Earl Camden, Royal George* and *Hope* hoisted blue ensigns, masquerading as men-of-war under Rainier's command, while the remaining Indiamen hoisted the red ensign. These ships made sail on the starboard tack but Linois was sufficiently encouraged to approach on the opposite tack, edging slowly towards the Indiamen throughout the forenoon with the intention of passing Dance's stern and falling upon the 'Country' ships to leeward.

An hour after noon Dance hoisted the signal to tack in succession, then bear down in line ahead and engage the enemy ship-to-ship. The *Royal George, Ganges* and *Earl Camden* led the Indiamen as they crowded on sail in the light breeze. Linois, his ships in close order, engaged the van of Dance's Indiamen, but as the rest came up he took flight, and for two hours the British pursued the *Marengo* and her consorts to the eastward, breaking off two hours before dark. On 28 February the 'fleet' finally met the 74s *Albion* and *Sceptre*, their assigned but tardy escort. Dance was knighted on his arrival in the Thames, and received a presentation sword; plate and money were awarded to the other commanders, and the directors of the Company distributed £50,000 among the officers and crews of the East Indiamen. Of Linois, Napoleon wrote to Denis Decrès that all his, Napoleon's, enterprises at sea failed because his admirals saw double 'and have discovered, I know not where, that war can be made without running risks . . . Tell Linois that he has shown want of . . . that kind of courage which I consider the highest quality in a leader.'

Despite his master's poor opinion of him, Linois cruised against British and Indian trade with considerable success after his defeat by Dance, able to restore and recruit his ships at either Île de France or the French factory at Pondicherry on the Indian coast. Irritating though they were to the British and Indian economies, Linois's small triumphs, were, however, a mere by-blow to the great campaign upon which the curtain was rising on the far side of the globe.

The entry of Spain into the war had necessitated the blockade of Ferrol, in addition to that of Cádiz and Cartagena, and Rear-Admiral The Honourable Alexander Cochrane was charged with this duty. Vice-Admiral Sir John Orde blockaded Cádiz and he was jointly responsible with Nelson for watching Cartagena. At the beginning of 1805, Nelson lay sheltering and repairing his weather-battered fleet in Sardinian waters; on 19 January his frigates informed him the Toulon fleet had sailed. The Trafalgar campaign had begun.

Unbeknown to Nelson, heavy weather had almost immediately driven Vice Amiral Pierre Villeneuve back to Toulon; however, the intelligence from his frigates that the French were steering south when last seen persuaded Nelson they had again gone to Egypt; he followed accordingly, but achieved nothing beyond an increase in anxiety.

Meanwhile, also in January, Contre-Amiral Burgues Missiessey had brokeout of Rochefort, Rear-Admiral Sir Thomas Graves having been driven from his station by appalling weather. Informed of Missiessey's escape, Admiral Cochrane left Ferrol in pursuit and Cornwallis replaced Cochrane's ships with some of his own. Missiessey was bound for the West Indies, to ravage British colonies and wait there for Villeneuve, and to this end he had with him troops and a park of artillery. However, Villeneuve's enforced return to Toulon meant that Missiessy, acting on his discretionary orders, returned to the Basque Road on 20 May, having attacked Dominica.

Villeneuve finally sailed from Toulon a second time on 30 March and, again avoiding Nelson, headed west to pass through the Strait of Gibraltar as originally planned. He raised the blockade of Cádiz, springing the Franco-Spanish ships-of-the-line there, and with them crossed the Atlantic, making for the West Indies. Mortified at having missed his quarry yet again, Nelson divided his fleet, leaving Rear-Admiral Bickerton in temporary command of the Mediterranean Fleet while he took his own squadron across the Atlantic after Villeneuve. This was against all precedent: Commanders-in-Chief did not abandon their stations; they informed the Admiralty of the state of affairs and left Their Lordships to make the appropriate dispositions. But Nelson was no conformist and, having guessed wrong once, was determined not to lose his enemy twice. 'I was in a thousand fears for Jamaica,' he wrote, apparently never suspecting the grand design of a French concentration in the Channel but thinking rather of Britain's major sugar-producing colony.

The grand French design had already somewhat miscarried, however. Ganteaume never got beyond the Goulet, hampered by specific orders to avoid a battle. With the British Channel Fleet waiting hungrily in the Iroise, Ganteaume was compromised. It was not so much that Napoleon's admirals invariably saw double, as their imperial master complained; they were often shackled by their orders, though ready enough to take refuge in them if they offered a soft option. Nelson, by contrast, was pleading his case for breaking with tradition: ' . . . surely it will not be fancied that I am on a party of pleasure . . . to the West Indies . . . I think the Ministry cannot be displeased.'

Fortunately, he was right. The reforms initiated by St Vincent had shaken Viscount Melville out of office at the Admiralty and the First Lord was now Charles Middleton, Lord Barham. As far as anyone could exercise and co-ordinate control over dispersed fleets and squadrons in those days when communications and intelligence relied on a telegraph system to the ports, the speed of wind-driven ships and the acuity of sea-officers, Barham could and did. He was a remarkable man, a humane captain who had been the first to introduce the three-watch system into British men-of-war, a man who had served with distinction as Comptroller of the Navy Board, and who as First Lord brought more experience to bear in his new post than perhaps any other officer then in the entire Royal Navy.

As Barham diligently drew together the threads of the Royal Navy's intelligence network and despatched his orders accordingly, Villeneuve's fleet entered Fort-de-France, taking His Britannic Majesty's sloop-of-war *Fort Diamond* in passing. The garrison were desperately short of water, their cistern having been cracked by an earth tremor, and Maurice was obliged to capitulate to *force majeure*. It was Villeneuve's only success, unless one counts the fact that he avoided the pursuing Nelson by a margin of about a hundred miles. In fact, on 4 June 1805 Villeneuve had not only received orders from Napoleon to raise the blockade of Ferrol but also knew of Nelson's arrival in the West Indies, and was anxious to be off. By the time Nelson learned of the Franco-Spanish departure for the Channel, Villeneuve was half-way back across the Atlantic. The little British *Épervier* overtook his fleet on her way to London with the news from Nelson.

Nelson, having divided something of the plan, set off, to race back to the Mediterranean. He arrived at Gibraltar on 19 July, and wrote to Barham that he had not 'obtained the smallest intelligence of the Enemy's Fleet'. In distant London, Barham had had word on 8 July of Villeneuve's likely course, from which he knew that Villeneuve was probably making for Brest, Rochefort or Ferrol, rather than returning to the Mediterranean. He reviewed the situation accordingly. Cornwallis was off Brest with two dozen sail-of-the-line; Stirling had half a dozen off Rochefort; Sir Robert Calder was off Ferrol with ten, and Collingwood off Cádiz with six. 'I think there is a chance of our intercepting the Toulon Fleet,' Barham wrote to Cornwallis, telling him to combine the Ferrol and Rochefort squadrons with his own ships and 'stretch out' into the Atlantic for a week before returning to station.

The British squadrons from Ferrol and Rochefort combined as planned, and on 22 July Sir Robert Calder intercepted Villeneuve. What followed was not the battle Barham and Cornwallis wanted. In misty weather Calder failed to bring the enemy to close action, though he captured two Spanish ships. Nightfall put an end to the action, and Calder was later censured for not having done his utmost. Cornwallis was furious: he had only just resumed his own station, fearing lest Ganteaume should have heard of his several days' absence and a little later learned that Villeneuve, having escaped Calder, had entered Ferrol.

Off Ushant the Channel Fleet was augmented by Calder and Stirling, plus some ships from Nelson. It seemed to be the end of the affair, but Napoleon, learning of Villeneuve's presence in Ferrol on 11 August, was soon angrily ordering Villeneuve to combine with Ganteaume at Brest *and* to force the issue by action if necessary. 'If with thirty ships my admirals fear to attack twenty-four British, we may as well give up all hopes of a navy,' the Emperor railed. He was already considering a postponement of his invasion plans – orders for the march across Europe had been drafted – but he had not quite given up hope. Villeneuve might yet secure the Channel and enable his legions to hop across it. But Villeneuve was a disturbed and indecisive man, and he feared his imperial master. On the day Napoleon learned of his presence in Ferrol, Villeneuve sailed, heading out into the Atlantic.

Off Cádiz, Nelson was by now both unwell and disaffected. He handed over to Collingwood and by 19 August he was back in England. After conferring with Barham at the Admiralty he joined Emma Hamilton at Merton, his house near London. The redoubtable Cornwallis, meanwhile had heard of the departure of the Combined Fleet from Ferrol and divided his own fleet, placing some under Calder and sending them south, hoping perhaps that Calder would redeem himself. A few days later Villeneuve ran into a Danish brig whose master told him he had been searched by an officer from the British man-of-war *Dragon* who had mentioned that a British fleet was in the offing. Inclined to believe this information, Villeneuve put about and, dodging Collingwood, ran safely into Cádiz on 20 August.

Napoleon sent Amiral Rosilly to supersede Villeneuve, and five days later gave orders for the Grand Army to begin its march east wards. Although these decisions were to lead to a series of campaigns that would extend Napoleon's power and Empire across the whole of Europe, they were ultimately to cost him the war.

Villeneuve now received an order from Napoleon to return to Toulon, and learned also that his successor was on his way. He gave orders to his Spanish second-in-command, Gravina, that the Combined Fleet would sail. Nelson too had received orders, to resume command of the Mediterranean Fleet, but off Cádiz, not Toulon. He rejoined *Victory* at Spithead on 14 September and on the 28th reached his station, whereupon Collingwood reverted to second-in-command. Close inshore, just off the mole of Cádiz, lay Nelson's eyes, the frigate *Euryalus*, commanded by The Honourable Henry Blackwood. On 20 October Blackwood signalled to Nelson that the enemy were coming out of port.

At daylight on 21 October 1805, after a night of alarms, the Franco-Spanish fleet were seen in a straggling crescent heading roughly north-west, attempting to get back to Cádiz after sighting the British fleet in the west. Beyond them to leeward lay Cape Trafalgar. The British fleet ran down before the light westerly wind in two columns, one led by Collingwood in *Royal Sovereign*, the other by Nelson in *Victory*. The British enveloped the centre and rear of the enemy, and by evening the Franco-Spanish fleet was shattered. Some of the ships in the van under Contre-Amiral Dumanoir le Pelley escaped, and in the gale that followed the British lost a number of prizes, but it was the victory of empowerment that Nelson, now mortally wounded, had sought – if not quite the victory of annihilation he most desired. It was to prove the penultimate but crucial fleet action of the war.

Nelson died in *Victory*'s cockpit before nightfall and the onset of the gale. The senior Spanish admiral, Gravina, was also mortally wounded. Villeneuve was taken a prisoner to London, where he witnessed his adversary's state funeral. Arrangements were made for his exchange, and in April 1806 he was shipped in a cartel to Morlaix. What happened next is uncertain. After they were exchanged Napoleon lionised Capitaine Lucas and Capitaine Infernet, who had fought their ships like tigers; but he prepared no such reception for his Commander-in-Chief. Villeneuve reached Rennes, and there on 22 April his body was found, with six stab wounds in the heart. It was said that the door to his room was locked from the inside, and that he had inflicted the fatal wounds upon his own person. Like John Wesley Wright, however, he had been murdered.

On the periphery of these great events others of a less momentous but still significant nature had taken place, in particular an encounter some distance off the north coast of Puerto Rico in the West Indies.

On the same day that Nelson arrived back in Gibraltar, 19 July 1805, a French frigate squadron composed of the 40-gun frigate *Topaze* and the corvettes *Département des Landes*, 22, *Torche*, 18 and *Faune*, 16, each of which had been sent from France with despatches for Villeneuve, fell in with a British frigate on *her* way from Jamaica to Barbados with despatches for Lord Nelson. Neither flag officer was any longer in the Antilles, and the French ships, wearing British colours, deceived the British commander into thinking he had run into some homeward-bound West Indiamen. He discovered his mistake too late, when Capitaine François Baudin's ships failed to answer his recognition signals and bore down towards him.

The victim of this ruse was none other than Captain Zachary Mudge, whose frigate *Blanche* was close hauled on the larboard tack, heading south-south-east, but now bore away in an attempt to escape. Most of the copper sheathing on *Blanche*'s bottom was missing and the consequent accumulation of weed slowed her, so she was soon overtaken by *Topaze*. Ranging up on the *Blanche*'s starboard quarter shortly before ten o'clock in the forenoon, Baudin opened fire. Mudge responded as the *Topaze* came within pistol shot, then shortened sail and prepared to fight. He could not escape, for the *Département des Landes* was coming up astern of *Topaze*, with *Torche* and *Faune* approaching from astern. Mudge tried to cross Baudin's bow and rake the *Topaze*, but Baudin suddenly clewed up his foresail and put his helm over, turning *Topaze* to larboard. As the two frigates swung, *Topaze*'s bowsprit fouled *Blanche*'s mizen shrouds, but a moment later Baudin crossed Mudge's stern and poured a heavy raking fire into *Blanche*. Although Mudge continued to resist for another forty minutes, the *Blanche* was by then making water, her sails were almost destroyed, her masts and spars were damaged, and seven of her guns had been dismounted. She was, moreover, virtually surrounded, with only the *Faune* out of range, so Mudge was obliged to strike his colours.

The *Blanche* was apparently so infected with dry rot that the French, finding her with her bilges full, set fire to her. There was some argument as to whether Mudge had done his utmost, but a court martial later acquitted him. Baudin, having failed to deliver his despatches, then headed towards Rochefort. He got nowhere near the port, however, for he ran into dispersed cruisers of the Royal Navy. The *Faune* was the first of his ships to be sighted, by the 20-gun ship-sloop *Camilla* on the evening of 20 August. Captain Robert Barlow, now commanding the 74-gun *Goliath*, joined the chase, and by eight in the morning Lieutenant de Vaisseau Charles Brunet struck his colours, thus releasing twenty-two of *Blanche*'s crew. *Camilla* and the captured *Faune* headed north, and Barlow steered south.

At about noon four sails were sighted from *Goliath*; one proved to be the British 64-gun ship *Raisonable* (Captain Josias Rowley), but the other three were Baudin's *Topaze*, the *Département des Landes* and *Torche*. Barlow and Rowley made sail in chase while Baudin signalled his squadron to disperse. The *Département des Landes* escaped, but Barlow ran down the little *Torche* and took her at about eight o'clock in the evening, releasing a further fifty-two of *Blanche*'s people. Rowley meanwhile had gone in pursuit of *Topaze,* and at daybreak on the 16th found her only three miles ahead of him. The wind was now dropping, but *Raisonable* carried the breeze longer than the leeward ship. Baudin opened fire with his stern-chasers as Rowley approached. Round- and grape-shot damaged *Raisonable* as she closed, then the wind dropped to a calm. After a brief hiatus a breeze sprang up; Baudin caught it first and stood away on the starboard tack. Although Rowley made after his enemy, *Topaze* was on her best point of sailing and made her escape, finally seeking refuge in the river Tagus. The British consul in Lisbon obtained the release of Mudge, his officers and crew from the French frigate, and they returned home to their court martial.

The campaign of Trafalgar had not quite finished on 21 October. It will be recalled that at the end of the battle Contre-Amiral Dumanoir le Pelley had escaped with the van division of the Combined Fleet. Dumanoir's natural destination was Toulon, but he knew that part of Nelson's fleet under Rear-Admiral Louis had, at the time of the battle, been sent in to Gibraltar to take on fresh water and stores (Jane Austen's brother Francis was among its officers). Dumanoir's chances of passing the Strait unmolested were therefore small, and he determined to head for a French Atlantic port.

However, Lord Barham had now flung a cordon of cruisers into the Atlantic. These consisted of sloops, frigates, and ships-of-the-line such as the *Goliath* which caught Baudin's ships. Another was Captain Thomas Baker's *Phoenix,* which was making for a rendezvous west of the Scillies with sealed orders.

At the end of October Captain Baker stopped some neutral vessels and learned of sightings of a squadron of French ships. He assumed these to be Amiral Zacharie Allemand's which, having escaped from Rochefort once the British blockade was raised, had been successfully harrying British trade. Unaware of the purport of his sealed orders, Baker decided that the slightest chance of locating Allemand probably over-rode all other considerations. He therefore opened his orders prematurely and, as their contents confirmed his judgement, went in search of Allemand.

Sailing south, Baker reached the latitude of Cape Finisterre, where on 2 November he saw four sails and gave chase until they turned on him. He thereupon continued south under a press of canvas, headed for the cruising station off Ferrol where he expected to find Sir Richard Strachan, who had been sent there from the Channel Fleet to look for Allemand. Stretching to the south, Baker now saw more sails ahead of him. When the vessels chasing him came in sight of the ships on the southern horizon they turned about, confirming Baker's opinion that his pursuers were probably French. To maintain contact with the enemy to the north, Baker turned *Phoenix* after them, meanwhile signalling to the ships to the south, which he judged were British.

Also in the vicinity, the *Boadicea,* 38 (Captain John Maitland), and *Dryad,* 36 (Captain Adam Drummond) had that same day caught sight of the French squadron. After nightfall they saw the ships to the south but, suspicious as to their identity and failing to make contact satisfactorily, stood away to the north-east.

Meanwhile Baker boldly approached these large vessels in the moonlight and, despite attracting gunfire from one of them, hailed her. She proved to be the 80-gun *Caesar,* Captain Sir Richard Strachan, commodore of a squadron consisting, besides *Caesar,* of the seventy-fours *Hero, Courageux, Namur* and *Bellona,* and the frigates *Santa*

*Margarita*, *Revolutionaire* and Fitzroy's *Aeolus*. Strachan's vessels were somewhat dispersed and Baker, having advised the commodore of the presence to the north-eastwards of a detachment of French, was ordered to round up the squadron and follow on.

Strachan bore away in a wind from the west-north-west, and by about midnight had seen the enemy in the moonlight, heading east-north-east under a crowd of sail. An hour or so later the moon set and thick, squally weather obscured the enemy, so Strachan shortened sail and waited for the rest of his squadron to join him. At this time Strachan lay about forty miles to the north-east of Cape Ortegal, on the north-west corner of Spain.

By daylight Strachan had mustered most of his squadron, and at nine o'clock the enemy were again seen to the northward. Baker's *Phoenix* and Captain Wilson Rathborne's *Santa Margarita* were ordered ahead to maintain contact. The wind was now at gale force from the south-south-west and the two frigates stormed in pursuit, with *Caesar, Hero, Courageux* and *Namur* behind them. *Bellona* was unable to keep up, while *Aeolus* and *Revolutionaire* pressed on to stop the enemy escaping.

The French squadron was not in fact Allemand's, but Dumanoir le Pelley's four survivors from Trafalgar, the 80-gun *Formidable* and the seventy-fours *Duguay Trouin, Mont Blanc* and *Scipion*. The chase ran on into the night. By the following morning, 4 November, the wind had eased to a moderate breeze and first *Santa Margarita* and then *Phoenix* caught up with and engaged the rearmost French vessel, the *Scipion*, galling her while Strachan's main body slowly caught up. About an hour before noon the wind shifted to the south-south-east, allowing Strachan to form line ahead and overtake his quarry. Dumanoir, seeing that an action was inevitable, headed north-east and reduced sail as he too formed line, slightly encouraged that *Namur* and *Revolutionaire* remained well astern.

Strachan hailed Captain The Honourable Alan Gardner aboard *Hero* and Richard Lee on the *Courageux* that he proposed to attack the centre and rear of Dumanoir's line, leaving *Duguay Trouin* in the French van unopposed. Thus *Caesar, Hero* and *Courageux* would respectively engage the flagship *Formidable* (Capitaine Jean Letellier), *Mont Blanc* (Capitaine Guillaume Le Villegris), and *Scipio*, (Capitaine Charles

Bellanger). The British ships, to windward, opened fire at about a quarter past twelve, Strachan hoisting the signal for close action. At this point, Capitaine Claude Touffet of the *Duguay Trouin* tried to tack, intending to cross *Caesar*'s bow and rake her, but the *Duguay Trouin* missed stays and failed to swing round. Strachan luffed to avoid her, crossed her bow and raked her in his turn, followed by *Hero*.

Dumanoir, followed by the other French ships, also tried to tack, but *Formidable*'s rigging had been damaged and she lost way and was overtaken by *Mont Blanc* and *Scipion*. These French ships managed to haul round onto the larboard tack, and the British wore or tacked in chase. The lightness of the wind was now hampering Strachan himself, but he was able to signal *Namur*, still working up from the south, to engage the French van, a signal he emphasised by drawing Captain Halsted's attention to it with two shotted guns fired in *Namur*'s direction. Strachan also signalled Gardner's *Hero* to lead the British line, *Caesar* being less than handy thanks to the damage she had sustained.

At about two in the afternoon *Hero* drew level with the *Scipion* and fired her starboard battery into her, bringing down her main topmast. *Scipion* dropped to leeward and *Courageux* fell upon her from upwind, with *Phoenix* and *Revolutionaire* engaging from leeward. *Hero* pressed on and slowly passed *Formidable* until she lay off Dumanoir's larboard bow. A little later *Namur* came up astern and Gardner left *Formidable* to Halsted, making sail in chase of *Mont Blanc*.

Strachan, meanwhile, had refitted *Caesar* and soon loomed up close to *Formidable* which, with only her foremast left standing, was just then striking to *Namur*. A moment or so later, at about ten past three, the dismasted *Scipion* also surrendered and was secured by the frigates. *Duguay Trouin* and *Mont Blanc* now attempted to escape, but Strachan and Gardner engaged them and within twenty minutes had forced their surrender. *Mont Blanc* had had her main and mizen shot away, and *Duguay Trouin* was mastless.

The action had been bloody and furious. The British lost 24 men killed and 111 wounded, but the French losses were terrible, 750 killed and wounded. Touffet was among the dead and Dumanoir and Bellanger were wounded.

In 1809, after his exchange, Dumanoir was censured for his tactics, and demanded a court martial. He was acquitted, but it is clear that he had run from an inferior force until his enemy had had time to concentrate against him. His squadron, though terribly beaten about, were all purchased into the Royal Navy. *Formidable* became the *Brave* and was used as a prison-ship, while *Mont Blanc* became a powder-hulk at Plymouth. *Scipion* and *Duguay Trouin* were recommissioned, the latter as *Implacable*; her original name was that of a famous French corsair from St Malo. Although hulked in 1855, *Implacable* remained in Portsmouth as a static training ship until 1948, when she was towed out into the English Channel where, with the ensigns of France and Britain flying above her, she was sunk by gunfire. Today her figurehead and stern-galleries may be seen at the National Maritime Museum at Greenwich.

Sir Richard Strachan, heir to a baronetcy at seventeen, became a rear-admiral on 9 November 1805, and the January following was appointed a Knight Commander of the Order of the Bath. His ships' companies received the formal thanks of both Houses of Parliament, the captains all received gold medals, and the first lieutenants of the ships-of-the-line were all promoted to commander. This must have been felt as a singular slight by Captain Baker and *his* first luff, Samuel Brown, who had been instrumental in bringing about the action. Still, Baker went on to a knighthood and flag rank and distinguished himself on various occasions, particularly in the defence of several major convoys, in the Baltic and elsewhere. His Baltic service led him to marry a Swedish noblewoman. At this remove of time it is impossible to know whether or not Baker was in good odour with the Admiralty on the occasion of his encounter with Dumanoir, but one officer who was decidedly not, had begun his amazing career as a frigate-captain in 1805.

Despite Lord Cochrane's obvious promise, the end of the peace in 1803 did not find him sent to sea in a crack frigate. Quite the contrary: he was sent instead to the 20-gun *Arab*, the former French privateer *Brave* (which, oddly enough, had been taken by the *Phoenix* in April 1798). The *Arab* was on convoy and fishery protection duties, a dull routine appointment which, St Vincent hoped, would prevent the young aristocrat from distinguishing himself. The old man, great though he was, was highly prejudiced against the nobility, and in St Vincent's eyes Cochrane's unfortunate outspokenness outweighed his virtues as a sea warrior. But in April 1804 St Vincent was swept from office, to be replaced by the Scotsman Henry Dundas, Viscount Melville. Whatever Melville's own vices as a venal politician, he was prepared to listen when another Scot, the Duke of Hamilton, told him that the most promising Scottish sea-officer was wasting his talents in an old tub called the *Arab*.

Taking heed of Hamilton's advice, Melville posted Cochrane into the brand-new 32-gun frigate *Pallas*, then arranged for him to cruise in an area potentially rich in prizes: the Azores. There was a catch, however; Cochrane certainly took several Spanish merchantmen, but through a clever piece of bureaucracy Admiral Young, the port-admiral at Plymouth, shamelessly helped himself to a flag-officer's share of Cochrane's prize money. Young had had his own clerk transcribe Cochrane's orders from the Admiralty and himself counter-signed them, thus tacitly implying that Cochrane was acting under *his* orders. It was good enough for the prize-courts, but not for Cochrane. Though at the time he could do nothing about it, it was just the sort of bureaucratic trick Cochrane detested, and he inveighed relentlessy against the corruption of a prize system so disproportionate in its rewards to those who took all the risks (though there were few risks run off the Azores).

Cochrane's prizes were sent in to Plymouth, attracting the notice of the newspapers. On 24 February the *Caroline* arrived with logwood and sugar from Havana; on 7 March 'came in a rich Spanish prize with jewels, gold, silver and a valuable cargo', and on the 23rd it was 'a most beautiful letter-of-marque [privateer] of fourteen guns, said to be a very rich and valuable prize to the *Pallas*, Captain Lord Cochrane'.

Among the prizes *Pallas* took was the Spanish ship *Fortuna,* carrying 432,000 silver dollars, and aboard was an elderly Spanish merchant whose treasure was forfeit to his captors. He and the *Fortuna*'s master had both previously suffered huge financial loss in similar circumstances in 1779, and they now pleaded with Cochrane. Characteristically, Cochrane proceeded to ask his crew if they would renounce 10,000 dollars of the *Fortuna*'s cargo, to be restored to the old men, and, at least according to Cochrane's own account, they cheerfully agreed. Such generosity notwithstanding, Cochrane began to recoup his own family fortunes from this cruise – though they nearly suffered a check when on the way home he ran into three French line-of-battle ships from Missiessey's squadron. Hard-pressed in a strong wind, the British frigate was in danger of capture when Cochrane resorted to one of his daring ruses.

Although the *Pallas* was already carrying more sail than was prudent, he sent his topmen aloft with additional stays and set these up to support even more canvas. But this failed to give *Pallas* the speed she wanted. A heavy sea was running and the conditions favoured the enemy's larger ships. Ever resourceful, Cochrane hit on another idea. Ordering his men to the halliards, clew and buntlines, Cochrane chose his moment and suddenly clewed-up or lowered every sail. He then put his helm over and, using *Pallas*'s way, wore ship under bare poles. Astonished, the French failed to react quickly enough and rushed impetuously past as Cochrane, standing away on the opposite tack, showed his pursuers a clean pair of heels.

As part of his acquired treasure, Cochrane had aboard his frigate three huge gold candle sticks originally intended for a Spanish cathedral. As he entered Plymouth at the end of his cruise on the gloriously sunny morning of 5 April, these gleamed at the *Pallas's* mastheads.

Such flamboyance was not appreciated in some quarters, but Cochrane's successes ensured that he never afterwards had to resort to the press-gang to man a ship. Few sea warriors could claim that.

# CHAPTER 12

## 'Firmness ... to the backbone'

The British naval victory off Cape Trafalgar was followed by the French military victory of Austerlitz. The news broke William Pitt's heart; 'Roll up that map,' the Prime Minister allegedly said, catching sight of a map of Europe, 'it will not be wanted these ten years.' It was a notably prescient remark, but Pitt did not live to know the accuracy of his prediction. He died in January 1806, replaced by Lord Grenville's comparatively short-lived ministry. Thereafter a succession of First Lords of the Admiralty culminated in the reinstatement of Viscount Melville in 1812. These men were not seamen but they were supported by several successive First Naval Lords who were. In the immediate post-Trafalgar period Rear-Admiral John Markham followed Barham, endorsing the old admiral's policy and setting the tradition for those who followed him in their turn. Writing to the then First Lord, Thomas Grenville, before returning to sea in command of the Channel Fleet, Earl St Vincent said: 'You will find in Markham firmness and integrity to the backbone, happily combined with ability, diligence and zeal.' These were the qualities which summed up the guiding principles of British naval strategy in the last, long phase of the war, the great period of attrition. It therefore becomes necessary to run ahead a little and establish the principal chronology of the land-war against which British sea-power was now in deadly opposition.

At the time that Villeneuve and Gravina were engaged with Nelson and Collingwood off Cape Trafalgar, an Austrian general named Mack was surrendering his entire army at Ulm, in Bavaria. Scarcely a shot had been fired: Napoleon had simply outmanoeuvred Mack. A few weeks later, at Austerlitz, Napoleon smashed a second Austrian army which was combined with a powerful Russian force. In October 1806 the Grand Army destroyed the Prussians at Jena-Auerstädt, reducing Prussia to passivity. Moving into East Prussia, the French clashed again with the Russians in a snowstorm at Preussich-Eylau in February 1807; finally, on 14 June, the Grand Army routed the Russians at Friedland, and Tsar Alexander sued for peace. At a meeting on a raft in the middle of the river Nieman at the frontier town of Tilsit, Napoleon and Alexander came to a secret compact which isolated Great Britain.

Among the clauses of this agreement was a plan to seize Denmark's fleet. Quite how remains to this day a mystery, but London heard of it. As a result, a British fleet and expeditionary force were sent to Copenhagen on a pre-emptive strike. The fleet was commanded by Sir James Gambier, the army by General Lord Cathcart (one of whose major-generals was the future Duke of Wellington). The troops were landed, to besiege and bombard the city until they had forced a capitulation which led to the surrender of the Danish fleet and naval arsenal. All the men-of-war in port or being built on the slipways were captured or destroyed.

The consequence of this high-handed action was that another British fleet had to be committed to the Baltic to protect British trade. This, despite the hostility of the governments of Denmark, Russia and Prussia, was still considerable, carried on under an extensive and much abused system of licensing, while Sweden, a vacillating and uncertain ally to Britain, remained an important source of naval stores, iron, tar, jute, flax, spar and ship-building timber. All this trade, often in convoys of up to a thousand merchant ships, had to run the gauntlet of Danish reprisals. The navigable passages of the Sound, the Great Belt and the Little Belt, were all flanked on either side by Danish islands or the Jutland peninsula. From these shores gunboats by the score would sally out and attack the convoys, even inflicting heavy damage on large ships-of-war when they were becalmed. In addition to this hit-and-run form of warfare, there were a few Danish cruisers which had escaped the rape of Copenhagen by being in Norwegian waters, Norway being then a possession of the Danish crown. The admiral responsible for this new theatre of operations was Rear-Admiral Sir James Saumarez, who flew his flag in *Victory*. Like that of the Mediterranean on the southern flank of Europe, the Baltic command was to prove of critical importance in this confrontational period.

In addition to Denmark, Franco-Russian diplomacy now sought to make an ally of Turkey, and in 1807, Sir John Duckworth was detached from Collingwood's Mediterranean fleet and sent with a powerful squadron to force the Dardanelles and demonstrate in force in the Bosphorus before Constantinople. The British fought their way through the narrow strait, with some dashing action led by Sir Sidney Smith, and Nisbet Willoughby once more conspicuously at the centre of it. During those operations against the Turks Willoughby, having suffered burns during the rescue of survivors from a flaming British man-of-war, was twice wounded in the head. One pistol-ball lodged permanently in his brain, another cut his cheek in two, and he was listed as being mortally wounded. Despite this dire prognosis, he recovered.

The diplomatic and naval negotiations with the Sultan – in which Willoughby played the part of messenger and Smith, despite his familiarity with the Sublime Porte, was denied any part – were incompetently handled. Arbuthnot, the British ambassador, was stricken with a mysterious illness at a critical time and the burden fell upon the bombastic and quite useless Duckworth, whose appalling irresolution reduced the matter to a farce. Far from over-aweing Sultan Selim III, he made the British navy a laughing-stock, and provided the French ambassador, General Sebastiani, with some excellent news to send to Paris.

When Duckworth met a Russian squadron under Seniavin, the Russian proposed they should join forces and return to Constantinople, but Duckworth declared that, 'Where a British squadron had failed, no other was likely to succeed,' and refused the offer of help. A few months later Russia was an enemy, but Seniavin in the Mediterranean and Kontr-Admiral Poustouchine in the Black Sea so effectively strangled Constantinople that the city was reduced almost to starvation, and on 19 June 1807 Seniavin destroyed the Turkish fleet at Lemnos.

Duckworth, meanwhile, exculpated his conduct with a curious if not amazing explanation which revealed his total incapacity. To Collingwood, the Commander-in-Chief who had succeeded Nelson in the Mediterranean, he reported that had departed from the Bosphorus because the Turks were 'so ignorant and foolhardy, that no rhetoric could persuade, no threats intimidate them'! Duckworth crowned his disastrous independent command in the Levant by failing to capture Alexandria, and was only saved from public censure by the fall of the government. Meanwhile, as Russia changed sides after Tilsit, Collingwood, the British Commander-in-Chief in the Mediterranean, was left to add the blockade of Seniavin's fleet at Corfu to his mounting responsibilities.

Despite this reverse, the Royal Navy had matters well in hand, and from the summer of 1807 until the two emperors fell out and Napoleon invaded Russia in 1812, while the whole of Europe was ranged against Britain, her 'wooden walls' served her well. Indeed, and due in part to her now unchallenged superiority at sea, Britain was even able to go over to the offensive on land. As early as 1806 Napoleon had created his brother Joseph king of the Neapolitan part of the Kingdom of the Two Sicilies. The consequent hostilities between King Ferdinand and the usurper occupied the attentions of a supporting British naval squadron under Sir Sidney Smith. Operating on the coast of Calabria, at the toe of Italy, Smith carried over the Strait of Messina a small force of British troops then in Sicily. These engaged and defeated a larger force of veteran French infantry at Maida, a remarkable little adventure which, while it demonstrated the potential of British infantry, distracted Smith from his principal duty of supporting the besieged garrison of Gaeta and earned him the censure of the British Government.

When in the spring of 1808 Napoleon virtually kidnapped the Spanish royal family and transferred King Joseph from Naples to Madrid, substituting his brother-in-law Maréchal Joachim Murat on the Neapolitan throne, the Spanish rose in insurrection. This gave the British Government the opportunity to intervene, and an army was sent to the Iberian peninsula. Initially, things went badly; the first expedition was withdrawn; the second, after a brilliant march into Spain, was driven back in a horrendous winter retreat through the mountains to Coruña where a fleet and transports under Rear-Admiral James Bowen took off the shattered remnants of Sir John Moore's army in January 1809. But that summer a new army was landed at Lisbon. Under the future Duke of Wellington it defeated the French at Talavera, fell back to Lisbon until the spring of 1811, being kept fully supplied by sea, and then began the long advance across Spain. The French were defeated at Salamanca in July 1812, at Vitoria in June 1813, and at Toulouse in April 1814. By then Napoleon had abdicated, and was soon exiled to Elba, whereupon an uneasy peace settled on Europe.

During the Peninsular War, Wellington admitted that 'it is our maritime superiority [which] gives me the power of maintaining my army while the enemy are unable to do so'. But Wellington's was not the only army supplied by the Royal Navy; the Spanish armies, fragmented and less effective, nevertheless tied down thousands of French troops, while the guerrilla partisans cut off all communications between the French posts. These were kept supplied and materially helped by the far-flung cruisers of the Royal Navy, who also operated elsewhere on the coasts of Europe, from the Aegean in the Mediterranean to the Gulf of Riga in the Baltic – anywhere they could in any way damage the military or economic strength of the French Empire. Thus, cruiser warfare became the offensive weapon of sea-power, while blockade remained the primary, unremitting and aggressive form of front-line defence.

A little after Trafalgar, in the winter of 1805, Lord Barham decided to ease the British naval blockade: 'It is to little purpose now to wear out our ships in a fruitless blockade during the winter.' Toulon was almost void of battle ships, Cádiz contained the wreckage of the Combined Fleet, and although a squadron under Salcedo lay at Cartagena, he was mewed up by the attentive Collingwood. Only in Brest did a sizeable fleet lurk, and Barham had decided it could be watched by frigates, releasing the reluctant Cornwallis from constant close blockade if the weather became bad. Barham argued that if the French emerged they would not get far, once their escape was made known and the Channel Fleet set on their trail. Moreover, the British ships were better off riding out the winter gales in Torbay than lying off Ushant.

In the decade following Trafalgar the French navy continued to build ships-of-the-line and cruisers of all classes, while the military success of Napoleon enabled him to add to his own fleets by taking over those of his allies, or by acquiring the men-of-war of neutral nations. Constantly at the back of the Emperor's mind lay a dormant plan to revive a mighty naval offensive against Great Britain; but in the event, its accomplishment was beyond his abilities.

Although the French admirals continued to lack both energy and temerity, a number of frustrated French captains accomplished some remarkable achievements. Taking advantage of bad weather, or a favourable slant of wind to evade the watching British, they invariably left the French Atlantic ports with two objectives: to resupply French possessions overseas in the West Indies and the Indian Ocean, and to disrupt and destroy British trade. Large French frigates were capable of carrying a considerable amount of military cargo, though such a lading hampered their sailing and fighting qualities, but the majority of French frigate captains considered they had done enough if they were home after a couple of months. The exceptions to this generality were those frigates which were sent to the Indian Ocean.

To effect this the French made up flying squadrons of three or four frigates, with a corvette in support, and they were sufficient in numbers to be a constant headache to the Royal Navy. Combined with the actions of French privateers, to which was later added the very serious interdiction of British trade by Danish gun-boats and the less effective, if more emotive, predations of American cruisers, these assaults constituted a significant challenge. Great Britain's reliance on her foreign trade for her survival, let alone her victory over the French Empire, cannot be over-emphasised. British merchant ships were even more ubiquitous than British warships, and it lay with the sea warriors commanding the cruisers of the Royal Navy to provide them protection.

In the winter after Trafalgar, however, with Barham relaxing the blockade and Cornwallis driven off station by bad weather, the situation seemed at first to favour the French. On 13 December 1805 Vice-Amiral Leissègues and Contre-Amiral Willaumez broke out of Brest, separating the next day. Leissègues's squadron consisted of the 130-gun *Impérial*, the 80-gun *Alexandre*, three 74s, *Jupiter*, *Brave* and *Diomède*, the 40-gun frigates *Comète* and *Félicité* and the corvette *Diligent*. His orders were to reinforce San Domingo with the thousand troops on board, then either to cruise for two months off Jamaica or, if the enemy were superior, to raid the fishery on the Grand Banks off Newfoundland. Willaumez, in the 80-gun French *Foudroyant* with five 74s, *Vétéran* (whose captain was Napoleon's youngest brother Jérôme), *Cassard*, *Impétueux*, *Patriote* and *Éole*, the 40-gun frigates *Valeureuse* and *Volontaire*, and two brig corvettes, was to cruise against British trade in the South Atlantic and off Martinique.

On 15 December the French were seen by lookouts in a convoy of twenty-three sail bound from Cork to the West Indies. The escort commander, Captain Charles Brisbane aboard the *Arethusa*, sent off his fellow escorts *Boadicea* and the sloop *Wasp* with the news, but the Admiralty did not learn of the break-out until Christmas Eve and it was the end of January 1806 before two flying squadrons were sent out in pursuit. One of these was under Vice-Admiral Sir John Warren, the other was commanded by Rear-Admiral Sir Richard Strachan. Their comprehensive orders took account of other squadrons then operating in the areas likely to be invaded by either of the French admirals, which included the expedition then on its way to retake the Cape of Good Hope from the Dutch.

Vice-Admiral Warren, flying his flag in the British *Foudroyant*, 80, had as his flag-captain John Chambers White. In support were the 90-gun *London* (Captain Sir Harry Neale), and five 74s, *Ramillies*, *Namur*, *Hero*, *Repulse* and *Courageux*. Warren was joined later by the frigate *Amazon*. Neither Strachan nor Warren succeeded in running down their quarry, but Warren ran into another French squadron.

In March 1806 Contre-Amiral Linois was on his way back to France in the 74-gun *Marengo*, in company with the 40-gun frigate *Belle Poule*, commerce raiding on the passage between St Helena and the Canaries. He was returning from his cruise in The Indian Ocean and his encounter with Dance. Just after midnight on the 13th sails were sighted to the eastward and Linois went in chase, believing them to be a convoy of merchant ships heading south-east. They were in fact Warren's flying squadron.

The *London* was upwind but, because of her poor sailing qualities, astern of the *Foudroyant*. On sighting the approaching sails Neale fired blue lights and Captain William Parker of the *Amazon* did the same, though he could see nothing of the enemy. Linois made off, but as dawn broke he realised he could not outrun the British ships. He ordered *Belle Poule* to escape, while *Marengo* engaged *London*. After an exchange of broadsides Linois sheered away, but *Marengo*'s gunnery had damaged *London*'s rigging and the pursuit was left to the other British ships, which were now approaching. Unluckily *Marengo* failed to get clear of both *London*'s guns and those of *Amazon* as she stormed past in chase of *Belle Poule*.

By nine o'clock in the forenoon the two frigates *Amazon* and *Belle Poule* were engaged in a running fight as, far astern, Warren's seventy-fours closed round *Marengo*. *Ramillies* opened fire and, with *Repulse* and *Foudroyant*, forced Linois to strike his colours an hour before noon. At about the same time, *Amazon*'s gunnery was forcing Captain Bruilhac to surrender the *Belle Poule*. British losses were light, but the *Marengo* suffered 63 men killed and 83 wounded, among whom were Linois and his flag-captain, Vrignault. Of Linois's original squadron, only the frigate *Sémillante* now remained a danger to British merchantmen in the Indian Ocean. His cruise justified Napoleon's condemnation of his abilities, though it might be said to have caused some concern in British quarters.

But what of Leissègues and Willaumez?

After sighting the French ships between Madeira and the Canaries, on 23 December Captain Brisbane's *Arethusa* met with a British squadron under Vice-Admiral Sir John Duckworth. Having heard from Commander Langford of the *Lark*, 18, that a French squadron had dispersed a British convoy, Duckworth had thrown up the blockade of Cádiz and was then seeking the enemy. He considered himself a second Nelson, and Brisbane's news provoked him to head north, leaving Madeira to the east. On Christmas Day 1805 Duckworth's ships went in chase of nine sails heading south; the next morning his squadron was extended many miles astern of his flagship, the *Superb*. Still under the command of Richard Goodwin Keats, *Superb* was well ahead of her consorts, but the disposition of his ships dissuaded Duckworth from engaging. Instead, he shortened sail and despatched the frigate *Amethyst* to carry the news to the Admiralty. Then, requiring water, he decided to head west for the Leeward Islands.

Duckworth's inexplicable action in allowing Willaumez (for it was he) to escape without further pursuit, thus compounded his original desertion of his station off Cádiz, where he was subordinate to Collingwood. On 12 January 1806 Duckworth anchored off Barbados, joining Rear-Admiral Alexander Cochrane in *Northumberland*, and *Atlas*, both of 74 guns. Both admirals remained ignorant of Leissègues's arrival in the West Indies until 1 February, when Duckworth was disturbed to learn that French line-of-battle ships had been sighted heading for San Domingo.

Duckworth now weighed and laid a course for San Domingo, where on 6 February he engaged Leissègues off Occa Bay in what was to prove the last fleet action of the war. Leissègues's squadron was broken, though the French frigates *Comète* and *Félicité* and the corvette *Diligente* escaped. Although in the battle Duckworth's ships endured ferocious gunfire from the French, the British casualties of 74 killed and 264 wounded were far lighter than the enemy's 1,500 men either killed or wounded. The captured *Brave* sank on her passage to Britain and the *Alexandre* was too damaged to be recommissioned, but *Jupiter* was added to the British fleet and named *Maida,* after Sir John Stuart's minor Calabrian victory. Duckworth was not granted further honours, the view being taken that only his success justified his desertion of Cádiz. As Barham wrote on the eve of his own retirement as First Lord of the Admiralty, the battle 'puts us out of all fear from another predatory war in the West Indies'.

And Willaumez? He was luckier, at least to start with, successfully destroying merchantmen in the South Atlantic and West Indies and avoiding both Rear-Admiral Cochrane and Strachan's questing squadron. Like Willaumez, Strachan was caught in a hurricane and his squadron dispersed, but by the middle of September three of the British ships had made their rendezvous off Cape Henry, Virginia. Here they sighted the *Impétueux* running for shelter in Chesapeake Bay under jury rig, and the seventy-fours *Bellona* (Captain John Douglas) and

*Belleisle* (Captain William Hargood) and the 36-gun frigate *Melampus* (Captain Stephen Poyntz) gave chase. Capitaine Alain Belair was forced to run the *Impétueux* aground and haul down his ensign. The wreck was burnt. Willaumez's squadron was now fatally weakened; the *Patriote* and *Éole* sought refuge in Chesapeake Bay, though only the *Patriote* returned to France. The *Valeureuse* reached the Delaware but never served again, *Cassard* got back home, and the French *Foudroyant*, after refitting in Havana, returned to Brest in February 1807.

Since October 1805 Commodore L'Hermitte had also escaped the blockade and had been cruising in the South Atlantic with a third French squadron consisting of one 74-gun ship, two frigates and a brig-corvette. L'Hermitte's orders were to divert units of the British Channel fleet, attack British posts on the coast of West Africa, thereby disrupting the lucrative slave-trade, then cross the Atlantic to create havoc among merchant shipping in the West Indies. Although his squadron was dispersed by a hurricane on 20 August 1806, L'Hermitte seized British slavers and merchantmen and captured the British sloop-of-war *Favourite*. On 27 September one of his dispersed frigates, the 40-gun *Président* (Capitaine Labrosse), was approaching the Biscay coast of France when she fell in with a squadron under Rear-Admiral Sir Thomas Louis in the *Canopus* and surrendered after a chase, to be purchased later into the Royal Navy.

L'Hermitte was supposed to be relieved by Jérôme Bonaparte, and the cruise was intended to be highly predatory, but miscarried in failing to capture an African base to assist the maintenance of the ships. Although he and his squadron failed to achieve what they might have, L'Hermitte himself was more fortunate than his colleague Labrosse, and his 74-gun *Régulus* managed to slip into Brest on 5 October.

The escape of Leissègues, Willaumez and L'Hermitte, though ineffective against the British and costly to the French, nevertheless emphasised the importance to British commerce of maintaining a constant close blockade on enemy ports. It was far more difficult to locate an enemy squadron at large in the vastness of the oceans, than to prevent it from leaving its home port. On the other hand, the waste of the resources entrusted to Leissègues and Willaumez temporarily reduced the Brest fleet to the impotence of that at Cádiz, and no ship-of-the-line got out during the remainder of 1806.

So much for the line-of-battle ships; frigates were another matter, even from Cádiz, where Capitaine Louis La Marre La Meillerie slipped his moorings on the evening of 26 February 1806. La Meillerie's 40-gun *Hortense* was accompanied by the *Hermione* and *Rhin*, both of 40 guns, the 36-gun *Thémis* and the brig-corvette *Furet*.

Offshore, Lord Collingwood, the British Commander-in-Chief, had eased the blockade to induce the French to sail, leaving only the 38-gun frigate *Hydra* and the sloop *Moselle*, 18, inshore. Collingwood's stratagem almost went awry when, on the 23rd, the wind increased in strength from the east and drove the two British cruisers off to leeward, allowing La Meillerie's squadron to get away to sea. Nevertheless, it was obvious to *Hydra's* Captain George Mundy that the French would take advantage of the favourable wind, and despite the darkness of the night of the 26th strange sails were spotted. *Hydra* and *Moselle* gave chase on a parallel course. About midnight Mundy ordered John Carden of the *Moselle* to go and look for Collingwood and let him know the French frigate squadron was at sea.

By dawn, Mundy's hard-driven frigate was overhauling the hindmost French vessel, the brig-corvette *Furet*, which hauled down her ensign after a single broadside from *Hydra*. La Meillerie left her to her fate, a decision which seems scarcely credible given the strength of the three French frigates as against the solitary *Hydra;* but the commodore probably had the usual orders to prosecute his mission, and if possible to avoid any action which compromised it. If so, La Meillerie had succeeded, getting the bulk of his laden squadron clear of the coast; now he was to vanish into the vast Atlantic.

That spring another French frigate squadron evaded the British blockade, bound on a predatory mission the like of which obliged the Royal Navy to deploy cruisers from Basra in the Persian Gulf to the North Cape of Norway, and from the Sunda Strait in Indonesia to the Denmark Strait off Greenland. Commodore Amand Leduc victualled his squadron for five months and left L'Orient in the early morning of 28 March 1806. He commanded the 40-gun frigate *Revanche* and had in company the 40-gun *Guerrière*, the 36-gun *Syrène* and the brig-corvette *Néarque* of 16 guns. Leduc was to cruise in the polar seas off the coasts of Iceland, Greenland and Spitsbergen to prey on British and Russian whaling vessels. He had previously served as master of a Dunkerque whaler, and his knowledge of the Arctic Ocean and the fisheries was invaluable.

Unfortunately for Leduc, in the early afternoon his squadron was seen off the Île de Groix by the British frigate *Niobe*, cruising there. Captain John Loring immediately made sail in pursuit but Leduc, following his orders, headed south to clear the coast under a press of sail. It was dark as the *Niobe* gradually overtook the corvette *Néarque*, whose commander fired rockets and a gun, and burnt flares in alarm. Leduc was unmoved, ready to sacrifice his small consort to the greater purpose of his mission; at ten o'clock in the evening *Niobe* came up close to the *Néarque* and, having fired a volley of musketry, accepted her surrender as Leduc disappeared into the darkness.

The ice field appeared to be late retreating in the spring of 1806, and most of the British whalers were unable to reach the Spitsbergen shore where the Right Whale usually congregated. In point of fact the pack-ice had moved south, opening clear water farther north. Captain William Scoresby, master of the Whitby whaler *Resolution*, having forced the pack, found himself in open water in latitude 81° 30′ North. He was fortunate and, unmolested by Leduc, made a successful voyage.

Encountering the pack-ice himself, Leduc began his search but found no quarry and as time passed became increasingly worried about running into British cruisers. This persuaded him to try to work north again, and at the end of May his squadron reached the ice a second time, in latitude 72° North. By 12 June Leduc was in sight of the distant ice-covered peaks of Spitsbergen, but he then ran into fog, in which they lost *Guerrière*. As a compensation, he now located the whaling fleet; hoisting Swedish colours, Leduc ran in among the whalers and captured a number before they could recover their boats and escape into the loose pack-ice.

Capitaine Paul Hubert of the *Guerrière* had also experienced a change of luck. On 22 June *Guerrière* captured and set fire to the homeward-bound whaler *Dingwall* of London, and three days later he took and burnt the *Simes* of Leith. Cruising further east, Hubert seized the merchant ship *Boyne* of Yarmouth on her way to Archangel on the White Sea coast of Russia; he put all his captives aboard a neutral Danish ship (which later landed them in the Shetlands), then took several more prizes before his crew began to show symptoms of scurvy.

News of the French squadron at large in the northern seas had by now reached London by way of Hull. The ability of the Admiralty to respond to such a report in those days before radio communications was again exemplified. Trade protection in the North Sea was vested in frigates, sloops and cutters operating on the east coast of Britain. The Admiralty knew of Leduc's presence in the north on 12 July. Immediately the frigates *Phoebe* of 36 guns and *Thames* of 32, then anchored in Leith Roads, were ordered to sail to Lerwick in the Shetlands. Meanwhile the 38-gun *Blanche*, now commanded by Captain Thomas Lavie and lying at anchor in The Downs, was telegraphed an instruction to proceed to Yarmouth Road, on the Norfolk coast. Here Lavie received detailed orders to take *Phoebe* and *Thames* under his command and seek out and destroy Leduc's squadron. But in Lerwick there was more up-to-date news from the landed prisoners; Captains Oswald and Taylor of the *Phoebe* and *Thames* learned that one of the French frigates was on her own and not far away. They did not wait for Lavie, but sailed north without delay. Lavie followed three days later, having himself discovered that *Guerrière* alone had captured several ships off the Faeroe Islands. In the late forenoon of 18 July *Blanche*'s lookouts reported a sail heading towards them from the east.

For his part Hubert, much in need of water, was making for the Faeroes, unaware that the sail ahead of him was a British man-of-war. Hubert beat to the westward as Lavie ran down towards him with the light south-westerly breeze behind him. At about three o'clock in the afternoon Hubert realised his mistake and turned away, setting every stitch of sail *Guerrière* would bear. A chase ensued, lasting until shortly before two in the morning of the 19th, when *Blanche* poured two broadsides into *Guerrière* before Hubert could open fire. For three quarters of an hour the two frigates hammered each other, but while the French gunners were unable to reduce *Blanche*'s rig the British shot away *Blanche*'s mizen topmast. Hubert hauled down his ensign, for further resistance was useless. His crew were enfeebled by scurvy, to which he had already lost thirty-seven men, while *Blanche* had accounted for a further fifty in killed and wounded. (A day after the *Guerrière*'s capture, Scoresby's *Resolution* passed the Faeroes, home-ward-bound, laden with whale blubber for the trying works of Whitby, able to pass upon his lawful occasions thanks to the exertions of Lavie and his frigate.) The *Blanche* and *Guerrière* arrived in Yarmouth Road on 28 July. Lavie was knighted for his victory, his first lieutenant, Henry Davies, was promoted to commander, and *Blanche*'s crew received their share of prize-money when *Guerrière* was purchased into the British navy.

Lavie's colleagues had not done so well: *Phoebe* and *Thames* missed *Revanche* and *Syrène*, which had taken on water in Iceland before cruising off Cape Farewell. Here the French enjoyed some success, taking the whaler *Molly* on 21 June and a few days later capturing the British privateer *Minerva* of Greenock. This vessel had assumed the French frigates to be Prussian whalers and had attacked them, whereupon Leduc's ships ran out their guns, compelling the astonished commander of the *Minerva* to haul down his colours. Leduc also captured a number of British and Russian merchantmen, freeing his prisoners in one of them, the *Rose*, whose master reached Hull with the news that the two French frigates were ravaged by scurvy. Three more British frigates, the *Amethyst, Princess Charlotte* and *Diana,* were now sent after Leduc, but they too laboured in vain.

By this time Leduc had taken the *Blenheim* and *Holderness,* after which he headed for home by way of the north coast of Ireland. Here he was chased on 28 August, but escaped to spend a few days off Cape Clear until on 14 September he bore away to reach L'Orient on the 22nd. He had destroyed one Russian and twenty-eight British vessels, mostly whalers, but the cost had been half his squadron. As for the state of his crews, the contrast with the increasing ability of the Royal

Navy to keep the sea for long periods was marked. The effect of the scurvy was profound, and demonstrates the true difference between the opposing navies. Although Leduc's cruise was regarded as a qualified success in terms of enemy trade destroyed, the tying-down of six Royal Naval frigates and the alarm it caused in the whaling ports, the real cost to France was considerable. Besides the manpower lost to disease and battle, she had given up two men-of-war, one of which was then commissioned against her, and none of the prizes were brought home, merely plundered and then burnt.

Having failed to find Leduc, the *Phoebe* and *Thames* proved a greater danger to their friends than their enemies, profiting from their cruise to the extent of pressing seamen out of the whalers, ignoring the exemptions their crews possessed and, on one occasion, exchanging eight prime seamen for thirteen Prussian prisoners taken out of a sealing brig!

At the time of Leduc's escape from L'Orient in the spring of 1806, the British blockading squadron lying off Rochefort was commanded by Vice-Admiral Thornbrough, one of whose roving frigates was the 32-gun *Pallas*. Thornbrough had given Captain Lord Cochrane orders to 'annoy the enemy', a duty Cochrane took literally. On the night of 5 April he sent *Pallas*'s boats up the River Gironde to seize a French 14-gun brig-corvette, the *Tapageuse,* which lay under two batteries about twenty miles upstream. This was successfully undertaken but the *Pallas*, awaiting the return of Lieutenant John Haswell and more than a hundred and fifty men, was herself vulnerable, so close inshore in enemy waters. At daylight Cochrane observed three sails coming in from the Atlantic, clearly French men-of-war bound for Bordeaux. With his customary resource, he briefed his forty remaining men and confined his furled sails with rope yarns. On his signal, a few nimble topmen cut these light lashings, the sails were set, and with the speed of a fully manned frigate *Pallas* made sail, heading to intercept the inward-bound vessels. Cochrane handled *Pallas* like a yacht, boldly driving at the three French corvettes and, firing a few guns, forced the 20-gun ship-corvette *Garonne* into shoal water, where she ran aground. Cochrane then headed *Pallas* for the remaining two brig-corvettes, the *Malicieuse*, 16, and the *Gloire*, 20 guns (not to be confused with a frigate of the same name). These were similarly headed off and forced to strike the seabed with such violence that their masts went over the side. By this time Haswell was approaching with *Tapageuse*, and Cochrane made off with her. Fully manned again except for his prize crew, Cochrane wrought havoc along the French coast, destroying three telegraph stations; then, having been joined by the brig-sloop *Comet* and the cutter *Frisk*, his little squadron stormed a battery of three 36-pounder guns on the Pointe de l'Aiguillon on 9 May.

On 14 May Cochrane was ordered by Thornbrough to reconnoitre Allemand's squadrons, lying at anchor in the roadstead behind the Île d'Aix. Standing inshore in a north-easterly wind, Cochrane's *Pallas* passed the 16-gun ship-sloop *Kingfisher*, whose commander was forbidden to get too close inshore, and brought *Pallas* to an anchorage from which he had an unobstructed view of the Basque and Aix Roads. The British frigate lay just within range of the shore batteries, and Contre-Amiral Allemand ordered the 40-gun frigate *Minerve* and the 16-gun brig-corvettes *Sylphe*, *Lynx* and *Palinure* to destroy the impertinent enemy. Allemand also ordered the 40-gun frigates *Armide* and *Infatigable* to prepare for action.

Capitaine Jacques Collet of the *Minerve* made all sail before the favourable wind, intending to catch the *Pallas* before she should escape. Cochrane was able to count Allemand's squadron of five ships-of-the-line, five frigates, one ship-corvette and three brigs before he perceived Collet's approach, whereupon he weighed anchor and hoisted his topsails; he then hove-to, enticing Collet on while holding his own fire. Once the *Minerve* and the brigs were within short range, *Pallas*'s gunfire shot down the main topsail yard of one of the brigs. Cochrane then hauled his yards and, as his gunners fired into the enemy, dodged among the shoals avoiding the gunfire of the shore batteries which now joined in.

At about one o'clock in the afternoon, *Pallas* was close to windward of the *Minerve*. She fired broadsides into her, and then closed to board. At this moment *Minerve* struck the bottom and stopped dead, and the *Pallas* collided with such an impact that her loaded guns were thrust inboard. Undaunted, Cochrane's gunners promptly discharged so devastating a broadside into *Minerve*'s hull that the French were driven from their weapons, leaving Collet almost alone upon his quarterdeck. Cochrane, observing the approach of *Infatigable* and *Armide*, cut loose from *Minerve*. He was aware that Allemand had also sent the 40-gun *Gloire* to secure the British frigate.

In the collision *Pallas* had lost her jib-boom, her spritsail yard, foretopmast, maintopsail yard, studding sail yards, a bumpkin and a cathead and bower anchor; but she drew less water than the shattered *Minerve*, and was able to set sufficient sail to draw off. Seeing Cochrane's plight, Commander Seymour had disregarded his instructions and now approached *Pallas* in *Kingfisher* to take her in tow. Neither *Infatigable* nor *Armide* followed, and Cochrane coolly withdrew, having gained at least the moral victory. The French refloated *Minerve*, and with the other three frigates she was to sortie again later in the year.

La Meillerie, it will be recalled, had escaped from Cádiz in February with the loss of the *Furet*. His squadron first resupplied Senegal, then proceeded to Cayenne before cruising fruitlessly against British commerce off Barbados for fifteen days. By the end of July La Meillerie's frigates were on the way back to Rochefort, and on the 27th they were seen from the 74-gun *Mars*, the look-out cruiser belonging to Captain Richard Keats's squadron then blockading the port. Giving chase, Captain Robert Oliver of *Mars* hoisted the signal for an enemy in sight, which was seen by the 64-gun *Africa*. La Meillerie's squadron again ran and the chase went on all night, until at daybreak *Mars* began to draw up with the *Rhin*, which had dropped behind her consorts. At this point La Meillerie decided to turn on his solitary British pursuer. The *Hortense*, *Thémis* and *Hermione* hauled round, and in line ahead on the larboard tack dropped back to support the *Rhin*. La Meillerie kept this up until *Mars* drew closer, whereupon he seems to have lost his nerve, for he put his helm over and left the *Rhin* to her fate.

Oliver now closed for the kill, but at about six in the evening a squall hit the two ships. It lay the frigate over, but allowed the big two-decker to range up on the *Rhin*'s lee-quarter. The *Mars* was cleared for action, her iron gun-muzzles ranged in two black and formidable rows, but Oliver first fired a warning shot, and Capitaine Michel Chesneau struck his colours. The *Rhin* was purchased into the Royal Navy and subsequently took a number of French corsairs, particularly in the Western Approaches. La Meillerie's conduct encouraged in the British fleet, a growing assumption of superiority against all odds, and tended to breed a dangerous conceit.

As one of the squadron off Rochefort, the *Mars* now exchanged both her captain and her local flag officer, for in the autumn Captain Oliver was relieved by William Lukin and Commodore Sir Samuel Hood, still in the 74-gun *Centaur,* was entrusted with the duty of watching the area. Along with *Mars*, Hood's squadron now consisted of the 98-gun *Windsor Castle* (Captain Charles Boyles), and the seventy-fours *Achille* (Captain Richard King), *Monarch* (Captain Richard Lee) and *Revenge* (Captain Sir John Gore), with the gun-brig *Atalante* (Commander Joseph Masefield) as despatch vessel.

In the first hours of 25 September 1806, Hood's squadron were about twenty miles off Chasseron lighthouse. The wind was northerly and Hood's ships were spread out on the larboard tack when the *Monarch* made the night signal that an enemy was in sight. Hood, thinking the strange sails might be line-of-battle ships, signalled his squadron to form line. Just as he discerned that the strangers were frigates, they in turn saw the British and, setting all possible sails, headed south-south-west, whereupon Hood ordered a general chase. *Monarch* was the leading vessel, with *Revenge* lagging some miles behind.

The French squadron, several of which had already encountered Lord Cochrane in May, had left Rochefort the previous evening, bound for the West Indies with stores and troops on board. Commodore Elénore Jean Soleil commanded four heavy 40-gun frigates, his own *Gloire*, with *Infatigable* (Capitaine Joseph Girardias), *Minerve* (Capitaine Joseph Collett) and *Armide* (Capitaine Jean Langlois), the 36-gun *Thetis* (Capitaine Jacques Pinsum) and the brig-corvettes *Lynx* and *Sylphe*. There was a heavy swell running under the rough wind-sea, and the conditions favoured the heavier British ships.

Burdened as the French frigates were with supplies for the West Indies garrisons, after four hours *Monarch* had almost caught up with the rearmost, the *Armide*. However, *Centaur* was eight miles astern, with the rest of Hood's squadron strung out far behind her. Langlois hoisted *Armide*'s colours and Captain Lee opened fire with *Monarch*'s bow-chasers, *Armide* returning fire from her stern-chasers. At about six o'clock in the morning the *Infatigable* hauled round towards Rochefort and tried to escape, but *Mars* followed her. The headmost and southerly French ships were the *Thetis, Lynx* and *Sylphe,* and these three raced on, outran the British ships and got away, but the *Gloire* and *Minerve* dropped back to the aid of the *Armide*. Langlois and Soleil now both opened fire on *Monarch* and inflicted considerable damage on her, for her crew were unable to open the lower-deck gun-ports because of the heavy swell. The *Monarch* was reduced to an unmanageable state in some twenty minutes, despite a heavy fire from her starboard battery, but *Minerve* was also damaged, and *Gloire* and *Armide* now made sail as *Centaur* approached.

Hood now took over the chase and engaged *Gloire* and *Armide*, leaving *Monarch* to batter the *Minerve* alone. The action ran on through the forenoon, until Capitaine Langlois of the *Armide* hauled down his ensign in submission to Hood. At about midday Girardias of the *Infatigable* struck to Captain Lukin of the *Mars* and he, having taken possession, made sail to join *Centaur*. Soleil could do nothing now but run, and the *Gloire* headed west with *Centaur* and the undamaged *Mars* setting every sail that would draw. At half-past two in the afternoon *Mars* began to fire on the fleeing *Gloire*, and within another half an hour, Soleil struck.

Soleil's ships had tried to thwart Hood's pursuit by damaging his ships' rigging and thereby escaping, but this had proved ineffective. British losses were nine dead and twenty-nine wounded, among them Hood, whose right arm had been shattered by a musket ball.

All four French frigates were relatively new ships of more than 1,000 tons each, and all were subsequently taken into the Royal Navy: *Minerve* as *Alceste, Infatigable* as *Immortalité*, and *Armide* and *Gloire* under their own names.

# CHAPTER 13

---

# 'Stand firm'

Throughout 1806 and 1807 there was significant action in the further flung reaches of Franco-British conflict. In August 1805 a military corps of 5,000 soldiers under the command of Sir David Baird was embarked in sixty transports and four East Indiamen, and under the escort of a naval force under Commodore Sir Home Riggs Popham reached Table Bay in early January 1806. After a brief campaign of less than a week Baird took possession of Cape Town on 12 January. On 4 March the 40-gun French frigate *Volontaire*, a solitary remnant of Willaumez's squadron, sailed blithely into Table Bay, deceived by the Dutch colours flying from the forts and the anchored shipping. When the 64-gun *Diadem* changed her ensign, *Volontaire*'s astonished captain was obliged to surrender, releasing two hundred British soldiers who had been captured out of their troop transports by Willaumez's ships in the Bay of Biscay.

The re-acquisition of the Cape of Good Hope was a necessary precaution, not merely to protect the trade of The Honourable East India Company but to deny the French a safe haven at the Cape and isolate their possession of the Île de France (Mauritius). This distant enemy base athwart the trade route to India and China was an increasing irritant to British commerce, supporting as it did both corsairs and French national frigates.

On 21 June 1806 the East Indiaman *Warren Hastings*, homeward-bound from China, was off the French island of Réunion in the southern Indian Ocean. During the late morning, as the East Indiaman ran before a stiff north-easterly wind, it was reported to Commander Thomas Larkins that a strange sail was in sight. The stranger was revealed as a frigate and Larkins, seeing her British colours, made the private signal; receiving no reply, he cleared away his 36 'cannonades'.

The stranger was the 40-gun French frigate *Piémontaise* (Capitaine Jacques Epron), and she quickly swung to range up the larboard quarter of the *Warren Hastings*. Epron attacked from the lee side, to disable the Indiaman and deprive her of her own fire-power as she heeled towards him in the strong wind. Running up French colours, Epron ran past the Indiaman, firing into her. Larkins fired back, but Epron tacked ahead of her and stood back along the *Warren Hastings*' larboard side a second time, so close that the yardarms of the two vessels barely missed each other. The Indiaman's port rigging and foremast were damaged and her ensign halliards were shot away, but Epron had not finished. *Piémontaise* put about again under the *Warren Hastings*'s stern and, reducing sail, ran slowly along her side yet again inflicting more damage, before tacking ahead of her and repeating the process.

Epron, turning again under the *Warren Hastings*'s stern, came close on her larboard port quarter and wrecked the Indiaman, shooting away her bowsprit and masts until only the main was left. The mess impeded the working of the after upper-deck guns, the gunroom was on fire, the tiller ropes were damaged and the surgeon's instruments had been scattered by a round shot. *Piémontaise* had suffered the loss of her own maintopsail, but her heavier armament and surplus of man power overwhelmed the *Warren Hastings,* and after a gallant defence of four hours Larkins struck his colours.

Unfortunately his ship, now uncontrollable, ran athwart the *Piémontaise* as she lowered a boat and this was interpreted as an act contrary to the rules of warfare. An infuriated French officer scrambled on board and stabbed Larkins. Lieutenant Moreau and his men were drunk, and a spate of bloodshed followed as the surgeon, the second officer, a midshipman and a boatswain's mate were all wounded. Larkins survived this shameful act, despite injury to his liver, while Epron took his prize in tow, reaching the Île de France on 4 July. It was to be some time before Larkins and his company were revenged.

In September Epron's frigate was on the Malabar coast of India where she attacked another Indiaman, the *Fame*. Once again the merchant master, James Jameson, made a gallant defence, inflicting seventeen casualties on the *Piémontaise*'s people at a cost of seven of his own, before submitting to superior force.

In the Indian seas the effectiveness of the British war effort had been compromised by the division of the East Indies station between two new rear-admirals – Pellew, who had relieved Rainier at Penang in January 1805, and Troubridge. The division between the two commands was no more than a bureaucratic nicety, but the purely arbitrary line chosen by Pellew as senior officer – 82° 30' East of Greenwich – made no strategic sense and thus tended to dislocate all attempts at co-ordination. Until Linois went home, Pellew's frigate squadrons were instructed to seek out and destroy him. In July 1806, his cruisers *Greyhound*, 32, and *Harrier*, 18, took the Dutch 36-gun frigate *Pallas* and two richly-laden Indiamen she was escorting. An attempt by the 74-gun *Sceptre* and the 38-gun *Cornwallis* to attack the French frigate *Sémillante* in the port of St Paul on the island of Réunion failed, and she escaped her fate, at least for the time being.

In June Captain Peter Rainier, nephew of the former Commander-in-Chief of the East Indies, was promoted post-captain at the age of twenty-one and given command of the 36-gun frigate *Caroline*. (This was nepotism of a high order, for little more than a year earlier Rainier had been a mere midshipman.) In October the young Rainier attacked shipping in Batavia Road and took the 36-gun Dutch frigate *Maria Reigersbergen* after an action of half an hour. The Dutch frigate was purchased into the service as *Java,* only to founder in foul weather along with Troubridge's *Blenheim* when bound for the Cape the following year. Meanwhile Pellew himself was busy promoting his own sons, and Fleetwood Pellew was posted into the frigate *Terpsichore* in time for Pellew's descent on Batavia in November, when he destroyed the shipping off the Dutch colonial capital.

Several spirited actions took place in the West Indies, one of the most remarkable of which involved the 'Saucy *Arethusa*', under the command of Captain Charles Brisbane. On 23 August 1806 *Arethusa* and the 44-gun *Anson* (Captain Charles Lydiard) were off the Cuba coast, near Havana. Early that morning they saw the Spanish frigate *Pomona* approaching, beating up for Havana in light airs against a strong current. The *Pomona* was carrying a valuable cargo, including specie, the small-denomination coinage used for trade payments, which she had loaded at Vera Cruz. Brisbane and Lydiard made sail to head her off. Unable to reach the entrance to Havana, *Pomona* was anchored under the guns of Moro castle close by. The castle was heavily armed, and had furnaces capable of heating shot. These were now lit, and Spanish gun-boats headed for *Pomona* to take off her specie and help with her defence.

Lydiard and Brisbane made ready to anchor close to *Pomona*, but the light wind delayed them, and by the time they had made their approach the gun-boats had interposed and the specie had been removed. At approximately ten o'clock in the morning Lydiard anchored *Anson* by the stern and engaged the gun-boats, each of which bore a long 24-pounder, while *Arethusa* anchored between *Anson* and *Pomona* and fired into the Spanish frigate. The gun-boats' gunnery proved poor, and though red-hot shot from the Moro guns started a fire aboard *Arethusa* it was quickly doused. After about half an hour the *Pomona*'s colours were lowered and the prize was brought out from under the enemy's guns. The *Pomona* was afterwards purchased into the Royal Navy as the *Cuba*.

A few days later Brisbane and Lydiard were bound on an even more daring enterprise.

Towards the end of 1806 the Commander-in-Chief at Jamaica, Vice-Admiral Dacres, once again received reports that the Dutch traders of Curaçao were anxious to acquire British protection and consequent relief from the strictures of the embago. Dacres therefore sent Brisbane, fresh from his exploit off Havana, to investigate. Brisbane left Port Royal on 29 November 1806 with a frigate squadron. Besides his own 38-gun *Arethusa*, he was accompanied by Lydiard in *Anson* and the 38-gun *Latona* (Captain James Wood). Off Aruba Island on 23 December they were joined by *Fisgard* (Captain William Bolton).

Brisbane made known his intention of approaching Curaçao on New Year's Day making for St Anne, on the south east coast of the island, whither the trade wind would swiftly carry the squadron. An hour after the turn of the year the frigates lay-to, hoisted out their boats and took them in tow. At five in the morning the yards were squared and they set course directly for the narrow entrance to St Anne, between Fort Amsterdam on the eastern side and the batteries opposite.

The 36-gun, 12-pounder Batavian frigate *Kenau Hasselaar* was moored just inside to cover the small port's approaches, supported by the ship-corvette *Suriname* of 22 guns and a pair of schooners. Beyond rose the Misselburg, a hill bearing a number of fortified positions. The summit was crowned by Fort Republiek the guns of which commanded the whole port.

At daylight Brisbane's squadron closed the coast flying a flag of truce, a device to encourage the Batavian authorities to parley. *Arethusa* led *Latona*, *Anson* and *Fisgard* in line astern. The garrison ignored the flag of truce and opened fire immediately, while a short-lived shift in the wind caused the *Fisgard* to ground briefly. Despite this frustration, the other men-of-war reached their assigned positions and anchored; as *Arethusa* did so, her bowsprit stuck over the town wall, so small was the port. In pursuance of his orders and the notion that a swift capitulation was likely, Brisbane held his ships' fire and, insouciantly disregarding the hostile gunfire, he leaned upon the *Arethusa*'s main capstan to write a note to the governor, giving him five minutes to surrender. This was despatched by a runner.

The governor ignored the note, the Batavian gunners continued to fire their weapons, and at exactly a quarter past six in the morning Brisbane hauled down the flag of truce. With a reverberating thunder the British frigates loosed off three or four broadsides, and a few minutes later Brisbane boarded the *Kenau Hasselaar* to haul down her colours himself. Captain Wood was then ordered to warp *Latona* alongside and take possession; and at about the same time, Lydiard of the *Anson* captured the *Suriname*.

Having thus seized the ships in the harbour, the four post-captains had themselves pulled ashore in their boats, and at the head of a party of seamen and marines stormed through several of the fortified gun emplacements, including Fort Amsterdam, where sixty cannon lay. By this means they reached the citadel and the town, which swiftly capitulated. The landing parties then returned to the frigates, which by this time had clapped springs on their cables and veered themselves to bring their broadsides to bear on Fort Republiek. After half an hour's bombardment the fort's guns ceased fire, and before noon on New Year's Day, 1807, most of the island was in British hands.

This dashing exploit cost the lives of only three Britons killed and fourteen wounded, but the Batavians suffered severely, losing some two hundred men. Kapitein ter Zee Cornelis Evertsz of the *Kenau Hasselaar* was dead and Kapitein Luitenant ter Zee Jan van Nes of the *Suriname* lay bleeding among the badly wounded. Brisbane and Wood subsequently received knighthoods, and all four British captains were presented with gold medals. Since John Parish first lieutenant of the *Arethusa*, had just been promoted, her second lieutenant, Henry Higman, and the first lieutenants of the other ships, William Mather, Thomas Sulivan and Samuel Jeffery, were all made commanders. A considerable sum in prize-money was also gained from this action, some deriving from the purchase of the *Kenau Hasselaar* into the Royal Navy as the *Halstarr*.

There was now a rash of taking islands. Following the revelations of the secret clauses of Tilsit and the seizure of the Danish fleet at Copenhagen, the Danish islands of Helgoland in the German Bight and Anholt in the Kattegat were garrisoned, the latter by Maurice, former commander of the *Fort Diamond*. It was Helgoland which posed the greatest threat to Napoleon's Empire, however, for it was through the German Bight that the embargo on the importation of British manufactures into Europe was continually broken, while the small British naval squadron attached to the island effectively blockaded the rivers Elbe, Weser, Jade and Ems to French commerce. Helgoland also acted as a recruiting post for young Hanoverians wishing to join the seven infantry battalions and three cavalry regiments of the King's German Legion which after 1809 operated with Wellington's army in the Peninsula. In addition, the island was useful as a 'listening post' through which agents made their way to and from

Hamburg. By this means word of the Spanish uprising of 2 May 1808 was conveyed to the Spanish troops of the Marquís de la Romana which were part of Maréchal Bernadotte's occupying army in Denmark. Romana's men, isolated from the rest of Bernadotte's army, were paraded and, by arrangement, withdrawn by a division of Saumarez's Baltic fleet under the orders of Rear-Admiral Sir Richard Keats; they were then repatriated to Spain, where they took up arms against their former French allies in the liberation of their native land.

Such were the possibilities inherent in sea-power. Wherever Britain could exert influence by these means, she did so. Cruisers were sent to operate on every European coast where the French and their allies used the sea or the coastal roads for the transport of military supplies.

Farther afield, Pellew, now sole Commander-in-Chief on the East Indies station, mounted an increasing offensive against the Batavian Republic's colonies, and grew more concerned about the French presence at Île de France. French corsairs from the island constantly menaced British trade. Their crews, when captured, were exchanged to release much-needed British seamen, and promptly returned to sea if they could evade the British blockade of the island. Because of the prevailing conditions the blockade of Île de France and the outlying islands was very difficult to maintain effectively, and the French were able to reinforce their base repeatedly. In 1806 the 40-gun *Cannonière* arrived after missing a rendezvous with Linois; on her way she had met a convoy of East Indiamen and out-fought and disabled the 74-gun escort *Tremendous*, whose gunnery was very poor. Having reached Île de France she was joined by Epron's *Piémontaise,* and these frigates then reinforced the *Sémillante.* When in 1807 the Admiralty recalled Troubridge – fatally, as has been mentioned for he was lost with his ship on the voyage – the blockade of Île de France was made a responsibility of the flag officer at the Cape of Good Hope, releasing Pellew to reduce the Batavians in Java. In the course of the next four years Pellew and his successor Drury defeated them comprehensively, taking Java and many other islands in a laborious series of under-resourced actions.

Pellew's personal concern was chiefly for his fortune, for that deep vein of cupidity was never far below the surface of the admiral's thoughts. He deliberately stationed his cruisers to intercept the Spanish treasure ships, and in March 1807, in the San Bernardino Strait young Captain Peter Rainier of the *Caroline* intercepted the *San Raphael*, bound from Lima to Manila carrying half a million silver dollars and a cargo of copper. Rainier's prize-money of £50,000, made him the richest post-captain in the navy, but Pellew's share as Commander-in-Chief was £26,000.

Even as he moved against the Batavians on the coast of Java, Pellew was after more prizes. He knew that the insular Japanese permitted two Batavian merchant ships to enter Nagasaki every year, and these were said to bear rich cargoes back to Java for transhipment to Amsterdam. He had been unable to catch these elusive and mysterious ships in 1807, and determined that he would not miss them a second time. Arranging for his son Fleetwood to take command of the *Phaeton,* he sent her north in the following September. On 5 and 6 October 1808 the younger Pellew reconnoitred Nagasaki, an intrusion which was to have unforseen consequences.

The entry of an armed warship into Japanese waters and the illegal and, in Japanese eyes, unwarranted landing of a party of curious British led by Pellew Junior, was a humiliation for the Shōgunate, and aroused their vengeance. The Shōgun ordered the Governor of Nagasaki and the five senior military officers of the province to commit suicide in atonement for the dishonour done to the Emperor. The Prince of Hirzen was confined for several months, in fear of execution. The three wretches who had acted as interpreters were obliged to drown themselves, and the inhabitants of the Prince's lands which lay around Nagasaki were forbidden to use their front doors for the period of His Highness's incarceration. Most significant, however, was the Shōgun's newly-kindled determination to establish a national Japanese navy. Thus to Pellew's exertion of sea-power to its uttermost limits in the cause of his greed may be attributed one of the most profoundly consequential decisions ever taken by an outraged government.

The sheer numbers of British men-of-war at sea now imposed an extremity of demand upon manpower resources, and desertions from

British ships were common where a chance of escape offered. Sympathetic to their plight and eager for the services of prime seamen or pressed and unwilling but competent tradesmen, the United States of America offered a safe refuge for men grown weary of the loss of liberty, the unvarying diet and the casual brutality that were the fate of the thousands of men who expended their lives in King George's service. The pursuit of deserters had become almost as much of an obsession with British officers as their 'right' to search neutral vessels for contraband of war on the high seas. A deserter who had swum to the American frigate *Essex*, lying off Spithead awaiting despatches from the American embassy, was recaptured after a Royal Naval lieutenant boarded the American man-of-war and demanded that the man be given up. Worse was to come, however, and while the right to search might not have become a *casus belli*, such incidents as the encounter between the *Leopard* and the *Chesapeake* were provocative in the extreme.

In June 1807 four men deserted from Royal Naval vessels off the American coast. The British consul at Norfolk in Virginia complained to Captain Stephen Decatur of the Norfolk Navy Yard that they were believed to have enlisted aboard the *Chesapeake*, then fitting for a voyage to the Mediterranean. Of the four men, three had been impressed some months earlier from an American merchantman, on the pretext that, as they had been born before the Treaty of Paris in 1783 which formally ended the American War of Independence, they were notionally 'British'. Decatur refused to give up the men and his decision was approved by James Madison, the Secretary of State.

The *Chesapeake* sailed on 22 June 1807, and that afternoon was hailed by Captain Salusbury Humphreys of the 50-gun *Leopard*, with a request that despatches might be placed on board for carriage to Gibraltar. Commodore James Barron agreed and hove-to, only to be confronted by a lieutenant demanding the surrender of the four deserters, which he naturally refused. On receiving his lieutenant's report, Humphreys ordered *Leopard* to open fire on the unsuspecting *Chesapeake*. Holes riddled her sails, rigging was cut away, twenty-one shot were lodged in her hull, and three dead and eighteen wounded lay upon her deck. The four deserters were given up, and the *Chesapeake* put back into port; Barron was subsequently court-martialled and dismissed from the United States Navy. Of the four 'Britons' thus recovered, one of the deserters was hanged and the other three were sentenced to 500 lashes (though one died prior to the sentence being carried out). The remaining two men were released on the plea of President Jefferson and returned to the *Chesapeake*. War between Britain and America was not really averted, though it seemed so at the time; it was merely postponed.

Humphreys' action was unnecessarily arrogant, but in the absence of a Draconian regime Britain would have had great difficulty – would perhaps have found it impossible – to maintain her fleet at sea. Injustice is inexcusable, but the events of 1775–83 and the present neutrality of the United States led inevitably to touchiness on both sides. As for the wretched seamen attempting to regain a measure of private liberty, desertion was as dangerous as enduring enemy fire, and had to be accepted as entailing a similar risk.

Few sea warriors gave much thought to their sailors as individuals, and while several dealt with them compassionately, there was always the consideration that they were a resource without which a sea-officer's reputation would amount to little. One captain who did consider his men as individuals – and who got scant credit for it from the naval establishment of the day – was Captain Lord Cochrane.

During the years 1806 and 1807, Thomas Cochrane had been making a political reputation for himself the details of which are beyond the scope of this narrative. Suffice it to say that he had stood for Parliament upon an anti-corruption platform, had in due course been elected an MP, and had proceeded to make a thorough nuisance of himself to the Government and the jobbing politicians of his day.

In February of 1808 Cochrane was posted to the 38-gun frigate *Impérieuse*, the former Spanish *Medea*, and directed to harass the enemy's coasts. His cruising station was to the east of Gibraltar, and on 19 February he destroyed a small flotilla of four Spanish gun-boats off Cartagena; on the 21st he attacked a French store-ship under the guns of Almeria, and in the succeeding six weeks he captured ten small coasting vessels and destroyed a signal tower on the Minorcan coast.

In April *Impérieuse* bombarded a fortified tower at Ciudadela in Minorca, and demolished a second on the Majorcan coast. Later that month, in the face of a body of Spanish troops among whom Cochrane dropped a few round-shot, *Impérieuse*'s boats watered from a river on the Spanish coast. On 8 May – *after* the Spanish uprising against the French had begun – Cochrane fired at a fort at the mouth of the Ebro and captured a xebec, then wrecked another flotilla of gun-boats he met off Cape Palos. By now Cochrane had learned of the political *volte-face* that had occurred in Spain, and immediately began to encourage Spanish resistance to French military occupation. Landing wherever he could, he did what ever he could to render the road that ran along the Catalonian coast useless to artillery and cavalry, audaciously wrecking the numerous French batteries maintained to protect coastal waters. Making contact with the Spanish guerrilla chiefs and acting with them, he assisted in the capture and destruction of the fort at Mongat, between Barcelona and Gerona.

By mid August *Impérieuse*'s boats were periodically landing seamen and marines as Cochrane destroyed a whole line of semaphore stations along the shore. He carried off the code books, but strewed burnt paper about to make it look as though the books had been destroyed. Consequently, the French did not bother to change their code, and Cochrane was able to read their messages. This facility he passed on to other cruiser commanders, most notably Captain Jahleel Brenton of the 38-gun frigate *Spartan,* who was similarly occupied.

Having been fired upon by some guns at La Ciotat, *Impérieuse* stood inshore and bombarded the town. Acting in concert, the two sea warriors Cochrane and Brenton then destroyed signal stations in the Gulf of Fos, took a battery at Port Vendres, fired rockets into Cette, burnt pontoons near Montpellier, and raided every coastal convoy they could find. When short of water, Cochrane sent his boats into the mouth of the Rhône, taking the trouble to demolish the rebuilt signal station at Fos while parties of his men filled up their frigate with fresh water.

By October *Impérieuse* was back on the Spanish coast, throwing shot at any detachments of French troops seen on the coastal roads, destroying convoys and capturing military stores, which Cochrane turned over to the guerrillas. The following month Collingwood sent him to relieve the naval garrison landed some time before at Fort Trinidad, a massively strong fortification on the road to Barcelona. Cochrane contrived to hold the position against several assaults, using every artifice he could think of to delay the inevitable capture by French troops and heavy artillery. On one occasion Cochrane – a tall man, it will be recalled – was out reconnoitring the French position with the future novelist Frederick Marryat, then a rather short midshipman doing duty as captain's clerk. Midshipman Marryat, betraying an inclination to duck the occasional musket ball that whined past them, was sternly told to 'stand firm' and do his duty as a bulwark for his commanding officer.

Cochrane's cruises culminated in December when *Impérieuse* captured a supply convoy to the besieged city of Barcelona, destroyed several batteries and sank some more gun-boats. Warmly commended by Collingwood, he received from the Admiralty, where his name awoke only prejudice, a reproach for expending too much powder and shot.

At the end of December 1807 Cochrane's uncle, Rear-Admiral Sir Alexander Cochrane, had left Barbados and, following the Treaty of Tilsit, taken the Danish islands of St Groix and St Thomas. Under the terms of the Peace of Amiens the French had retained Guadeloupe, Martinique, Guiana and San Domingo, though this last colony was threatened by the neighbouring hostile black state of Haiti and, after May 1808, by the Spanish at Puerto Rico.

The protection of British commerce remained a priority, one pursued aggressively by the destruction of safe havens for the swarms of corsairs that operated for profit from French-held islands. The French navy constantly attempted to resupply their West Indian possessions, in the teeth of the British Navy's hounding-down of enemy cruisers known to have escaped the blockade, that vital cornerstone of British naval policy. An increasing British stranglehold on West Indian waters effectively kept the remaining French colonies under siege, and by 1808 the plight of Martinique had become desperate. In August the three corvettes *Diligente*, *Sylphe* and *Espiègle* were loaded with supplies for

Captain Lord Cochrane

Captain David Porter (USN)

Captain Sir William Hoste

Captain Sir Charles Brisbane

Captain James Lawrence (USN)

Captain Sir Philip Broke

Captain Isaac Hull (USN)

Captain William Bainbridge (USN)

Commodore Sir Nathaniel Dance of
the Honourable East India Company

Commander John Wesley Wright

Captain James Bowen

The youthful Captain Fleetwood Pellew

*Centaur* hoists a gun up Diamond Rock, January 1804

The brig-sloop *Speedy* rescues survivors from *Queen Charlotte* off Livorno, March 1800

Cause of war: *Mercedes* explodes, October 1804

*Shannon* captures *Chesapeake*, June 1813

*Juno* escapes from Toulon, January 1794

the island, but upon sailing were seen in the Bay of Biscay by the British 18-gun sloop *Comet* (Commander Cuthbert Daly) which forced Lieutenant de Vaisseau Louis Clément of the *Sylphe* to strike. On the 16th the remaining two corvettes fell in with the 38-gun British frigate *Sibylle* (Captain Clotworthy Upton), which took *Espiègle*. *Diligente* again escaped, until she was spotted by the little *Recruit* (Commander Charles Napier), off Antigua on 6th September. A hot action followed, but *Recruit*'s mainmast fell, whereupon Commander Lemaresquier raked his enemy and ran for Martinique. *Recruit* limped back to Carlisle Bay in Barbados, Napier nursing a smashed thigh, the femur of which stuck through his flesh, his only lieutenant mortally wounded, and the ship under the command of her sailing master.

A further attempt was made to pass reinforcements and stores to Martinique in November 1808. Commanded by Capitaine Jacques Pinsum, the 40-gun frigate *Thétis* slipped out of L'Orient, only to be seen off Île de Groix by the 36-gun frigate *Amethyst* (Captain Michael Seymour) on the evening of the 10th. Signalling an enemy's escape to other British ships offshore, Seymour made sail in pursuit. At about nine that night the two frigates, both running before the wind, fired their chase guns. It seemed inevitable to Pinsum that *Amethyst* would overhaul *Thétis,* so he suddenly hauled *Thétis* onto the starboard tack, intending to pass ahead of the British frigate and rake her. Seymour was vigilant enough to turn *Amethyst* inside *Thétis,* however, and the two vessels swung through a complete circle before running off before the wind again, *Amethyst* now slightly ahead of *Thétis*. Pinsum now crossed *Amethyst*'s stern, intending to rake her, but *Thétis*'s jib-boom fouled on *Amethyst*, and Pinsum which aborted the manoeuvre. When the jib-boom had torn clear, both frigates ran on as before, neck-and-neck. At about ten o'clock *Amethyst* drew ahead, whereupon Seymour put his helm over, crossed *Thétis*'s bow and fired a raking broadside into her before turning away to run before the wind again. At this point the mizen masts of both vessels fell.

Pinsum decided to settle the issue by boarding, and called his crew and the troops he had embarked to make ready. But as the frigates collided the French were assailed by a furious cannonade and a succession of broadsides which devastated *Thétis,* dismounting thirteen guns, smashing in her sides and scything through the assembled boarders. A few minutes after midnight, the Amethysts boarded and took *Thétis*, her decks deserted but for the sole living occupant of the quarterdeck, Lieutenant Dedé, who submitted his sword. As he did so, the two masts remaining to the *Thétis* crashed to the deck. Pinsum and 134 officers, seamen and soldiers were killed, to British losses of 19 killed and 51 wounded.

The French sent more stores out to Martinique from Cherbourg in November, but only a few ships got through, and the island fell to an expeditionary force of ten thousand troops from Barbados under Rear-Admiral Sir Alexander Cochrane and Lieutenant-General Beckwith in January 1809. Faced with an overwhelming force, Vice-Admiral Villaret-Joyeuse, the captain-general, eventually capitulated on 24 February, after a spirited resistance.

A final effort to relieve Martinique was made by Commodore Troude, who left France early in 1809, with three seventy-fours, *Courageux, Polonais* and *D'Hautpoult*, and two former frigates, *Félicité* and *Furieuse*, both armed as store-ships. When he reached the West Indies and learned of Martinique's capture, Troude made instead for Les Saintes. Hearing of this, Cochrane decided to take the little archipelago, but Troude and his men-of-war slipped away. He was seen by *Hazard,* and reported to Cochrane. Offshore with Cochrane's flagship the *Neptune* were *York, Pompée, Polyphemus* and *Recruit*, and a general chase began. *Pompée* and *Recruit* caught up with Troude's *D'Hautpoult* and opened fire. Cochrane's *Neptune* then came up, but the French ships increased their distance and only the *Recruit* was able to hang onto their coat-tails during the night. Commander Charles Napier's leg had mended and the 18-gun *Recruit* annoyed the heavier French vessels through the hours of darkness, compelling them to yaw and fire broadsides at her. By the evening of 15 April 1809 *Pompée* had again caught up and the French were forced to scatter. *D'Hautpoult* steered to the west-north-west, with *Pompée* astern, while *Neptune* and *Recruit* followed *Courageux* and *Polonais*. The chase ran on into the 16th, when the frigates *Latona* and *Castor* joined *Pompée*. Before daylight, *Castor* was close enough to disable *D'Hautpoult* until *Pompée* arrived to force Troude to close action. British men-of-war were now arriving from every point of the compass, and shortly after five in the morning *D'Hautpoult* submitted. Napier was placed in command of her, and soon afterwards made post-captain.

*Courageux* and *Polonais* escaped to Cherbourg, but the store-ships *Furieuse* and *Félicité* were not so lucky. They left Les Saintes on the night of 15 April and discharged their desperately-needed cargoes at Guadeloupe, then sailed from Basse-Terre on the night of 14 June, only to be chased until the 18th, when the *Latona* caught up with and captured the *Félicité*. *Furieuse* was free until she ran into the 20-gun sloop *Bonne Citoyenne* on 15 July in mid Atlantic. Commander Mounsey manoeuvred his fast, formerly French corvette skilfully and in seven hours exhausted his ammunition, firing 129 broadsides to the *Furieuse*'s 70. Mounsey then worked athwart *Furieuse*'s hawse to board, upon which *Furieuse* struck and was taken in to Halifax.

In November 1809 an Anglo-Spanish force attacked and took San Domingo; thus, of all the French Antilles there remained to the Empire only Guadeloupe. French frigates had been running supplies through intermittently and in the autumn of 1809 *Renomée* and *Clorinde*, both of 40 guns, and the former 40-gun *Loire* and *Seine*, reduced to store-ships of 20 guns, were sent out from France. They were chased off Antigua on 13 December by *Junon* (Captain John Shortland), and the sloop *Observateur* (Commander Frederick Wetherall). *Renomée* received *Junon* with a devastating broadside and *Clorinde* immediately engaged, while *Loire* and *Seine* raked from ahead and astern. Captain Shortland was wounded five times, but did not strike until a quarter of his crew had fallen. So shattered was the *Junon* that she was burnt by her captors, and Shortland died of his wounds on 21 January 1810.

Meanwhile Wetherall in the *Observateur,* knowing the destination of the French, had run ahead to contact Captain Ballard of the *Blonde*, the British frigate off Guadeloupe. Informed of the situation, Ballard joined *Thetis,* and the two 38-gun frigates, together with the two 18-gun sloops *Hazard* and *Cygnet,* lay in a cordon between Les Saintes and Guadeloupe. On 16 January Ballard was reinforced by the 18-gun sloops *Scorpion* and *Ringdove*. On the 17th *Castor*, 32, arrived with the French in pursuit astern. Seeing the waiting British squadron ahead, the French turned round and headed for the shelter of the shore batteries at Guadeloupe. As Ballard went after them, more British men-of-war arrived on the scene, and by the next day he had been joined by the 36-gun frigate *Freiya* and the 74-gun *Sceptre*. On the 18th the British attacked in force, but *Renommée* and *Clorinde* slipped away along the shore to the northward. *Sceptre* and *Freija* engaged the shore batteries, which were also attacked by a landing party from the sloops under Cameron of *Hazard*, while *Thetis* and *Blonde* fired on the two store-ships. Both soon capitulated, but they caught fire and their cargoes were lost.

The game was up. The British frigate *Melampus*, 36, had taken the brig *Béarnais*, 16, off Guadeloupe on 14 December 1809; *Rosamond*, 18, had seized her consort the *Papillon* on the 19th; on 11th January 1810 Ballard despatched *Scorpion* to Basse-Terre, Guadeloupe, to cut out the 16-gun brig *Oreste,* and on the 21st, Hayes of the *Freija* took some small vessels in Baie Mahaut. Finally, on the 27th, Rear-Admiral Sir Alexander Cochrane arrived from Martinique with 7,000 troops under Beckwith. They marched across the mountains to corner General Ernouf in Basse-Terre. After a few days of skirmishing, Ernouf capitulated on 6th February. In the succeeding fortnight Beckwith and Cochrane mopped up the remaining small Dutch colonies of St Martin, St Eustatius and Saba. Thus, excepting the black republic of Haiti, the entire West Indies were in the hands of either Great Britain or her new ally, Spain.

The war in the West Indies was ended in a final bizarre act. After the death of Dessalines, Britain recognised both the Haitian kingdom of King Christophe and the adjacent Dominican Republic of President Pétion as independent sovereign states. In early 1812 a renegade from Christophe's navy, a former corsair named Gaspard, was illegally raiding trade in the 44-gun frigate *Améthyste,* formerly the French frigate *Félicité,* sold to King Christophe after being taken by the *Latona*. In February 1812 Gaspard's piratical vessel lay in the Bight of Léogane while Captain Yeo's elderly frigate *Southampton* was lying at Port-au-

Prince. Yeo slipped to sea under cover of darkness on the 2nd and challenged Gaspard's legitimacy the following day. Gaspard responded with a broadside, precipitating an action in which *Southampton* shot away *Améthyste*'s main and mizen masts, causing terrible slaughter and killing Gaspard. After her surrender to Yeo, the refitted *Améthyste* was restored to King Christophe.

Thus ended the war in the West Indies. The Royal Navy's numerous and ubiquitous cruisers wrecked all French ambitions there, guaranteeing the deployment of British troops wherever they were considered necessary. The climate was highly destructive to any shore-bound garrisons, but the actions of the Royal Navy robbed France of the economic value of her sugar islands.

# CHAPTER 14

## 'Remember Nelson'

In the period between Tilsit and the outbreak of war with the United States, the cruisers of the Royal Navy were engaged world-wide in both offensive and defensive warfare. The tedious business of trade convoys, to which was now added the escort of military transports to the Iberian Peninsula, went on as a matter of routine. In the East as in the West Indies, cruisers were used systematically to reduce enemy possessions, while in the Baltic Sea, North Sea, Irish Sea and English Channel the war with French, Danish and Dutch privateers was at its height.

Meanwhile Great Britain's principal battle fleets, supported by semi-independent cruisers, continued the wearing work of blockade. The Channel Fleet continued to maintain its relentless patrols off the French Atlantic ports, with Saumarez in the Baltic and Collingwood in the Mediterranean coping with complex diplomatic issues on top of their strategic commitments. Occasionally a single cruiser would be required to enforce policies that Government demanded.

Nominally neutral after Tilsit, Constantinople was in the throes of a power-struggle after the Russian victory of Lemnos, and British relations with the Turks remained strained after the shambles of Duckworth's mission. Generally there was a desire not to press the Turks too hard, though the boats of the *Glatton* and *Hirondelle* had cut out a specie-laden Turkish ship from the harbour of Sigri on Mytilene (modern

Lesbos) on 1 March 1807. But the only formal agreement concluded between the two countries was 'an understanding' that Turkish men-of-war would avoid cruising in the Aegean or attempt to exact tribute from the Greeks. To ensure this, Collingwood had left Captain John Stewart in the 42-gun frigate *Seahorse* among the Sporades. However, the Turks were determined, and not without reason, to extirpate a nest of rebellious Epirots engaged in piracy from the Gulf of Salonika; knowing that only a lone British frigate was in the area, they sent a squadron to attend to the matter.

Anchored off Skíros on 1 July 1808, Stewart heard of Turkish ships-of-war off Chiliodhromía in the Northern Sporades. He weighed and made sail in search of them. In heavy squalls *Seahorse* was compelled to triple-reef her topsails, but by late afternoon of the 5th the weather had moderated. *Seahorse* caught sight of two men-of-war, and gave chase. All three ships were heading south in a northerly breeze and Stewart cleared for action as *Seahorse* began to work up onto the wind-ward quarter of the larger of the two strange vessels. Stewart now perceived that his larger quarry was an Ottoman ship, and was aware that she would be better manned than *Seahorse,* which in addition to suffering the chronic shortage of men prevalent throughout the Royal Navy had men absent in prizes. Darkness fell and the three ships turned to the westward, with the light wind on their starboard quarters; it was half-past nine in the evening before *Seahorse* drew close to the starboard side of the 52-gun *Badere-I-Zaffer,* whose smaller consort *Alis Fezzan,* 26, was to leeward. The *Seahorse* loomed very close to *Badere-I-Zaffer* and Stewart called upon his pilot, a Gibraltarian who had been a slave of the Turks and spoke their language, to hail the *Badere-I-Zaffer* and demand her surrender.

This peremptory summons was ignored by Albay (Senior Captain) Scandril Kichuc-Ali, and Stewart ordered a double-shotted broadside fired into the Ottoman ship. Scandril immediately returned fire and a fierce action began, with Scandril edging away to allow the *Alis Fezzan* to engage *Seahorse.* As soon as Yarbay (Junior Captain) Duragardi-Ali's guns could fire across *Badere-I-Zaffer*'s stern and hit *Seahorse,* Scandril turned his ship to starboard with the intention of running alongside *Seahorse* and boarding her. Divining this, Stewart had *Seahorse*'s helm put hard over, hauled his yards round and luffed up sharp into the wind, continuing the swing until he had come round onto the larboard tack and exposed his starboard battery to the enemy.

Frustrated, Scandril now wore round, passing his stern through the eye of the wind, and both vessels then ran back to the eastwards, some distance apart but on converging courses. Duragardi-Ali also paid off his ship before the wind, and at about ten o'clock found *Seahorse* surging up on his port quarter, taking the wind from *Alis Fezzan*'s sails and rapidly over-hauling him. Stewart fired his starboard broadside into the Turkish sloop, caused an explosion on board and in fifteen minutes had reduced her to a wreck. Duragardi-Ali luffed under the stern of *Seahorse* and broke off the engagement.

Stewart next stood on after *Badere-I-Zaffer*, closing her so fast that at half-past ten he ordered *Seahorse*'s topgallant yards dropped and the fight resumed. Both vessels squared their yards before the breeze, which had now worked round to the north. For some time *Seahorse*'s starboard guns fired at *Badere-I-Zaffer*'s port battery, until Scandril again attempted to run on board his assailant; but as he did so *Seahorse* scraped ahead of *Badere-I-Zaffer*, cutting down a crowd of boarders mustered on the Turkish ship's forecastle with grape from her stern chase guns. Both ships suffered slight damage, and the *Badere-I-Zaffer* now caught up with *Seahorse*. Stewart reopened fire, but with his larboard battery exchanging fire with *Badere-I-Zaffer*'s starboard guns. At this point the Turk's mizen topmast fell.

It was now almost midnight, and the *Badere-I-Zaffer*'s guns were falling silent. Stewart repeatedly summoned *Badere-I-Zaffer* to surrender, but there was no reply, even as her two remaining topmasts fell. Stewart crossed the Ottoman's stern, then ranged up close on his opponent's port quarter to repeat his summons. Scandril replied with the discharge of some quarter guns, whereupon *Seahorse* 'instantly discharged her starboard broadside'. By now it was after one in the morning of 6 July; both antagonists hove-to on westerly headings and their exhausted crews dropped asleep at their posts, although the *Seahorse* fired an occasional gun 'to keep the Turks awake'.

At daylight *Badere-I-Zaffer* was seen to be making way, her shredded courses squared before the wind and her ensign still aloft. *Seahorse* made sail after her, ran across her stern and raked her yet again with her starboard broadside. Captain Scandril remained sitting on his quarterdeck, determined not to surrender to the infidels despite the wreckage all about him. By now his crew had had enough, however, and a few of his officers seized him and hauled down the Ottoman colours. Brought aboard *Seahorse*, Scandril was reluctant to give up his Damascus sword, but the British prize crew under Lieutenant Downie were already taking possession of their shattered prize. The *Badere-I-Zaffer* was wrecked aloft, hulled and leaking. Out of a total company of 543 men, she had lost about 170 killed and 200 wounded, many fatally. The under-manned British frigate's sea-time and experience had told against her enemy, and Stewart's ship-handling had been superb, particularly in a night action. *Seahorse* had suffered the minor loss of her mizen topmast, though her sails were shot through. Her crew had fared far better than their enemy, losing only five men killed and ten wounded out of a company of 251 men and boys.

The *Seahorse* arrived at Miconi with her prize in tow. On the way Scandril, who had been returned to his captured ship, tried to blow her up. At Miconi it took three days to re-rig *Badere-I-Zaffer* and render her sea-worthy. Stewart sent her crew back to Constantinople in Greek vessels, then towed *Badere-I-Zaffer* to Malta. There she was sold to Maltese traders who loaded her with Egyptian cotton and despatched her to London. She then made a voyage to Brazil and back, before being broken up at Deptford. After the action *Seahorse* took a British plenipotentiary to Constantinople, and there she passed *Alis Fezzan* in a dismantled state. The diplomatic initiative resulted in a peace treaty being signed on 5 January 1809 with Mahmud II, the new sultan who had emerged triumphant from the intrigues in the Topkapi.

Elsewhere in the Mediterranean, while Collingwood and his successors Cotton and in due course Sir Edward Pellew maintained the blockade of Toulon, the French vassal kingdoms of Naples and Italy along with the south coasts of France and Spain were all targets for intimidation by British cruisers. These also maintained a watch upon smaller ports, to reinforce the blockade and to hamper the movements of all hostile merchant shipping or men-of-war making their way towards the arsenal of Toulon from their building yards at Spezzia or Livorno.

The ingenuity and determination of British frigate captains, though occasionally verging on the reckless, gained them a fearsome reputation. On 22 May 1810 Captain Murray Maxwell of the *Alceste* chased some small French feluccas into the heavily fortified bay of Agay on the Gulf of Fréjus. That night Maxwell sent two boats into the bay, which was covered by batteries. One, led by Lieutenant Wilson, failed to storm a battery; the other, commanded by Henry Bell, the master, was exposed to a heavy fire before the seamen and marines managed to spike the guns in the second battery. *Alceste* then lay offshore for three days, until the night of the 25th when Maxwell sent Bell and a midshipman named Adair in two armed boats to lie in a rocky cove; he then stood out to sea, as though abandoning his attack on the convoy. As the coasters resumed their passage next morning, Bell and Adair attacked them, taking four in spite of gunfire from ashore and a sharp resistance from the feluccas' crews.

Off Corsica at dawn on 26 May 1811 the 20-gun brig-corvette *Arbeille* fell in with the British 18-gun sloop *Alacrity* (Commander Nesbit Palmer). The *Arbeille* was a converted American brig, and under Lieutenant de Vaisseau Ange de Mackau she hove-to and awaited the British sloop. De Mackau, a competent seaman, ably raked *Alacrity* several times, shooting not at her rigging but along her decks, wrecking her rudder head and tiller and causing severe casualties. Palmer was wounded early in the action, went below to have a cut hand dressed and failed to reappear on deck. His lieutenant, Thomas Rees, was badly wounded, but sat upon a gun and exhorted the crew until he was killed. Soon afterwards the master was wounded and, since his mate had been mortally wounded, command of *Alacrity* fell upon the gunner, who demurred. The boatswain, James Flaxman, thereupon fought the ship hard until Palmer sent up word from below that he should surrender. Flaxman, now wounded himself, grabbed a pistol from the binnacle and roared out that he would shoot the first man who touched the ensign halliards, but the gunner insisted, and *Alacrity* submitted. Palmer contracted tetanus poisoning from his trivial injury, and was accordingly allowed the dignity of having 'died of his wounds', thus avoiding dishonour. De Mackau distinguished himself, was promoted and became a baron of the French Empire.

Such British reverses were the exception. All along these coasts and up the Adriatic to the lagoons of Venice, men like Cochrane and Brenton mercilessly plagued the enemy. The ships and their commanders acquired almost legendary status. Captain The Honourable Henry Duncan followed Cochrane into the *Impérieuse*; Brenton's *Spartan* was joined by the 32-gun *Success* (Captain John Ayscough) and scored some notable coups; Captain James Brisbane fanned the *Belle-Poule's* reputation under British colours. Captain Sir Peter Parker of the *Menelaus* was proving a most able cruiser commander when he was killed in action ashore fighting in America, while in successive command of the frigates *Thames* and *Euryalus,* Captain 'Mad Black Charlie' Napier, who had been made post after the capture of the *D'Hautpoult* in the West Indies, was actively acquiring his famous nickname. In later life, as 'Carlo de Ponza', he was to command a Portuguese fleet and defeat the rebel Miguellites off Cape St Vincent. An eccentric, he would insist on his officers wearing uniform while he sported odd garments, a habit he took with him to the Baltic when he commanded a British fleet there during the 'Crimean' War. By then Napier was in his sixties and his conduct was less than satisfactory, but as a young man his mixture of dash and disregard for convention made him an inspiring sea warrior.

The luckiest of these sea warriors was William Hoste, who was destined to fight the last formal battle of the war. Hoste had gone to sea in 1793, a protégé of Nelson. Having served as a lieutenant in the *Theseus* at the Battle of the Nile, he was promoted and followed Thomas Masterman Hardy as commander of the brig-sloop *Mutine*. In 1808 he arrived in the Adriatic in the 32-gun frigate *Amphion* to harry the coasts of Italy. At that time the provinces of Dalmatia and Illyria and the island of Corfu were in French hands, and required blockading. The Venetian navy had been seized by the French, and the shipyards of the former republic were engaged in building ships for Napoleon.

In the summer of 1810 Hoste was thirty years old, and senior officer of the frigates stationed in the Adriatic. In company under his orders he had the 32-gun frigate *Cerberus* (Captain Henry Whitby, a protégé of Admiral Sir William Cornwallis) and the 38-gun frigate *Active* (Captain James Gordon). As a base the squadron used an anchorage on the Dalmatian island of Lissa which they had named Port St George. Hoste had so successfully 'annoyed the enemy' during the summer that a French squadron was sent to reinforce the Venetians and wrest domination of the Adriatic from him. This the French considered as possible as it was desirable: the Strait of Otranto, commanded by the French-held island of Corfu, should have been closed to British ships, making the Adriatic a French lake and permitting free trade throughout the area.

On 29 September 1810, the Franco-Venetian squadron was formed at Chioggia near Venice under Commodore Dubourdieu in the 44-gun *Favourite*; the *Favourite*'s captain was Louis Le Marre La Meillerie. On 6 October Dubourdieu was off Ancona, where *Amphion* and *Active* found him. Having left *Cerberus* at Lissa, Hoste withdrew to the east, with Dubourdieu in half-hearted chase. The French commodore did not persist, but returned to his anchorage off Ancona. Reaching Lissa, Hoste signalled Whitby to weigh, and with *Cerberus* and the newly-arrived sloop *Acorn* returned across the Adriatic towards Ancona, only to find the anchorage now empty.

Hoste now headed south, expecting Dubourdieu to have made for Corfu; but finding no trace of the French, he returned to Lissa. Here he discovered that Dubourdieu had seized Port St George, captured Hoste's prizes anchored in the bay, and driven into the hills the party left in charge of the signal station. He had then retired to Ancona, and there he lay at anchor until 11 March 1811, when he embarked 500 soldiers. His squadron now consisted of the French 44-gun frigates *Favourite*, *Flore* (Capitaine Jean Péridier) and *Danaë* (Capitaine Villon), and the Venetian frigates *Corona*, 44 guns (Capitano Pasquaglio), *Bellona* (Capitano Duodo), the 32-gun *Carolina*, (Capitano Baralovich), the corvettes *Principessa Augusta* of 18 guns (Capitano Bolognini), the 10-gun *Principessa di Bologna* (Capitano Raggio) and the lesser craft

*Lodola,* of 2 guns, and *Eugenio,* 6. Dubourdieu's intention was to deprive Hoste of Lissa prior to annihilating the British squadron.

Hoste's three frigates, now without *Acorn* but with the 22-gun sloop *Volage* (Captain Phipps Hornby), encountered Dubourdieu in the early hours of 13 March off the north point of Lissa. In a strong north-north-westerly wind, Hoste made the night signal to chase, which required the British to get to windward of the enemy. At daylight Dubourdieu came down from the north in two divisions, *Favourite, Flore, Bellona* and *Principessa Augusta* forming the weather or starboard division, with *Danaë, Corona, Carolina* and the others in the lee or larboard division. Hoste led his ships across the enemy's track on the starboard tack, with *Active, Volage* and *Cerberus* following in his wake and the signal 'Remember Nelson' flying from *Amphion*'s masthead.

Perhaps himself remembering Nelson, Dubourdieu sought to break the British line in two places, but the close formation of the British cruisers and the ferocity of their gunfire foiled him. As the action began in mid forenoon *Favourite*'s decks were swept by a hail of hundreds of musket balls discharged from a howitzer aboard *Amphion,* and Dubourdieu fell. Finding themselves close inshore about forty minutes later, Hoste's squadron wore round onto an easterly course. *Cerberus*'s rudder was fouled by a shot, compromising her position in the line, but Hornby swung the little *Volage* inside her to take the leading position on the port tack. Meanwhile *Favourite* ran aground, passing out of the action, to leave Capitaine Péridier's *Flore* leading the Franco-Venetian weather division. As Hoste headed away to clear the island, *Flore* ran across *Amphion*'s stern and hauled her yards onto the port tack, taking station on *Amphion*'s starboard and lee quarter. Following Péridier, Capitano Duodo of *Bellona* came up on Hoste's larboard quarter.

Meanwhile *Danaë,* leading the allied lee column, wore onto the larboard tack to engage *Volage,* the *Corona* and *Carolina* following. The British sloop was close enough to damage the enemy with her 32-pound carronades, but Duodo hauled out of range – whereupon Hornby of *Volage* unwisely increased his charges, until his carronades broke their breechings and split their slides, reducing *Volage*'s armament to her 6-pounder bow chasers. Whitby's *Cerberus* had by now been engaged by *Corona* and endured a punishing fire from the Venetian frigate, a sharp contrast to her consort *Carolina*, whose Baralovich hung back from the action.

Having avoided *Active* to attack the weaker *Volage*, *Danaë* was now caught by Gordon as he pressed up to assist his consorts ahead. *Active's* intervention saved the *Cerberus* and *Volage*, whose opponents now disengaged to the eastward, making sail.

Hoste, fighting off both *Flore* and *Bellona*, now coolly crossed ahead of *Flore*, to pour shot into her lee bow until she struck her colours. But Duodo equally boldly passed astern of *Flore* and raked *Amphion*, whereupon Hoste wore *Amphion* to approach *Bellona* on the opposite tack. *Amphion's* broadsides brought down *Bellona's* Venetian colours, and a few shot at *Principessa Augusta* caused her to sheer away. Leaving a boat to take care of the prizes, Hoste ran up the signal for a general chase, wore round again and stood after his other three vessels, only to see the surrendered *Flore* making sail.

Hoste was furious that the *Flore's* officers, having struck, now took advantage of the fact that *Amphion* had been so engaged at the time that Hoste had been unable to take formal possession of his prize.

*Cerberus* and *Volage* were not able to pursue, so *Amphion* and *Active* went after the retreating enemy, *Danaë* having made sail to cover the escape of *Flore*. *Active* was now in pursuit of *Corona*, and eventually engaged her from her lee beam until, after about forty minutes, Pasquaglio capitulated. *Carolina* and *Danaë* now joined the *Flore* and the smaller vessels running for the shelter of the guns of Lessina, an island to the eastward.

Damage and casualties were heavy on both sides. The British suffered 45 killed and 145 wounded, with Hoste among the latter. In *Bellona* Duodo was among the seventy-odd casualties, and died of his wounds; Péridier of *Flore* was also badly wounded. Dubourdieu had died at the outset and his flag-captain, La Marre Le Meillerie, also lay dead among *Favourite's* 150 casualties. Hard aground, *Favourite* was set on fire by her crew before they scrambled ashore to give themselves up to two British midshipmen left on Lissa in charge of the signal station and the prizes. These young men had not been idle bystanders during the action, for the Venetian schooner *Lodola* had entered St George's Bay, where

Capitano Cotta summoned the Sicilian privateer *Vincitoire* to surrender, to which her master agreed. The midshipmen promptly put off in boats, and drove off the *Lodola* and retook *Vincitoire.*

Hoste remained in the Mediterranean, transferring into *Bacchante* the following year and distinguishing himself at Cattaro and Ragusa. He was made a Knight of Austria and created a baronet in 1814, becoming a Knight Commander of the Order of the Bath in 1815. In 1822 he was appointed to command the Portsmouth guardship *Albion,* and in 1825 he was made captain of the Royal Yacht *Royal Sovereign.* But Sir William's health was broken, and he was involved in tortuous wrangles over prize-money; he was not destined to make old bones, and died in 1828. He was more fortunate than most of his generation of sea warriors, for his close early connection with his Norfolk neighbour ensured that his statue was placed next to Nelson's in St Paul's Cathedral.

By this time command of the Mediterranean from Constantinople to Gibraltar was firmly in the hands of the British: but it was otherwise in the Baltic, where only the Franco-Russian breach of 1812 ended the anxieties of Sir James Saumarez.

Saumarez had to ensure that as little disruption as possible took place to the importation of those commodities necessary for the maintenance of the British navy. These naval stores came from both the neutral and belligerent states bordering the Baltic Sea, those from the latter under license, breaking Napoleon's 'Continental System'. The greater the encouragement of Russian trade, which the Russian economy desperately required, the more likely was it that a rift would open between the bosom friends of Tilsit, Napoleon and Tsar Alexander. War had been formally declared between Sweden and Russia in 1808, and from his flagship *Victory*, usually anchored in Vinga Sound on the coast of south-west Sweden, Saumarez did everything possible to assist the Swedes in prosecuting it.

The dimension of Saumarez's responsibilities is simply illustrated by three convoys of 1810. In late May, 362 outward-bound vessels were escorted by the *Princess Carolina*, 74, the former Danish *Prindsesse Carolina*; in late July 332 merchantmen had only the escort of the frigate *Hussar.* The homeward convoy passing simultaneously through the Great Belt was of 220 ships, escorted by the frigate *Fisgard* and the brig-sloop *Renard*.

It was always the weather that posed the greatest threat to wind-driven ships, and the winter of 1811 proved a hard one. Thirty ships of a homeward-bound convoy of seventy-two vessels were wrecked in a storm, driving ashore near Nysted in the entrance to the Great Belt. As the remnant waited for the weather to moderate, they were joined by three line-of-battle ships, the 98-gun *St George*, flying the flag of Rear-Admiral Reynolds, which had been damaged in the same storm, the *Defence* and the *Cressy*. When conditions improved the merchantmen and warships left the Skagerrak, only to run into another storm, the wind in which rose to hurricane force. The jury-rigged *St George* fell to leeward, running aground on the Jutland coast with the loss of all but six of the 850 souls on board. *Defence*, a Trafalgar ship, was also wrecked, losing 518 men, only a dozen surviving. Further south in the North Sea another convoy of 120 sail was dispersed and its escort of the 74-gun *Hero*, and the sloop *Grasshopper* were lost.

Saumarez could do little about the weather, but the dispositions of his cruisers were carefully made to protect trade passing through the Great Belt, off Langeland and Nyborg, and in The Sound near Copenhagen. In Hangö lay a Russian fleet of nine line-of-battle ships, two 50-gun ships, eight frigates and corvettes, two brigs and two cutters under Vitse-Admiral Hanikov. A weak and poor-quality Swedish fleet of seven sail-of-the-line and some frigates, almost a third of whose crews were suffering from scurvy, was anchored off Oro nearby, and Saumarez sent Rear-Admiral Sir Samuel Hood in *Centaur*, with *Implacable* (Captain Thomas Byam Martin), to stiffen them. Hood joined Konteramiral Nauckhoff's Swedish squadron on 20 August 1808, and the following evening Hanikov's Russians loomed in the offing before withdrawing. On the 22nd reinforcements brought Nauckhoff's line-of-battle ships to ten. Next day Hanikov reappeared, making a bold approach before again retiring to the south.

Early on the 25th the Anglo-Swedish squadron got under weigh in pursuit of the Russians, catching sight of them off Hangö Udd, the south-western extremity of Russian-occupied Finland. Here Nauckhoff transferred the worst of his sick to the *Frederic-Adolph* for passage to Karlskrona before resuming the chase. By four o'clock on the morning of 26 August the pursuit was being led by the two copper-bottomed British ships, with the 74-gun *Implacable* two miles ahead of *Centaur* and the Swedes a dozen miles astern. Martin beat on to windward, convinced by the press of sail and wide dispersal of his ships that Hanikov (who had previously served with the Royal Navy) was anxious to avoid action. In due course the rearmost Russian, the 74-gun *Sevolod*, crossed *Implacable*'s bow on the starboard tack, and Martin immediately altered course to pursue. Two hours later *Sevolod* tacked again and, as she crossed *Implacable*'s bow, opened fire. Martin fired back, then turned into *Sevolod*'s wake and began to run up under her lee. By half-past seven the two men-of-war were within 'pistol-shot'. *Implacable* shot away *Sevolod*'s colours, the Russian guns fell silent, and about thirty minutes later Kapitan Rudnov struck his pendant.

Astern of *Implacable*, Sir Samuel Hood had watched Martin engage *Sevolod*, but had also seen that Hanikov had reversed his squadron and was running down to the support of *Sevolod*. Hood hoisted the recall, obliging Martin to abandon *Sevolod,* which was taken in tow by a Russian frigate as *Implacable* withdrew. The two British ships fell back towards Nauckhoff, some ten miles to leeward, giving Martin an opportunity to refit his rigging. This completed, the two British ships hauled their wind and dashed after the Russians again. Nauckhoff's heavy ships were still some miles away, but the 66-gun *Tapperheten* and the Swedish frigates were closer. Despite this, Hanikov again avoided action and the Russians, taking advantage of a wind-shift to the north-east, headed for Ragersvik (close to modern Tallin). Approaching this refuge, the *Sevolod* ran onto a shoal; after Hanikov's other ships had safely anchored, the Russian admiral sent boats back to get her refloated. By lightening her and carrying out anchors, *Sevolod* was hauled off the shoal and by the evening was being towed into Ragersvik by the boats of the Russian squadron.

This was the moment when Hood appeared, to run *Centaur* alongside *Sevolod,* fouling her bowsprit. As the two ships collided, *Centaur*'s guns fired into *Sevolod* at point-blank range until *Sevolod*'s bowsprit, caught in *Centaur*'s mizen rigging, had been lashed by *Centaur*'s officers under a storm of musketry. A fierce mêlée raged for possession of both ships as *Sevolod*'s anchor was let go.

*Implacable* now anchored a cable away and, baring her teeth, compelled the Russians to surrender the *Sevolod* a second time. But this was not the end of the affair, for *Centaur* and *Sevolod* now dragged astern onto the shoal, and Hanikov ordered two of his ships out of Ragersvik to recapture *Sevolod* and, if possible, take *Centaur*. The British managed to heave *Centaur* into deep water, and abandoned their chances of carrying off the *Sevolod* by setting her ablaze. Equally frustrated, the Russian ships re-anchored.

On 30 August Saumarez anchored off Ragersvik to join Nauckhoff and Hood. In addition to *Victory*, he had in company the line-of-battle ships *Mars, Goliath* and *Africa*. By this time Hanikov had taken due precautions, mooring his ships so that their broadsides commanded the approach, erecting batteries on East Raga island and fortifying the anchorage with chain booms. The extent of the defences was reconnoitred by Captain Bathurst of the frigate *Salsette* and Captain Trolle of the Swedish frigate *Camilla*, but not before fireships had been made ready to send into Ragersvik. Saumarez blockaded Ragersvik until October, when the ice had began to form. He then retired to Karlskrona with Nauckhoff, leaving Hanikov to escape to Kronstadt before the onset of winter. There were to be no further major confrontations in the Baltic until Russia resumed her place as an ally of Great Britain.

The greatest challenge to Saumarez, and in fact to British maritime supremacy in the post-Trafalgar period, was that of the angry Danes. The 'Mosquito-war' which they waged against all British shipping passing through their waters was particularly effective. Danish gunboats attacked the convoy rendezvous at Malmö, on the coast of Sweden, causing havoc, and even Saumarez's expedient of attaching ships-of-the-line to convoys often misfired, especially when the wind fell away to a calm. In June 1808, the 64-gun *Dictator* was attacked in Kiøge Bay and was compelled to withdraw, and a worse incident occurred in October. Mustering a convoy of 137 merchantmen at

Malmö, the bomb-vessel *Thunder* and some small gun-brigs were joined by the 64-gun *Africa*. To cover the passage of the convoy through The Sound, Captain John Barrett anchored *Africa* off Amager Island as a deterrent; the ship's presence only acted as a lure for the 'mosquitoes'. Twenty-five gun- and mortar-boats, supported by seven armed launches and manned by some 1,600 men, pulled out from Copenhagen and surrounded the *Africa*. In the calm they took station ahead and astern of the British ship, where no bow-chasers and only a pair of stern-chasers could respond, and battered her for four hours. Twice Barrett's ensign halliards were shot through, and twice the Danes thought them-selves victorious; in the end they failed to capture the *Africa* and were obliged to withdraw, but somewhat more than the moral victory lay with them.

So dangerous was The Sound considered that during the following year it was prohibited, and all British convoys were forced to undergo the more intricate navigation of the Great Belt. But even here saftey could not be guaranteed: in May 1809 the *Melpomene* (Sir Peter Parker) was caught in a calm and, although she was within five miles of the 74-gun *Temeraire*, subjected by a score of gun-boats to a battering so severe that she was shortly afterwards sent home for a thorough dry-docking and repair before being despatched to the Mediterranean.

The Danes were also able to open an effective if modest offensive with the handful of cruisers left to them after the British rape of Copenhagen in 1807. These were most successful when operating from the remoter waters of Danish Norway, where they could hide among the fjords and islands. Commander William Dillon was in command of the ageing brig-sloop *Childers*, the same little vessel upon which the guns of Pointe St Mattieu had fired at the beginning of the wars many years earlier. One dark night in March 1808 Dillon was scouring the coast of Norway when he fell in with the Danish brig-of-war *Lügum* (Kaptajn Wulff). Dillon awaited moonrise and then attacked. *Childers* was so rotten that *Lügum*'s shot passed right through her sides and soon reduced her to a sinking condition. Wulff withdrew, however, and Dillon made Leith Road, his men constantly pumping the *Childers*. In June Wulff and some gunboats fell on the British brig-sloop *Seagull* and compelled her to surrender. So successful was the *Lügum* that she formed the core of a small Danish squadron fitted out to prey on British trade passing through the Skagerrak.

In 1810 these Danish brigs were back, damaging the 36-gun frigate *Tribune* (Captain George Reynolds), on 12 May. In July they fell upon a convoy of forty-two merchantmen bound for the Orkneys and Leith, driving off the single escorting gun-brig, the *Forward*, and taking the *entire convoy* as prizes. At the end of the month the same brigs engaged the 10-gun cutter *Algerine* and the 12-gun brig-sloop *Brevdrageren,* but were driven off. They were back on station the following year, when they captured the 12-gun brig *Safeguard* and fought off the brig-sloops *Chanticleer* and *Manly*. By 1812 the Danes had commissioned a 40-gun frigate, the *Nayaden,* and Saumarez, learning of this, anticipated her appearance with the brigs in the Skagerrak. He despatched the 64-gun *Dictator* (Captain James Stewart) with three brigs, *Calypso*, *Podargus* and *Flamer*, specifically to hunt her down. On the evening of 6 July 1812 Stewart located *Nayaden* with the brigs *Lollane, Kiel* and *Sampsø* anchored behind some rocky islands off Mardø near the Naze of Norway. Stewart ran in so close to the cliffs that *Dictator*'s yardarms are said to have almost brushed them and, deliberately running the bow of his ship aground so that the wind swung her broadside to *Nayaden,* 'literally battered to atoms' the Danish frigate.

As in the Mediterranean, so in the Baltic, Saumarez's detached ships not only protected British imports from enemy raids but kept up their own war against enemy commerce, principally the coasting trade along the Baltic shore of the German states. And during the five winters that Saumarez withdrew from the frozen Baltic, his ships either refitted at home or were used to support Wellington in the Peninsula.

When the Tsar finally lifted his embargo on trade with Britain, legalising what had been going on clandestinely for some time, the Royal Navy immediately came to the aid of the Russians. On the left wing of the Grand Army's fatal invasion of Russia in 1812, the Army Corps of Maréital Macdonald advanced across Courland and invested the city of Riga; Byam Martin's *Implacable* was there in the Gulf of Riga, stiffening Russian resolve to defend the city until, in the wake of

Napoleon's winter retreat, Macdonald sought terms. Saumarez had by then returned home following the death of his daughter Mary, but before he hauled down his flag the wreck of the Grand Army was crossing the Beresina in confusion, and his contribution to the downfall of Napoleon had been made.

Tall, courteous and handsome, James Saumarez was 'rather ceremonious in his manner, but without the least tincture of affectation or pride'. He was, however, by his own admission an irritable man, piqued by his lack of a peerage. It was eventually granted in 1831, five years before his death, and was richly deserved, for Saumarez was an able if not an exceptional commander, both of individual ships and as a commander-in-chief or 'armed-diplomat'. He fought one of Britain's most persistent and tenacious enemies, the Danes, in a long battle for the very roots of Britain's power. But it was a war over trade, lacking a single fleet action, and therefore failed to attract its due appreciation until almost too late.

# CHAPTER 15

---

# 'My Lord, you *must* go . . . '

In 1809 the British Admiralty received their biggest scare from a break-out of a French fleet in the post-Trafalgar period. But although the blockade of Brest was raised, such was the efficiency of the British squadrons and the cruisers that the enemy fleet never left the French coast.

News of the British decision to systematically reduce the French West Indian islands was known in Paris at the end of 1808, and Contre-Amiral Willaumez at Brest was ordered to sail, as soon as he could evade British vigilance, to release Commodore Troude's three sail-of-the-line and five frigates from L'Orient, then to make for the Basque Roads. Here he would be joined by three more line-of-battle ships and frigates and a troopship then lying off Rochefort under Commodore Faure. Willaumez was then to proceed to reinforce Martinique and attack British commerce in the Antilles.

Admiral Gambier was at the time commanding the blockade of Brest. He was no Cornwallis, and strong westerly gales in mid February 1809 persuaded him to withdraw from his station off Ushant. Before he returned, Willaumez's squadron had slipped its moorings and headed south. The solitary sentinel, Captain The Honourable Charles Paget of the 74-gun *Revenge,* followed them, making for Commodore John Beresford who lay off L'Orient in *Theseus,* with *Valiant* and *Triumph* in company. The daylight was already waning, but soon after meeting

263

*Revenge*, with Beresford steering to the eastwards, French and British came in sight of one another.

Contre-Amiral Gourdon's division wore round to pursue, with the rest of Willaumez's ships following, at which Beresford tacked to the westward and formed line of battle. As they drew away from L'Orient, however, the French hauled their wind and resumed their mission, for Willaumez knew he had lost the element of surprise, and that any delay would compromise his objectives. Willaumez tried to deceive Beresford by heaving-to and furling his sails, as though anchoring off L'Orient, then resetting sail after dark. Unfortunately for the French the night proved windless, and at daylight they were still only off the Île de Groix. The wind that day was in the north-west, so Willaumez despatched word to Troude and set course with the fleet for the Pertuis d'Antioche, the passage between the isles of Oléron and Aix where the Rochefort ships were to rendezvous.

With Willaumez heading for L'Orient, Beresford ghosted east-south-east along the coast during the quiet night and, although Willaumez was ahead of him, by the forenoon of 23 February Beresford was again in touch with the enemy as the French passed inshore, with the British astern and to seaward, of Belle-Isle. During daylight they lost touch, which allowed Willaumez to approach the Île de Ré after dark. The wind had now veered to north-east, and ahead of him was stationed the British squadron, blockading the Basque and Aix Roads which lay behind the Île d'Oléron guarding the estuary of the Charente and the port of Rochefort.

Here, at anchor off the Chasseron lighthouse on Oléron, lay Sir Robert Stopford in the 80-gun *Caesar* with the 74-gun ships *Defiance* and *Donegal* and the frigates *Naiad* and *Emerald*. Further north, off the Baleine light on the Île de Ré, was Stopford's lookout frigate, *Amethyst* (Captain Michael Seymour). The moment Seymour saw the approach of Willaumez's fleet he fired up rockets, and Stopford weighed anchor to head north, sighting Willaumez about midnight. Stopford was too late to prevent the French entering the Pertuis d'Antioche at dawn, but despatched *Naiad* north to inform Gambier. Captain Thomas Dundas of *Naiad* shortly thereafter spotted three suspicious sails and, still within sight of Stopford, signalled their presence, whereupon Stopford stood to the north, leaving *Emerald* and *Amethyst* to watch Willaumez.

These strange sails were the 40-gun frigates *Calypso*, *Cybèle* and *Italienne*, under Commodore Pierre Jurien, the only three French vessels to have sailed from L'Orient, because Troude's heavier ships were tidebound. Jurien had been chased by the British frigate *Amelia* and the brig-sloop *Dotterel*, the lookout ships of Beresford's squadron, had avoided contact with Beresford's main force; nevertheless, Captain The Honourable Frederick Irby of *Amelia* and Commander Anthony Abdy of *Dotterel* had kept so close to Jurien that he had twice had to haul round and fire at his pursuers, delays sufficient to compromise him now. With a shift of the wind and the approach of Stopford the unfortunate Jurien was cornered on his native coast, and turned to head for the protection of shore batteries at Les Sables d'Olonne. *Amelia* and *Dotterel* followed, Irby a third time ranging up astern of *Cybèle*, wearing under the French frigate's stern and firing into her as he passed.

Jurien anchored his ships under the shore batteries of Les Sables d'Olonne, clapped springs on his cables and waited upon events. Stopford formed a line, with *Defiance* in the van and *Amelia* in the rear. The coast was now thronged with spectators as Captain The Honourable Henry Hotham anchored *Defiance* close to Jurien's ships and opened fire. At close range the *Defiance*'s gunfire proved deadly, and burning gun-wads ignited fires aboard *Italienne* and *Cybèle*. Hotham kept up this pressure with support from the other British men-of-war, and to get out of range the French vessels cut their cables and drifted inshore as the tide flooded. All three were soon aground and virtually wrecked; with the tide on the ebb, Stopford disengaged, and by nightfall on 24 February 1809 he was back off the Chasseron light to join Beresford in the investment of the Basque Road.

In the anchorage, Willaumez's force, now joined by that of Commodore Gibert Faure, consisted of the 120-gun *Océan*, the 80-gun *Foudroyant* and *Ville de Varsovie*, the 74-gun ships *Tourville*, *Aquilon*, *Tonnerre*, *Regulus*, *Cassard*, *Jemmappes* and *Patriote* (the *Jean Bart* had run aground and become a wreck), the 40-gun frigates *Elbe*,

*Indienne*, *Pallas* (not to be confused with Cochrane's old frigate) and *Hortense*, the brig-corvette *Nisus* and the store-ship *Calcutta* (the former British Indiaman). The relief of Martinique was now abandoned: Willaumez sought to secure his defences by dragging a heavy boom made of chains stapled to logs across the passage into the anchorage

Gambier, meanwhile, had been thrashing about since hearing of the French escape on 23 February. He had sent Duckworth with eight sail-of-the-line to head Willaumez off from the Mediterranean and Toulon, and himself headed back towards Plymouth. On the way *Naiad* caught him up and told him of Willaumez's whereabouts. Gambier telegraphed the news to the Admiralty and, heading south again, joined Stopford off the Île d'Oléron on 7 March. Informed of the destruction of Jurien and content that, with Stopford and Gambier united off Rochefort, the immediate escape of Willaumez was unlikely, Their Lordships at the Admiralty remained cautious. The weather might favour the French, and there were political anxieties over the annual West India trade and the military operations then in train. Their Lordships decided to anni-hilate Willaumez where he was.

Fire- and rocket-ships were to be prepared, and transports and bomb-vessels were ordered for the purpose. However, this was potentially an extremely dangerous operation. The opinions of senior officers, in-cluding Gambier, who thought that fireships were 'a horrible mode of warfare', were against it, while the Board of Admiralty itself, led by Lord Mulgrave, could not contemplate failure and sought to evade all responsibility for the outcome.

Into this convoluted and highly politicised situation sailed Captain Lord Cochrane, who had just entered Plymouth in *Impérieuse* after his daring raids on the Spanish coast of Spain. Scenting a solution, Mulgrave called Cochrane in and candidly explained the situation. Cochrane, still an opposition Member of Parliament and a hated figure to Portland's government, appreciated that failure would be synonymous with ruin. He knew the ground, however – and he thought the plan too tame. What was required was something more terrible. Mulgrave listened indulgently: this was what he wanted to hear. Cochrane was then ordered to draft a plan at once, whereupon Mulgrave took it through to the Board, assembled in the adjacent room. They immediately approved it, provided that Cochrane, a sacrifical scapegoat, commanded the operation.

Cochrane declined the honour; he was ill and tired, and knew the jealousy such an appointment would arouse. But Mulgrave would not brook a negative answer. Next day he called Cochrane back: 'My Lord, you *must* go. The Board cannot listen to further refusal … Rejoin your frigate at once. I will make you all right with Lord Gambier … Make yourself easy about the jealous feelings of senior officers.'

On 3 April 1809 *Impérieuse* anchored in the Basque Road where Gambier was as disposed as Mulgrave had been to regard Cochrane's arrival as providential. Their meeting was interrupted by an enraged Rear-Admiral Eliab Harvey, who insisted that the honour of leading the attack should be his, as second-in-command, and added an infuriated damnation of Gambier, his procrastinations, his 'methodistical … conduct and vindictive disposition'. Harvey was sent home in his flagship, the *Tonnant*, 80, and Cochrane ordered to make his preparations.

Similar emotions were stirring French breasts; Pellew's old friend Capitaine Jacques Bergeret of the *Ville de Varsovie* had written to Paris denouncing Willaumez's failure to force an action off L'Orient on Beresford's weaker squadron. The prescient Bergeret did not share either Willaumez's or Napoleon's opinion that ships were safe in Aix Road. As a result of his letter to Denis Décres, the Minister of the Marine, both Bergeret and Willaumez were replaced, the latter by Zacharie Allemand.

Gambier's fleet now lying in the Basque Road was formidable. The Commander-in-Chief flew his flag in the 120-gun *Caledonia*, and with him were the two 80-gun ships *Gibraltar* and Stopford's flagship *Caesar*; eight seventy-fours, *Hero, Donegal, Resolution, Theseus, Valiant, Illustrious, Bellona* and *Revenge*; the heavy frigate *Indefatigable*, 44; the two thirty-sixes *Emerald* and *Aigle*; the thirty-twos *Unicorn* and *Pallas*; the sloops *Dotterel, Foxhound* and *Lyra*; the gun-brigs *Insolent, Encounter, Conflict, Contest, Fervent, Growler* and *Martial*; the schooner *Whiting*; and the hired cutters *King George* and *Nimrod*.

Cochrane's *Impérieuse* was anchored close to the special vessels he was preparing for the operation. Mulgrave's designated ships had not yet arrived, so Cochrane took over eight transports and the frigate *Mediator*, converting them to fire-ships filled with barrels of tar and other flammable material. Strips of tarred canvas were festooned everywhere, and vents were cut to feed the flames and allow them to ascend rapidly. Cochrane personally supervised the equipping of three 'explosion vessels', reinforced to compress the explosive force of 1,500 casks of gun-powder which were tamped down with sand. Hundreds of 10-inch mortar shells were laid over the powder-casks, then several thousand hand grenades covered the whole infernal conglomeration. A fifteen-minute fuse ran aft to the stern.

On the 10th, the dozen promised fire-ships arrived with a single bomb-vessel, the *Aetna,* and Cochrane told Gambier that he was ready. Gambier now delayed, saying the fire-ship crews might be murdered by the French. 'If you choose to rush to self-destruction that is your own affair,' he sanctimoniously informed Cochrane, 'but it is my duty to take care of the lives of others, and I will not place the crews of the fireships in palpable danger.' Cochrane was dumbfounded; the conditions were right, but the naval Commander-in-Chief was indulging in a fit of Christian conscience! On reflection, however, Gambier recalled his professional duty and gave way.

On the afternoon of 11th April 1809, *Impérieuse* moved near the Boyart Shoal and Cochrane assembled his vessels. Joining Cochrane, the *Caesar, Aigle, Unicorn* and *Pallas* were to pick up the crews of the expendable vessels, and their boats would be available for any other service. *Whiting, King George* and *Nimrod* were all fitted with Congreve rockets while *Aetna,* covered by the *Indefatigable* and *Foxhound*, positioned herself to shell a fort covering the approach. *Emerald, Beagle, Dotterel, Conflict* and *Growler* were sent east of Aix to create a diversion, and *Lyra* and *Redpole* were fitted with lights to mark the shoals, an essential precaution in the strong tide and north-westerly wind. Cochrane's detachment left the rest of Gambier's fleet anchored between six and nine miles from the enemy.

Observing the activity of the British, Allemand had anchored his ships in three lines lying roughly north-to-south, heading north. Reckoned from the Île d'Aix, the easternmost line was made up of

*Elbe, Tourville, Aquilon, Jemmappes, Patriote* and *Tonnere.* Lying parallel a cable to the westward, with their broadsides covering the intervals, in the main line, was the central trot of *Calcutta, Cassard, Regulus, Océan, Ville de Varsovie* and *Foudroyant.* A shorter line another half-mile farther west consisted of the frigates *Pallas, Hortense* and *Indienne.* Beyond the anchorage the heavy boom of anchor cables, timbers and spars stretched for about two miles, barring the channel. On the late afternoon of 11 April, Allemand gathered the fleet's boats, alerting the 2,000 conscripted soldiers on Aix and the artillerymen in the shore batteries to the likelihood of an attack. He had also taken the precaution of striking the top-hamper of his ships-of-the-line, though the frigates were ready to weigh anchor if required to intervene. Allemand could do little more except console himself with the cold comfort that, according to Napoleon, 'Nothing can be more insane than the idea of attacking a French squadron at Île d'Aix . . . '

Midshipman Marryat wrote that 'the night was very dark, and it blew a strong breeze directly in upon . . . the enemy's fleet.' At half-past eight the explosion vessels, the fire-ships and the *Mediator* cut their cables, were swung round and, with a two-knot tide under them, bore down upon Allemand's lines, followed by some of the squadron's boats. Cochrane was aboard the leading explosion vessel, Marryat the second, and their first objective was to blast their way through the defensive boom. An hour later, after passing the lights of *Redpole* and *Lyra,* Cochrane ordered his men into the boat towing astern, lit the fuse, and scrambled down after them. Only at this point did they realise they had left their pet dog behind. Returning to rescue their mascot, they then pulled smartly away. Close astern, Marryat did likewise, and a few moments later the dark night was illuminated by the first explosion. The concussion was tremendous: just inside the floating boom, Allemand's boats were swamped and scattered by the wave thrown up. Paradoxically, Cochrane was saved by having had to return for the dog, for his boat still lay inside the radius of the debris falling out of the sky. After the detonation and the passing wave there was 'nothing but a heavy rolling sea . . . all having again become silence and darkness'.

The boom was blown apart by Cochrane, and the effect of Marryat's vessel exploding was more psychological than physical. The stunned French watching apprehensively aboard their ships wondered how many more dreadful explosion vessels the mad English possessed. In fact the third explosion vessel was run into by a prematurely-abandoned fire-ship and failed to explode at all, for the fuse blew out, but this was just the beginning of the plan's failure, as *Mediator* and the other fire-ships sailed down through the breach in the boom. Several of them had been ignited too early, and the majority of the twenty finally prepared either ran aground, or ran harmlessly up the centre of the channel in the grip of the tide. Cochrane was furious as he clambered aboard *Impérieuse* to watch his meticulously-planned attack miscarry through a lack of nerve on the part of the volunteers.

Notwithstanding this, for aught the French knew, the few fire-ships which drove into Allemand's 'safe haven' were more explosion vessels. The approaching fires piercing the blackness of the night played havoc with notions of distance and perspective. *Aetna*'s mortars thundered, the shells arcing through the sky to blow up on or over the Île d'Aix, Congreve's rockets blazed across the sky, and the rumble of gunfire from the sloops beyond Aix combined with the misdirected French gunnery from the batteries on Aix and the ships in the anchorage, to produce a scene of sublime horror. As the fire-ships approached and the flames licked up into their rigging, the rockets lying upon their yards ignited and flared out on either beam to add to the hellish atmosphere. One fire-ship *was* handled brilliantly, crashing into the *Régulus*, her grappling irons fouling as the French seamen frantically hacked at their two anchor cables; she then broke clear, only to run into the *Tourville*. *Hortense* cut her cables to avoid one fire-ship, hoisted sail and fired her guns into another, but her shot hit her neighbours. Allemand's *Océan*, deeply laden with stores for Martinique, cut her cable and ran aground. A moment or two later a second well-directed fireship crashed into *Océan,* followed by the *Tonnere* and the *Patriote*, both of which collided with the flag-ship as they strove to manoeuvre in the strong tide. Despite this fatal onslaught, Allemand's seamen managed to thrust the fire-ship clear before the *Océan* caught alight.

Most of the fire-ship crews escaped by a hard pull to windward, though a few men were killed and some fell into the hands of the French. At daylight Cochrane was mollified by what appeared to be a scene of devastation. Only *Foudroyant* and *Cassard* still floated; all the other French vessels were aground. *Océan* was afterwards refloated, but beyond the flagship, *Aquilon* and *Ville de Varsovie* had struck rocks, and near them lay *Régulus* and *Jemmappes* on a softer seabed. The *Tonnere* was bilged on the Pontra Rock, and close to the wreck of the *Jean Bart* lay the *Calcutta*. *Patriote* and *Tourville* were stuck on the muddy flanks of the Île Madame, *Elbe* and *Hortense* were on the Fontenelles, *Indienne* lay on the mud off Pointe Aiguille, and the *Pallas* had come to rest under guns of the Barques fort at the estuary of the River Charente. The ebb tide had finished what Cochrane had begun.

Cochrane now signalled to Gambier that eleven French ships were aground, and requested support to annihilate the enemy; at twenty minutes to seven he signalled that only two were afloat. But during the forenoon, as the tide flooded again, Allemand began to rally his men, and an agitated Cochrane transmitted 'enemy preparing to heave off'. Gambier summoned all captains aboard *Caledonia*, then moved closer to Aix and re-anchored. He considered the attack a great success, of which he made sure by ordering *Aetna*, with *Growler*, *Conflict* and *Insolent* in support, to add a little piquancy to the situation by firing at the French batteries and ships. He also ordered *Valiant, Bellona and Revenge* to anchor farther in, and to take with them the frigates and sloops, a movement that suggested the whole British fleet was going to approach. *Cassard* and *Foudroyant* now cut their cables and made for the Charente, only to run aground, joining the *Jemmappes, Patriote, Océan* and *Régulus*, which had refloated only to go aground again.

As he watched the enemy making for the Charente and the safety of Rochefort, then saw Gambier's fleet re-anchor again, Cochrane grew incandescent. Throwing caution to the winds, he ordered *Impérieuse* under way and headed towards the French, flying provocative signals for assistance which he thought Gambier must, in all conscience, honour.

As Cochrane anchored *Impérieuse* to batter *Calcutta, Aquilon* and *Ville de Varsovie*, he also ordered *Insolent, Growler* and *Beagle* to move in closer. Gambier, now compromised, reluctantly instructed some vessels to assist Cochrane. *Indefatigable* arrived first, just as *Calcutta* lowered her colours, but the others took some time to work up against the tide. Nevertheless, by four in the afternoon the *Valiant*, *Revenge*, and *Pallas* had arrived to anchor in a half-moon, with springs on their cables to enable them to cannonade the three French ships on the Palles Shoal. Just as *Theseus* arrived to help, *Aquilon* and *Ville de Varsovie* capitulated, while the crew of *Tonnere* set fire to their ship, abandoning her before she exploded. The *Calcutta* had also been set alight, and her cargo of ammunition now blew up. Boats from *Valiant* set fire to *Ville de Varsovie* and *Aquilon,* which caused a panic aboard *Tourville.*

When the tide had risen sufficiently, Cochrane took *Impérieuse* into the Charente with *Pallas, Beagle, Conflict, Contest, Encounter, Fervent, Growler, Whiting, Nimrod, King George* and *Aetna,* to fire into *Océan, Régulus* and *Indienne. Beagle* engaged *Océan* for five hours, until the falling tide compelled Cochrane to order a retirement. That afternoon *Redpole, Dotterel* and *Foxhound* all arrived with letters from Gambier ordering Cochrane to withdraw. On the 14th *Patriote, Hortense, Elbe* and the French *Pallas* hauled themselves upstream out of trouble, while *Tourville* and *Océan* ran aground once again. The next day Cochrane finally withdrew, leaving things in the hands of Captain George Wolfe of *Aigle. Impérieuse* embarked Gambier's flag-captain, Sir Harry Neale, with Gambier's despatch and sailed for England. By the end of the affair *Jemmappes, Océan, Cassard, Foudroyant* and *Tourville* had all clawed their way into Rochefort; *Indienne* was burnt, leaving only *Régulus* exposed, and on 19 April she was shelled by the newly arrived bomb-vessel *Thunder* – whose 13-inch mortar promptly split. This fiasco drew the curtain down. Gambier, considering he had 'done his utmost', sailed for home.

Courts martial judged the French commanders: De la Roncière of *Tonnere* was cleared, Lacaille of *Tourville* was dismissed and imprisoned for two years, Proteau of *Indienne* was confined for three months, and Lafon of *Calcutta* was shot. These wretched officers paid the penalty for Willaumez's initial timidity.

But there were worse things in store for the British. Harvey was dismissed, and though he was later reinstated to his rank, he was never afterwards employed. The stupid Gambier damned Cochrane with faint praise. Despite appointment as a knight of the Order of the Bath, Cochrane, to whom such honours meant little, remained so resentful that he used his position as an MP, to oppose the customary thanks of Parliament to Lord Gambier. Mulgrave prophesied that it was an action which 'will not only prove injurious to the Government, but highly detrimental to yourself'. Cochrane was headstrong: 'I do not recognise Lord Gambier's services ... for none had been rendered'. Mulgrave tried coercion, threatening 'high displeasure', to which Cochrane blithely replied, 'The displeasure of the Government will not for a moment influence my Parliamentary conduct ... ' As a final effort, Mulgrave promised Cochrane three frigates and the Mediterranean, if he would absent himself; but Cochrane was a man of arrogantly unshakeable if misguided principle, and the oh-so-obvious *douceur* was in direct contravention of his sternest precepts.

Gambier demanded a court martial to approve his conduct, and it duly assembled aboard *Gladiator* at Portsmouth between 26 July and 4 August. The court was composed of jobbers favourable to Gambier. It was presided over by his friend Sir Roger Curtis, supported by Admiral Young, Cochrane's old enemy from Plymouth dockyard, and the self-serving Sir John Duckworth. Cochrane was not called except to give evidence, and was then brow-beaten and forbidden to ask questions. Gambier's conduct was judged to have been correctly tempered by the caution proper to a Commander-in-Chief and, it was implied, by high considerations lying outside the professional judgement of a mere junior post-captain. Gambier's claims to mature caution arose from judgements based upon the British charts of the Aix roadstead. Cochrane countered by asserting that the British charts were inaccurate, that the navigation was less complex than they indicated, and that he had had experience of the area over several years. He himself had navigated on French charts, but these were ruled to be inadmissible, because their accuracy could not be proven, a state of war then interrupting intercourse between France and Great Britain! Accordingly, Gambier was 'most honourably acquitted', and Cochrane humiliated.

Cochrane had ensured his own obloquy. Given leave, he then sailed in his own yacht to Malta, and set about exposing the injustices inherent in the naval prize system. In the House of Commons Cochrane also continued to work for reform in the Royal Navy, deploring the pittances paid to disabled officers in contrast to the huge pensions paid to Admiralty civil servants. Since many of these officials came from aristocratic families, Cochrane further drew down upon his own head the hatred of the Establishment.

In 1814 the Establishment had its revenge, aided, ironically enough, by a member of Cochrane's own family, an uncle named Andrew Cochrane-Johnstone. Cochrane-Johnstone was a disreputable MP who sat for a rotten borough and used his parliamentary privilege to escape his creditors. In 1814 he implicated his nephew in a notorious stock-exchange fraud based upon the assumption that Napoleon had been killed in action, the Russians were approaching Paris, and the war was over. The news sent a volatile government stock called Omnium sky-high: when the truth leaked out, the market crashed, but not before those in the know had made a profit of 70 per cent.

Cochrane was drawn into the conspiracy through having met the officer carrying the momentous news at his house, and having offered him a change of clothes after his journey from France. He was also known to have breakfasted with his uncle on one of the fatal few days of the speculation. The extent to which Cochrane was actively involved with the hoax remains uncertain. There is no proof of his absolute innocence, but neither is there any concrete proof of his guilt. Certainly he had invested £36,000 of his prize-money in Omnium, but he had also left standing instructions with his broker to sell if the price rose by 1 per cent, a perfectly legal, modest and businesslike arrangement.

In the subsequent prosecution at the Old Bailey, held before the anti-Radical reactionary Lord Ellenborough, Cochrane was thoroughly if circumstantially implicated, and condemned. A solicitor who had appeared for Gambier during his court martial acted for the prosecution, one of Cochrane's witnesses was deliberately sent to sea, and the denial by one of the known conspirators that Lord Cochrane had had anything to do with the affair was ignored. Cochrane was fined and sentenced to imprisonment, after standing in the public pillory – a vindictive refinement that was remitted when it was realised that it was likely to precipitate a riot in Cochrane's favour. He was expelled from the House of Commons and the Royal Navy, and locked up in the King's Bench Prison. Here he learned that the Prince Regent had ordered his degrading: his knight's banner was torn down from Westminster Abbey, and his spurs were ceremoniously struck off a proxy in Palace Yard. By this time the war *had* ended: Napoleon, then in his short exile on Elba, deplored the treatment meted out to the man he had dubbed *Le Loup de Mer*.

Cochrane went into exile, taking his wife Kitty with him. Seeing her as a teenager, walking in Hyde Park, he had instantly decided to marry her. Tall and red-haired, Cochrane is said to have been engaging in appearance, and he succeeded in persuading Kitty Barnes to wed him. She bore him five children and accepted the extraordinary vicissitudes of life with her remarkable cock-sure husband. Cochrane left Britain to fight for the liberation of Chile and Peru from the Spanish, and Brazil from the Portuguese, before commanding the Greek navy in their war of liberation against the Ottoman Turks. In 1848, on the instigation of Albert, the Prince Consort, he was reinstated in his rank and honours, to serve as Commander-in-Chief on the North American station between 1848 and 1851. He died as Admiral The Earl of Dundonald at the age of 85 in 1860. A remarkable, opinionated, headstrong and brilliant seaman he was always his own man, and always concerned for the seamen he commanded. Whatever his deficiencies as a politician, as a sea warrior he was supreme.

Despite the subsequent wranglings in London, the attack on Allemand's fleet had a profound psychological effect on French admirals, and the destruction and damage to the ships in the Aix Road was considerable. Yet as far as the British public were concerned, 1809 was the year of an even greater disaster. A large naval force had landed an army under Lieutenant-General The Earl of Chatham on the Dutch island of Walcheren. The expedition's objective was the seizure of Antwerp – Carthage to London's Rome, and therefore to be destroyed as a prime objective of the war – along with the elimination of a large number of men-of-war in the Schelde under Contre-Amiral Missiessy. The British naval force was commanded by Rear-Admiral Sir Richard Strachan, supported by other flag-officers such as Keats; the army by the Earl of Chatham, brother of the late Prime Minister, William Pitt. The whole vast enterprise miscarried, and the troops were bogged down on Walcheren where they became infected by the 'Walcheren-fever', a marsh-ague better known medically as malaria. Soldiers and seamen died in droves, and the invasion became a fiasco. It was the subject of a little quatrain:

> Sir Richard, longing to be at 'em,
> Stood waiting for the Earl of Chatham.
> The Noble Earl, with sabre drawn,
> Stood waiting for Sir Richard Strachan.

It was in the Iberian Peninsula, not the Low Countries, that the British army made its great contribution to encompass Napoleon's ruin. Wellington went over to the offensive in the spring of 1811, defeating Masséna at Fuentes de Oñoro. In 1812 Wellington's troops stormed the border fortresses of Cuidad Rodrigo and Badajoz, thrashed Marmont at Salamanca and entered Madrid, to fall back on Portugal for the winter and resupply by sea. The following June Wellington defeated Maréchal Jourdan and King Joseph at Vitoria and advanced to the Pyrennes, crossing the Bidassoa into France on 7 October 1813.

Sir Home Popham exemplified the co-operation offered to Wellington throughout this campaign by the Royal Navy. Popham's orders allowed him a free rein, but he was expected to co-operate with the Spanish, annoy the French, and render Wellington such assistance with supplies as he might be able.

Although the regular Spanish army had some success, it was to the fearsome Spanish guerrillas that Wellington looked to keep the French constantly anxious about their communications.

So, on the northern, Biscay, coast the Royal Navy and the Spanish guerrilla *partidas* tied down 120,000 French soldiers under Général Cafarelli by hit-and-run raids, the ships often transporting the guerrilla forces to strike at French strong-points. Popham's ships carried a large quantity of small-arms with which to supply the guerrillas, and extra detachments of marines. In June Popham landed a 24-pounder through the surf, then had it hauled by men and oxen to a commanding high-point, from where it cannonaded a French-held fort at Lequeito. The place was then stormed by Don Gaspar el Pastor's partisans, and the captured garrison was taken into captivity aboard *Magnificent*. Popham next destroyed a fort at Bermeo which the garrison had abandoned, then raided Plencia. On 25th June, Popham ordered the frigate *Surveillante,* (Captain Sir George Collier) to form line astern and his 74-gun *Venerable* led *Surveillante* into Bilbao, firing at Algorta fort with spherical case-shot. He then attempted to land guns at Guetaria, but withdrew them on the approach of a French column. Popham also co-operated with Francisco Longa. The two men met at Castro Uriales, west of Bilbao, systematically seeing off a relieving force and laying siege to the French stronghold, which fell on 8 July. Popham left a marine detachment in possession and went to join Mariano Renovales in an attack on Bilbao itself. At Portugalete on the 10th, the guerrillas ran into the French and Popham ran into a gale. When the gale abated Popham returned to Guetaria, this time with the guerrilla leaders Jauregui and Espoz y Mina. On 17 July guns were successfully landed and operations were under way when a French column drove off Jauregui and the attempt was again frustrated.

Popham's force was now enlarged, and he sailed to assist the partisan forces under Porlier and Longa, who were besieging Santander without heavy cannon. Popham mounted a battery on Isla de Mouro and cannonaded the Castello de Ano. Then he concerted a plan with the Spanish, landing marines at Sardiniero Bay ready to storm the defences with Longa and Porlier's men. Next, leaving *Venerable* offshore, Popham boarded *Surveillante* and led his other frigates, the *Medusa*, 32, and *Rhin*, 38, into the harbour and anchored. The assault was made on the 27th. The guerrillas, marines and seamen took the Castello de Ano, blowing it up the next day; on the night of 2 August the French slipped out of the town. The capture of Santander delivered a safe haven into the hands of the British, providing Wellington with his much-needed supply port in the north.

Wellington, held up at Burgos by a lack of siege artillery, finally agreed to his staff's suggestion that he obtain 24-pounders from Popham's ships at Santander. Two were landed and hauled laboriously inland, reaching Reynosa, 50 miles away, on the 18th, before Wellington impatiently abandoned the siege and withdrew to Ciudad Rodrigo, leaving the French a respite in which to deal with the guerrillas. The *Venerable* was ordered home and Popham, to his chagrin, never returned for the final phase of the Peninsular War. He was consoled by receiving his flag in 1814, but it was left to Collier to render assistance to the guerrillas in the following spring. On 5 April 1813, with guns landed by Collier, Mina took Tafalla to the south of Pamplona. Collier went on to render assistance in the taking of San Sebastián. But Wellington was now crossing Spain on his final advance, and Santander became the principal supply port.

Despite providing Wellington with this important logistical stepping-stone, Popham, a man who had run extraordinary risks, both militarily and politically, having led an extempore and foolish attack on the Rio de la Plata. Yet he is hardly known today except for being credited as the inventor of the naval code that allowed Nelson to transmit his famous 'England expects . . . ' signal at Trafalgar. Like many other outstanding sea warriors of his day, his curious reputation lies obscured by the long shadow of Horatio Nelson's.

# CHAPTER 16

---

## 'To purge the eastern side of the globe'

A few months before the rupture between Napoleon and Tsar Alexander which led to the fatal march of the Grand Army on Moscow, the Emperor of the French was again meditating the invasion of England. The majority of the invasion vessels prepared for 1805 had been moved into the Schelde, hence the Walcheren expedition, but a number remained at Boulogne, whither travelled Napoleon, intending to hold a marine review on 20 September 1811.

The *prames peniches* and gun-boats were gaily bedecked with bunting, and Napoleon boarded a gorgeously decorated barge to inspect the craft assembled under the command of Contre-Amiral Baste. Unfortunately, lying at anchor just beyond the breakwaters was the British 38-gun frigate *Naiad* (Captain Philip Carteret). Her presence angered Napoleon, and he ordered her driven off. Clapping a spring on his anchor cable when he saw the approaching *prames*, Carteret opened fire on the gun-boats as soon as they cleared the entrance to Boulogne, keeping them at bay for two hours and then beating off the reinforcements that a desperate Baste and a furious Napoleon threw in. A second attack next day was met by *Naiad* and the brig-sloop *Castilian* of 18 guns, the 10-gun brigs *Rinaldo* and *Redpole*, and the smaller 8-gun *Viper*, all of which had arrived that morning. It ended with the capture of the 12-gun *prame Ville de Lyon* after she was boarded by the *Naiad*'s crew.

The merit of this otherwise insignificant little action was its practical demonstration to the Emperor of the French that his power did not extend beyond the arms of his own breakwaters. It was a fact of increasing relevance, for while the British navy was about to receive a shock from the impact of war with America, the strangulation of every French naval enterprise was all but complete.

There is an air of desperation in the attempts of the French to maintain their dwindling overseas bases and to prosecute their *guerre de course* in the last years of the war. It cannot be denied that they tried, and cruisers like Capitaine Jacques Epron's *Piémontaise* had runs of exceptional success. Epron, it will be recalled, took the Indiaman *Warren Hastings* off the French island of Réunion in the southern Indian Ocean in June 1806. Having captured a number of Country ships, *Piémontaise* was sighted by Rear-Admiral Drury on 20 January 1808 as he was on his way to Madras. A few weeks later Epron learned of the late departure of three Indiamen from Bombay, and made for Cape Comorin to intercept them before they acquired a naval escort.

On 6 March Epron saw his quarry and made sail towards them, but to his consternation they were not without escort, and at the sight of a British frigate Epron made sail to run. Captain George Hardinge of the 36-gun *San Fiorenzo* spread his wings in hot pursuit, and just before midnight had worked *San Fiorenzo* up alongside *Piémontaise*. The broadsides thundered and the gun flashes stabbed the night as Epron's gunners desperately aimed high to cut away the rigging of the British frigate. In ten minutes Epron had disabled his adversary and dropped Hardinge astern. Patiently, *San Fiorenzo*'s people knotted and spliced, then made sail again and caught up with their enemy at dawn on 7 March. At half-past six in the morning, as the sun rose on the beautiful coast of Sri Lanka, Epron wore and opened fire on the *San Fiorenzo* coming up hand-over-fist. Again *Piémontaise*'s guns aimed high, while *San Fiorenzo*'s were laid horizontally; once again, after two hours the *San Fiorenzo*'s masts and sails were wrecked. At a quarter-past eight Epron ceased his fire and made sail eastwards, but the *Piémontaise* was badly hulled and Epron's crew were at the pumps as he dropped Hardinge out of sight over the horizon astern.

The British crew worked all day to repair the damage, then made sail: at midnight they could see *Piémontaise* in the distance, pale in the moonlight. By nine in the forenoon *San Fiorenzo* was once more bearing down upon her quarry. In addition to the accretion of weed and barnacles occasioned by her long service in tropical waters, *Piémontaise* was now water-logged and sluggish, her pumps working continuously. Frustrated, Epron hauled up and accepted action. Hardinge's reward for his persistence was to be killed in *Piémontaise*'s second broadside; command of *San Fiorenzo* fell upon Lieutenant William Dawson, who for an hour and twenty minutes maintained a vicious cannonade of the French frigate. At the end of this period Epron struck the tricolour.

The *Piémontaise* had had a large crew, along with numerous Lascars from prizes who had been put to the pumps, but 49 men had been killed and 92 wounded; besides her captain, *San Fiorenzo* had 13 killed and 25 wounded. Few single ship actions demonstrate so readily the differences between the tactics of aiming high and aiming low. Had Epron's frigate proved the faster ship, she would have escaped after the first encounter, but the superior sailing of the *San Fiorenzo* and the industry of her people in refitting her secured the victory. By extending the action Epron had exhausted his supplies of 18- and 8-pound shot, and was reduced to using only his 36-pounder carronades. Nevertheless, he was beaten by an enemy who dismissed the French tactic of disabling to rely upon a more brutal annihilation.

After her masts fell on 9 March Dawson took *Piémontaise* in tow, and arrived at Colombo on the 13th. The *Piémontaise* was only four years old, and after extensive repair was purchased into the Royal Navy under her own name. Dawson was made a post-captain, but died in 1811.

Epron's fate was to prove universal: while French corsairs continued to plunder British commerce with devastating effect, even on the south coast of England itself, the French navy's sallies had all the character of forlorn hopes. To the end they attempted to send out powerful flying squadrons comprising three of their fine, heavy frigates, usually accompanied by a corvette. The destination of these groups was almost invariably Île de France, and it was in the Indian Ocean that the last act of the great naval drama between Great Britain and France was played out.

The French archipelago in the Indian Ocean was highly dependent upon military stores from France. At first single frigates had been sent out in support, but these rarely broke the British blockade. In April 1809 the 40-gun *Niéman* (Capitaine Jean Dupotet) had left the Gironde, but late on the evening of the 5th, she ran into the British 36-gun frigates *Emerald* (Captain Frederick Maitland) and *Amethyst* (Captain Michael Seymour).

Despite the onset of night Seymour retained contact with the French frigate in a fresh easterly breeze, and by midnight *Amethyst* was firing ranging shots at the fleeing *Niéman*. In due course Seymour had almost overtaken Dupotet, and fired his starboard broadside; but Dupotet wore round, only to be followed by the experienced Seymour, who then crossed *Niéman*'s bow and raked her several times. At one point the two ships collided, before drawing apart and pounding at each other until three o'clock in the morning of 6 April. At this point the *Niéman*'s hammocks in the nettings were alight and her mizen mast and main topmast fell, a second fire starting in her main top as the first was extinguished. Next, the remainder of the *Niéman*'s mainmast fell, but at this time *Amethyst* lost her own main and mizen, depriving Seymour of the ability to manoeuvre. Duportet's fate was sealed, however, for Captain Robert Mends had been steering the 'Saucy Arethusa' towards the thunder of the guns and the *Niéman* fell into British hands, once more depriving Île de France of food and stores.

Since 1803 the Île de France had been under the governorship of Général Decaen, an intransigent anglophobe who, while thwarted in his personal ambition to make a name for himself by driving the British out of India, nevertheless acted vigorously in maintaining his isolated archipelago as an outpost of French imperialism. In addition to its geographical isolation, the Île de France's position in the trade winds made it difficult to blockade, so that access was rarely effectively impeded by the British. But, with the exception of Epron, it was not until 1808 that active French frigates arrived to contest the mastery of the Indian Ocean, and Decaen was gratified to receive supplies and reinforcements aboard the new frigates *Manche*, 40, *Caroline*, 40, *Bellone*, 44 and *Vénus*, 44, the commander of which, Jacques Hamelin, was appointed commodore.

Under Lieutenant de Vaisseau Jean Ferretier, the *Caroline* reached the Bay of Bengal and in February 1809 captured the Indiamen *Streatham* and *Europe*, while Hamelin in *Vénus* captured the Company's armed brig *Orient* off the Great Nicobar on 26 July 1809. Hamelin next joined *Manche* and the corvette *Creole* and bombarded Tappanooly on the west coast of Sumatra in mid October. In November, off Achin Head, Hamelin's ships took the Indiamen *Windham*, *Charlton* and *United Kingdom*, while *Bellone* took the British sloop *Victor* and later a Portuguese man-of-war, the 52-gun *Minerva*.

It was obvious that the British blockade was still ineffective, although attempts were made to strengthen it. The neighbouring island of Rodriguez was occupied by Lieutenant-Colonel Keating and 600 men from Bombay, with the intention providing the blockaders with a source of wood, water, vegetables and poultry. At this point the 'immortal' Josiah Nesbit Willoughby reappears to play a crucial role in coming events. After being diagnosed 'mortally' wounded in action against the Turks during his patron's feeble demonstration at Constantinople, Willoughby went on sick-leave. He was then sent out to South America and joined the 18-gun *Otter*, in which he was part of Home Popham's disastrous adventure on the shores of the Rio de la Plata, which lies outside the scope of this book. Retiring to the Cape of Good Hope, Willoughby was promoted on merit to the command of the *Otter* in April 1808. The sloop was one of the ships now assigned from the Cape of Good Hope to blockade Île de France.

When Ferretier's *Caroline* returned from the Bay of Bengal with her prizes she found the British off Île de France in some force, and ran into St Paul's on the adjacent island of Bourbon. Aboard the 64-gun *Raisonnable* Commodore Josias Rowley, in charge of the little squadron off Port Louis, decided to cut her out. He embarked a detachment of troops from Rodriguez, assigning the attack to Captain Robert Corbet of *Nereide* who would have under his orders the 36-gun frigate *Sirius* (Captain Samuel Pym), *Otter* and *Sapphire*, and the Company's schooner *Wasp*. The troops under Keating were supported by seamen and marines under Willoughby, and all embarked in *Nereide* for the assault. The landing, made on 21 September 1809, was successful and the *Caroline* and her prizes, *Streatham* and *Europe,* together with the captured British privateer *Grappler* and some smaller vessels, fell back into British hands.

On the 22nd French troops approached, and Willoughby landed and destroyed a warehouse containing the silk from the captured Indiamen, worth £500,000. He coolly re-embarked, and after a truce had been arranged the British removed all stores and prize cargoes from the remaining warehouses before retiring. The *Caroline,* built at Antwerp in 1806, was commissioned by Corbet as His Britannic Majesty's frigate *Bourbonnaise,* and Willoughby replaced Corbet in *Nereide.*

At the end of December the British 32-gun frigate *Magicienne* arrived off the island to recapture the Indiaman *Windham* as the French prize-crew tried to make Port Louis; but on 2nd January 1810, as Rowley's ships lay unseasonally becalmed offshore, a coastal breeze allowed *Bellone* and *Manche* to slip into Port Louis with their prizes, the men-of-war *Minerva* and *Victor* and the Indiamen *Charlton* and *United Kingdom.* A little later Hamelin's *Vénus* followed. In March, when the blockade was lifted at the onset of the cyclone season, Decaen sent Duperré to sea again in *Bellone*, with the recommissioned *Minerva* (now *Minerve*) and *Victor.*

Decaen's problems were increased by his success, for he had to support not only his garrison, the native population and the crews of French naval frigates, but a large and shifting population of privateersmen and their hapless prisoners. Among these was the luckless Commander Matthew Flinders, whose great surveying voyage had been ended by the refusal of the French at Port Louis to honour their government's passport, on the grounds that it was made out for a different vessel from that in which Flinders had arrived. Flinders's remarkable surveying voyage had accomplished much, greatly increasing knowledge of Australian waters, but the dangers had been considerable and the *Investigator* had been wrecked. The wretched man was compelled to kick his heels for eight years before he was released. Returning home to write up his travels, he died in 1814 on the day *A Voyage to Terra Australis* was published.

During his confinement on the island Flinders must have watched the corsairs come and go in an agony of frustration. From Port Louis,

Robert Surcouf and his ilk continued to plunder both East Indiamen and the 'Country' ships, bringing much-needed rice and other necessities to the island, and enabling Decaen to support a sufficient number of French national frigates to worry the British Commander-in-Chief of the East Indies station – now Vice-Admiral William Drury, Pellew having returned home in 1809.

Despite the recaptures, which only involved the various parties in prolonged wrangles in the prize courts, these depredations by Decaen's cruisers caused a great outcry among the influential merchants of Madras, Calcutta and Bombay, and the Governor-General of India, Lord Minto, was driven to declare his intention 'to purge the Eastern side of the globe of every hostile or rival European establishment'. Minto and Drury began to plan for the reduction of the Mauritian islands, as they referred to the Île de France and Île de Bourbon. While troops and transports would be supplied from India, Rear-Admiral Albemarle Bertie at the Cape was to provide the warships at the end of the cyclone season.

Meanwhile Commodore Hamelin lay at Port Louis in *Vénus*, with *Manche* and the corvette *Entreprenante*. The *Bellone, Minerve* and *Victor* were still at large, but in response to Decaen's appeals to France for help the 36-gun *Astrée* had just arrived from Cherbourg.

On 30 April Willoughby arrived from the Cape in *Nereide* to discover a merchant ship and a schooner anchored under the guns of the little port of Jacolet. That night he landed, spiked a battery, defeated some militia, and seized two guns. At daylight he saw another battery, forded an intervening river and stormed into this too. Willoughby's men then captured two anchored ships; one, the schooner *Estafette,* was French, but the second was an American merchantman and was therefore released before Willoughby withdrew. Later he landed upon Flat Island, off Île de France, intending to exercise his men, but a musket he was using burst its breech, fractured his jaw and exposed his larynx. This would have prevented a less determined man from joining the attack on the French archipelago, but in a couple of months Willoughby was ready for action.

At the beginning of July Drury's frigates *Diomede* and *Ceylon* escorted the troop convoy to Rodriguez. A few days later they were joined by Rowley's frigates *Boadicea, Nereide, Sirius, Iphigenia* and *Magicienne,* and the attack was made on Île de Bourbon. On 7 July, 950 men under Lieutenant-Colonel Frazier landed unopposed at Grande Chaloupe, west of St Dénis, the island's capital. A second landing was made under Keating three miles further east. Here Willoughby, swathed in bandages, stormed ashore at the head of his seamen and fought his way into Forte Ste Marie for the night. Next day Keating joined Frazier, and the French surrendered that evening. On the following morning *Sirius*'s boats seized the shipping in St Paul's and prevented the corsair *Édouard* of Nantes from escaping with despatches after a twelve-hour pursuit by *Sirius*'s barge.

As a prelude to the main assault on Île de France it was thought desirable to occupy Île de la Passe, in the entrance to Grand Port, as a base from which to win over the populace with a persuasive proclamation. Bad weather aborted the first attempt, but on 13 August Captain Pym sent in *Sirius*'s boats, captured the batteries and accepted the capitulation of the garrison. Pym's seamen and marines were replaced next morning by the grenadier company of the 69th Regiment landed from *Nereide*. Pym then resumed the blockade of Port Louis, leaving behind Willoughby in *Nereide* with the 14-gun-brig *Staunch* (Lieutenant Benjamin Street).

On 17 August 1810 Willoughby started to distribute the propoganda leaflets in his characteristic style, unlikely as it was to conciliate the locals. Landing near Grand Port with a small force of soldiers, seamen and marines, he marched inland, destroyed a battery, blew up a magazine and carried off a 13-inch mortar. Next day he landed at Grande Rivière, wrecked the signal station and retired, without receiving a scratch from 700 idle French militia close by. Sending Street to Port Louis, Willoughby went ashore again on the 19th when he discovered that during the forenoon the *Bellone, Minerve* and *Victor* had arrived with their prizes: these were the Indiamen *Ceylon* and *Windham*, captured for the second time. Willoughby hurriedly reboarded *Nereide* and hoisted both the tricolour and a private signal he had found in a signal-book picked up at Grande Rivière, thus enticing the French ships to approach. As the *Victor* passed *Nereide*, Willoughby shifted his colours and opened fire, as did the British-manned guns on Île de la

Passe, at which *Victor* immediately struck, coming to an anchor close under *Nereide*'s quarter. However, when *Minerve* and *Ceylon* had passed, firing on *Nereide* as they did so, *Victor* weighed and followed them into port.

The *Nereide*'s gunfire had proved ineffective. Willoughby's predecessor, Robert Corbet, was a brutal commander whose crew had mutinied the previous year. He was an obsessive and punctilious ship-handler, considering 'smartness' the very thing; but he had neglected gunnery practice, and Willoughby, despite his energetic approach to naval service, had done little to remedy the deficiency.

Seeing what had happened Duperré, still outside in *Bellone*, ordered his prize-master in *Windham* to head away to the westwards. He then bore down towards the entrance, firing into *Nereide* as he took *Bellone* past her and into Grand Port. Willoughby sent the ship's launch off with Lieutenant Henry Deacon to see Pym: Willoughby asked Pym to send *Sirius,* and he himself would take his boats in after the French. To keep the enemy awake until Pym arrived, Willoughby had the mortars on Île de la Passe shell Duperré, forcing the French ships to move farther up the harbour.

Offshore next day, Pym saw *Windham* and chased her under the batteries at Rivière Noire. Taking two boats, Lieutenant John Watling of *Sirius* volunteered to cut her out, but he forgot to check that his boarding party had brought small-arms, and boarded the *Windham* brandishing his boats' foot-stretchers! Incredibly, he re-captured the Indiaman without loss. From the captured prize crew he learned how matters stood at Grand Port, and passed the information to Pym. Pym then sent *Windham* to Rowley at St Paul's, Île de Bourbon, and set sail himself for Grand Port. Rowley in turn despatched *Magicienne* to Port Louis to pick up Henry Lambert's *Iphigenia* and Street's *Staunch,* with instructions to rendezvous with him off Grand Port.

Meanwhile, at Grand Port, Duperré had anchored his ships with springs on their cables in a rough crescent protected by coral reefs. By this means their broadsides commanded the approach to the inner anchorage.

As *Sirius* ran in towards the coast she encountered Lieutenant Deacon in *Nereide*'s barge. Now fully briefed, Pym sailed into Grand Port the next morning, the 22nd. Seeing Pym approaching, Willoughby sent his men to the capstan and, as *Sirius* sailed past, *Nereide* weighed in her wake. Pym's precipitate action proved foolhardy in the extreme, for within minutes *Sirius* had missed the unmarked channel and run hard aground. Willoughby immediately dropped an anchor and lowered boats to assist, but *Sirius* was not refloated until early on the 23rd when she was re-anchored close to *Nereide*.

By mid afternoon that day *Iphigenia* and *Magicienne* had joined *Sirius* and *Nereide*, and all four British frigates renewed the attack. The plan called for *Nereide* to anchor between *Victor* and *Bellone*; *Sirius* to anchor directly abeam of *Bellone*; and *Magicienne* to take station between the captured Indiaman *Ceylon* and *Minerve*, with *Iphigenia* abeam of the latter. As they sailed in, *Sirius* and then *Magicienne* ran aground. *Iphigenia* dropped her stream anchor astern, then ran on and let go her bower under-foot, by which time she was abreast of the *Minerve*. Lambert opened a furious cannonade at pistol-shot range, aiming her quarter guns at *Ceylon*. Realising that the operational plan was compromised, Willoughby anchored *Nereide* with a spring on her bower cable and engaged the much heavier *Bellone*. As the battle began, artillery ashore joined in, and a pall of smoke was soon hanging over Grand Port, while the concussion of the guns reverberated like incessant thunder round the bay.

As the tropic night fell, *Ceylon* drifted aground. The *Minerve*, her cable shot away, fell foul of *Bellone*'s cable and both ships ran ashore; as they did so, *Minerve*'s guns severed *Nereide*'s spring. *Nereide*, in consequence, swung under the influence of the wind and lay to her bower anchor, exposing her stern to a raking fire from *Bellone*. With consummate *élan* Willoughby cut his cable, let go his opposite anchor, veered cable and brought his starboard broadside to bear. The grounded *Minerve*'s guns were now hidden behind *Bellone*, but *Nereide* continued to be hammered until every one of her guns had been knocked off their carriages, damaged by shot or otherwise rendered useless. Moreover, her stern was on the bottom. Just before eleven o'clock Willoughby sent a boat to *Bellone*, 'to say we had struck, being entirely silenced and a dreadful carnage on board'. Duperré ignored Willoughby's capitulation. It had now begun to rain, and a few minutes after midnight *Nereide*'s mainmast fell. Still *Bellone*'s guns and those in the shore batteries continued to fire, until the frigate's mizen, to which a Union flag had been nailed, crashed down, whereupon Duperré ordered a cease-fire. As the sun rose on 25th *Nereide* fell to the French; of her company of 291 men and boys, all but 52 had been killed or wounded; as for the immortal Willoughby, he had merely suffered a splintered cheek, been wounded in one eye and had the other torn from its socket! Along with his ship's company he passed into French hands, a prisoner.

During that day Captain Lucius Curtis ordered *Magicienne*'s crew to abandon and burn her. Lambert warped *Iphigenia* out, intending to assist Pym's *Sirius*, but the latter remained so firmly aground that she too was set on fire, and blew up before the morning was over. Pym sent Watling by boat to inform Rowley of the disaster. Watling was chased by the *Entreprenante*, but by pulling along the breakers he reached Île de Bourbon early on the 27th with news of the British defeat.

Hamelin left Port Louis in *Vénus* with *Manche* and *Astrée* and, meeting *Entreprenante*, learned of the situation at Grand Port. He arrived off Grand Port at about five in the afternoon, putting an end to *Iphigenia*'s slow progress down the harbour. Hamelin demanded Lambert's surrender, and after the despatch of a boat to Bourbon, Lambert capitulated, on condition that *Iphigenia*'s crew and the island's garrison be sent by cartel to the Cape, not to serve again until formally exchanged. These assurances were dishonoured, and all were imprisoned on the island. The Île de France was proving a costly nut for the British to crack.

Briefed by Watling, Rowley approached in *Boadicea*, only to discover the situation to be worse than he had expected. He was chased away from Grand Port on 29 August by *Vénus* and *Manche,* but returned a few days later. Hamelin had withdrawn to Port Louis, but nothing could be done, and Rowley went back to St Paul's Bay in what was now called Réunion. The tables were now nicely turned by Capitaine Bouvet, who arrived on the scene on 9 September, and, with a squadron consisting of *Iphigénie* (formerly *Iphigenia*), *Astrée, Entreprenante* and *Victor,* blockaded Réunion.

That same day the martinet Captain Corbet, now in command of the 38-gun *Africaine,* called at Rodriguez on his way to Madras. Hearing of the disaster at Grand Port, instead of proceeding on his voyage he put back for Réunion. Arriving off the island early on the 12th he saw Bouvet's ships *Iphigénie* and *Astrée* being chased by *Boadicea, Otter* and *Staunch*. Corbet failed to catch up with the chase before nightfall, but at two o'clock next morning he lay off Port Louis close to *Astrée* and *Iphigénie*, with *Boadicea* only five miles away. Clearing *Africaine* for action he opened fire, only to fall mortally wounded. Lieutenant Joseph Tullidge fought on for two hours, by which time *Africaine* was wrecked aloft and of her company of 295 souls, 49 were dead and 119 wounded. Moreover, as there was no sign of *Boadicea* coming to *Africaine's* aid to balance the unequal struggle, Tullidge struck to Bouvet. He was an unfortunate victim of Corbet's cruelty, for suspicions lingered that *Africaine's* brutalised crew had failed to do their utmost in support of their hated commander.

Too late, a shift in the wind now allowed *Boadicea* to approach; but seeing *Africaine* flying French colours, Rowley went in search of *Staunch* and *Otter*. Having located them, he returned to the scene, whereupon Bouvet abandoned *Africaine,* which was retaken and escorted into St Paul's Bay. *Boadicea*, *Otter* and *Staunch* next went in chase of *Iphigénie* and *Astrée*, but were unable to catch up with them. They in turn captured the Bombay Marine's *Aurora*, carrying her triumphantly into Port Louis on 22 September. But the bad news for the British did not end there. Five days earlier the 32-gun British frigate *Ceylon* (Captain Charles Gordon), coming from Madras to join Rowley, had been chased off Grand Port by *Vénus* and *Victor*. By midnight, *Vénus* had overtaken *Ceylon* and opened fire. The action allowed *Victor* to manoeuvre athwart *Ceylon's* hawse and rake her. Gordon and thirty other men were wounded and ten killed as Gordon ordered her ensign lowered.

Coming up at dawn onto *Boadicea's* quarterdeck as she lay anchored in St Paul's Bay, Rowley was mortified to see the two French ships and their prize nine miles away. He immediately sent his men, among whom were fifty volunteers from the *Africaine*, to the capstan and weighed in chase, hoisting the signal for *Otter* and *Staunch* to follow and emphasising it with a gun. *Vénus* lay-to, to defend her prize, directing *Victor* to slip the tow of *Ceylon* and escape. Hamelin engaged *Boadicea* as she came up, but surrendered after a brisk action of ten minutes in which nine men were killed and fifteen wounded. Aboard *Ceylon* Lieutenant Philip Gibbon took back his ship and rehoisted British colours. All the ships returned to St Paul's Bay where the *Africaine* lay and where *Vénus*, though she was in poor condition, was recommissioned as *Nereide*, in replacement of the captured Willoughby's frigate.

By October 1810 Vice-Admiral Bertie, commanding at the Cape of Good Hope and sick of waiting for the troops promised by London to effect the capture of Île de France, acted on his own initiative. On the arrival of the brand-new frigate *Nisus* from Britain he hoisted his flag and left Table Bay on 4 September. Bertie met Rowley on 15 October, and shifted his flag into *Africaine*. With *Nisus* (Captain Philip Beaver), *Boadicea*, *Nereide* (the former *Vénus*), *Ceylon* and *Staunch*, Bertie now reconnoitred Île de France, receiving fire from the batteries at Port Louis, before leaving Rowley off the island with *Boadicea*, *Nisus* and *Nereide* and running on to Rodriguez.

The invasion was to be under the direct command of Captain Beaver of *Nisus* (with whom, years earlier, the young Thomas Cochrane had quarrelled), specially selected as he was considered an expert in landing operations. Rowley, advised by Willoughby who knew the coast well, had already sent Street of the *Staunch* to carry out a meticulous survey of the north coast of Île de France. Under cover of night Street, helped by Lieutenant Blakiston of the Madras Engineers and the masters of *Boadicea* and *Africaine*, had discovered a perfect landing beach at Mapou Bay, hidden by the island known to the British as Gunner's Quoin. Unfortunately one of *Nisus*'s boats had been captured, but the approach to Mapou Bay was secretly buoyed the night before the invasion.

The force under Bertie now consisted of his flagship *Africaine*, 38, *Illustrious*, 74, *Cornwallis*, 44, the 38-gun frigates *Boadicea*, *Nisus*, *Clorinde*, *Menelaus* and *Nereide*, the 36-gun *Phoebe* and *Doris*, and the 32-gun *Cornelia*, *Psyche* and *Ceylon*. There were also the sloops *Hesper*, *Eclipse* and *Hecate*, all of 18 guns, the 16-gun *Actaeon*, the gun-brig *Staunch*, the armed ship *Emma*, and the hired auxiliaries

*Egremont*, *Farquhar* and *Mouche*. Including the ships' marines, there were 6,848 soldiers under the overall command of General Abercromby embarked in transports. Bertie ordered the fleet to leave Rodriguez on 22 November.

The landing had been carefully planned. Its first wave consisted of 1,555 men in forty-seven ships' boats. These were covered by a dozen additional boats armed with either 6-pounders or the frigates' boat carronades, with two bearing small howitzers, all manned by 160 seamen and Madras artillerymen. The troops were a scratch battalion of infantry made up largely of the light and grenadier companies of the 12th, 33rd, 56th, and 59th Regiments, and when embarked in the boats presented 'a most magnificent and interesting spectacle'. It was about two hours after noon on 29 November 1810 as they pulled away from the fleet offshore; 'the breeze . . . [was] particularly favourable, and the day one of the finest that could be chosen'.

The troops and seamen landed unopposed; the enemy, retreating, blew up a magazine at Fort Malartic in Grand Bay when they knew the British were ashore. There were the customary upsets. Beaver lost his signals book when his gig was swamped while towing astern of *Nisus*. 'It was as well', he lamented, 'to be able to disembark and advance without a struggle, for circumstances did not combine as I could have wished. A strong tide made to the westward, which prevented the flat and heavy boats from preserving the necessary order . . . ' He need not have worried; all the soldiers were ashore by nine in the evening and the advance guard had moved forward under Keating's command three and a half hours earlier. Keating skirmished with the retreating garrison from Fort Malartic before bivouacking for the night.

The second wave of troops landed at daylight on the 30th; Keating, meanwhile, reached the River Tombeau and halted to await the rest of the force. He could see Port Louis beyond the river, and watched as Decaen, galloping up on his horse, received a graze from a musket ball. Port Louis was indefensible from a land attack and could not withstand a siege, for the French Governor had only some two thousand regular troops upon which he could depend. Decaen's Creole militia had been neglected by Paris, while his own iron regulation had kept them under the utmost privation: their ardour for the distant Emperor's honour was consequently not great. Decaen himself had long since despaired of implementing his imperial master's dream of invading India. He knew he was rotting while his peers found glory and fortune in Europe, but he drew up his force outside Port Louis under the command of his deputy, Vandermaesen, and prepared to make a stand.

Beaver's *Nisus* supported Abercromby's advance on the seaward flank. The frigates' boats kept the troops supplied direct from the sea and provided Abercromby with a floating headquarters. On 1 December 1810 the British confronted Vandermaesen, turned his flank and assaulted his front. Vandermaesen's men broke and fled, and the next morning Decaen called a truce. 'After much extravagant bravado and insolence on the part of Governor de Caen [*sic*], the Isle of France was surrendered by capitulation on the 3rd,' wrote Beaver, adding, with petulant outrage: 'I wish I had been of greater consequence . . . the terms were rather demanded than supplicated, and are far too advantageous for such an undeserving and inferior garrison . . . they are actually allowed to march with their arms, the eagles and fixed bayonets.'

But neither Abercromby nor Rowley was a fool. A late hurricane was possible and, although the promised troops had finally arrived from the Cape, they wanted the costly adventure concluded. Since the objective had been achieved and Mauritius, as it must now be called, was no longer French, the parading of a few discredited eagles was not of much importance.

Finally, and to the relief and satisfaction of Rowley, Pym, Willoughby and the other sea warriors, the French frigates *Bellone*, *Vénus*, *Manche*, *Minerve*, *Astrée* and *Iphigénie* all fell into British hands, as did the corvette *Victor*, the brig *Entreprenante*, two dozen French merchant ships, the other *Ceylon* and her sister East Indiamen *United Kingdom* and *Charlton*, along with some other prizes. The battered hulk of Willoughby's *Nereide* was also retaken, but given up as unserviceable. Willoughby, his colleagues, officers and ship's company were liberated, as was the unfortunate Commander Matthew Flinders, whose long days of unjustified captivity were over.

Willoughby went home with his crooked jaw, and his empty eye-socket covered by a black patch. Examined at Surgeon's Hall, he was awarded a pension of £300 but refused to retire. He volunteered to serve with the Russian army and was again taken prisoner by the French, after giving his horse and his Cossack attendant to two wounded Russian soldiers. Capture involved him in the Retreat from Moscow, and the redoubtable Willoughby marched with the Grand Army back to France, to be released after Napoleon's first abdication in 1814. He was appointed a Knight of the Order of the Bath and a Knight Commander of Hanover, and ended his remarkable career in command of the large 42-gun frigate *Tribune* from 1818 until his retirement on half pay in 1822. Seniority eventually elevated him to the rank of rear-admiral, and he was appointed a naval aide-de-camp to the young Queen Victoria. Cruel, heartless and arrogant, he was withal fearless in action, and while his men doubtless disliked him, they would follow him to the death. Incredibly, this excessively courageous and indisputably successful sea warrior was also the compiler of 'a very estimable volume' entitled *Extracts from Holy Writ and various Authors, intended as Helps* [*sic*] *to Meditations and Prayer, principally for soldiers and seamen*, which was distributed *gratis* in the army and navy. This worthy work notwithstanding, Nesbit Josiah Willoughby was not quite immortal, for in 1849, at the age of seventy-two, what remained of him was finally summoned to his Maker.

# CHAPTER 17

---

## 'Don't give up the ship'

With the capture of Île de France, the cruiser war against the French was more or less over, and in due course the ships and men dispersed, leaving not a mark upon the vast expanse of the Indian Ocean.

Indeed, the number of cruisers Sir Samuel Hood, in command from 1812, was able to retain was a matter of some delicacy, for a new threat had arisen, manifestations of which might yet appear in the eastern seas. Hood was not to see it materialise, for malaria killed him in December, but it was real, and it came from powerful enemy cruisers.

But they were no longer Spanish, or Dutch, or French. Now they were American.

A long war breeds its own imperatives. It assumes a priority in the lives of its protagonists, and it disregards the legitimate rights of those not immediately concerned with its horrors. As a consequence it is likely to draw in and implicate others, which is what happened with the United States in 1812.

A major factor in the rupture between America and Great Britain, of which the first manifestations have already been seen, was the attitude of the latter's sea warriors in cases of desertion. Desertion, for the Royal Navy's officers, was a domestic problem, set apart from the abstruse legalities of the right of search and legalistic definitions of the contraband of war, but the arrogance of the sea warriors sent to do the dirty-work involved in reclaiming deserters upset the Americans, hyper-sensitive in the pride of new nationhood.

To the grim British veteran, cousin Jonathan was a touchy stripling, who should pipe down, or risk a good thrashing for his impertinence. To the proud young officers of the equally youthful United States Navy, the half-brutalised John Bull was a cruel and despotic affront to the sanctity of their own quarterdecks. It might be added that, though their prospects ashore were vastly better, quite a few British seamen who deserted to the American navy found a taste for flogging equally prevalent among Yankee officers.

America had been outraged by the action taken by Captain Salusbury Humphreys, a dark-visaged man of a mien sinister enough to fuel the most extreme fantasies, when he ordered the guns of *Leopard* to fire into the *Chesapeake*. The affair died down, but was not forgotten. Then, four years later, on 1 May 1811, the British frigate *Guerriere*, cruising off New Jersey, stopped the American merchant brig *Spitfire* and removed a 'deserter' named John Deguyo, who was said to be a citizen of the United States. President Jefferson, pushed beyond his tolerance, ordered Captain John Rodgers to sea in the 44-gun United States frigate *President* to recover Deguyo. On the dark and blustery night of 16 May the *President*'s lookouts saw a vessel lying-to on a station regularly occupied by British men-of-war. An exchange of hails was followed by a peremptory exchange of fire which lasted for fifteen minutes before the strange ship's guns fell silent. Seeing his opponent's top-hamper fallen about her decks, Rodgers drew off until daylight. Dawn revealed not the *Guerriere* but the small British ship-sloop *Lille Belt*, a Danish prize of 22 guns. Rodgers had killed eleven men and wounded twenty-one. As Humphreys had translated his orders literally, so had Rodgers: the result was war.

Although the American navy was small, its seventeen cruisers were effective, and in the main fast, heavily-armed and able ships. American guns bore dispart sights which were by no means common among their adversaries. Ship for ship they were formidable, and against them most of the Royal Navy's frigates and sloops were growing old, were not over-armed, were usually under-manned and, significantly, had generally become lax in the matter of gunnery. The preponderant might of the Royal Navy, however, was overwhelming. In 1812 the Admiralty had 978 vessels available to it; 584 men-of-war were in commission at sea, more than 480 of which were 'cruizers'. To man this prodigious fleet, 145,000 seamen and marines were under orders; there were 777 post-captains on the Navy List, 566 commanders and 3,163 lieutenants. When the British Admiralty turned their full attention to the blockade of the American eastern seaboard it was to prove as watertight as the strangulation of Napoleon's European empire: but until that happened, the cruisers of the United States Navy were as dangerous to British commerce as those of the French, Dutch and Danish had been.

On 21 June 1812 Rodgers, now a commodore, sailed to interdict the British convoys leaving the West Indies. Rodgers' squadron consisted of *President*, the 44-gun *United States* (Captain Stephen Decatur), the 38-gun *Congress* (Captain John Smith), and the sloops *Hornet*, 18, and *Argus*, 16. Two days later they sighted the British 36-gun frigate *Belvidera*, whose captain, Richard Byron, had been warned of the possibility of war and made sail. Rodgers gave chase, and by noon *President* had almost overhauled the *Belvidera*. Clearing for action, Rodgers himself personally fired the first bow chaser. With the first three ranging shots nine men aboard *Belvidera* were incapacitated, but then a gun burst aboard the *President*, killing and wounding sixteen men; Rodgers was hurt, and the event engendered mistrust of the remaining guns aboard *President*. Byron now fired his own stern chaser, causing six more casualties. With a shattered leg, Rodgers bore up and delivered his larboard broadside, losing ground as Byron ran on, firing his stern guns and repairing his rigging. Byron now cut loose his anchors, threw his boats overboard and pumped sixteen tons of fresh water over the side, slowly increasing *Belvidera*'s speed and escaping to Halifax with the news of hostilities.

Though Rodgers missed his main objective, he subsequently crossed the Atlantic, captured eight British merchantmen, and returned to Boston on 31 August. After only two months at sea, scurvy had broken out in his ships. Meanwhile, on 9 July Captain David Porter took the 32-gun American frigate *Essex* to sea, captured a military transport out of a convoy escorted by the *Minerva*, 32, and the British ship-sloop *Alert*, a converted collier armed with 16 guns.

Next to sail was Captain Isaac Hull, who left the Chesapeake on 12 July in the 44-gun *Constitution* intending to join Rodgers. Four days later he ran into the scratch British squadron which had been hurriedly assembled at Halifax. This consisted of the 38-gun *Shannon* (Captain Philip Broke), the elderly 64-gun *Africa* (Captain John Bastard), *Guerriere* (Captain Richard Dacres), Byron's *Belvidera* and the 32-gun *Aeolus* (Captain Lord Townshend). Broke had captured the little American brig *Nautilus*, but the wind then fell away to a calm and his squadron was now dispersed. Before dawn next morning Hull saw the *Guerriere* and both he and Dacres made sail to engage, Dacres signalling to the other British ships on the horizon. Receiving no response, Dacres decided they must be Rodgers's ships, and sheered away.

Daybreak revealed Broke's ships under every scrap of canvas they could hoist in the light airs, and it was now Hull's turn to run. By six in the morning it was dead calm. Hull rolled long 24-pounders aft, while Broke summoned the boats from all his ships to tow *Shannon* after the enemy. Hull at first did likewise, but seeing the gap diminish, he ran his kedge anchor half a mile ahead by means of two cutters, then had his people walk back on the joined ropes while the cutters ran out another anchor. This kedging proved a marginally faster method of progressing than towing, and as the enemy crews toiled at their tasks, occasional puffs of wind gave each ship steerage way for a few moments, at one point even allowing Dacres to fire a few guns. Hull pumped his drinking water out, and soused his sails so that they held what wind there was; the British did likewise. As the forenoon wore on Byron mustered help from the other ships and had anchors run ahead from *Belvidera*, but the occasional shot among the boats was a deterrent. In the late afternoon a light breeze gave the exhausted men a rest, but at sunset it fell calm, and out went the boats again. About midnight a breeze arose, and all the boats were hoisted inboard. In the breeze *Constitution* drew away out of extreme cannon shot, and continued to open out her distance during the following day. That evening a squall swept down and Hull, smartly dousing sail, felt the *Constitution*'s hull tremble as she forged through the sea at 11 knots. Broke's ships followed, but Hull had the lead as the squall passed, and at eight o'clock on the morning of 20 July, Broke gave up the chase.

Reaching Boston, Hull resupplied *Constitution*. He had to borrow the money to do so. Without orders and to avoid further financial embarrassment, he then sailed again to cruise off Nova Scotia, laying a deliberate trap for a British cruiser. On the afternoon of 19 August 1812 Hull's lookouts saw a familiar sail to leeward: the *Guerriere*. Dacres had been detached by Broke, anxious about Rodgers's where-abouts, to return to Halifax and re-store. Captain Dacres was twenty-eight years old, the over-confident son of an unpopular admiral, and a sea warrior about to swallow a bitter pill. His opponent was a veteran of Tripoli, a commander of considerable experience and, as he had shown a few weeks earlier, a consummate seaman. He was about to demonstrate that he could fight, too, and with his heavier ship the outcome was not much in doubt.

A fresh north-westerly wind blew over a grey sea lying under a lower-ing, cloudy sky. Dacres clewed up *Guerriere*'s courses, backed his main topsail and hove-to on the starboard tack, clearing his ship for action as *Constitution* bore down with the wind astern, her courses hauled up in the clew garnets and her iron teeth rumbling out through the opening gun ports. Dacres had seven Americans in his crew; he ordered them below, out of harm's way, but one remained at his gun. As *Constitution* approached, Dacres hauled his main yards round, fired his starboard broadside and then wore round to fire his larboard: neither did any damage. Dacres wore again, and exchanged fire with *Constitution*'s bow chasers as Hull yawed a little. This manoeuvre was repeated as the range shortened and then Dacres, having failed to wing his opponent, ran off before the wind, but kept his courses in the bunt-lines. Hull let his forecourse and fore topgallant draw, and shortly after six o'clock in the evening *Constitution* ranged up on *Guerriere*'s larboard beam. Hull stayed his first lieutenant's enthusiasm to open fire, then shouted, 'Now, boys! Pour it into them!'

The thunder and flashes of broadside fire erupted while small-arms sputtered viciously from the tops, incapacitating a number of officers on both ships. Within fifteen minutes *Guerriere*'s mizen fell over the side, so that she slewed round. 'By heaven, that ship is ours!' Hull shouted. Putting his helm over, he swung *Constitution* to starboard, crossed *Guerriere*'s bow and raked her. But *Constitution* fouled *Guerriere*'s bowsprit in her mizen rigging, and as this tore free *Guerriere* swung and her forward starboard guns battered Hull's cabin. At the same time, however, in breaking free her foremast fell across the mainstay, and this pulled the mainmast down. *Guerriere* now lay unmanageable, rolling in the sea so that water slopped in through her gun ports and several guns broke loose. Hull ran off before the wind, rove new braces, wore round, and returned to cross Dacres's bow a second time.

In the moments during which the two ships lay entangled, *Constitution*'s quarterdeck had filled with men eager to board *Guerriere* and put the hated British to the sword, but the motion of the two frigates made the leap too hazardous. Dacres had run forward at the head of his men to repel the boarders, and together with several men on either side of him was shot by musketry. The ball hit him in the back but he refused to leave the deck.

Now, as *Constitution* lay again under *Guerriere*'s lee bow, Hull sent Lieutenant George Read scrambling across to demand Dacres's submission. Dacres, wincing with pain, commented that all his masts had gone, and the assumption might be made. When *Guerriere*'s mizen fell taking the ensign with it, a Union flag had been run up its stump; it was now lowered. It was all over. Of *Guerriere*'s crew of 282, fifteen were killed and sixty-three were wounded, six mortally. *Constitution*'s losses were seven killed and seven wounded out of 456, though three of the wounded also died, following amputations. Dacres boarded *Constitution* to proffer his sword, which Hull refused. A few hours later *Constitution*'s yards were hauled and she made sail for Boston, leaving the hulk of the wrecked *Guerriere* burning in her wake.

The result of this action was largely psychological: 'The exultation of the Americans was as natural as was the depression of the British ... both feelings were exaggerated.' After a swift exchange, Dacres was tried and acquitted at Halifax, but it was only the first, if the most dramatic, of a number of humiliations for the British. On 18 October the 18-gun brig-sloop *Frolic* (Commander Thomas Whinyates) was escorting a homeward West India convoy when the American 18-gun ship-sloop *Wasp* (Master Commandant Jacob Jones), fell upon her. Whinyates hove-to to engage and cover the escape of the convoy to leeward. Both sloops had been damaged in a gale, and the weather was still rough as they ran off before the wind, rolling heavily. Although the *Frolic*'s rate of fire was fast, the shot went high; *Wasp*'s was deadlier, slower and precise. While Whinyates's gunners dismembered *Wasp*'s spars and rigging, Jones's repeatedly hulled *Frolic*. In the end, the *Wasp* fell athwart *Frolic*'s hawse and raked her. When the Americans succeeded in boarding the wildly rolling and pitching *Frolic*, they found they had swept her crew clear. Only a few remained on their feet, and neither the badly wounded Whinyates nor Lieutenant Frederick Wintle could stand without support; *Wasp* had lost ten men. But Jones's triumph was short-lived, for within hours he and his prize had been taken by Captain John Poo Beresford in the 74-gun *Poictiers*.

The object-lesson was clear enough. Whinyates's reckless courage yielded him nothing. He had employed French tactics – if he had employed tactics at all – in aiming high. Jones had demonstrated what the British seemed to have forgotten, that gunnery won naval battles. But Jones learned a lesson too: that ultimate victory goes to the big battalions.

For Britain, ashes were to be heaped upon ashes. In October Rodgers, now recovered, sailed again, his squadron deliberately dividing. The *President* and *Congress* achieved little, taking a dozen merchant vessels and chasing Woodley Losack's *Galatea* and the *Nymphe*, now commanded by Captain Farmery Epworth, before returning to Boston at the year's end. *Argus* came home at the same time, having had a narrow escape from pursuit, though she had actually taken a prize in the process of running. But in mid Atlantic Decatur's *United States* had run into the new British 38-gun frigate *Macedonian*.

Some time previously Decatur had met the *Macedonian*'s captain, John Carden, and Carden, had told Decatur he had little doubt of the outcome of any encounter between their ships, declaring that the Americans had no battle experience. Carden was a punctilious martinet, a harsh disciplinarian and an unpopular officer who was fond of the lash, as was his first lieutenant, David Hope. The two believed in 'smartness', and in the subordination of all else to this worthy objective. The two officers had been at some pains to man their ship with prime seamen, weeding out the lazy and slack. Moreover, they insisted on gunnery training, though for them this had more to do with firing fast and simultaneously on command, than with permitting mere seamen gun-captains to exercise intelligent individual fire control.

These exemplary 'Macedonians' were at divine service on Sunday, 25 October 1812 when the *United States* was seen bearing down upon the British frigate over a sparkling sea. Calling in at Madeira on his way to the West Indies, Carden had learned that the United States frigate *Essex* was at large, and as he threw up the church service and beat to quarters he assumed the approaching ship was the *Essex*. Carden exhorted his men to recall Nelson's famous signal, but with his next breath instructed his junior midshipmen, boys in their early teens, to shoot any man deserting his station in action.

Aboard the *United States* Stephen Decatur affected contempt for such unimportant matters as uniform, and was wearing a straw hat as his frigate cleared for action. Curiously, Decatur's crew included a considerable number of former British seamen, three or four actually related to Macedonians and several who had been bargemen to Nelson. These men, like all seafarers in the war, were unable to abandon their trade, and sought the most congenial place to exercise it. From being providers of patriotic manpower, they had changed in the long, tedious period after Trafalgar, into mercenary hawkers of marketable skills; such was the degenerating tendency of prolonged hostilities.

The engagement opened at long range. The heavier American guns damaged the *Macedonian*, and the damage worsened as they came onto parallel courses shortly after nine o'clock. A storm of shot riddled the British frigate as she wore to run east and to the north of her opponent as the range closed between them. Both ships backed their mizen topsails to slow their progress and steady their gundecks. Carden, to windward, was surprised at the rapidity of the enemy's rolling fire. At a quarter-past ten Decatur backed his main topsail and fired his larboard broadside. A cannonade at short range followed and *Macedonian* began to lose her spars and sails, and with them the power of manoeuvre. *United States* drew ahead as *Macedonian* drifted down wind. Decatur took *United States* clear, then wore to windward and ran down to rake *Macedonian* and round up to leeward. It was a quarter-past eleven when Carden ordered his colours struck.

Decatur had lost twelve men killed and wounded, while Carden's ship suffered thirty-eight killed and sixty-six wounded. *Macedonian* had lost her mizen mast, her main topmast and her fore topmast; she had been hulled more than a hundred times, and several of her larboard guns were dismounted. Decatur abandoned his cruise and lay hove-to in the open ocean for two weeks without seeing another ship as he refitted the *Macedonian*. Having re-rigged his prize, he took her in triumph to New London and she was commissioned into the United States Navy under her own name.

Carden was acquitted for the loss of his ship when tried at Bermuda in the following March, but the court considered he had suffered from 'over-anxiety to keep the weathergage', and that this had fatally delayed a close action. Since both sides attested to the raw courage of the *Macedonian*'s crew, the fault lay with their leader. Carden, like many British commanders of the post-Trafalgar period, had become complacent, too ready to assume that he would win even against unequal odds. It was a dangerous conceit. That Decatur commanded one of the finest-regulated men-of-war ever commissioned was enough to tip the scales, against *any* opponent, but Carden's over-reliance upon the punctilio of formal gunnery at the expense of effectiveness, contributed to his downfall. It was, however, defective leadership which sealed his fate: he lacked the vision of a man like Cochrane, who won his men's hearts and minds by eschewing the bullying superiority men like Carden considered their birth-right.

In October the *Constitution* was at sea again, on passage to the South Atlantic under Captain William Bainbridge with the 18-gun brig-sloop *Hornet* (Master Commandant James Lawrence). Off the coast of San Salvador on 13 December 1812, where they were supposed to meet the *Essex*, the Americans fell in with the 20-gun British ship-sloop *Bonne*

*Citoyenne*. The enemy vessel being of equal force to the *Hornet*, Lawrence conceived the curious notion of challenging her to single combat. Bainbridge gave assurances that he would not interfere but Captain Pitt Greene declined – not out of cowardice, but because aboard *Bonne Citoyenne* was specie to a value of £500,000, the safe carriage of which would guarantee Greene himself a rake-off of £5,000. Bainbridge did not attempt to cut her out but left Lawrence to blockade her, and pressed on for his cruising station in the South Atlantic.

In the forenoon of 29 December the *Constitution* was some thirty miles off the Brazilian coast when she sighted a sail which was bearing down in chase. This was the British 38-gun *Java*, with a prize of an American merchantman, the *William*.

The *Java*, was actually the French-built *Renommé*, taken in the Indian Ocean. She was commanded by Henry Lambert, who had brought her home to Britain from Mauritius, where he had fought at Grand Port. In August the *Java* had been fitted out to carry Lieutenant-General Hislop, the new Governor, to Bombay, along with his staff, stores, a detachment of troops, and a quantity of copper for the bottoms of men-of-war then being built in the Wadia shipyard. All had gone well until Lambert came to man her. It was found necessary to enlist sixty Irish landsmen, fifty rebellious seamen from the sloop *Coquette*, several drafts of pressed men, some 'volunteers' from prison ships, and a disproportionate number of boys from the Marine Society. The final eight deficiencies in her full complement of 300 were made up by genuine volunteers from a seventy-four at Spithead. With the general's staff and supernumeraries embarked, Lambert's ship contained 397 persons. Such a ship was cluttered and her company consumed more water than she could carry with her, so that Lambert was obliged to stop and take some aboard, the delay that threw her into Bainbridge's way; moreover, when she took *William*, a master's mate and nineteen prime seamen had to be put aboard as prize crew. On 28 December Lambert had ordered gunnery practice, and six rounds of unshotted cartridges were fired in broadsides. It was the first time most of *Java*'s crew had manned a gun.

On the 29th, Lambert brought *Java* up on *Constitution*'s weather (starboard) quarter as Bainbridge clewed up his courses. At two in the afternoon, almost neck-and-neck, the ships opened fire. Despite her gunners' lack of practice, *Java*'s early broadsides did great execution and Lambert edged closely to sweep the American with grape and musketry. *Java*, by far the faster ship, ran ahead, but Bainbridge anticipated Lambert wearing and did so himself in the smoke that now hung over the protagonists' decks; both ran parallel, reaching across the wind, *Java* to windward of the *Constitution*. Again *Java* drew ahead, again *Constitution* wore inside her and again they came parallel, now heading east. Bainbridge luffed to close the distance, enabling Lambert to draw ahead and avoid the worst of *Constitution*'s broadside gunfire. But the cohesion and rapidity of fire from *Java*'s ill-served guns now began to falter; Lambert was losing his precarious advantage conferred by *Java*'s speed.

Bainbridge, wary of being raked, let fall his fore and main courses, swiftly driving up under *Java*'s lee and, shooting away the British frigate's bowsprit. The acceleration enabled Bainbridge to wear, while *Java* floundered in stays, her headsails lost with her bowsprit. Bainbridge crossed Lambert's stern at two cables distance and raked her; then, as *Java* slowly swung, her starboard broadside responded and both ships ran off with the wind free on their larboard quarters, *Java* still in the windward station. But it was *Constitution*'s guns which were now dealing death and destruction as Bainbridge steadied her deck with a backed mizen topsail. Bainbridge was plying grape from his carronades and his sharpshooters in the tops were picking off men on *Java*'s upper decks. Despite this galling fire, Lambert's ill-assorted company stuck to their guns as their captain saw his sails shot away, his rigging flying loose, his men falling like corn stalks under the scythe as *Java*'s hull shuddered to the impact of round shot.

Lambert's last resort was to carry his adversary by boarding. Summoning his seamen and marines, he put his helm over and ran *Java* at *Constitution*'s main chains. As her broken bowsprit loomed, *Constitution*'s guns raked *Java*. The British boarders fell back, *Java*'s foremast fell, bringing down the main topmast, and the broken spar fouled in the *Constitution*'s mizen rigging. This held *Java* long enough for the Yankee guns to rake her again while the American sharpshooters prevented a soul crossing to the *Constitution*'s deck. Then *Constitution*'s impetus carried Bainbridge clear, and Lambert managed to get his ship before the wind; but Bainbridge, now ahead, wore his ship and then luffed her up under *Java*'s stern, raked with her starboard batteries, wore again, and ranged up to fire her larboard guns.

Still the *Java*'s crew fought their ship as both frigates again ran parallel, almost dead before the wind. The flashes from the gun muzzles ignited the ropes and canvas hanging over *Java*'s starboard gangway, and water was continually used to douse this. The first lieutenant, Henry Chads, was wounded, but took command as Lambert was shot through by a musket ball. *Java*'s upper deck was wrecked, and her masts fell until she wallowed like a log and one by one her guns fell silent, their servers exhausted. At half-past four *Constitution* drew ahead and Bainbridge luffed up to windward, setting his men to refitting. An hour later, a red ensign still fluttered above *Java*'s deck. Hauling round, Bainbridge ran down and hove *Constitution* to, athwart *Java*'s bow. To the shattered British there seemed to be little wrong with her beyond the shot-holes in her sails, and her positioning to rake them once more was intolerable. Chads struck his ensign. It was almost six o'clock.

Against American losses of 10 killed and 25 wounded, *Java* suffered 22 killed and 102 wounded, many, including Lambert, mortally. Boys as young as thirteen-year old Midshipman Keene were among the casualties. Bainbridge reported that *Java* had been 'exceedingly well handled and bravely fought'. When Bainbridge restored to General Hislop some of the personal effects looted by the American boarding party, Hislop in turn presented Bainbridge with a sword. 'Our gallant enemy', Chads wrote, 'treated us most generously.' Other sources record that the British seamen were manacled, which they well may have been, for they had proved dangerous; but the officers were paroled.

The *Java* was not worth salvaging and was burnt. Lambert died of his wound on 4 January 1813, his sole triumph the curtailment of Bainbridge's cruise. *Constitution* headed for San Salvador where *Hornet* still lay confining *Bonne Citoyenne* in neutral waters, though she had retaken the *William*. Here Lambert was buried with military honours in the Portuguese fortress of Fort San Pedro. At the court martial on

*Java*'s loss, held aboard *Gladiator* in Portsmouth on 23 April 1813, Chads was honourably acquitted; he was made a commander shortly afterwards, a captain two years later, and died in 1868 a full admiral and a Knight Grand Cross of the Order of the Bath.

After Bainbridge's departure for home, *Hornet* remained blockading the *Bonne Citoyenne* until 24 January 1813, when the British 74 *Montagu*, flagship of the Brazilian station, arrived on the scene. Lawrence stole away under cover of night, leaving Pitt Greene to savour his small fortune.

A month later Lawrence was off the Demarara River, where he discovered two British brig-sloops, the *Peacock* and *Espiègle*. The latter lay at anchor behind the river's bar, but the *Peacock* (Commander William Peake), was approaching from seaward. A short action was fought in which the British in the lee position fired uselessly upwards, but the lee guns of the *Hornet* pierced the *Peacock*'s hull so that in the course of a quarter of an hour she was reduced to a sinking condition. Her crew were badly mauled and Peake paid the ultimate penalty for his incapacity. His ship was aptly named and as aptly nick-named 'the yacht', for the fastidious attention paid to the order and brilliance of her decks, the polish of her brass and the neatness of her ropes. As for her guns, her carronade breechings were parcelled in canvas and the elevating screws gleamed with polish – so unused had small cruisers on remote stations become to fighting for their living that they had lost the knack. Instead, their commanders diverted their crews' energies to the assiduous pursuit of 'smartness'.

On this occasion another fundamental tenet of British naval philosophy was also missing, for the commander of *Espiègle*, John Taylor, failed to go to his consort's aid and later affected not to know of the affair. He was dismissed the service after a court martial, though since the evidence against him was inconclusive he was later reinstated, with a heavy loss of seniority. Lawrence, returning home to America in *Hornet* as yet another Yankee hero, was saved for a worse fate.

Those reflecting on this series of disasters had ample food for thought. Superior American gunnery, poor British leadership and the inferior quality of their ships' complements were part of the problem, but so too was the worn-out state of the British frigates' compared with their freshly fitted-out adversaries. Of the inherent courage or tenacity of the Royal Navy's officers and men in these actions there is little doubt, and contemporary commentators sought every possible excuse to mitigate the sobering facts. 'In the name of God,' lamented *The Times* in December 1812, 'what was done with . . . [our] immense superiority of force? . . . Oh, what a charm is hereby dissolved! What hopes will be excited in the breasts of our enemies!' London wondered, and the Admiralty fumed. When they heard the news aboard the cruisers of the Royal Navy, opinion was unanimous. What was required to see off cousin Jonathan were ships in which all these weaknesses had been foreseen and eliminated.

In real terms Rodgers' cruise had been ineffective and the number of prizes he and his colleagues had taken was disappointing, but this fact had been totally eclipsed by the dazzling demolition of the British frigates. The British had actually done rather better. Despite Jefferson's embargo of outward trade and his delay in declaring war so as to enable American merchant ships at sea to reach the safety of home ports, they had taken enough American merchantmen to hint at what a regular blockade might mean to the American economy. Jefferson's tactics themselves back-fired, by limiting American commerce, but the most frustrating element for the Americans, and the greatest success for the British, lay in the near-perfection of the Royal Navy's convoy system. This was as tedious as unopposed blockade, but it was a war-winning strategy that has escaped the notice of most naval histories, precisely because of its lack of drama.

Convoys were susceptible to the predatory privateers of France and Denmark, and now of the United States, but although the impact of the war against British trade was potentially significant and worried ship-owners, merchants and Their Lordships of the Admiralty, the cruisers of the Royal Navy successfully contained it. Scores of French privateers were captured, so that, with one or two notable exceptions like Robert Surcouf's Indian Ocean cruises in *Revenant*, the investing *armateurs* found the viability of their business questionable, and their profits disappointing. On balance the Danes did better and the Americans best of all – but, as we have repeatedly seen, the efforts of the commerce-raiding naval cruisers of all its enemies, though temporarily troubling, never overwhelmed the Royal Navy. There were however two notable exceptions to this generalisation, and they were both American.

On the outbreak of war with America Admiral Sir John Warren was in command of the North American station with two local flag officers, one of them Sir Edmund Nagle, as subordinates. Though their resources were slender, from Christmas 1812 these officers steadily stepped up the formal blockade of the eastern seaboard. To counter the power of the big American frigates the British hurriedly built a few 24-pounder frigates of fir, but they were based on the *Endymion* and were smaller than the *Constitution*. Three 74-gun third rates were also quickly cut down and these razées were more effective, retaining their 32-pounders. But, fast as the reaction was, it was the spring of 1813 before it began to bite, after which it swiftly reduced the American economy, creating widespread distress and making the war, and Jefferson's government with it, unpopular.

The *President* and *Congress* sailed that spring but between them took only sixteen prizes, including the British naval schooner *Highflyer*. Returning to port, the *Congress* was found to be so worn-out that she was laid up. Decatur's *United States*, the newly recommissioned *Macedonian* and the *Hornet* sailed, only to be chased back into New London. Lieutenant William Allen of the 16-gun brig-sloop *Argus* was more successful. Having conveyed an American ambassador to France, he proceeded to raid commerce in the English and St George's Channels; but as he could not send home his twenty prizes, he had to burn them. Occasionally, however, his hard-worked crew took advantage of their cargoes, and after plundering a wine-laden prize from Oporto on the night of 14 July 1813 they were sore-headed when at five o'clock the next morning the 18-gun British brig-sloop *Pelican* was seen bearing down.

Allen had been Decatur's first lieutenant in the action with *Macedonian* and made no attempt to escape, though the coast of Pembrokeshire was only fifteen miles under his lee. He opened fire; *Pelican's* Commander John Maples responded, and within seconds Allen had had a leg shot off. Mortally wounded, he refused help and stayed on deck until he passed out. The first lieutenant was next wounded and the second lieutenant, also named Allen, was left to fight the *Argus.* Maples tried to rake, but Allen was equal to the occasion and luffed up and backed his main topsail, so that *Argus* lay athwart *Pelican's* bow. The raking broadside was poorly aimed and both ships bore away, engaging in a running duel in which *Argus* was the loser. As her rigging was systematically shot away, the over-indulgence of her crew contributed to diminish their morale. Maples fore-reached and ran across *Argus's* starboard bow, his men ready to board. Faced with this *fait accompli,* Allen struck.

William Allen's raids had caused sensations in London and Liverpool, since the news of every capture so close to British shores was swiftly carried to Lloyd's and the shipping houses of Liverpool. But worse was to come, for in distant waters a colleague of Allen's was engaged in the most successful anti-British commerce raid of the entire period.

It will be recalled that Captain David Porter's *Essex,* sailing in July 1812, had been the first American in the war to take a British warship, the former collier *Alert.* It had been intended that *Constitution, Hornet* and *Essex* should rendezvous and operate together, but Hull had had family business to attend to, sailing was delayed, and Bainbridge took his place. By then Porter had already gone, bound for the South Atlantic and a long cruise for which he had extra stores and sixty men above *Essex's* normal complement.

Porter was a dark, headstrong young man, who had made a name for himself at Tripoli harbour where he had been imprisoned with Bainbridge after the loss of *Philadelphia.* The son of a Revolutionary War sea-officer, he had sailed with Truxtun, seen action in the Quasi-War with France aboard *Constellation* in her fight with *Insurgente,* and formed part of the captured frigate's prize-crew. In the Caribbean on trade protection, aboard the man-of-war schooner *Experiment,* he had fought Haitian pirates; in Baltimore, Maryland, he had stabbed a drunk who attacked him; in New York he had drunk copiously with the writer Washington Irving; in Washington he had fallen impetuously in love and, when ordered out of Miss Evalina Anderson's house by the fifteen-year-old beauty's brother, threatened the young man with defenestration. As a newly-married couple in New Orleans, Porter and Evalina adopted a young man named David Farragut, who afterwards joined Porter as a midshipman in *Essex* and, later still, commanded the Union navy in the Civil War, gained two victories at New Orleans and Mobile, and became the first admiral in the United States Navy.

After taking the *Alert* and a troopship, the *Samuel and Sarah*, out of a convoy escorted by the British frigate *Minerva*, mentioned earlier, Porter made several more captures, then put in to the Delaware to land his despatches. Here he received instructions about joining Bainbridge and left again on 28 October for the South Atlantic, where he seized several more merchantmen including one, the *Nocton*, carrying specie. Failing to locate Bainbridge and hearing from a Portuguese merchant ship that an action had been fought between a British and an American frigate, Porter decided to double Cape Horn and make for the South Pacific. He had a hard time of it, but reached Valparaíso and, thanks to the anarchic conditions prevailing in Chile, was welcomed there. At the time many of the Spanish colonies of South America were in rebellion taking advantage of Spain's involvement in Napoleon's wars to throw off the colonial yoke imposed from Madrid. Chile was largely in rebel hands, the American consul was friendly to anti-imperialists and favoured their cause, and Porter was consequently able to refit *Essex* in comfort.

As for his presence in the Pacific, Porter could claim that this was to afford protection to the American sperm whale fishery; in fact, his real objectives were the whalers of Great Britain. To his crew he had already issued a written proclamation: 'The unprotected British commerce on the coast of Chile, Peru and Mexico will give you an abundant supply of wealth; and the girls of the Sandwich Islands shall reward you for your sufferings during the passage round Cape Horn.' Neither statement proved wholly true, for though *Essex* took numerous prizes, not one reached a friendly port where its value could be realised, and the girls of the Sandwich Islands rewarded Porter's sailors with the syphilis their enemy had left behind on their own visits of exploration two generations earlier.

On leaving Valparaíso Porter captured a Peruvian privateer, the *Nereyda*, which owing to a loose and tacit alliance with Britain had been taking American sperm-whalers. Next Porter recovered one of the *Nereyda*'s prizes, the Nantucket whaler *Barclay*: it was just the beginning. The *Essex*'s cruise proved to be an extraordinary affair, with Porter dominating a large portion of the largest ocean on the planet for a year. He destroyed the British whaling trade, taking thirteen whalers in succession, amounting to some 60 per cent of the whole, and punctuating these captures with rather bombastic proclamations to his crew. One whaler, the *Georgiana*, he armed as a consort and sent to take her own prizes. Porter also armed a second auxiliary, the whaler *Atlantic*, renamed *Essex Junior*, and put Lieutenant John Downes in command of her. At Valparaíso, trying to sell his prizes, Downes heard that news of their cruise had reached London. He went after Porter, finding him in the Galapagos Islands on 30 September 1813, fitting out more auxiliary warships. Porter took his extemporised squadron to Nuku Hiva in the Marquesas where he enjoyed a seven-week idyll careening *Essex*, and with characteristic pomposity annexed the island to the United States. His men, more interested in fornication than imperialism, divided their time between refitting their ship and miscegenating. As Bligh had, after this prolonged period of licence, Porter found his crews mutinous when they received orders to put to sea again. Unlike Bligh, Porter threatened to blow them all up: *Essex* and *Essex Junior* left Nuku Hiva on 13 September 1813.

Porter left his prizes to colonise the Marquesas, but the plan went wrong: the men turned mutinous, combined with the British prisoners and sailed one whaler, the *Seringapatam*, to New Zealand. Lieutenant Gamble, left as 'governor', manned the *Sir Andrew Hammond* and set off for the United States, leaving the remaining prize burning in 'Massachusetts Bay'. Gamble was captured by a British ship off Hawaii and not repatriated until after peace had been signed.

Porter meanwhile had been to Mocha Island, south of Valparaíso, to water and reprovision. Unaccountably, when he might with more profit have made directly for home, he then sailed north to Valparaíso. Here he invoked the neutrality laws when Captain James Hillyar in the 36-gun British frigate *Phoebe* and the 18-gun ship-sloop *Cherub* (Commander Thomas Tucker) sailed into port. Hillyar ran in provocatively close, exposing his bow to raking fire from the *Essex*, then rounding to and hailing Porter, announced that he had no intention of violating Chilean neutrality. Porter was furious, and stated afterwards that he had had the British ship at his mercy; but Hillyar had called his bluff and tested his mettle. Porter had not seized the initiative.

The *Phoebe* and *Cherub* anchored and there followed days of flaring insults, both formal and informal. Flags bearing slogans declaring 'free-trade and sailors' rights' were run up to *Essex*'s mast trucks; pendants declaring loyalty to King and Country ran up the *Phoebe*'s. *Cherub*'s crew sang in the evening more sweetly than the Americans, Porter generously admitted, but 'those of the *Essex* were more witty and to the point'. Boat crews swore at each other, officers maintained a frigid formality, and at the residence of the American consul Porter and Hillyar discussed the terms for an engagement. It was an interesting confrontation, firebrand American and cautious, experienced Briton. Needless to say, the two could not agree; so Hillyar weighed *Phoebe*'s anchor and lay offshore.

Finding himself blockaded, Porter tried to provoke Hillyar by burning the former British whalers lying in port, but Hillyar declined to react. A middle-aged man of solid achievements, James Hillyar had no interest in bravado; he had had a long war, and he was only anxious to beat the Yankee and go home to his family. Porter, on the other hand, felt the outcome was sufficiently doubtful as to threaten to dull the brilliance of his reputation. For a whole month he vacillated, consumed with anxiety and thwarted ambition. The preponderance of carronades in *Essex*'s main batteries had always been a sore point with Porter; now they haunted him as he contemplated Hillyar's long 18-pounders. Porter finally decided that when conditions were right, he would abandon *Essex Junior* and make a run for it.

Meanwhile Hillyar remained patiently on his station. In the end, as so often happens at sea, the weather decided the matter, and Porter had no choice. On 28 March 1814 a southerly gale rendered Valparaíso untenable, *Essex*'s cable parted, and Porter was compelled to stand offshore. He who hesitates is lost, and his luck had run out.

As soon as *Essex* was clear of Vaparaíso, Hillyar and Tucker bore down, and Porter made a dash to round the headland of Punta del Angeles. As he did so a squall struck *Essex* and carried away her main-topmast. Farragut later maintained that Porter should have run out to sea; instead he tried to return to port, found himself unable to do so, and was forced to anchor *Essex* in a small bay three miles from Valparaíso. Although *Essex* lay within territorial waters, Hillyar determined to attack before dark.

It was four in the afternoon as the British ensigns ran up the mastheads of *Cherub* and *Phoebe* and they closed in on the *Essex*. Porter too hoisted battle ensigns, and ran springs to his cables; but these availed him little, for they were not rigged when the action opened and, when they were, were shot away. Tucker, making for the *Essex*'s starboard bow, was soon driven off, but *Phoebe* took station across *Essex*'s stern and her 18-pounders scythed *Essex*'s decks with raking broadsides. Porter compensated for his loss of springs by running three long 12-pounders aft and firing them to such effect that Hillyar and Tucker backed away. A long way from home, they could afford to lose few men, and fewer spars. Hillyar re-engaged but, having suffered some damage aloft, withdrew a second time to knot and splice, and maintain command of his ship in the rapidly failing wind. At half-past five *Phoebe* was anchored off *Essex*'s larboard quarter. Tucker kept *Cherub* under weigh and, manoeuvring out of range of *Essex*'s carronades as Porter had fearfully apprehended, began to knock the American to pieces with her bow chasers.

Porter could not sustain this devastation and cut his cable, closing with *Phoebe* so that his carronades began to take effect. *Cherub* hauled out of the fight as Hillyar now used his sails to draw out of range of the American carronades. The *Phoebe*'s 18-pounders resumed their bombardment; the result was now no longer in doubt, but Porter refused to strike, despite the needless slaughter of his men. Hillyar's first lieutenant, William Ingram, begged his captain to close and board and put an end to the 'deliberate murder'. But Hillyar, properly, wished to preserve his own men, and the matter lay in Porter's hands, not his; a moment or two later, Ingram fell dead with a splinter in his head. Aboard *Essex,* the carnage was awful and confusion was growing. Porter sent a midshipman to shoot a man who ran from his gun, and the lad found the coward being chased by another seaman who was dragging the remains of his severed leg round the deck as he attempted to do the middy's work for him. Elsewhere, acts of selfless courage were taking place.

Finding himself unable to close and board *Phoebe,* Porter decided to run *Essex* aground, but as she drew close to the bluffs the wind shifted, blew the frigate's head round, and again exposed her to *Phoebe's* raking fire. The light wind now gently thrust *Essex* towards *Phoebe,* just as Downes arrived in a boat with some men left behind in Valparaíso. Hillyar avoided the slow, fortuitous advance of his enemy, and withdrew as Porter dropped his sheet anchor and fired every gun he had left. *Phoebe* was by now badly damaged, both aloft and in her hull, and for a moment or two Porter hoped she might drift out of range in the light airs. But then *Essex's* cable parted, and the game was up. Drifting helplessly herself, she endured a further storm of shot until a fire below drove men to rush on deck with their clothes alight. The instruction to jump overboard in such circumstances to extinguish the flames was taken as a general order, and many seamen did so. Some drowned, others reached the shore terribly wounded. In the mayhem, out of 255 on board *Essex,* fifty-eight lost their lives in the fighting, sixty-six were wounded, and thirty-one were drowned. *Phoebe* lost four killed and seven wounded; *Cherub* one killed and three wounded, including Tucker.

Hillyar's violation of Chile's neutrality was made much of in Porter's account of events, and he sneered at Hillyar's excessive caution and his refusal to engage in a ship-to-ship duel which left *Cherub* out of the action. Hillyar's violation of Chilean neutrality was indeed indefensible, though the Chileans were not materially hurt by it. He was otherwise a naturally careful man, not a death-or-glory hunter. Porter's ship's company had paid the price for his fear that his reputation might be even slightly diminished. He *was* at a disadvantage with his short-ranged carronades and missing main topmast, but Hillyar was no fool, neither was he a coward for capitalising on the advantages within his grasp. Porter's crew had fought their ship with unsurpassed courage, and a devotion that went far beyond the legitimate expectations of government. Porter himself was a victim of hubris and he might have better served his men by preventing an excessively 'unnecessary effusion of blood'.

Captain Hillyar sailed north and, in the execution of his orders, destroyed the fur trading posts on the Columbia River before turning his attention to the whaling ships of the United States. After all, Cousin Jonathan had to be punished for his presumption. In fact, by the time Hillyar and Porter had fought their action off Valparaíso, British sensibilities had been mollified by another fought not on the threshold of an emerging new South American republic, but on the doorstep of Boston itself.

Like Porter, Captain James Lawrence, was a man eager to make a name for himself; and, also like Porter, he had conceived the romantic notion of a ship-to-ship duel, when as commander of the *Hornet* he was blockading the specie-laden *Bonne Citoyenne* at San Salvador. In May 1812, as a full captain, he was placed in command of the *Chesapeake*, many of whose crew refused to re-enlist because of lack of prize money. Instead they signed on in privateers, and were replaced by a draft from *Constitution* and new recruits which included forty British and some Portuguese. Two of Lawrence's lieutenants were midshipmen, acting up. In short, *Chesapeake*'s crew at the time of her sailing was of poor, untrained quality. A few weeks' cruise would have knocked heads and worked up the ship, but Lawrence was now afflicted by the same personal hubris as Porter, amid a more generally prevailing feeling of smugness. A sense was growing among the Yankees that they were as naturally superior to the British as the British considered themselves to be to the French – and had considered themselves to be to cousin Jonathan, until he gave them their come-uppance. For the ambitious Americans it was time Britannia's trident was wrested from her!

Lawrence might have been able to suppress these destructive sentiments, at least until his ship was in a fighting condition, but unfortunately they were daily aroused by the news that a British frigate lay a-cruising just outside Boston, and Boston was incensed. The British frigate had been on the North American station for some time, and Porter's *Essex* had only just avoided her the previous summer. She was His Britannic Majesty's frigate *Shannon,* one of the *Leda*-class, 38-gun, 18-pounder frigates built on the lines of the French frigate *Hebe*, captured in 1782, and one of the most numerous group of cruisers ever built for the Royal Navy. Captain Philip Broke came from Suffolk, where his family held land on the banks of the lovely River Orwell. He had taken command of *Shannon* on 14 September 1806, commissioning her as a new ship, and had immediately begun to train up a motley crew into expert gunners. Unlike many of his colleagues, Broke had long ago got round the restrictive Admiralty instructions about limiting expenditure on practice shooting by disregarding them and underwriting some of the cost himself. Using dispart sights and holding individual gunnery shoots at floating targets made of casks, he had added competition between guns to the corporate effect of broadside firing, giving small prizes to gun-crews who did well. Broke also regularly exercised his crew at small-arms, cutlass and pike drill, and it was common for him to appear abruptly on deck and order a cask thrown overboard. He would then order a particular gun's crew to sink it, urged on by their fellows.

Thus *Shannon*, under Broke's command, combined all the decisive virtues that had been lacking in part or in total from her defeated sisters. Moreover, Broke himself, while neither a firebrand nor a martinet, was no cautious career-officer like Hillyar in the distant Pacific. As an officer and a gentleman of honour, Broke smarted under the humiliation the American's parvenu navy had inflicted upon his own service, and he was not averse to a trial of strength. By way of a local boat he had sent into Boston a challenge to Lawrence, offering a single ship duel in a position to be agreed beforehand, giving Lawrence the chance to get clear of Boston and shake his crew down. Fatally, it seems the American captain never received it. At all events, as *Chesapeake*'s anchor was weighed at noon on 1 June 1813, the masts of *Shannon* broke the skyline. *Chesapeake* stood out to sea, passing the lighthouse on the Brewsters, heading for the *Shannon*.

Eighteen miles east of Boston light, heading south-east with her deeply reefed main topsail and topgallant aback, *Shannon* lay hove-to under fighting canvas and waited for the *Chesapeake*. With the American frigate standing out towards him under a press of canvas, Broke can have been in little doubt of Lawrence's intentions. It was about half-past five when Lawrence drew close and took in his studding sails, struck his royal yards and shortened down. As the two frigates came in range, heading a little north of due west, Lawrence hauled up *Chesapeake*'s forecourse and broke out battle ensigns at her three mast-heads.

Lawrence appeared to Broke to be heading to cross *Shannon*'s stern to rake, and Broke ordered his men to lie down and not expose them-selves. In fact Lawrence had no such idea but instead seemed determined to try a slogging match, for he luffed up fifty yards from the *Shannon*'s starboard quarter and squared his mainyards, so placing the two enemies yardarm to yardarm in a quixotic manner. Broke had made his pre-parations carefully. *Shannon*'s guns were loaded alternately with two round shot and a keg of musket balls, and one round shot and one double-headed shot. All fire was to be held until William Mindham, gun-captain of the fourteenth gun in the starboard battery, had his weapon aimed at the *Chesapeake*'s second larboard gun-port. Mindham did as he was bid, and as he jerked his lanyard and the gun lock's hammer struck the frizzen, the first shot rang out. It was ten minutes to six as, in succession from the stern and rippling forwards, the *Shannon*'s guns roared and recoiled inboard. The iron stormed across the gap and struck the Americans. *Chesapeake* responded with a murderous broadside, but despite her backed sails she was carrying her way and going too fast. Lawrence luffed up into the wind a little to check her as *Shannon*'s gun crews leapt like fiends about their artillery pieces.

From the tops of *Shannon*, the whole length of the enemy seemed clouded by gunsmoke and splinters. The boatswain, fourth lieutenant and sailing master were killed; the men at *Chesapeake*'s wheel were systematically wiped out, and the *Chesapeake* luffed again as rigging fore and aft was shot away. Exposing her larboard quarter to *Shannon*'s gunfire, her stern was beaten in, and an arms chest on the quarterdeck was blown up by a grenade tossed down on *Chesapeake's* deck from *Shannon*.

Now Broke noted that *Chesapeake* was gathering sternway, so he put his helm over, swung to larboard and kept his mizen topsail a-shiver, spilling wind. But the *Shannon's* jib-stay was shot away, and with her jibs masked in the lee of *Chesapeake* she failed to bear away. At six o'clock the *Chesapeake's* larboard quarter fell on board the *Shannon's* starboard main chains and held there as *Shannon's* after bower anchor caught in the wreckage of *Chesapeake's* quarter.

As the two ships came together, Lieutenant John Law of the Royal Marines shot Lawrence as he stood in full-dress uniform on his quarter-deck. Broke ran forward, the decks of his own ship slippery with blood, his gunners still toiling at their grim task. Seeing the enemy seamen flinching, Broke shouted for the two ships to be lashed, for the guns to cease fire and for boarders to storm the enemy quarterdeck. In passing a lashing, Broke's boatswain, William Stevens, had his arm hacked off by an American cutlass and fell riddled with musket balls; incredibly, he survived.

The dangerous cult of personality activated by a charismatic commander now exerted its baleful influence: one of his young acting lieutenants helped carry the much-admired and mortally wounded Lawrence below. The American court martial held later was less than impressed by this act of devotion, judging the unfortunate officer to have deserted his post. Lawrence's last command, 'Don't give up the ship!', has become axiomatic in the United States Navy, even though it was not to be obeyed that fell evening.

Broke himself led the first boarders, a score of men from the *Shannon's* quarterdeck. At the appearance of the British most of the American seamen on the *Chesapeake's* upper deck ran below, and only a handful of marines, one corporal and nine men, along with Samuel Livermore, the chaplain, were left to confront them. Livermore fired a pistol at Broke, who cut him down for his charity. Broke then checked the impetuosity of his men until they could be joined by parties under Lieutenants Falkiner and Broom, and more under the first lieutenant, George Watt. Several, including Watt, were shot by *Chesapeake's* mizen topmen, before a long 9-pounder was swung on them, the breech quoins knocked out, and a charge of langridge cleared them from their perch aloft. Simultaneously, *Shannon*'s fore and main topmen under Midshipmen Smith and Cosnahan had cleared *Chesapeake*'s main top. Cosnahan had sat astride *Shannon*'s starboard main yardarm and fired loaded muskets handed him by his sailors, while Smith had led five men along *Shannon*'s foreyard and then onto *Chesapeake*'s mainyard as they lay together, side by side.

As Broke's boarders drove the remnant few resisting their progress forward along the deck, some of them dived overboard, and other American seamen began to tumble down into *Chesapeake*'s main gun deck with the news that the British were in possession of the quarterdeck. One of the officers commanding a battery, Lieutenant George Budd, calling for men to follow, led a counter-attack up the companionways, checking the advance of the British along the gangways and killing the *Shannon*'s purser and Broke's clerk. Budd was knocked back down the ladder as, alarmed by the noise above him, Lieutenant Ludlow, although mortally wounded while commanding his division of guns, dragged himself on deck with a few men; he and his followers were cut to pieces. With confusion below, the remaining handful of defenders made a last stand on the forecastle.

Broke, still leading the attack, parried a pike thrust and was struck by a clubbed musket which bared his skull to the bone. As he fell he was saved by Mindham, and a deadly fight ensued which ended only when the British had killed every man standing against them. A few volleys of musketry fired down the companionway finally secured the *Chesapeake,* and her colours were lowered. They were struck by Lieutenant Watt, sufficiently recovered from his wound in the foot, who called across to *Shannon* for a British ensign to hoist. In the confusion he bent it on the halliards *below* the American Stars and Stripes, and as the United States flag rose superior to the British, a volley of shots swept the after deck. This took the top of Watt's head off and killed the men about him, to the mortification of the British still aboard *Shannon* when they realised their mistake. Someone rectified Watt's error and, as the British colours rose to *Chesapeake*'s gaff, Mindham eased the wounded and shaken Broke onto a carronade slide, pointing out the moment of triumph. It was about five minutes past six in the evening; less than fifteen minutes had passed since Mindham opened the action.

It was a Pyrrhic victory. As Broke reported, 'the enemy fought desperately, but in disorder.' His own losses were thirty-three killed or mortally wounded and fifty-nine wounded, more than were sustained in any other victorious action in the war. But Lawrence, who soon afterwards died of his wounds, had lost forty-seven killed and ninety-nine wounded, fourteen mortally.

The *Shannon* had been heavily punished, though not as badly as her opponent, from which 362 shot were taken, more than twice the number counted in *Shannon*'s hull. Lieutenant Provo Wallis took *Shannon* and her prize into Halifax, where cheering crowds lined the heads. Aboard *Shannon* her people remained silent, out of respect for the wounded Broke lying below. He had been severely hurt, and suffered headaches for the rest of his life; he was made a baronet for his victory, and died a rear-admiral in 1841. Lawrence and Budd were buried at Halifax with full honours. Wallis and Falkiner were both made commanders, and the *Chesapeake* was purchased into the British navy though never commissioned. Soon after the end of the war she was sold and broken up. Her figurehead was preserved, and some of her timbers remain in a mill built near Portsmouth.

The propaganda value of the victory was considerable, outweighing its real merits. Cousin Jonathan's pride had been dented, but while London went wild with triumphant excitement, John Bull ruminated. 'It was as well Broke met Lawrence and *Chesapeake*', Admiral Sir Isaac Coffin remarked drily, 'and not Hull and *Constitution*.'

# CHAPTER 18

---

# 'The ship is safe'

The cruiser war with America went on after Lawrence and Porter had been defeated. The *President* under Rodgers had escaped the blockade in a May fog and took a number of prizes in the North Atlantic and North Sea during the summer of 1813. On 5 September 1813, the gun-brig *Enterprise*, having taken a number of British privateers, fought a savage and bloody action in which both commanders were killed, defeating the British gun-brig *Boxer* off the Maine coast. The American sloop *Adams* took ten British merchant vessels before being chased into the Penobscot River and burned in the summer of 1814. That spring the *Constitution* had sailed on a cruise but took only four vessels in three months, and on 29 April a newly-commissioned American sloop named *Peacock* took the 22-gun British sloop *Epervier*. The *Peacock* captured ten merchant vessels before returning home, and a new *Wasp* took the sloop *Reindeer* in June, sank the 18-gun *Avon* on 1 September, but then foundered with all hands.

As the Allies beat Napoleon to the gates of Paris and the Emperor of the French abdicated on 6 April 1814, the might of the Royal Navy turned its attention on the coast of the United States. The British blockade now really tightened its grip on American trade, sapping the country's will to fight on. After a struggle the American naval flotillas on the Great Lakes triumphed, but the hawks in Congress were thwarted in their intention of acquiring Canada for the Union. The British extended their blockade by landing and burning coastal seaports associated with privateering, and even set fire to the White House after consuming President Madison's victory dinner laid out ready on the tables. This vindictive act provoked protests in Britain, where public opinion had no taste for land operations against the Americans, provided they conceded superiority at sea. Peace negotiations were soon opened in Ghent, and a preliminary settlement had been reached when a British force, landed at New Orleans under the command of Wellington's brother-in-law, was beaten by General Andrew Jackson.

The news of the peace agreed on Christmas Eve did not reach America for some weeks, and on 14 January 1815 Stephen Decatur slipped out of New York in the *President* in a snowstorm and a gale of wind, bound on a commerce-raiding mission. At eight that filthy night the *President* ran hard aground on Sandy Hook, to be beaten on the shoal by the heavy swell until she could be sailed off on a rising tide. Hogged and with sprung spars, Decatur was unable to work *President* back into port, and had to make a dash eastwards along the coast. He ran instead into the waiting British, commanded by Captain John Hayes in the 56-gun *Majestic*, one of the razéed seventy-fours converted for the North American war.

With the *Majestic* were the 40-gun *Endymion* (Captain Henry Hope), and the 38-gun frigates *Pomone* and *Tenedos*. A chase ensued, the powerful *Majestic* leading the British squadron and occasionally firing after the *President*. But during the day the wind, so strong the night before, fell away and the *Majestic* dropped back, Hope's *Endymion* taking the lead. In due course Hope ranged up on Decatur's quarter, to a position where *President* could not bring a gun to bear, and opened fire. When Decatur swung to fire a broadside and board, Hope turned away, evading contact.

After dark Decatur headed south, hoping to throw off the pursuit, but *Endymion* followed and a running fight ensued, broadside to broadside. Decatur, unable to escape his faster pursuer, began to destroy her, knocking *Endymion*'s rig to pieces and depriving her of her motive power. Hope's frigate fell astern and Decatur fired a parting shot. But the *President*'s masts were already badly strained from her grounding, and she was making water. Nor was she alone, for *Pomone* was coming up astern, passing the wallowing *Endymion* with her eleven dead and fourteen wounded, while behind *Pomone* were *Tenedos* and *Majestic*. Just before midnight *Pomone* was close enough to fire two broadsides. Decatur could do no more; he was wounded, and his butcher's bill was long, twenty-four killed and fifty wounded. He struck his ensign and a boat from *Tenedos* took possession of *President*, returning to *Majestic* with Decatur, who handed his sword to Hayes. In a gale two days later, all *President*'s masts went by the board, as did two of *Endymion*'s; the latter also had to jettison guns to save herself.

The *Constitution* made a last cruise, under Captain Charles Stewart, and was off Madeira in February 1815, long after peace had been concluded. Here, under a moon on the evening of the 20th, she out-fought the 22-gun *Cyane* and the 20-gun *Levant* in detail. Taking his prizes to the Cape Verde Islands, Stewart had to leave hurriedly when the *Leander* and *Newcastle*, both of 50 guns, and the 40-gun *Acasta* approached. A chase followed in which the *Cyane* escaped, to reach America, and the British ships were drawn off in pursuit of the *Levant,* which they failed to recognise, thinking her an American frigate. Stewart too got away, and in due course reached New York. The *Levant* doubled back to the Cape Verdes, where the British prisoners left ashore turned the guns of a battery upon her. Caught in a cross-fire that took no notice of Portuguese neutrality and damaged houses in Porto Praya, *Levant*'s colours came down.

The *Hornet* and *Peacock* had followed Decatur out of New York a week later. Captain James Biddle reached Tristan d'Acunha on 23 March and fell in with the British 18-gun brig sloop *Penguin* (Commander James Dickinson). An action followed in rough weather, but the British gunnery was poor and an attempt to board resulted in half *Penguin*'s spars being torn down. In the close-quarters fire-fight Dickinson was killed, and then, as the vessels drew apart, *Penguin*'s foremast fell. Riddled with shot and ungovernable, she was surrendered by her first lieutenant, James M'Donald.

*Hornet* and *Peacock* made a rendezvous and headed for their new cruising station in the East Indies. They went in chase of an Indiaman, only to discover that she was the new 74-gun *Cornwallis* (built in India, for whose hull Lambert's *Java* had loaded copper sheathing). The faster *Peacock* soon outran her large pursuer, but *Hornet* was chased for two days as Biddle jettisoned almost everything except a single gun. *Cornwallis*, though fast, demonstrated no particular expertise in her gunnery, and in the end a shift of wind enabled Biddle to escape and return home.

The *Peacock* continued on her course and in the Indian Ocean took four Indiamen. Captain Lewis Warrington reached the Sunda Strait in June, and on the 30th encountered The Honourable East India Company's small cruiser *Nautilus*, a vessel very inferior to *Peacock*. Lieutenant Charles Boyce of the *Nautilus* informed Warrington of the peace, but the American chose to disbelieve him and demanded his surrender. After the exchange of two broadsides and the murder or mutilation of fifteen men, Boyce complied. It was the last action of a dirty and largely unnecessary war, the most lasting benefit of which was to check the overweening pride of the sea warriors of Great Britain.

During this furious aside with the United States, the Royal Navy had continued its war with Napoleon and the French Empire. Until the very end of the war French flying squadrons tried to break out, and occasionally succeeded, but in the effectiveness of the British blockade lay the ultimate success of British strategy. Aggressive and costly, it drained British resources, particularly manpower, for Britain's prime seamen, as well as her most experienced commanders, were employed in the battle-squadrons, not in her over-stretched cruisers. The unremitting vigilance, the seamanship and navigation, were backed up by good logistics and communications, a slow but steady advance in technology, a better quality if still tedious diet, and a fine administration.

As has already been noted, far more British ships, especially cruisers, were lost to the dangers of navigation and stress of weather than fell to all the efforts of her combined enemies during the period 1793 to 1815 – more than 340 of them. The fate of the 38-gun frigate *Blanche*, whose exploits have featured in these pages, was typical. Off Ushant in a westerly gale on 4 March 1807, she was pinned on a lee shore, driven aground and wrecked, with the loss of all but forty-three men, who fell into the hands of the French.

In the age of wind-driven ships, the only recourse officers and men had to combat the might of natural forces was their skill as seamen, and the finest example of this was the conduct of Captain John Hayes, to whom Stephen Decatur later surrendered his sword. On the wild night of 16 December 1812 Hayes was in command of the 74-gun *Magnificent*, lying at anchor in the entrance of the Basque Roads. The ship's topmasts had been struck down, and their yards lowered to reduce resistance to the wind aloft. Despite these precautions *Magnificent* began to drag her anchor, and while letting go a second anchor to hold the ship, Hayes was alarmed to see the breakers on a shoal less than five hundred yards dead to leeward. The gale continued to rise, the wind booming in *Magnificent*'s rigging as rain lashed across her decks. Moreover, the sea was increasingly heavy, bursting upon the bow, and the tide was onshore. Ironically, a previous *Magnificent* had been lost off Brest in March 1804 when she struck 'an unknown rock'; and Hayes was determined that his own ship should not share the same fate. He boldly resolved 'to do his utmost' to save his ship, and to claw offshore.

Coolly he mustered his crew and gave detailed instructions. A spring was clapped onto the small bower cable and the fore and main top and topgallant yards were sent aloft again outside their housed masts. As this work was proceeding, one anchor cable parted, but the other held for the time being. Having made the sails ready in light stoppings, Hayes braced his lower yards for the starboard tack, sent his men to their stations and told his crew to do exactly as he ordered with absolute obedience.

'Cut the cable!' Hayes shouted, whereupon the *Magnificent*'s head failed to fall off the wind. A moment later the parting of the spring made her broach, at which Hayes set his fore topsail, squared his main and mizen topsail yards, but left the mainyard braced round. As the wind came abeam, the mizen topsail was set and the helm put hard over, forcing *Magnificent* to swing. The main course and main topsail were instantly set, the mizen yards were sharply braced and the ship flew round, to head away from the shoal now only a stone's-throw away. As *Magnificent* stood out to sea, Hayes announced to his silent ship's company, 'The ship is safe!' This splendid example of club-hauling was to earn the captain the soubriquet 'Magnificent' Hayes.

As the long war inevitably reduced the quality of British ships and gunnery, the few French cruisers slipping to sea had the pick of officers and men mewed up by the enemy's blockade. These last emerging French frigates were in first-class condition, new-built, heavily armed and with coppered hulls. Though the French had a weakness in their crews' lack of experience and inability to keep the sea, the last frigate actions with them, like the encounters with the Americans, were not always British victories.

One of these late sallies was made by the 40-gun *Iphigénie* and *Alcmène* (Capitaine Jacques Emeric and Capitaine Alexandre Ducrest du Villeneuve), which left Cherbourg on a six-month cruise but were captured in January 1814 off the Canary Islands by the 74-gun *Venerable* (Captain James Worth). The *Venerable* was flying the flag of an old sea warrior, Rear Admiral Philip Durham, who had seen the war through from beginning to end.

So too had Sir Edward Pellew, who was blockading Toulon with the Mediterranean squadron. In the closing months of the war, Pellew came close to fighting a fleet action with Vice-Amiral Maurice Emeriau off Cape Sicié, but fate denied him that final glory. Perhaps it disapproved of his nepotism and considered he had profited enough. Pellew's success earned him a peerage in 1814; his sons were both senior naval officers and one, Pownall, sat as a Member of Parliament.

Aboard his flagship at the end of the war – the 120-gun *Caledonia*, the largest line-of-battle ship to have been built in Britain – he had his son-in-law as flag-captain and his brother Israel, now a rear-admiral, as his Captain-of-the-Fleet or chief-of-staff. Israel, having survived the explosion of his own frigate, had commanded the 74-gun *Conqueror* at Trafalgar. During the battle one of his officers, sent aboard a surrendered French battleship to accept the sword of her captain, had been asked to whom he capitulated. He was told to Captain Pellew; the Frenchman expressed his relief. There was no dishonour attached to striking to Sir Edward Pellew. It was not Sir Edward, he was informed, but his brother. 'My God,' the Frenchman is supposed to have exclaimed, 'there are two of them!'

On 2 February 1814, while 'Magnificent' John Hayes was cruising in *Majestic* between the Azores and Madeira on the lookout for the *Constitution*, he saw and chased the American privateer *Wasp* (not to be confused with the man-of-war of the same name). The chase ran through the night, and the next morning suspicious sails were seen in the offing; Hayes relinquished his chase and *Majestic* went to investigate. The strange squadron consisted of the 40-gun French frigates *Atalante* (Capitaine Mallet) and *Terpsichore* (Capitaine François Breton), with two prizes. Breton wished to fight, telling Mallet that between them they could overwhelm the seventy-four, but Mallet signalled his consort to make sail, and a chase began. By noon *Majestic* was coming within range of *Terpsichore,* and three hours later she began firing her bow chasers after the French frigate. For two hours, slowly overhauling Breton's ship, the big British third-rate lifted and fell in the increasingly heavy seas as a gale rose, her sails drawing, and the sparkle of gunfire rippling along her sides. The gunsmoke was whipped away in the wind as the shot whined over *Terpsichore*, whose gunners responded manfully until a few minutes before five o'clock when Breton, abandoned by his colleague Mallet, struck his colours. Hayes let *Atalante* go, for the conditions were deteriorating and he wished to secure his prize. The *Terpsichore* was a new ship, built at Antwerp in 1812 to a Sané design, but although she was taken into the Royal Navy, the end of the war meant that she was never afterwards fitted for service.

Mallet did not prosper by his cowardice, for he was spotted off the south coast of Brittany on 25 March by Captain Sir Peter Parker's frigate *Menelaus* and chased into Concarneau Bay, not far from L'Orient. Parker had already retaken one of Mallet's prizes, and now he sent in Lieutenant James Seagrove and Midshipman Frederick Chamier to challenge Mallet to come out and fight. Mallet declined. Thus did the cruiser war end not with a bang, but a whimper: a French frigate blockaded in a French bay by a British frigate of equal force.

Upon Napoleon's first abdication in April 1814 he was conveyed into exile on the Isle of Elba by Captain Thomas Ussher in the 38-gun frigate *Undaunted*. On the north coast of France, coming out of exile, Louis XVIII was conveyed back to France in the Royal Yacht *Royal Sovereign*, escorted by a squadron consisting of the 98-gun *Impregnable* (Captain Henry Blackwood) and flying the flag of Admiral of the Fleet HRH The Prince William, Duke of Clarence. ('Silly Billy', a professional if not outstanding naval officer, succeeded his brother George IV as William IV in 1830.) Additional escort was provided by the British frigate *Jason*, the Bourbon French frigate *Polonais*, two Russian frigates, and two yachts of the Trinity House.

Louis was obliged to flee Paris when Napoleon escaped from Elba, but the campaign of 'The Hundred Days' ended with the total defeat of the Emperor of the French at Waterloo on 18 June 1815. During this campaign there were two cruiser actions, both in the Mediterranean. The British 74-gun *Rivoli*, a captured French ship commanded by Captain Edward Dickson, intercepted the 40-gun *Melpomène* (Capitaine Joseph Collet) as she was on her way to Naples to embark the Emperor's mother. Then, on the eve of Waterloo, a fierce engagement between the 22-gun corvette *Légère* and the 18-gun brig-sloop *Pilot* resulted in the former escaping, having wrecked the British sloop's rigging. There were a few other final sparks in the West Indies, where the Bonapartist Comte de Linois initially rejected Rear-Admiral Philip Durham's demand that Guadeloupe submit to Bourbon rule. Finally, on the coast of France, Captain Charles Malcom of the frigate *Rhin* (herself a notable apprehender of privateers), along with the *Menelaus* and *Havannah*, the sloops *Fly* and *Ferret* and the schooner *Sealark*, destroyed a coastal convoy on the Breton coast. But there was to be no climactic equivalent of Waterloo for the careworn men and ships of the British Royal Navy; they merely had the last word.

After the rout of Waterloo, Napoleon fled west. Loyal Bonapartists had put together a plan to spirit him to a quiet retirement in the United States, and Capitaine Baudin of the *Bayadère* was waiting eagerly to receive his Emperor. The frigate *Infatigable* and an American ship, the *Pike*, were also in the Gironde, while Capitaine Philibert and Capitaine Ponée were at Rochefort with the 40-gun frigates *Saale* and *Méduse*. It was thither Napoleon went, only to be confronted with a small blockading squadron led by Captain Frederick Maitland in the 74-gun *Bellerophon*. Messages were sent to Baudin, but it was too late: escape was impossible and, after negotiations with Maitland, Napoleon was pulled out to *Bellerophon* and threw himself on the mercy of his most implacable foes, the British.

Maitland took him to Torbay, where the curious British flocked out in hundreds of boats to catch a view of the Corsican Ogre, while the Allied Governments decided what to do with him. At British insistence, they decided clemency was out of the question. 'General Bonaparte' would be exiled on the remote island of St Helena, in the South Atlantic, 'the most isolated . . . unsocial place in the world'. The 74-gun *Northumberland* hoisted the flag of Sir George Cockburn, recently returned from North America, left Plymouth, embarked the quondam Emperor, and carried him into exile and out of history. The Great War was over, the Grand Army dispersed and, for a while at least, Britannia's trident was supreme.

As a young general, Bonaparte had perceptively declared: 'Let us concentrate all our activity upon the [French] navy, and [thereby] destroy England. That done, Europe is at our feet.' Had he taken his own advice, Napoleon might well – as one notable naval historian said – have written the name of France from Kerry to the Celebes. But he failed to understand the management of sea-power, and the French navy lost all the advantages it undoubtedly possessed in 1793 and again in 1803. Great Britain's blockade was *the* decisive factor in the Great War, but without the support of her widely dispersed cruisers to protect her vital trade and to hold off *any* threat of local superiority in *any* quarter of the globe, the effectiveness of the blockade would have been significantly – perhaps crucially – reduced.

Towards the end, under enormous strain, the sea warriors of the Royal Navy had managed to stave off disaster. The legacy of their exertions was a century of relative peace and stability throughout the world. During this period, their heirs and successors put down the very slavery that had contributed to the wealth of their country during

'The Great War with France'. They were also engaged in another task, for in the long peace they surveyed and charted the greater part of the globe, making up for the near-disastrous lack of decent British charts in a great explosion of hydrographical and exploratory enterprise.

At the conclusion of the war the ships of the Royal Navy were rapidly laid-up, their crews cast ashore, unemployed and hungry, an embarrassment to the state. The case of many of the seamen became desperate, and for a while revolution seemed a prospect the British would have to face. Among these now forgotten men and their families, personal tragedies were frequent. A few of the maimed gained pensions and perhaps a place at Greenwich Hospital; some went back to sea in the merchant ships from which they had been pressed; the landsmen recruited by means of the Quota Acts reverted to their former occupations, but most, whatever their origins, lived on their memories.

It was often little better for the officers. The exceptions, those who had made fortunes out of prize money, revelled in their wealth; but the vast majority languished on half pay in genteel penury, their thwarted ambitions aggravated into bitterness by social pretensions. Perhaps the adaptable young did best; some who had served as midshipmen later recalled the days of their youth in long-winded autobiographies; a few, like Marryat and Chamier, became novelists of note. In the foxing pages of *Peter Simple* and *Ben Brace* can still be found the tragi-comic social round of the sea-life, the japes of odd characters set amid the routine of a frigate sent 'to cruise against the enemy'. Here too can be discerned still the faint noise of the wind, a cheerful song and the scrape of a fiddle setting the bare-soled feet of the capering mariners to a madcap dido to while away a dog-watch. Also audible in the reader's imagination are the imperative cries of command, the thin rattle of the marine snare-drum and the terrible thwack of the lash; while beyond, in the far distance, the occasional thunder of the guns. But under the bright flutter of the imagined bunting, below the taut grey canvas and the black, straining rigging, amid the smoke and flashes, the glint of steel and the spark of flint on frizzen, the cries of the dead and dying echo yet.

At the end of it all, the price paid by British seamen for their nation's freedom was high.

332

# Chronology

of the main events during the French Revolutionary and
Napoleonic Wars

(Major political and military events are shown in bold type)

| | | |
|---|---|---|
| **1789** | | **French Revolution.** |
| **1793** | January | **French Revolutionaries execute King Louis XVI and declare war on Great Britain** following incident with the British brig-sloop *Childers*. Revolutionary France is at war with most of Europe, united against her in **the First Coalition.** |
| | August–December | The Royal Navy support the French royalists at Toulon until their eviction by the Revolutionary armies. |
| **1794** | Spring | British capture Martinique and St Lucia from the French. |
| | June | **Defeat of the French on the 'Glorious First of June'** by a British fleet commanded by Lord Howe. The French grain convoy covered by the French fleet reaches France. |
| **1795** | March | Action between British (under Hotham) and French squadrons off Genoa. |

333

| | | |
|---|---|---|
| | June | 'Cornwallis's Retreat' off Belle Île before superior numbers of French men-of-war. |
| | | Lord Bridport's engagement off Île de Groix. |
| | July | Hotham's second action in Mediterranean. |
| | | Rainer captures Trincomalee in Ceylon (Sri Lanka) followed by all the Dutch possessions in Ceylon and India. |
| | August | Cape Colony taken from the Dutch. |
| 1796 | Summer | More West Indian islands are taken from the French. |
| | August | British squadron overwhelms Dutch squadron at the Cape of Good Hope. |
| 1797 | January | Abortive French expedition to Ireland. |
| | | Pellew destroys the *Droits de l'Homme*. |
| | February | **Battle of Cape St Vincent; Jervis defeats Spanish fleet.** |
| | | British take Trinidad. |
| | July | Nelson bombards Cádiz, then makes disastrous attack on Tenerife. |
| | October | **Battle of Camperdown: Duncan defeats Dutch fleet.** |
| | | **French defeat Austrians and conclude peace of Campo Formio which terminates the First Coalition.** |
| 1798 | January | **Rebellion in Ireland.** |
| | June | **Irish rebellion suppressed at Vinegar Hill.** |
| | Summer | **French expedition to Egypt.** Malta captured on the way and India threatened. Nelson initially fails to locate French. |
| | August | **Battle of the Nile; Nelson destroys French fleet anchored in Aboukir Bay.** |
| | Autumn | French expedition against Ireland under Bompart. |

|  |  | French successes ended at Ballinamuck and Irish hopes dashed at Killala. |
|---|---|---|
|  | October | Warren defeats Bompart's firgates off Tory Island. |
|  | November | Minorca taken from Spanish. |
| 1799 | June | **Second Coalition formed** against France, consisting of Great Britain, Austria, Russia, Kingdom of the Two Sicilies (Naples) and Turkey. |
|  | August | Further Dutch men-of-war taken at Den Helder. |
| 1800 | February–March | Capture of *Généreux* and *Guillaume Tell* off Malta. |
|  | Summer | **French defeat Austrians at Marengo and Hohenlinden.** |
|  | September | French garrison in Malta surrenders to British. |
|  | October | Bonaparte arrives back in France from Egypt. **Tsar Paul takes Russia out of Second Coalition because of increasing hostility towards Great Britain.** |
|  | November | **Bonaparte becomes First Consul of France and attacks Austria in her Northern Italian provinces.** |
|  | December | **Baltic States of Denmark, Russia, Sweden and Prussia revive Armed Neutrality of the North against British interference with their trade.** |
| 1801 | January | **Austria makes peace with France at Lunéville and the Second Coalition collapses, to leave Great Britain isolated.** |
|  | March | **Assassination of Tsar Paul and accession of Alexander I.** |
|  | April | **British naval operations against the Armed Neutrality of the North. Battle of Copenhagen;** Sir Hyde Parker commands fleet but attack on Copenhagen led by Nelson. **Denmark, followed by Russia and Sweden, sue for peace with Britain.** |

| | July | Saumarez's action off Algeçiras followed by his pursuit of Moreno's Franco-Spanish squadron. |
| 1802 | March | **Peace of Amiens. France, Spain, The Batavian Republic (The Netherlands) make peace with Great Britain. Britain retains Ceylon and Trinidad. Cape Province returned to Dutch; Egypt evacuated by French and returned to Turkey; independence of Portugal and Ionian Islands guaranteed. France agrees to leave Naples and Britain to evacuate Malta and to remove French lilies from Royal Arms. During the peace France intervenes in the German states, Switzerland and Italy, so Britain declines to leave Malta. First Consul Bonaparte also sends an expedition to Haiti to suppress the independence of the Black Republic of Toussaint L'Overture.** |
| | August | **Bonaparte becomes First Consul for Life.** |
| 1803 | May | **War breaks out again.** French revive preparations to invade Britain by establishing encampments along Channel coast. |
| 1804 | March | **The Duc d'Engien is executed as a warning by Bonaparte to French royalists and to governments sympathetic to their cause. The event spurs the formation of the Third Coalition, led by Britain and backed by Russia, Austria and Sweden, with some German states.** |
| | May | **After a plebiscite, Bonaparte becomes Napoleon, Emperor of the French.** Samuel Hood takes Surinam. |
| | December | Moore's frigates precipitate **war with Spain** by attacking Bustamente's squadron off Lagos. **Napoleon crowned in Paris.** |
| 1805 | May | **Napoleon crowned King of Italy in Milan.** |

| | | |
|---|---|---|
| | Summer | French invasion plans mature. Villeneuve's fleet escapes from Toulon and is joined by Spanish. |
| | July | Calder's unsatisfactory mid Atlantic brush with Villeneuve's Combined Fleet. |
| | October | **Battle of Trafalgar; Nelson decisively defeats Franco-Spanish Combined Fleet under Villeneuve and Gravina.** Death of Nelson, and subsequently of Gravina and Villeneuve. |
| | | Dumanoir le Pelley's van squadron escapes. |
| | November | Le Pelley engaged by Strachan and taken off Cape Ortegal. |
| | December | **French Grand Army, having given up attempt to invade Britain, marches east, envelops Austrian army under Mack at Ulm and defeats Austro-Russian army at Austerlitz. Austria forced to make peace.** |
| 1806 | January | **Prime Minister William Pitt dies, broken-hearted, as the Third Coalition collapses.** |
| | | Home Popham retakes Cape Colony from the Dutch. |
| | February | Duckworth's action off San Domingo secures West Indies. |
| | July | Small British force landed by Royal Navy defeat French at Maida. |
| | October | **Napoleon's Grand Army inflicts a heavy defeat on Prussia at Jena-Auerstädt. The pursuit destroys the Prussian army and Prussia sues for peace, ending the short-lived Fourth Coalition. From Berlin Napoleon institutes his famous Continental System excluding British goods from Europe. This is followed by successive reinforcing decrees and is opposed by Britain's Orders in Council, by which the countervailing announcement was made that the European Continent was in a state** |

of economic blockade which would be enforced by the Royal Navy.

| | | |
|---|---|---|
| 1807 | February | Duckworth's disastrous mission to Constantinople. |
| | June | Incident between HMS *Leopard* and USS *Chesapeake*. Battle of Lemnos: Russian fleet under Seniavin defeats Turkish fleet. |

**Having beaten the Russians at Eylau in February, Napoleon's Grand Army inflicts a greater defeat on the Tsar's armies at Friedland, forcing Alexander I to make peace. The two emperors meet at Tilsit and declare an alliance, again leaving Britain alone against France, which now occupies Denmark and leaves Sweden isolated. The fleets of Portugal and Denmark are to be taken over by the French, but London quickly learns of this plot.**

| | | |
|---|---|---|
| | September | Lord Gambier lands an army under Lord Cathcart for the bombardment of Copenhagen and pre-emptively seizes the Danish fleet. Danish gunboats thereafter attempt interdiction of British convoys through their waters, with considerable success. |
| | November | **French invade Portugal;** Portuguese fleet escapes to Brazil. |
| 1808 | April | **Napoleon usurps Spanish throne and establishes** his brother Joseph as King of Spain. |
| | May | **Spanish insurrection against French rule begins Peninsular War and the 'Spanish ulcer'.** |
| | July | Spanish force defeats French at Baylen. |
| | August | **British government send first expeditionary force to Iberian peninsula.** |
| 1809 | January | British expeditionary force retreats to Coruña |

where it is evacuated by the Royal Navy and a fleet of transports.

February     British take Martinique for the second time.

April     **Austria, concerned about French ambitions in Spain, seeks a new alliance with Britain and the Fifth Coalition is formed.**

Lord Gambier sent to destroy French fleet in the Basque and Aix Roads. Lord Cochrane's explosion vessels and fireships attack the anchored French.

**British expeditionary force returns to Iberian peninsula and in July Wellington inflicts first of a series of defeats on the French at Talavera. The campaign lasts until 1814, when Wellington's army attacks Toulouse. Wellington is supplied throughout by British seapower.** British cruisers act in support of the Spanish guerrilla armies on the Biscay and Mediterranean coasts of Spain.

July     **French decisively defeat Austrians at Wagram.** Napoleon subsequently divorces Josephine and marries the 'Austrian mare', the Grand Duchess Marie-Louise.

July–     Strachan's support of Lord Chatham's disast-
September     rous expedition to Walcheren and the Schelde. This is intended to support Austria, but her defeat and Chatham's failure **end the Fifth Coalition.**

1810     February     Drury takes Amboyna from the Dutch. These follows the systematic reduction of Dutch possessions in the East Indies. Java falls in August after Drury's death.

August     French defeat attempt by British frigates to take Île de France (Mauritius).

December     **Alexander takes Russia out of the Continental**

System due to economic difficulties.
British take Île de France from French.

| | | |
|---|---|---|
| 1811 | March | Hoste's frigate action against Dubourdieu off Lissa. |
| | May | USS *President* opens fire on HMS *Lille Belt,* the final *casus belli* between Britain and the United States. |

British frigates take Tamatave, Madagascar, destroying last eastern base of the French navy.

**1812**   June    **Napoleon invades Russia supported by Austrian, Neapolitan and Prussian troops,** claiming that Alexander has broken the terms of the Treaty of Tilsit by allowing trade between Russia and Britain. **Alexander immediately seeks a new alliance with Britain and the Sixth Coalition is formed.** Saumarez, British C-in-C Baltic, much preoccupied with Danish 'Mosquito-war', operates in support of Russia.

**Great Britain and the United States of America at war.**

              September    **Battle of Borodino, after which the Grand Army occupies Moscow.**

              October    **Retreat from Moscow begins. Grand Army wastes away. Prussia and Austria abandon their alliance with Napoleon.**

**1813**   May    Napoleon raises fresh armies and engages Russian, Prussian and Austrian armies as these countries join the Sixth Coalition. **The vast campaign continues until the Allies reach the gates of Paris in April 1814.**

              September    Americans triumphant on Lake Erie.

**1814**   April    With the Allies in Paris, **Napoleon abdicates** and is taken to exile in Elba by HM Frigate *Inconstant*.

**Louis XVIII is taken back to France** in the British Royal Yacht escorted by ships of the Royal Navy, the Russian Navy and French frigates flying the Bourbon lilies.

|          |          |
|----------|----------|
| August   | **British capture and burn Washington.** |
| September | **The European Allies meet for the Congress of Vienna, which lasts until June 1815.** |
|          | Americans defeat the British on Lake Champlain. |
| December | **Peace of Ghent ends war between Great Britain and the United States** but does not prevent Battle of New Orleans in January 1815. |

| | | |
|---|---|---|
| 1815 | March | **Napoleon escapes from Elba and returns to Paris. In conference at Vienna the Allies form the Seventh Coalition, a continuation of its predecessor.** |
| | June | **After hurling back Blücher's Prussians, Napoleon turns on Wellington. Reinforced by Blücher, the allies rout Napoleon at Waterloo.** |
| | | **Napoleon surrenders** to Captain Maitland of HMS *Bellerophon* off Rochefort. He is later conveyed to his final place of exile, St Helena, in *Northumberland*. **End of the Napoleonic War.** |

| | | |
|---|---|---|
| 1821 | May | Napoleon dies of stomach cancer on St Helena. |

# Select Bibliography

The naval wars of 1793–1815 are covered by numerous books, many of them focused upon Nelson or the great fleet actions of the era, but these are outside the scope of the present work. This select bibliography is intended to provide the interested reader with a starting-point for further study or amusement, and to represent the chief sources to which I have referred. What follows is only a short list of those books which extend beyond the obsession with Nelson. Many titles once hard to obtain have recently been reprinted, and I have indicated modern editions where these are available.

Although somewhat dry and devoid of personal interest, the two great standard histories are William James's *The Naval History of Great Britain* (Richard Bentley, 1847) and William Laird Clowes's *The Royal Navy, a History* (volumes 4, 5 and 6: Sampson Low, Marston and Co., 1899). More recent editions of Laird Clowes's work (and in substantial portions of the history he was only the editor) have been published by the AMS Press, New York (1966), and Chatham Publishing, London, (1999).

Several scholarly general studies of the period have been produced, and among the best are:

A.T. Mahan, *The Influence of Sea Power upon the French Revolution and Empire, 1793–1812* (two volumes) and A.T. Mahan, *Sea Power in its Relations to the War of 1812* (two volumes). Both were published by Sampson Low, Marston and Co. in London and by Little, Brown and Co. in Boston, the first in 1892, the second in 1905. These famous studies by an American naval officer were born out of a great admiration for Nelson, and are not without their deficiencies; however, they remain a monumental body of work.

G. Marcus, *A Naval History of England:* Volume 2, *The Age of Nelson* (Allen and Unwin, 1971; republished by Applebaum, Sheffield, 1977), is a far lesser-known study by a under-rated, detached and readable historian which vividly conveys the whole conduct of the war. Marcus's complementary *Heart of Oak* (Oxford University Press, 1975) covers the organisational and strategic management of the Royal Navy during the same period.

C. Northcote Parkinson, *Britannia Rules; The Classic Age of Naval History, 1793–1815* (Alan Sutton, Gloucester, 1987) is a short but excellent study by an historian whose other works, which are now difficult to obtain, include biographies of Pellew and studies of the war in India, China and the East Indies.

A highly readable account of the naval component of the War of 1812 between Britain and the United States may be found in C.S. Forester's *The Naval War of 1812* (Michael Joseph, 1957). For the Quasi-War with France and the Tripolitanian campaign, *The Commodores*, by L. Guttridge and J. D. Smith (P. Davies, 1970) is commended.

The social life aboard ship is vividly brought to life in John Masefield's *Sea Life in Nelson's Time* (Conway Maritime Press, 1984; originally published 1905). There are however a number of more modern books about the wider social, logistical and administrative issues, of which Michael Lewis's *A Social History of the Navy, 1793–1815,* (Allen and Unwin, 1960), remains of great value; Brian Lavery's *Nelson's Navy: The Ships, Men and Organisation, 1793–1815* (Conway Maritime, 1989) is of equal stature; both Peter Kemp and Christopher Lloyd have produced studies of the lower deck, though these range over a wider period. Nicholas Rodger's *The Wooden World,* though it deals with the Royal Navy of a slightly earlier period, nevertheless offers a monumentally comprehensive review of what was, at the time, the greatest organisation on the face of the earth.

The despatches of captains and admirals are to be found in the many volumes produced by the Navy Records Society for its members, while the number of naval memoirs, as of naval biographies, is relatively small. However, although the originals may still be found in dusty corners of second-hand bookshops, new editions of several first-hand accounts have been republished by Chatham Publishing of London. A few sea-warriors like Sir Sidney Smith and Sir Edward Pellew have attracted their own biographers, but the vast majority lie forgotten in their graves. Cochrane, as might have been expected of him, wrote his own *Autobiography of a Seaman,* a pell-mell, self-exculpatory account which is, none the less, a rattling good read.

Further contemporary opinion, gossip and comment by sea-officers, along with potted biographies of sea-warriors, navigational details, despatches and anecdotes, are to be found in *The Naval Chronicle,* published annually from 1798. Single volumes have hitherto been expensive, but a new abbreviated edition by Nicholas Tracy has been produced in five volumes by Chatham Publishing and provides a rich lode for those willing to dig a little. For the true, eccentric flavour of life aboard a man-of-war as it was lived and endured, however, the curious reader is recommended to try the pages of Captain Frederick Marryat (one of Cochrane's midshipmen), particularly his masterpiece, *Peter Simple.*

The Vintage Naval Library is to be complimented for republishing William O' Byrne's *A Naval Biographical Dictionary,* but this has the limitation of including only officers alive at the date of its first publication in 1849, by John Murray. A complete list of those sea warriors involved. *The Commissioned Sea-Officers of the Royal Navy between 1660 and 1815,* was published in 1994 by the Scolar Press of London for the Navy Records Society. This contains the known dates of promotions, etc., but no further biographical details.

The best studies of the great naval mutinies at Spithead and The Nore in 1797 are B. Dobrée and G. Manwaring's *The Floating Republic,* (first published in 1935, but reprinted in 1987 by The Cresset Library, an imprint of Century Hutchinson Ltd), and James Dugan's *The Great Mutiny* (André Deutsch, 1966).

Brief details of individual ships are to be located in David Lyon's *The Sailing Navy List* (Conway Maritime, 1993; originally a limited edition), while the history and development of the frigate during the period covered in this work is best elucidated by Robert Gardiner in his *Frigates of the Napoleonic Wars* (Chatham Publishing, 2000).

Details of the handling of large sailing vessels are comprehensively treated in John Harland's *Seamanship in the Age of Sail* (Conway Maritime, 1984).

For the abstruse elements fringing the sea-life, Geoffrey L. Green's *The Royal Navy and Anglo-Jewry, 1740–1820* (published by the author in 1989) makes a valuable contribution to our understanding of what made the naval scene tick. Richard Hill's admirable *The Prizes of War: The naval prize system in the Napoleonic Wars, 1793–1815* (published jointly by the Royal Naval Museum and Sutton Publishing, Gloucester, 1999) delves into the real-life complexities of the great gamble upon which many sea-warriors staked their reputations.

Vivid contemporaneous images of the whole period, from the American War of Independence to the end of the Napoleonic Wars, may be found, along with informed comment by numerous modern contributors, in the copiously illustrated six volumes of the *Chatham Pictorial Histories,* while many contemporary ship-board terms may be verified in the *Marine Dictionary* of William Falconer (originally produced in 1780, but reprinted by David and Charles, Newton Abbot, 1970).

This list is very far from even attempting to be exhaustive. For the imaginative enthusiast there are many titles to be discovered and many voyages and exploits to be enjoyed from the comfort of a chair, entirely avoiding the rigors of sea-duty itself. Such are the pleasures of reading history.

# An explanation of sailing and other terms with a brief glossary

(For the names of individual sails, reference should be made to the drawing of HM Frigate *Seahorse* in the end-papers)

Frigates, like ships-of-the-line and ship-sloops, were **ship-rigged,** that is to say they bore three masts, a **fore, main and mizen,** each of which carried horizontal **yards.** The lower of these on the fore and main masts bore the **course;** above the course on all masts was the **topsail,** and above that, the **topgallant.** The top and topgallant yards could be lowered to reduce windage and top-weight when the sails they bore were **furled or doused.** Occasionally a royal was set above the topgallant, but it was customary at this time to hoist a royal yard and sail up from the deck. All these sails were said to be 'square'. On the stays between the masts were hoisted triangular **staysails,** with triangular **jibs** and one square **sprit sail** set from the **bowsprit** forward. The quadrilateral sail set abaft, or behind, the mizen mast was known as the **spanker,** or **driver.** Its upper edge was set along a spar called a **gaff,** from which at sea a warship's **ensign,** or **colours** were flown. The lower edge was extended along a **boom.** This sail, the staysail and jibs were said to be 'fore-and-aft' sails. In light winds additional sails could be set from booms extended from the yard arms of the fore and main masts through rings called boom-irons. These were called studding sails (pronounced 'stuns'ls').

A **brig** was a smaller, two-masted vessel, having a fore and mainmast. The latter bore the spanker. The term **sloop,** synonymous with the French **corvette,** referred to smaller men-of-war, below the rating of

347

frigates and ships-of-the-line. The latter were the battleships of the day. Smaller cruisers bore a variety of rigs, mostly fore-and-aft in character, such as the single-masted **cutter,** the twin-masted **schooner,** or the two- or three-masted **lugger.** French naval luggers were called *chasse-marées* or sea-hunters.

**East** and **West Indiamen** were ship-rigged; other merchantmen could be ship-rigged, or rigged as brigs, snows (a two-masted rig similar to a brig), schooners, luggers and so on, while local rigs such as the **xebec,** tartane and polaccra were to be found in the Mediterranean and elsewhere.

Privately-owned vessels fitted out for war and the acquisition of prizes and prize-money were called **privateers.** They had to obtain a license from their government and this was called a **Letter of Marque and Reprisal,** so the privateers themselves were often called 'letters of marque'. The French excelled at this form of warfare and their privateers and the men who manned them were known as **corsairs.** The principals fitting out such craft were called *armateurs.*

Sails were set, usually by hoisting the upper yards and the triangular jibs and staysails. The course were let to fall and their lower corners, or **clews,** either led forward by ropes called **tacks,** or drawn aft by ropes known as **sheets.** The yards were swivelled and thus trimmed to the wind by **braces.** The triangular sails were trimmed by sheets, as was the spanker which was **brailed up** when being furled. Square sails could be reduced in area by **reefing,** that is by lowering the upper yards a little, then drawing the horizontal head of the sail partially back to the yard by means of **reefing tackles** and then resecuring it with **reef points.** This reduced the area and the centre of effort. Course yards were not lowered when reefing their sails.

In manoeuvring, the sails could be **backed** against the wind, and the sails of each mast could be individually trimmed to exert leverage and swing the ship. Sails could also be backed allowing the wind to blow on their forward surfaces and arrest movement. When a ship was **hove-to,** some of her sails drew while others were backed, thus holding her more or less stationary in the water. (Heaving-to was usually resorted to in very heavy weather, as it eased the strain on men and gear. A ship 'stopped' for any other reason was generally said to be **lying-to**, as might be required when waiting for a boat which was inspecting a neutral merchantman for war contraband.) When the spanker was backed, it was said to be **chapelled**. Nothing, however, ever prevented a sailing vessel from drifting under the pressure of the wind. Even without sails set, a ship was susceptible to this wind-drift, which was called **leeway**.

Even at anchor this pressure caused problems, and in extreme conditions not only the upper yards were lowered but so too were the course yards and the topgallant and topmasts (see Captain Hayes's extrication of the *Magnificent* in Chapter 18). A man-of-war carried three principal anchors, the heaviest of which was called the **sheet-anchor,** the two slightly lighter anchors the **best bower** and **small bower.** They were difficult to handle, but could be carried out by boats to haul a ship ahead in a calm (if the water was shallow enough to reach the bottom), or to haul her off a sand-bank, etc. This was called **kedging,** and a ship also usually bore another smaller anchor for this purpose, known as the **kedge anchor**. A ship lying to a mooring buoy or to two anchors in a fleet anchorage was said to be **moored;** the process of getting her ready for sea, or un-mooring, took some time. When a ship raised her anchor she was said to weigh it, and thus was **getting under weigh.** However, once she was moving through the water, she was said to be **making way.**

A ship sailing with the wind behind her was said to be **running before the wind.** As she turned and brought the wind round onto one bow or the other, she was said to be coming onto **the starboard tack** when the wind blew against her starboard bow, or onto **the larboard tack** if the wind blew on to her larboard bow. The **starboard side** of a vessel is that part of her lying to the right of the centreline when one is standing aft and looking forward. The **larboard** is the opposite, and the term larboard was, by the end of the war, being replaced by **'port'.** The side of the ship upon which the wind is blowing is said to be the **windward side.** The opposite side is the **leeward** (pronounced 'loo'ard') **side.**

Although different ships performed differently and their speed and manoeuvrability could change depending upon their trim, how deep-laden they were, and so on, generally speaking a ship sailed fastest when the wind was at right angles to her centreline, when it was said to be **on the beam.** A running wind blowing over either the starboard or port quarter, was said to be **a quartering wind.** A square-rigged ship such as a frigate or ship-of-the-line could not point at a closer angle than about seventy degrees to the wind. It was therefore necessary to proceed to windward by a laborious series of zig-zags, known as tacks. When **tacking** or **beating to windward** the yards were **braced sharp up,** as nearly in line with the hull as was possible. The lower corners of the courses were trimmed by hauling the ropes, also known as tacks (see above), well forward. When a vessel changed tacks by turning her bow through the eye of the wind she was said to be going about, or tacking, and she was helped by allowing the sails on her foremast to come aback for a few moments until she paid off on the new tack, whereupon they were trimmed the other way. The main and mizen yards were trimmed as she went through the wind and they were partially masked by the backed foresails. Occasionally, from the strength of the wind or the size of the waves, a ship stopped and would not come round; in this condition she was said to be **'in irons'.** The remedy for this was to turn the other way and put the stern of the ship through the wind, or **wear ship.** This always worked, but it meant taking the ship round in a circle and a lot of ground was lost to leeward.

The ability of a captain and crew to make their ship respond to the prevailing wind was important when engaging an enemy. Once battle was inevitable – as, say, after a pursuit – the lower corners of the courses were usually lifted to the yard arms, or **clewed-up.** The ropes doing this were the **clew garnets.** The **buntlines** gathered the bulk of the sails up so that they could be furled along the yards by the **gaskets.** Courses and topgallants came in first in a rising wind, the topsails being the primary manageable and deepest-reefed sails in a ship when fighting, or when sailing in strong winds.

The carrying-out of these manoeuvres called for considerable expertise on everyone's part. Crack frigates prided themselves on the smartness with which they executed such manoeuvres – which could, as Cochrane demonstrated, be vital to save the ship. However, some captains placed an almost fetishistic importance on 'smartness', often to the detriment of gunnery or the unhappiness of their crews.

When a ship went into action her crew was summoned to their stations by the marine drummer **beating to quarters**. The ship was prepared for battle by removing the temporary bulkheads that made up individual officers' cabins, sanding the decks to prevent slipping when blood ran on them, preparing cartridges and seeing that the ready-use shot was in the cup-shaped lodgements behind the guns known as **garlands**. Meanwhile the surgeon prepared his instruments, the carpenter his wedges and plugs, and the whole ship **cleared for action.**

This was quickly achieved, with the majority of the men manning the guns. These varied in weight of metal depending upon the weight of shot they threw. The  main armament of **'great' guns** could vary on a frigate between 12-pounders and 24-pounders, depending on her size, and the weight increased during the progress of the war. Thus a frigate in 1793 might have been a 32-gun, 9-pounder, at the end a 44-gun, 24-pounder. The official establishment of guns included only a ship's main armament and did not take account of upper deck **carronades**, named after the Carron Company of Stirlingshire in Scotland, developers of this light-weight, short-barrelled weapon which was very effective at short range against both ships and men. Nor did it include the small anti-personnel **swivel guns** mounted in the fighting tops. (A type of cheap and inferior gun mounted in merchant ships for self-defence was called, confusingly, the **cannonade**.) In the bow and stern of a ship were mounted **the chase** or **'chace' guns** for attack or defence in pursuits. By the end of the eighteenth century the **flint-lock** mechanism had replaced the slow-match held in a linstock for firing the guns, while towards the end of the war increasing use was made of **dispart sights** for aiming them.

It was common practice when opening an engagement to cause the maximum amount of devastation by firing a simultaneous discharge of guns known as a **broadside** using **double-** or even **triple-shotted**

**guns,** that is to say, guns loaded with two or three **round-shot,** or round-shot and anti-personnel **grape** or **langridge** shot. Other forms of projectile, such as **bar** and **chain shot,** were fired to reduce a ship's rigging and render her unmanageable. The Royal Navy tended to batter an enemy's hull, and a vessel sustaining damage to her hull was said to have been **hulled.** Most advantage could be obtained by manoeuvring one's ship across the bow or stern of an enemy, where one's own guns could do the maximum execution with little risk from the enemy. This was called **raking.** When a ship gained ground on an opponent and overtook her, she was said to **fore-reach** upon her.

# Additional Glossary

**Admiral**      a senior officer in command of a group of ships (see **Squadron** and **Fleet**) and having a flag-captain under him to actually command his flag-ship. He was distinguished by flying a flag appropriate to his rank as either a rear-, vice or full admiral. A few very senior officers were appointed Admirals-of-the-Fleet. An admiral had full tactical discretion and had withal to combine the skills of a strategist with those of a diplomat.

**Cartel**      A merchant ship specially fitted and licensed to exchange prisoners under a conventional scale of exchange. An agent for each government resided in London and Paris throughout the war to facilitate this.

**Colours**      a ship's national ensign, which she 'wore', all other flags being 'flown'.

**Commissioned**      the act of bringing a ship out of Ordinary, manning and fitting her out for sea-duty and active service (see **Ordinary**).

**Commodore**    the senior of a group of captains whose ships were acting in concert. A temporary appointment, rather than a rank. Although not a flag-officer, a commodore flew a broad pendant to distinguish his ship for the duration of his appointment (see **Admiral** and **Flag-Officer**).

**Coriolis**    a force generated by the rotation of the earth which spins wind and tides off to the right in the northern hemisphere. Thus, in the English Channel the height of high water is greater on the French side than on the English coast opposite.

**First Lieutenant** the commissioned officer next in seniority to the captain, who assumes command in the event of the latter's incapacity.

**Flag-captain**    the captain commanding an admiral's flag-ship.

**Flag-officer**    a general synonym for an admiral.

**Fleet**    a large group of ships acting in concert under a senior admiral and usually comprising two or more squadrons (see **Squadron**). The collective noun could also apply to a nation's combined men-of-war.

**Master**    the traditional and ancient name for the commander of a merchant ship. He might be styled 'captain' by courtesy or, as in the case of the masters of East Indiamen, 'commander' by rank, but his legal function was that of the ship's absolute master (see **Sailing Master**).

353

**Navy Board**  a subsidiary Board of Commissioners responsible for the maintenance of the fabric of the British fleet. Other subsidiary boards were the Sick and Hurt Board and the Victualling Board (see **Their Lordships**).

**Ordinary**  a ship was said to be in Ordinary when she was laid up in a dockyard port with a skeleton crew to maintain her fabric. Her masts, guns and stores were taken out of her and placed in storage (see **Commissioned**).

**Sailing Master**  also known as the 'master'. The warrant-holding navigating officer who, usually through his previous experience in merchant ships, was responsible for the stowage of stores, etc. in the hold and for the fabric of the vessel (see **Master**).

**Sheer-hulk**  an old ship moored permanently in a dockyard, in which the masts had been replaced by heavy crossed spars known as sheers (a primitive form of crane), by which means masts were hoisted in and out of men-of-war as they were commissioned or decommissioned.

**Squadron**  a group of warships acting in concert under a senior of officer, who could be up to the rank of rear-admiral (see **Fleet**).

**Start**  To start a seaman meant to hit him with a rattan cane, or rope's end usually for tardiness. These canes and rope 'starters' were carried by the boatswains and their mates.

**Strike**  to haul down one's colours (or ensign) and 'strike' them was a token of submission and surrender.

**Their Lordships**  the abbreviated term for 'The Lords Commissioners for the Execution of the Office of Lord High Admiral'. The professional and political Board of Admiralty with powers delegated from the Sovereign. They were responsible for the administration and strategic direction of the Royal Navy (See **Navy Board**).

**Truck**  The cap on top of a mast which was fitted with sheaves by which means flags could be hoisted.

**Veer**  To slack away, the opposite of hauling.

# Index

NOTE: Ranks and titles are generally the highest mentioned in the text

Abdy, Commander Anthony,  265
Abercromby, General Sir John,  292–3
Abercromby, Lieut.-General Sir
     Ralph,  68, 144–5
Aboukir Bay,  144
  battle of (1798),  112, 114, 119
a'Court, Midshipman Edward,  182
Acre,  121–3
Adair, Midshipman James,  251
Adam, Captain Charles,  151
Addington, Henry (later Viscount
     Sidmouth),  164, 169
Admiralty
  and attack on Willaumez's fleet,  266
  and blockade of Brest,  100
  hydrographic surveying and
     charts,  65–6
  and Leduc's operations in northern
     seas,  221
  orders seizure of Dutch ships in
     British ports,  53
  organises Channel squadrons,  37–8
  and payment of seamen's wages,  13
  recompenses Robert Jeffrey,  184–5
  and Spithead mutinies,  55–6, 90–1,
     93, 100
  telegraph system,  82
Adriatic,  252–3
Affleck, Commander Lutwidge,  177
Agay, France,  251

Aix, Ile d',  264–73, 275
Albert, Prince Consort,  275
Alexander I, Tsar of Russia,  210, 261,
     279
Algeciras,  159–61, 165
Allemand, Amiral Zacharie-Jacques-
     Théodore,  50–1, 82–3, 203,
     224–5, 267–71, 275
Allen, Second Lieutenant (USN),  310
Allen, Lieutenant William
     (USN),  309–10
Alvear, Capitán and Doña,  191
Amboyna,  69, 180
American War of Independence (1775–
     83),  54
Amiens, Peace of (1802),  2, 163, 171–
     2, 192, 240
Ancona,  253
Anholt (island),  234
Antilles,  263
Antwerp,  6, 169, 275–6
Arbuthnot, Charles,  211
Armed Neutrality,  5, 161–2, 163
Army of England (French),  173
Arnold, Benedict,  21
Aruba Island,  232
Audierne Bay,  90
Austen, Lieutenant Francis,  202
Austerlitz, battle of (1805),  171, 209–
     10

Austria, 54, 80, 119, 140, 163, 210
Ayscough, Captain John, 252

Bainbridge, Captain William
    (USN), 167, 303–7, 310–11
Baird, General Sir David, 229
Baker, Admiral Sir Thomas, 202–4,
    206
Ball, Captain Alexander, 141–2
Ball (master's mate on *Nymphe*), 26
Ballard, Captain Volant, 243–4
Ballinamuck, Ireland, 105
Baltic, 163, 210–11, 247, 256–62
'Band of Brothers', 112
Banda (island), 69, 180
Bantry Bay, Ireland, 86, 120
Baralovich, Capitano (Venetian), 253,
    255
Barbados, 225
Barbary coast (North Africa), 166
Barcelona, 240
Barham, Sir Charles Middleton, 1st
    Baron, 6, 197–9, 209, 213–14,
    217
Barker, Lieutenant, 45
Barlow, Captain Sir Robert, 1–2, 4, 6,
    10, 84–5, 150, 187, 190, 201–2
Barrett, Captain John, 260
Barron, Commodore James
    (USN), 167, 237–8
Barton, Captain Robert, 157–8
Basra, 219
Bastard, Captain John, 298
Baste, Contre-Amiral Pierre, 279
Batavia (East Indies), 113, 193, 231
Batavian Republic see Netherlands
Bathurst, Captain Walter, 259
Baudin, Capitaine François, 201–2,
    330–1
Bazely, Captain Henry, 146
Beauclerk, Captain Lord Amelius, 79
Beaver, Captain Philip, 291–3
Beckwith, Lieut.-General Sir
    George, 242, 244
Bedford, Captain William, 176
Belair, Capitaine Alain, 217
Belhomme, Lieutenant, 39
Bell, Lieutenant George, 89
Bell, Henry, 251
Bellanger, Capitaine Charles, 204–5
Belle-Ile, 59, 130, 140, 143–4
Bengal, Bay of, 172

Benghazi, 158
Beresford, Captain John Poo, 263–5,
    301
Bergeau, Capitaine Jean-Pierre, 109
Bergeret, Capitaine Jacques, 75–7,
    267
Bergevin, Capitaine Mathieu, 110
Berkeley, Midshipman the Hon.
    Frederick, 182–3
Berkeley, Captain Velterers, 99
Bernadotte, Maréchal Jean, 235
Berry, Captain Sir Edward, 112–13,
    142–3
Bertie, Rear-Admiral Albemarle, 285,
    291–2
Bickerton, Rear-Admiral Sir Richard
    Hussey, 196
Biddle, Captain James (USN), 325
Bilbao, Spain, 277
Biscay, Bay of, 100
Black Legion (French), 96
Blackwood, Captain the Hon.
    Henry, 142–3, 199, 330
Blakiston, Lieutenant (Madras
    Engineers), 291
Blankett, Rear-Admiral John, 54, 116,
    145
Bligh, Captain William, 93, 136, 312
Bolognini, Capitano (Venetian), 253
Bolton, Captain William, 232
bomb vessels, 10
Bompart, Commodore Jean-
    Baptiste, 28–30, 106–8, 116
Bonaparte, Jérôme, 176, 215, 218
Bonaparte, Joseph, 212
Bonavie, Lieutenant de Vaisseau
    Jean, 151
Boston, Massachusetts, 317–18
Boulogne, 279
Bourne, Lieutenant Richard, 103–4
Bouvet, Contre-Amiral François-
    Joseph, 85–6
Bouvet, Capitaine Pierre, 289–90
Bowen, Rear-Admiral James, 125–7,
    213
Bowen, Captain Richard, 80, 127, 129
Boyce, Lieutenant Charles, 326
Boyles, Captain Charles, 41–2, 226
Brace, Commander Edward, 107,
    109–10
Brenton, Captain Jahleel, 174–5, 239,
    252

Brest
  actions at,  127
  blockaded,  7, 99–101, 104, 119,
    121, 139, 151, 189, 213, 218
  blockade raised (1809),  263
  Bruix leaves and regains,  119–20
  French break out from (1805),  214–
    15
  French fleet in,  57–9
  and invasion threat to Britain,  81,
    83–5
  reconnoitred,  1, 4, 6, 47–8, 58–9
  restocked,  97
  ships built at,  121
Breton, Capitaine François,  329
Bridport, Alexander Alexander Hood,
    1st Viscount
  and attempted French invasion of
    Ireland,  85–6, 106
  and Bruix's break-out from
    Brest,  119–20
  commands Channel Fleet,  61, 81,
    96, 100
  and *Culloden* mutiny (1794),  55–6
  relieved by St Vincent (1800),  139
  shares profits from capture of
    *Hyène*,  98
  and Spithead mutiny (1797),  91
Briggs, Lieutenant Joseph,  117
Brisbane, Captain Sir Charles,  151,
    215–16, 232–4
Brisbane, Captain James,  252
Brisbane, Commander William,  44
Britain
  blockade in Europe,  145–6, 326
  French declare war on (1793),  6–7
  French invasion threat to,  81, 84,
    95, 102, 170–1, 173, 187–8, 197
  imperial expansion,  2
  merchant marine and trade,  7
  merchant shipping losses,  164
  neutral convoy interceptions and
    searches,  145, 161, 163
  reliance on foreign trade,  214
  resumes war with France
    (1803),  169–70
  seeks European Coalition,  170
  signs Peace of Amiens,  183
  whalers attacked,  220, 311–12
British Ships, Naval
  *Acasta*,  325
  *Achille*,  226

*Acorn*,  253–4
*Actaeon*,  291
*Active*,  94, 253–4
*Adamant*,  103
*Aeolus*,  203–4, 298
*Aetna*,  268, 270–2
*Africa*,  225, 259–60, 298
*Agamemnon*,  65
*Aigle*,  267, 272
*Alacrity*,  251–2
*Albion*,  195, 256
*Alceste* (earlier French
    *Minerve*),  224–7, 251
*Alcmène*,  72, 132
*Alert*,  298, 310–11
*Alexander*,  142
*Alexandria see Régénérée* (French
    Ships)
*Algerine*,  261
*Alliance*,  122
*Amazon*,  73–6, 84, 87–8, 215–16
*Ambuscade* (sometime French
    *Embuscade*),  28, 30–1, 106, 108,
    111, 116–18, 187
*Amelia* (earlier French
    *Proserpine*),  77, 79, 106–8, 130–
    1, 140, 144, 265
*America*,  54
*Amethyst*,  140, 144, 147, 216, 222,
    241–2, 264–5, 282
*Amphion*,  92–3, 187, 190–1, 252–5
*Andromeda*,  147
*Anson*,  37, 60–1, 65, 106–10, 124,
    232–3
*Antelope*,  189
*Apollo*,  22, 79
*Aquilon*,  130
*Arab* (formerly French privateer
    *Brave*),  206–7
*Archer*,  171
*Ardent*,  176
*Arethusa*,  38–9, 47–8, 58–60, 65,
    215–16, 231–3, 282
*Argo*,  73–4, 124, 127
*Aristocrat*,  70–1
*Arrogant*,  115
*Artois*,  22, 38, 47–8, 60, 124–5
*Atalante*,  42, 226
*Atlas*,  217
*Autumn*,  171
*Avon*,  323
*Bacchante*,  256

Badger, 102
Beagle, 268, 271–2
Beaulieu, 151–3
Belle-Poule (earlier French), 172, 193, 215–16, 252
Belleisle, 29, 217
Bellerophon, 331
Belliqueux, 148
Bellona, 203–4, 217, 267, 271
Belvidera, 297–8
Biter, 147
Black Joke, 126
Blanche, 61–4, 181–2, 192, 201–2, 221–2, 326–7
Blenheim, 169, 222, 231
Blonde, 243–4
Bloodhound, 171
Boadicea, 106, 176, 203, 215, 286, 289–91
Bonne Citoyenne (earlier French), 69, 243, 303–4, 306–7, 316
Boston, 28–31
Bourbonnaise see French Ships: Caroline
Boxer, 147, 323
Boyne, 57, 92
Brave see French Ships: Formidable
Brilliant, 144
Caesar, 110, 160, 203–5, 264, 267–8
Caledonia, 267, 271, 328
Calypso, 261
Camilla, 201
Canada, 107–8, 111, 139
Canopus, 218
Captain, 95, 140, 144
Caroline, 231, 236
Carysfort, 43
Castilian, 279
Castor, 42–3, 242–3
Centaur, 193, 226–7, 257–9
Centurion, 49–50
Cerberus, 131, 253–5
Ceylon, 285, 290–1
Chanticleer, 261
Charlotte, 222
Cherub, 313–15
Childers, 1, 260
Clorinde, 291
Clyde, 129–30
Colossus, 124, 178

Comet, 147, 224, 241
Concorde, 38–40, 60, 65, 73–4, 76, 157
Conflict, 267–8, 271–2
Conqueror, 328
Constance see French Ships: Constance
Coquette, 304
Cornelia, 291
Cornwallis, 231, 291, 326
Courageux, 144, 203–5, 215
Crescent, 38, 45–6, 66
Cressy, 257
Culloden, 55–7, 92, 95
Cumberland, 125
Cyane, 325
Cygnet, 243
Cynthia, 144
Daedalus, 116, 188
Danaë, 94, 146
Daphne, 59
Dart, 147
Defence, 147, 257
Defiance, 264–5
Diadem, 229
Diamond, 38, 47–8, 58–9, 64, 70, 103, 140
Diana, 47, 222
Dictator, 259, 261
Diomede, 49–50, 285
Director, 136
Donegal (earlier French Hoche), 106, 108, 110–11, 190–1, 264, 267
Doris, 79, 86, 107, 110, 140, 151–3, 174, 176, 191
Dotterel, 265, 267–8, 272
Dragon, 199
Druid, 45, 125
Dryad, 79
Duke of York, 65, 73, 84–5
Eclipse, 291
Égyptienne (earlier French), 144–5, 176
Emerald, 99, 264–5, 267–8, 282
Emma, 291
Encounter, 267, 272
Endymion, 309, 324–5
Epervier, 323
Espiègle, 307
Espion see French Ships: Atalante
Ethalion, 106–8, 111, 132

*Euryalus*, 199, 252
*Eurydice*, 45, 103
*Excellent*, 95, 130
*Fairy*, 146
*Falcon*, 147
*Favourite*, 218
*Ferret*, 130, 330
*Fervent*, 267, 272
*Fisgard* (formerly French
    *Résistance*), 96, 110–11, 140,
    147, 232–3, 257
*Flamer*, 261
*Flora*, 37–9, 47
*Fly*, 330
*Fortune*, 65
*Forward*, 261
*Foudroyant*, 107–8, 141–2, 215–16
*Fox*, 13, 54, 114, 116
*Foxhound*, 267–8, 272
*Freija*, 244
*Frisk*, 224
*Frolic*, 301
*Galatea*, 38, 48, 60, 301
*Gibraltar*, 267
*Gipsy*, 192
*Gladiator*, 184, 273
*Glatton* (converted East
    Indiaman), 80, 247
*Goliath*, 201–2, 259
*Grappler*, 176, 284
*Grasshopper*, 257
*Greyhound*, 231
*Growler*, 267–8, 271–2
*Guerriere*, 296, 298–300
*Halstarr see* Dutch Ships: *Kenau
    Hasselaar*
*Hannibal*, 159
*Harpy*, 146, 171
*Harrier*, 231
*Havannah*, 330
*Hazard*, 242–4
*Hebe*, 64–5, 317
*Hecate*, 291
*Hector*, 158
*Hercule see* French Ships: *Hercule*
*Hermione see* Spanish Ships:
    *Hermione*
*Hero*, 203–5, 215, 257, 267
*Heroine*, 188
*Hesper*, 291
*Highflyer*, 309
*Hirondelle*, 247

*Holderness*, 222
*Hound*, 111
*Hussar*, 256
*Hydra*, 103, 219
*Hyena* (later French *L'Hyène*), 28,
    30, 98
*Illustrious*, 267, 291
*Immortalité* (1; earlier French), 189
*Immortalité* (2; earlier French
    *Infatigable*), 224–7
*Impérieuse* (earlier Spanish
    *Medea*), 190–1, 238–40, 252,
    266–8, 270–2
*Impétueux*, 120, 139, 144
*Implacable* (earlier French *Duguay
    Trouin*), 204–6, 257–9, 261
*Impregnable*, 330
*Incendiary*, 157
*Inconstant*, 44
*Indefatigable*, 37, 65–6, 73–6, 87–
    90, 98, 120, 144, 190–1, 267–8,
    272
*Insolent*, 267, 271
*Intrepid*, 115
*Invincible*, 55
*Iphigenia* (later French
    *Iphigénie*), 286–90, 293, 328
*Iris*, 188
*Irresistible*, 99
*Jason*, 61, 65, 97, 101–2, 330
*Java* (earlier Dutch frigate) *see* Dutch
    Ships: *Maria Reigersbergen*
*Java* (earlier French
    *Renommé*), 243–4, 304–7, 326
*Juno*, 32–4
*Junon*, 243
*Kangaroo*, 107, 109, 156
*Kent*, 158
*King George*, 267–8, 272
*Kingfisher*, 224–5
*Lark*, 216
*Latona*, 232–3, 242–4
*Leander*, 112–13, 121, 325
*Leda*, 44, 317
*Leopard*, 237, 296
*Levant*, 325
*Leviathan*, 124–5, 180
*Liberty*, 70
*Licorne*, 22
*Lille Belt* (earlier Danish), 296
*Lion*, 142
*Lively*, 190–1

*Loire see* French Ships: *Loire*
*London*, 215–16
*Lyra*, 267–9
*Macedonian* (later US
   *Macedonian*), 55, 301–3, 309
*Magicienne*, 284, 286–9
*Magnanime*, 107–8
*Magnificent*, 277, 327–8
*Majestic*, 324–5, 329
*Malta see* French Ships: *Guillaume
   Tell*
*Manly*, 261
*Marlborough*, 140
*Mars*, 60, 101–2, 178, 225–7, 259
*Martial*, 267
*Mediator*, 268–70
*Medusa*, 190–1, 277
*Melampus*, 38–40, 64–5, 107–9,
   217, 244
*Melpomene*, 110, 260
*Menelaus*, 252, 291, 329, 330
*Merlin*, 176
*Mermaid*, 109
*Minerva*, 174–5, 298, 311
*Minorca*, 142
*Minotaur*, 140
*Modeste*, 188
*Monarch*, 226–7
*Moselle*, 219
*Mutine see* French Ships: *Mutine*
*Naiad*, 131–2, 264, 266, 279
*Namur*, 139, 203–5, 215
*Nemesis*, 147
*Neptune*, 242
*Néréide*, 145, 192
*Nereide*, 283–9;, *see also* French
   Ships: *Vénus*
*Newcastle*, 325
*Niger*, 64
*Nimrod*, 267–8, 272
*Niobe* (earlier French *Diane*), 143,
   220
*Nisus*, 291–3
*Northumberland*, 141, 217, 331
*Nymphe*, 20, 23–8, 38–40, 96, 301
*Observateur*, 243
*Oiseau see* French Ships: *Cléopâtre, La*
*Orestes*, 103
*Orpheus*, 180
*Otter*, 283, 290
*Pallas*, 60, 207–8, 223–5, 267–8,
   272

*Peacock*, 307
*Pelican*, 80, 309–10
*Penelope*, 142
*Penguin*, 325
*Phaeton*, 23, 38, 60, 69, 126, 236
*Phoebe*, 84–5, 90, 150, 221–3, 291,
   313–15
*Phoenix*, 202–5
*Piémontaise* (earlier French), 230–1,
   235, 280–1
*Pilot*, 330
*Pique see* French Ships: *Pique*
*Plantagenet*, 176
*Podargus*, 261
*Poictiers*, 301
*Polyphemus*, 90, 242
*Pomone* (38–gun), 324–5
*Pomone* (44–gun; earlier
   French), 39–41, 60, 97
*Pompée*, 160, 165, 242
*Prince George*, 127
*Princess Carolina* (earlier Danish
   *Prindsesse Carolina*), 256
*Proserpine see* French Ships: *Bellone*
*Psyche*, 291
*Quebec*, 62, 66, 69
*Queen Charlotte*, 92, 125–7, 140
*Railleur*, 146
*Raisonnable*, 202, 283
*Ramillies*, 101, 125, 215–16
*Raven see* French Ships: *Aréthuse*
*Recruit*, 183, 241–2
*Redpole*, 268–9, 272, 279
*Reindeer*, 323
*Renard*, 257
*Renown*, 144, 147, 157–8
*Repulse*, 139, 215–16
*Resistance*, 114
*Resolution*, 267
*Resource*, 188
*Retribution see* Spanish Ships:
   *Hermione*
*Revenge*, 226, 263–4, 267, 271–2
*Revolutionaire* (earlier French
   *Révolutionnaire*), 48, 66, 73–4,
   84, 109, 203–5
*Rhin* (earlier French *Rhin*), 219,
   225, 277, 330
*Rinaldo*, 279
*Ringdove*, 243
*Rivoli*, 330
*Robust*, 96, 107–8, 110–11, 152

Romney, 32, 44
Rosario, 147, 176
Royal George, 56, 139
Royal Sovereign, 60, 200
Russel, 180
Safeguard, 261
St Albans, 41
St George, 257
Salisbury, 23
Salsette, 259
San Fiorenzo, 96, 130-1, 280-1
Sandfly, 103
Santa Margarita (earlier
    Spanish), 47, 77-8, 203-4
Sapphire, 283
Sceptre, 180, 195, 231, 244
Scorpion, 243-4
Seagull, 178, 260
Seahorse, 248-50
Shannon, 176, 298, 317-21
Sibylle, 241
Sirius, 283, 286-9
Skylark, 330
Southampton, 244-5
Spartan, 239, 252
Spartiate, 43, 178
Speedy (later French Le Saint
    Pierre), 154-6, 159, 165, 174
Spitfire, 60
Stag, 116, 144
Standard, 60
Staunch, 286-7, 290-1
Success, 141, 157-8, 252
Superb, 160, 187, 216
Surprise (earlier French Unité), 74,
    134-5
Surveillante, 277
Swiftsure, 41-2, 159
Sybille, 114, 150-1
Sylph, 106-7
Syren, 64
Tartar, 44
Temeraire, 260
Tenedos, 324-5
Terpsichore, 80, 127, 129, 231
Terrible, 110
Thames (sometime French
    Tamise), 78, 140, 221-3, 252
Theseus, 122-3, 130, 192, 252,
    263, 267, 272
Thetis, 243-4
Thistle, 184

Thunder, 260, 272
Thunderer, 127, 176
Tigre (earlier French), 61, 121-3
Tonnant, 267
Tremendous, 94, 235
Tribune, 261
Triton, 96-7, 132
Triumph, 187, 190, 263
Trusty, 46
Undaunted, 330
Unicorn, 77-8, 86, 147, 267-8
L'Unité, 188
Uranie, 151-2
Valiant, 263, 267, 271-2
Vanguard, 124
Vencejo, 188
Venerable, 53, 159-60, 277-8, 328
Vestal, 188
Victor (sometime French), 151,
    283-6, 288-91, 293
Victorious, 180
Victory, 95, 187, 199, 200, 211,
    256, 259
Ville de Paris, 152
Viper, 147, 279
Virginie (earlier French), 59, 75-7,
    115
Volage, 254-5
Wasp, 147, 215
Whiting, 267-8, 272
Winchelsea, 23
Windsor Castle, 226
Yarmouth, 92-3
York, 242
Zealous, 114
British Ships (Other)
    Alfred (East Indiaman), 194
    Atlantic (whaler; later US
        auxiliary), 312
    Aurora (Bombay Marine ship), 290
    Boddam (East Indiaman), 114
    Bombay Castle (East
        Indiaman), 149
    Bounty (armed transport), 134
    Boyne (merchantman), 220
    Canton (East Indiaman), 114
    Carleton (schooner), 21
    Caroline (Cochrane's prize), 207
    Ceylon (East Indiaman), 286-8, 293
    Charlton (East Indiaman), 283-4,
        293
    Cumberland (merchantman), 86

*Dingwall* (whaler), 220
*Dutton* (East Indiaman), 66–7
*Earl Camden* (East Indiaman), 194–5
*Egremont* (auxiliary), 292
*Europe* (East Indiaman), 283–4
*Exeter* (East Indiaman), 149, 194
*Fame* (East Indiaman), 231
*Farquhar* (auxiliary), 292
*Fly* (Bombay Marine packet), 114
*Ganges* (East India Company brig), 194–5
*Hope* (East Indiaman), 194–5
*Investigator* (survey vessel), 284
*Juno* (merchantman), 177
*Kent* (East Indiaman), 149
*Lord Nelson* (East Indiaman), 177–8
*Minerva* (privateer), 222
*Molly* (whaler), 222
*Mouche* (auxiliary), 292
*Nautilus* (East India Company cruiser), 326
*Nocton* (merchantman), 311
*Ocean* (East Indiaman), 114
*Orient* (East India Company brig), 283
*Porpoise* (surveying tender), 194
*Princess Augusta* (royal yacht), 188
*Raymond* (East Indiaman), 115
*Resolution* (whaler), 220, 222
*Royal Charlotte* (royal yacht), 188
*Royal George* (East Indiaman), 194–5
*Royal Sovereign* (royal yacht), 256, 330
*Samuel and Sarah* (troopship), 311
*Seaflower*, 146
*Seringapatam* (whaler), 312
*Simes* (whaler), 220
*Sir Andrew Hammond* (whaler), 312
*Streatham* (East Indiaman), 283–4
*Taunton Castle* (East Indiaman), 114
*Thomas and John* (privateer), 178
*Triton* (East Indiaman), 149
*United Kingdom* (East Indiaman), 283–4, 293
*Warren Hastings* (East Indiaman), 229–30, 280
*Wasp* (East India Company schooner), 283

*Wasp* (revenue cutter), 125
*Windham* (East Indiaman), 283–4, 286–7
*Woodcot* (East Indiaman), 115
*Woodford* (East Indiaman), 114
Broke, Captain Sir Philip, 298–9, 317–21
Broom, Lieutenant, 319
Brown, Mather, 126
Brown, Mr (Master of *Ambuscade*), 117
Brown, Lieutenant Samuel, 206
Brueys, Amiral François-Paul, 112
Bruilhac, Capitaine Alain, 193, 216
Bruix, Amiral Eustache, 119–21, 170
Brunet, Lieutenant de Vaisseau Charles, 201
Brussels: French occupy (1793), 6
Buchanan, Captain John, 124–5
Budd, Lieutenant George (USN), 320–1
Bulteel, Captain Rowley, 148
Burgess (*Nymphe* seaman), 26
Burgess, Captain Richard, 73
Burgoyne, General John, 21–2
Burke, Commander Henry, 178
Burke, Lieutenant Walter, 153
Bustamente, Contra-Almirante Don Josef, 190–2
Butterfield, Lieutenant William, 102
Byard, Captain Thomas, 107
Byron, Captain Richard, 297–8

Cádiz
   as blockade station, 81, 140, 159–60, 171, 196, 198–200, 213
   Duckworth leaves, 216–17
   Keith plans raid on, 144
   La Meillerie escapes from, 219, 225
   and Nelson-Cornwallis attack on Spanish fleet, 190
   Spanish sail from, 119–20
   Villeneuve raises blockade, 196
Cafarelli, Général Maximilien, 276
Calais, 189
Calder, Rear-Admiral Sir Robert, 158, 198
Camaret Bay, near Brest, 151–2
Campbell, Commander Patrick, 147
Camperdown, battle of (1797), 95
Canada, 5, 82–3, 323
Cape François, Haiti, 178–9, 182

Cape Henry, Virginia, 217
Cape St Vincent, 94–5
Cape Town, 229
  see also Good Hope, Cape of
Carden, Captain John, 111, 219, 301–3
Caribbean see West Indies
Cartagena, 140, 171, 196, 213, 238
Carter, Lieutenant Edmund (Royal
  Marines), 70
Carteret Bay, Cherbourg Peninsula, 64
Carteret, Captain Philip, 279
Cathcart, General William Schaw, 10th
  Baron, 210
Cawdor, Pryse Campbell, 1st
  Baron, 96
Ceylon, 61, 164
Chads, Admiral Sir Henry, 306–7
Chalas, Capitán de Fregata Don
  Raimondo de, 133
Chamier, Captain Frederick, 2, 329,
  332
Channel Fleet ('Western Squadron',
  RN), 7, 36, 59, 86, 93, 100, 171,
  247
Channel Islands, 45–6
Chatham, General John Pitt, 2nd Earl
  of, 275
Chatham, William Pitt, 1st Earl of, 28
Cherbourg, 174
Chesapeake Bay, 217–18
Chesneau, Capitaine Michel, 225
Chile, 311–15
China: British trade with, 172, 229
China Seas, 114–16
Christi-Pallière, Capitaine Jean, 156,
  165
Christian, Rear-Admiral Cloberry, 66,
  68
Christophe, Henri (King Henri I of
  Haiti), 244–5
Ciudad Rodrigo, Spain, 276, 278
Clarence, Admiral of the Fleet Prince
  William, Duke of (later King
  William IV), 330
Clément, Lieutenant de Vaisseau
  Louis, 241
Cochrane, Rear-Admiral Sir
  Alexander, 183, 196, 217, 240,
  242, 244
Cochrane, Kitty (née Barnes), 275
Cochrane, Captain Thomas, Lord (later
  Admiral 10th Earl of Dundonald)

antagonises Establishment, 274
and attempted destruction of French
  fleet at Ile d'Aix, 266–74
captured by Linois, 156–7, 159
career and character, 15, 154–5,
  303
commands Arab, 206
commands Pallas along French
  coast, 223–5
consideration for men, 154, 238,
  303
convicted over stock exchange fraud
  and exiled, 275
defeats Gamo, 155–6
harasses Spanish coast, 238–40
later career and reinstatement, 275
marriage and children, 275
in Mediterranean, 252
political career, 238, 266, 274
quarrels with Beaver, 291
released, 165
takes Généreux to Minorca, 141, 154
takes prizes, 207–8
transferred to Pallas, 207
in West Indies, 217
Cochrane-Johnstone, Andrew, 274
Cockburn, Admiral Sir George, 331
Coffin, Admiral Sir Isaac, 321
Coghlan, Jeremiah, 67, 147–8
Colby, Commander David, 111
Cole, Captain Francis, 45, 73–4, 84
Collet, Capitaine Jacques, 224
Collet, Capitaine Joseph, 226, 330
Collier, Commander George, 151,
  277–8
Collingwood, Captain Cuthbert
  blockades Cartagena, 213
  blockades Rochefort, 172
  at Cádiz, 198–9, 217
  at Cape St Vincent, 95
  commends Cochrane, 240
  eases Cádiz blockade, 219
  humanity to seamen, 55
  Mediterranean command, 212, 217,
    247–8, 250
  on natural hazards, 124
  sends Cochrane to relieve garrison at
    Fort Trinidad, 239
  serves in Culloden, 57
  at Trafalgar, 199, 209
Colpoys, Vice-Admiral Sir John, 55,
  83–5

Conseil, Capitaine, 62–4
Continental System, 169, 256
convoy protection: as Royal Navy
    responsibility, 8–9, 11, 308
Cooke, Captain John, 96
Copenhagen
  battle of (1801), 161–2, 180, 234
  besieged and bombarded
    (1807), 210
Corbet, Captain Robert, 283–4, 287,
    290
Cordova, Almirante Don José de, 95
Corfu, 212, 252–3
Cork, Ireland, 77
Cornwallis, Charles, 1st Marquess
  of, 171
Cornwallis, Vice-Admiral the Hon. Sir
  William
  and attack on Spanish fleet, 190
  blockades Brest, 189, 198
  commands Channel Fleet, 151, 171
  and conquest of Egypt, 164
  and *Culloden* mutiny (1794), 55
  Nelson leaves *Victory* for, 187
  promotes Maxwell, 153
  'Retreat' and rescue of *Mars*, 59–60
  supports Henry Whitby, 253
  and Trafalgar campaign, 196, 199
Corsica, 31, 81
Coruña, 9, 127, 177, 191, 212
Cosnahan, Midshipman Hugh, 320
Cotta, Capitano (Venetian), 256
Cotton, Admiral Sir Charles, 250
Coudin, Capitaine Jean-Daniel, 105,
  148–9
Countess, Captain George, 106–8
Courtenay, Captain George, 28–31
Courtenay, Mrs George, 35
Craig, Major-General Sir James
  Henry, 54
cruisers: defined, 10
Cunningham, Captain Charles, 129–
  30
Curaçao, 145, 181, 192, 232–4
Curtis, Captain Lucius, 289
Curtis, Rear-Admiral Sir Roger, 91,
  273
Curzon, Captain the Hon. Henry, 60,
  120, 144

Dacres, Vice-Admiral James, 232
Dacres, Lieutenant, 21

Dacres, Captain Richard, 298–300
Dale, Commodore Richard
  (USN), 166
Dalrymple, Alexander, 65
Damietta, 123
Dance, Commodore Sir Nathaniel (East
  India Co.), 194–5
Danish Ships, Naval
  *Brevdrageren*, 261
  *Freja*, 161
  *Kiel*, 261
  *Lollane*, 261
  *Lügum*, 260–1
  *Nayaden*, 261
  *Prindsesse Carolina*, 256
  *Provesteen*, 180
  *Sampsø*, 261
Dardanelles, 211
Davies, Commander Henry, 222
Dawson, Captain William, 281
Deacon, Lieutenant Henry, 287
Decaen, Général Charles Mathieu
  Isidore, comte, 172, 282, 284–5,
  292–3
Decatur, Captain Stephen, 167, 237,
  297, 301–3, 309, 324–5, 327
de Courcy, Captain the Hon.
  Michael, 107–8, 139
Decrès, Contre-Amiral Denis, 142–3,
  195, 267
Dedé, Lieutenant Joseph, 242
Deguyo, John, 296
Denmark
  and Armed Neutrality, 161–2
  Bernadotte in, 235
  fleet and islands seized, 210, 234,
    240
  frigate intercepted, 146
  harasses British in Baltic, 210–11,
    214, 259–62, 308–9
  *see also* Danish Ships
Denmark Strait, Greenland, 219
Dennis, John, 184
Desaix, Général Louis, 123, 140
Desgarceaux, Commodore, 39–40
Désirade, West Indies, 61
Dessalines, Jean Jacques, 178–9, 182,
  244
Devaux, Brigadier-General Pierre,
  baron, 159
Diamond Rock (Martinique) *see* Fort
  *Diamond*, HMS

Dickinson, Commander James, 325
Dickson, Captain Edward, 330
Digby, Captain Henry, 132–3
Dillon, Commander William, 260
Dixon, Captain Manley, 142–3
Djezzar Pasha, Achmed, 122, 139
Dominican Republic, 244
Douglas, Captain Sir Andrew
 Snape, 23, 38
Douglas, Captain John, 217
Dover, Strait of, 173
Downes, Lieutenant John (USN), 312,
 315
Downie, Lieutenant George, 250
Doyle, Major-General Sir John, 61
Drummond, Captain Adam, 203
Drury, Vice-Admiral William, 235,
 280, 285
Dubourdieu, Commodore
 Bernard, 253–5
Duckworth, Rear-Admiral Sir John
 captures Minorca, 119
 in Dardanelles, 211
 defeats Leissègues, 217
 Gambier sends to intercept
  Willaumez, 266
 at Gambier's court-martial, 273
 leaves Cádiz but fails to engage
  Willaumez, 216–17
 negotiates with Turks, 211–12, 247
 in West Indies, 172, 180–1, 217
 and Willoughby, 180–1
Ducrest, Capitaine Alexandre, 328
Dumanoir le Pelley, Contre-Amiral
 Pierre-Etienne, 159, 200, 202,
 204–6
Duncan, Vice-Admiral Adam, 53–4,
 69, 80, 93, 95, 123
Duncan, Captain the Hon. Henry, 252
Dundas, Captain Thomas, 264
Duodo, Capitano (Venetian), 253–5
Duperré, Capitaine (of *Bellone*), 284,
 287–9
Dupotet, Capitaine Jean, 282
Duragardi-Ali, Yarbay, 248–9
Durham, Rear-Admiral Philip, 56, 60,
 65, 106–9, 124, 328, 330
Dutch, the *see* Netherlands
Dutch East Indies, 145
Dutch Ships, Naval
 *Alliante*, 54
 *Amboyna*, 180

*Avontourier*, 193
*Blanche*, 124
*Contest*, 124, 267, 272
*Kenau Hasselaar* (later HMS
 *Halstarr*), 233–4
*Lutine*, 124
*Maria Reigersbergen* (later HMS
 *Java*), 231
*Nassau*, 124
*Pallas*, 231
*Suffisante*, 54
*Suriname*, 233
*Victorieuse*, 54
Dutch West Indies, 145, 192
Duthoya, Lieutenant de Vaisseau
 Morce, 174
Duval, Lieutenant Thomas, 114

East India Company (British)
 ships harassed by French, 149, 194–
 5
 uses Cape of Good Hope as
  haven, 229
East Indies station, 114
Edwards, Lieutenant John, 30–1
Edwards, Captain Valentine, 180
Egypt
 French army capitulates in, 145,
  163
 French expedition to, 111–12, 115–
  16, 120–1, 123, 144–5
 Napoleon orders Ganteaume
  to, 157–8
Elba, 158–9, 329
Eliot, Commodore John, 23
Ellenborough, Edward Law, 1st
 Baron, 274
Elliott, William, 16
Ellison, Captain Joseph, 45–6, 60
Elphinstone, Vice-Admiral Sir
 George, 54, 69
Emeriau, Vice-Amiral Maurice, 328
Emeric, Capitaine Jacques, 328
English Channel: naval encounters
 in, 37–41, 99, 127
Epron, Capitaine de Frégate
 Jacques, 146, 230–1, 280–2
Epworth, Captain Farmery, 301
Ernouf, Général Jean-Augustin,
 baron, 244
Erqui, Brittany, 70–1
Espoz y Mina, Francisco, 277–8

Evertsz, Kapitein ter Zee
    Cornelis, 234
Exmouth, 1st Viscount *see* Pellew,
    Admiral Sir Edward

Faeroe Islands, 221
Falkiner, Commander Charles, 319,
    321
Farragut, Admiral David, 311, 314
Faulknor, Captain Jonathan, 47
Faulknor, Captain Robert, 61–3
Faure, Commodore Gilbert, 263
Ferdinand I, King of the Two
    Sicilies, 121, 167, 212
Ferretier, Lieutenant de Vaisseau
    Jean, 283
Ferris, Captain Solomon, 159
Ferrol, 120, 144, 172, 195, 197–9
fireships, 10
Fishguard, 96
Fitton, Acting Lieutenant
    Michael, 192
Fitzgerald, Lord Edward, 81, 83
Fitzroy, Captain Lord William, 55
Flaxman, James, 251
Flinders, Commander Matthew, 194,
    284, 293
Foote, Captain Edward, 64
Forester, C.S., 2
*Fort Diamond*, HMS (i.e. Diamond
    Rock, Martinique), 193, 197, 234
Fort Malartic, Île de France, 292
Fort Trinidad, Spain, 240
Fort-de-France, Martinique, 193, 197
Fradin, Capitaine Jean, 78
France
    amalagamates Mediterranean fleet
        with Spanish, 80–1, 120, 160
    Britain resumes war with
        (1803), 169–70
    Channel coast raided, 173
    coastal trade harassed, 70
    convoys harassed and captured, 97
    disposition of fleet, 57–9
    European military conquests, 171,
        210
    expansion in Europe, 4
    expedition to Egypt, 111–13
    expeditions against Ireland, 81, 83–
        6, 90–1, 105–11, 163
    failed attempt to recover St
        Marcouf, 103–4

Grand Army retreats from
    Moscow, 262
    lacks sea power, 331
    losses in West Indies, 243–5
Napoleon's Consulate
    established, 139
    naval conditions, 19–20, 37, 57,
        328
    and naval conventions, 36
    naval presence in West Indies, 172
    naval successes and offensive
        (1796), 82–3
    navy strengthened after
        Trafalgar, 214
    navy suffers from scurvy, 221–2
    operates in northern seas, 219–23
    plans expedition against India, 111–
        12, 114–15
    privateers captured, 308
    resumes war with Russia
        (1812), 256, 261, 279
    revolutionary threat to Britain, 4–5
    ship losses, 64
    signs Treaty of Amiens, 163
    successes and status in Europe, 164
    threatens invasion of Britain, 81,
        84, 95, 102, 170–1, 173, 187–8,
        197
    wars with Britain (1793–1815), 2,
        6, 170, 173
    *see also* French Ships; *and* individual
        places
Franklin, John, 194
Frazier, Lieut.-Colonel, 286
French Ships, Naval
    *Affronteur*, 174
    *Africaine* (later HMS
        *Africaine*), 150, 290–1
    *Albion*, 181–2
    *Alcmène*, 328
    *Alerte*, 47
    *Alexandre*, 61, 215, 217
    *America*, 28–9
    *Anacréon*, 106
    *Aquilon*, 265, 269, 271–2
    *Arbeille*, 251
    *Aréthuse* (later HMS *Raven*), 130
    *Armide* (later HMS *Armide*), 224–7
    *Aspic*, 69
    *Astrée*, 285, 289–90, 293
    *Atalante* (corvette), 83–4, 90
    *Atalante* (frigate), 172, 329

*Atalante* (later HMS *Espion*), 41–2
*Athenaise, L'*, 180
*Babet*, 39–40
*Bayadère*, 330
*Bayonnaise*, 116–18, 176, 187
*Béarnais*, 244
*Bellone*, 282–9, 293
*Bellone* (later HMS *Proserpine*), 106,
   108, 111, 177–8
*Berceau*, 193
*Biche*, 106, 108, 110
*Bonne Citoyenne see* British Ships:
   Bonne Citoyenne
*Brave*, 215, 217
*Bravoure*, 157
*Brûle-Gueule*, 115
*Brutus*, 45
*Calcutta* (earlier East
   Indiaman), 266, 269, 271–2
*Calliope*, 97
*Cannonière*, 235
*Caroline* (later HMS
   *Bourbonnaise*), 282–4
*Cassard*, 215, 218, 265, 269, 271–2
*Censeur*, 83
*Cerbère*, 148–8
*Chevrette*, 151–3
*Chiffon*, 174–5
*Chiffone* (later HMS
   Chiffone), 150–1
*Clarisse*, 149
*Cléopâtre, La* (later HMS
   Oiseau), 24–8
*Clorinde*, 179, 243–4
*Cométe*, 215, 217
*Concorde*, 28–9, 31, 105, 110, 148
*Confiance*, 149
*Constance* (later HMS
   Constance), 96–7
*Coquille*, 106, 108, 111
*Cornélie*, 130
*Courageux*, 242–3
*Coureuse*, 64
*Courier*, 49
*Courier National*, 64
*Creole*, 283
*Curieux*, 193
*Cybèle*, 49–50, 113, 265
*Danaë*, 45, 253–5
*Département des Landes*, 200–2
*Desaix*, 156–7, 165
*Désirée*, 147

*d'Hautpoult*, 242–3, 252
*Diane see* British Ships: *Niobe*
*Diligente*, 215, 217, 240–1
*Diomède*, 215
*Droits de l'Homme*, 86–90, 91
*Duguay Trouin see* British Ships:
   Implacable
*Duquesne*, 83
*Édouard*, 286
*Elbe*, 265, 269, 271–2
*Embuscade see* British Ships:
   Ambuscade
*Engageante*, 39–40
*Entreprenante*, 285, 289, 293
*Éole*, 28–9, 215, 218
*Épervier*, 51, 176, 198
*Espérance*, 64
*Espiègle*, 240–1
*Espion* (earlier HMS *Espion*), 47
*Estafette*, 285
*Étourdie*, 70
*Expériment*, 51
*Faune*, 200–1
*Favourite*, 253–5
*Félicité* (later Haitian
   Améthyste), 45, 51, 215, 217,
   242–5
*Flèche*, 150–1
*Flore*, 253–5
*Formidable* (later HMS *Brave*), 61,
   204–5
*Forte*, 113
*Foudroyant*, 215, 218, 265, 269,
   271–2
*Fougueux*, 59
*Franchise*, 105, 110, 148–9
*Fraternité*, 85–7
*Friponne*, 82
*Furet*, 219, 225
*Furieuse*, 242–3
*Garonne*, 223
*Généreux*, 112–13, 141, 154
*Gentille*, 64
*Gloire* (1), 223
*Gloire* (2; later HMS *Gloire*), 64,
   225–7
*Guerrière*, 219–22
*Guillaume Tell* (later HMS
   Malta), 142–3
*Hercule* (later HMS *Hercule*), 101–
   2, 192
*Hermione*, 219, 225

*Hoche see* British Ships: *Donegal*
*Hortense,* 219, 266, 269–72
*Hyène, L' see* British Ships: *Hyena*
*Immortalité* (1), 106–11
*Immortalité* (2), 330
*Impérial,* 214
*Impétueux,* 215, 217
*Indienne,* 265, 269, 271–2
*Infatigable* (l; later HMS
    *Immortalité*), 224–7
*Infatigable* (2), 330
*Insurgente,* 310
*Iphigénie see* British Ships: *Iphigenia*
*Italienne,* 265
*Jean Bart,* 49, 64, 265, 271
*Jemappes,* 265, 269, 271–2
*Jupiter* (later HMS *Maida*), 215, 217
*Justice,* 144–5
*Légère,* 78–9, 330
*Levrette,* 41
*Liberté,* 64
*Lodi,* 144
*Loire* (later HMS Loire), 106, 108–
    12, 146, 243
*Lynx,* 224, 226–7
*Malicieuse,* 223
*Manche,* 282–5, 289, 293
*Marengo,* 172, 193, 195, 215–16
*Medée,* 80, 105, 110, 148–9, 194
*Méduse,* 330
*Melpomène,* 330
*Minerve see* British Ships: *Alceste*
*Minerve* (earlier Portuguese
    *Minerva*), 283–8, 293
*Mont Blanc,* 204–5
*Muiron,* 123
*Mutine* (later HMS *Mutine*), 51, 90,
    113, 252
*Néarque,* 219–20
*Nestor,* 59
*Niéman,* 282
*Nisus,* 266
*Océan,* 265, 269–72
*Oreste,* 244
*Palinure,* 224
*Pallas,* 146, 266, 269, 271–2
*Patriote,* 42, 215, 218, 265, 269–70,
    272
*Petit Diable, Le,* 98
*Piémontaise see* British Ships:
    *Piémontaise*
*Pique* (later HMS *Pique*), 62–4, 158

*Polonais,* 242–3, 330
*Pomone see* British Ships: *Pomone*
*Poursuivante,* 177
*Preneuse,* 115
*Président,* 218
*Prompte,* 64
*Proserpine see* British Ships: *Amelia*
*Providence,* 176
*Prudente,* 49, 113
*Régénérée* (later HMS
    *Alexandria*), 113, 145
*Régulus,* 218, 265, 269–72
*Renommée see* British Ships: *Java*
*Réolaise,* 97
*Républicain,* 58
*Résistance see* British Ships: *Fisgard*
*Résolue,* 39–40, 106, 108–11
*Réunion,* 45
*Revanche,* 219, 222
*Revenant,* 172, 308
*Révolution,* 87
*Rhin see* British Ships: *Rhin*
*Romaine,* 106, 108, 110
*Saale,* 330
*Sagesse,* 129–30
*Saint Antoine,* 160
*Saint Pierre, Le see* British Ships:
    *Speedy*
*Sans Pareil,* 43
*Scévola,* 45
*Scipion,* 204–6
*Séduisant,* 84
*Seine* (later HMS *Seine*), 113, 149, 243
*Sémillante,* 106, 108–10, 130, 172,
    193, 216, 231, 235
*Stanislaus,* 22
*Surveillante,* 179
*Sybille,* 44
*Sylphe,* 224, 226–7, 240–1
*Syrène,* 219, 222
*Tamise see* British Ships: *Thames*
*Tapageuse,* 223
*Tartu* (later HMS *Urania*), 90
*Terpsichore,* 329
*Terrible,* 174
*Thémis,* 219, 225
*Thérèse,* 147
*Thétis,* 226–7, 241–2
*Tonnere,* 265, 269–72
*Topaze,* 200–2
*Torche,* 200–2
*Tourterelle,* 64

*Tourville,* 265, 269–70, 272
*Tribune,* 77–9
*Unité see* British Ships: *Surprise*
*Valeureuse,* 215, 218
*Vautour,* 96, 176
*Vengeance,* 51, 96, 130, 149
*Vénus* (28–gun), 105, 110
*Vénus* (44–gun; later HMS
  *Nereide*), 282–5, 289–91, 293
*Vertu,* 113
*Vestale,* 80, 129–30
*Vésuve,* 65
*Vétéran,* 215
*Ville de Lyon,* 279
*Ville de Varsovie,* 265, 267, 269,
  271–2
*Volontaire,* 47, 215, 229

French Ships (Other)
  *Afrique, L'* (corsair), 60
  *Atalante* (corsair), 176
  *Bellone* (privateer), 177–8
  *Côte d'Or* (transport), 172
  *Éclair, L'* (corsair), 180
  *Emilie* (corsair), 149
  *Général Dumourier* (corsair), 23
  *Justine* (troopship), 90
  *Marie-Françoise* (transport), 172
  *Ranger* (corsair), 98
  *Vengeur* (privateer), 36, 70–2
  *Vénus* (privateer), 176
Friedland, battle of (1807), 210
frigates
  described, 10
  squadrons, 64
Fuentes de Oñoro, battle of
  (1811), 276

Galles, Morard de *see* Morard de
  Galles, Vice-Amiral
Gambier, Admiral James, 1st
  Baron, 263–4, 266–8, 271–3
Gamble, Lieutenant (USN), 312
Ganteaume, Contre-Amiral
  Honoré, 123, 157–9, 161, 173,
  197–8
Gardner, Vice-Admiral the Hon. Sir
  Alan, 92, 139, 204–5
Gaspard, Capitaine Mayor-Michel-
  Pierre, 129
Gaspard (French/Haitian
  corsair), 244–5

Gates, General Horatio, 21
Gaze, Mr (mate of *Nymphe*), 20
*Gazette de France,* 189
Genoa, 61, 140
George III, King
  at Weymouth, 46
  and *Nymphe* victory, 27–8
  renounces claims on French
    throne, 164
Gibbon, Lieutenant Philip, 291
Gibraltar, 81, 157–60, 198, 202
Girardias, Capitaine Joseph, 226–7
'Glorious First of June' (1794), 36, 43,
  120, 126, 130
Goa, 162
Good Hope, Cape of, 9, 20, 54, 69,
  94, 164, 215, 229, 283
Gordon, Captain Charles, 290
Gordon, Captain James, 253, 255
Gore, Captain Sir John, 132–3, 190,
  226
Gosset, Lieutenant Abraham, 70
Gourdon, Contre-Amiral Antoine-
  Louis, comte de, 264
Grasse, François-Joseph-Paul de, 130
Graves, Rear-Admiral Sir
  Thomas, 196
Gravina, Almirante Don
  Federico, 199–200, 209
Great War (with France, 1793–1815):
  outbreak, 2, 4, 19
Greene, Captain Pitt, 304, 307
Grenada, West Indies, 68
Grenville, Thomas, 111, 209
Grenville, William Wyndham Grenville,
  Baron, 73, 209
Grey, Lieut.-General Sir Charles, 49
Guadeloupe, 61–2, 240, 243–4, 330
Guernsey, 46
Guiana, 240
Guieysse, Capitaine Pierre, 151
Guillotin, Capitaine Jean, 105
gun-brigs, 11
Guthrie, James, 155–6

Haggit, Captain William, 103
Haiti *see* San Domingo
Halgan, Lieutenant de Vaisseau
  Emmanuel, 130
Halifax, Novia Scotia, 172, 297–8,
  321
Hallowell, Captain Benjamin, 159

Halsted, Captain, 205
Hamburg, 234
Hamelin, Commodore Jacques, 282–5, 289, 291
Hamilton, Archibald Douglas-Hamilton, 9th Duke of, 206–7
Hamilton, Captain Sir Edward, 134–5
Hamilton, Emma, Lady, 121, 142, 199
Hamilton, Sir William, 142
Hamond, Captain Graham, 190
Hanikov, Vitse-admiral Piotr, 53, 257–9
Hanover, 54
Harcourt, duc d', 72
Hardinge, Captain George, 280–1
Hardy, Admiral Sir Charles, 173
Hardy, Général Félix-Jean, 106
Hardy, Captain Thomas Masterman, 112, 187, 252
Hargood, Captain William, 28–30, 115, 217
Harvey, Rear-Admiral Eliab, 47, 267, 272
Haslar (hospital), 13
Haswell, Lieutenant John, 223
Havana
  naval action off, 232
  Spanish shipbuilding in, 81
Hayes, Captain John, 244, 324–5, 327–8, 329
'head-money', 24
Helgoland, 234
Heliopolis, 123
Herbert, Captain the Hon. Charles, 106, 131, 140, 144
Hesse-Cassel, 54
Higman, Commander Henry, 234
Hillyar, Captain James, 313–17
Hislop, Lieut.-General Sir Thomas, 304, 306
Hoche, General Lazare, 80
Holland, Commander John, 150
homosexuality, 13
Hood, Captain Alexander, 101–2
Hood, Admiral Samuel, 1st Viscount, 31–2, 61, 73
Hood, Admiral (Sir) Samuel
  blockades Alexandria, 121
  commands Courageux, 144
  commands Venerable at Algeciras, 159–60
  death from malaria, 295
  defeats Soleil off Rochefort, 226–7
  engages Russians in Baltic, 257–9
  escapes in Juno from Toulon, 32–4
  in Leeward Islands, 172
  Martinique victory, 192–3
  in Nelson's 'Band of Brothers', 112
  qualities, 32
  and US threat, 295
Hope, Lieutenant David, 302
Hope, Captain Henry, 324
Hornblower, Captain Horatio (fictional figure), 2
Hornby, Captain Phipps, 254
Horton, Captain Joshua, 146
Hoste, Captain Sir William, 252–6
Hotham, Captain the Hon. Henry, 265
Hotham, Captain William, 103
Hotham, Vice-Admiral William, 61
Houat (island), 140
Howard of Effingham, Charles, 2nd Baron, 14, 225
Howe, Admiral Richard, Earl, 36–7, 43, 59, 61, 66, 91, 93, 125–6
Hoxton Hospital, London, 13
Hubert, Capitaine Paul, 220–1
Hull, Captain Isaac (USN), 298–300, 310, 321
Humbert, Général Jean-Joseph-Amable, 87, 105, 107, 110
Humphreys, Captain Salisbury, 237–8
Hunt, Captain Anthony, 65, 73, 76
Hyères, 61

Île de Bourbon, 285–7, 289
Île de France (Mauritius)
  British invade and capture, 283–93, 295
  and capture of Warren Hastings, 229–30
  as French base, 49–50, 69, 172, 195, 235, 281
  supply difficulties, 57, 282
  Surcouf in, 149
Île de la Passe, 286–7
Île de Yeu, 61
Ilfracombe: French force lands at, 96
India
  Britain acquires, 5
  France plans expedition against, 111–12, 114–16, 163, 293

trade vessels threatened, 49–50, 69,
80, 149, 150, 172, 229, 235, 280,
285
Indian Ocean
French activities in, 99, 116, 172,
193, 214, 280–4, 295, 308
US activities in, 326
see also Île de France
Infernet, Capitaine Louis, 200
Inglis, Captain Peter, 86
Ingram, Lieutenant William, 314
Ionian Islands, 121
Irby, Captain the Hon. Frederick, 265
Ireland
coasts patrolled, 77
French invasion attempts on, 81,
83–6, 90–1, 105–11, 116, 163,
173
Irish Guard (frigates), 77, 79, 86, 107
Irving, Washington, 311
Italy, 54, 80, 140, 163

Jackson, Andrew, 324
Jacob, Capitaine Louis, 108
Jaffa, 122
Jamaica, 172, 196
Jameson, Commander James, 231
Janvrin, Lieutenant, 159
Japan: provoked by Pellew, 236
Jauregui y Jauregui, Don Gaspar ('El
Pastor'), 277
Java, 115, 235–6
Jefferson, Thomas, 166, 238, 296,
308–9
Jeffrey, Robert, 183–5
Jeffrey, Commander Samuel, 234
Jena-Auerstädt, battle of (1806), 210
Jenkins, Captain Henry, 116–18
Jervis, Vice-Admiral Sir John see St
Vincent, Earl of
Jones, Master Commandant Jacob
(USN), 301
Jones, Captain John Paul, 96, 166
Jourdan, Maréchal Jean-Baptiste, 276
Jurien, Commodore Pierre, 148, 265–6

Karamanli, Yusuf, Pasha of
Tripoli, 166–7
Keating, Lieut.-Colonel Henry, 283,
286, 292
Keats, Rear-Admiral Sir Richard
Goodwin

in blockade of Rochefort, 225
captains Galatea, 38, 48, 60
command in Baltic, 235
with Duckworth in pursuit of
Willaumez, 216
and French invasion attempt on
Ireland, 106–7
pursues Moreno and Linois, 160
serves under Nelson, 187
in Walcheren expedition, 276
Keene, Midshipman, 306
Keith, Admiral George Keith
Elphinstone, Baron (later
Viscount)
abandons raid on Cádiz, 144
blockades enemy ports, 140
as Commander-in-Chief of 'Lisbon
and the Mediterranean', 121
commands North Sea, 171
defence against invasion threat, 189
and French threat to Egypt, 157–8
promotes Cochrane, 154
pursues Bruix, 120
pursues Perrée, 141
raids French coast, 173
sails to Aboukir Bay, 144
Kerr, Lieutenant Alexander, 30
Killalla Bay, Co. Mayo (Ireland), 105,
107
King, Captain Richard, 226
King's German Legion (British), 234
Kingsmill, Vice-Admiral Sir Robert
Brice, 77, 86, 107, 109
Kléber, Général Jean-Baptiste, 122–3
Kosseir, 116, 145

Labrador, 82
Labrosse, Capitaine Guillaume, 218
Lacaille, Capitaine Charles, 272
La Ciotat, Spain, 239
La Crosse, Commodore Jean, 86–9, 95
Lafon, Capitaine Jean, 272
Laforey, Captain Sir Francis, 43, 103
La Guayra (South America), 94
Lake, Lieut.-General Gerard (later
Viscount), 105
Lake, Commander the Hon.
Warwick, 181–5
Lambert, Captain Henry, 287–9, 304–
6, 326
La Meillerie, Capitaine Louis La
Marre, 219, 225–6, 253, 255

Landolphe, Commodore Jean-
    François,  148
landsmen,  12–13
Langara, Almirante Juan de,  32, 82
Langford, Commander Frederick,  216
Langlois, Capitaine Jean,  226–7
Larkins, Commander Thomas,  230
La Rochelle,  7
La Romana, Pedro Caro y Sureda,
    Marquís de,  235
Laroque, Capitaine Jean-Baptiste,  96
Lavie, Captain Sir Thomas,  221–2
Law, Lieutenant John (Royal
    Marines),  319
Lawrence, Captain James (USN),  303–
    4, 307, 316–19, 321, 323
Leblond-Plassan, Capitaine,  176
Leclerc, Général Victor,  163
Leduc, Commodore Amand,  219–23
Lee, Captain Richard,  204, 226–7
Leech, Samuel,  55
Leeward Islands,  172
Le Havre,  70
Leissègues, Vice-Amiral Corentin-
    Urbain,  214, 216–18
Lejoille, Capitaine,  113
Le Large, Madame,  74
Lemaresquier, Capitaine Jean,  241
Lemnos,  247
Lennox, Commander Charles,  113,
    115
Letellier, Capitaine Jean,  204
Le Villegris, Capitaine Guillaume,  204
Lewis, Lieutenant Frederick,  120
L'Héritier, Capitaine Louis,  101
L'Hermite, Capitaine Jean,  115
L'Hermitte, Commodore Jean,  218
Lhuillier (French officer),  43
line-of-battle ships,  10
Linois, Contre-Amiral Charles, comte
    de
    attacked by Saumarez,  159–60, 165
    capitulates to Cole,  74
    captured in attack on Atlantic
        convoy,  41–2
    captures Cochrane,  156–7
    Dance bluffs and eludes,  194–5
    in Île de France,  172, 193, 231, 235
    refuses to give up Guadeloupe,  330
    surrenders to Warren,  215–16
Lisbon,  213
Lissa (island, Dalmatia),  253–5

Livermore, Samuel,  319
Lloyd's of London,  8
Longa, Francisco,  277
L'Orient,  7, 57, 61, 83, 130, 147, 219,
    241, 263–5, 267
Loring, Captain John,  179–80, 220
Losack, Commander Woodley,  151–3,
    301
Louis XVI, King of France,  4, 6
Louis XVIII, King of France,  330
Louis, Rear-Admiral Sir Thomas,  189,
    202, 218
Lucas, Vice-Admiraal Engelbertus,  69
Lucas, Capitaine Jean,  200
Ludlow, Lieutenant Augustus
    (USN),  320
Lukin, Captain William,  226–7
Lumsden, Captain George,  90
Lunéville, treaty of (1800),  163
Lydiard, Captain Charles,  232–3

Macao,  162
McBride, Rear-Admiral John,  19
Macdonald, Maréchal Jacques,  261–2
M'Donald, Lieutenant James,  325
Mack, General Karl,  209–10
Mackau, Lieutenant de Vaisseau Ange
    de, baron,  251–2
M'Kinley, Lieutenant George,  69
Macnamara, Captain James,  131
Madeira,  162
Madison, James,  237, 324
Magendie, Capitaine Jean-
    Jacques,  150
Mahan, Alfred Thayer,  3
Mahé,  150–1
Mahmud II, Ottoman Sultan,  250
Maida, battle of (1806),  212
Main, Lieutenant Dawson,  117
Maitland, Captain Frederick,  282,
    331
Malacca,  180
Malcolm, Captain Charles,  330
Mallet, Capitaine,  329
Malta,  140–3, 159, 164, 169
Man, Rear-Admiral Robert,  81
Maples, Commander John,  310
Mapou Bay, Île de France,  291
Marengo, battle of (1800),  140, 163
Markham, Rear-Admiral John,  209
Marmont, Maréchal Auguste,  276
Marquesas,  312

Marriot, Sir James,  43
Marryat, Captain Frederick,  2, 240,
   269–70, 332
Martin, Captain Thomas Byam,  77–8,
   99, 110, 140, 257–8, 261
Martinique,  49, 192–3, 215, 240–2,
   263, 266
Masefield, Commander Joseph,  226
Massaredo y Salazar, Almirante Jose
   Maria,  120
Masséna, Général André,  140, 276
'master and commander',  10
masters (sailing masters),  11
Mather, Commander William,  234
Maurice, Lieutenant James,  193, 197,
   234
Mauritius see Île de France
Maxwell (gunner of Surprise),  136
Maxwell, Lieutenant Keith,  152–3
Maxwell, Captain Murray,  251
Mediterranean
   actions in,  61, 80, 251–6
   Collingwood commands in,  212,
      217, 247–8, 250
   French reinforce power in,  120
   Nelson commands in,  171, 187, 189
   Royal Navy leaves (1796),  81, 84
   Royal Navy returns to,  112, 119
Melville, Henry Dundas, 1st
   Viscount,  169, 197, 206–7, 209
Ménage, Général,  106
Mendoza, Capitán Don Juan de,  132
Mends, Captain Robert,  282
Menou, Général J.F., baron de,  144–5
Meriton, Commander Henry,  149,
   194
Middleton, Sir Charles see Barham, 1st
   Baron
Mikonos,  44
Milbanke, Admiral Mark,  23
Miller, Captain Ralph,  122–3
Milne, Captain David,  63–4, 150
Minchin, Captain Paul,  64
Mindham, William,  318, 320–1
Minorca,  119, 141
   see also Port Mahon
Minto, Gilbert Elliot, 1st Earl of,  285
Missiessey, Contre-Amiral
   Burgues,  196, 207, 276
Mongar, Spain,  239
Moore, Captain Graham,  64, 107–9,
   190–2

Moore, General Sir John,  127, 191,
   213
Morard de Galles, Vice-Amiral Justin,
   comte de,  20, 35, 83–7, 95
Moreau, Lieutenant,  230
Moreno, Vice-Almirante Don Juan
   de,  159–60, 165
Morris, Lieutenant Amherst,  26–8
Morris, Commodore Richard
   (USN),  166
Motard, Capitaine Léonard,  193
Mould, Lieutenant Richard,  183
Moulston, Commodore (US seaman in
   French service),  77–9
Mounsey, Commander William,  243
Mudge, Captain Zachary,  181–3, 192,
   201–2
Mulgrave, Henry Phipps, 1st Earl
   of,  266–7, 273
Mullon, Capitaine de Frégate
   Jean,  25–7
Mundy, Captain George,  219
Murat, Maréchal Joachim,  212
Murray, Captain Sir George,  38–9,
   124, 187
Murray, William,  117
Muskein (French boat builder),  103

Nagasaki, Japan,  236
Nagle, Admiral Sir Edmund,  38, 47–8,
   60, 124, 309
Napier, Commander Charles,  241–3
Napier, Admiral (Sir) Charles ('Mad
   Black Charlie'; Carlo de
   Ponza),  100, 252
Naples,  212
Napoleon I (Bonaparte), Emperor of
   France
   abdication and exile to Elba,  213
   at Boulogne marine review
      (1811),  279–80
   breach with Alexander I,  279
   and British breach of European
      import,  234
   campaign in Egypt,  111–12, 116,
      120–1, 139
   campaigns in Italy,  80, 140, 163
   on capture of HMS Minerve,  175
   condemns disgracing of
      Cochrane,  275
   Continental System,  169, 256
   criticises Linois,  195, 216

and death of Wright, 189
designs on India, 111–12, 116, 293
elected Emperor, 170
European conquests, 171, 210, 212, 214
exiled to St Helena, 331
first abdication and exile (1814), 294, 323, 329–30
as First Consul, 139
and French commanders at Trafalgar, 200
Hundred Days and defeat at Waterloo, 330
and importance of sea power, 331
marches east across Europe, 199
marches on Syria, 121–3
orders Ganteaume to Egypt, 157–8, 161
orders Villeneuve to combine with Ganteaume, 198
on Peace of Amiens, 164
and Peninsular War, 276
prepares for invasion of England, 170–1, 173, 198
quits Egypt, 123
rearms and reorganises in peacetime, 164, 168–9
retreat from Moscow, 261–2
ridicules English, 16
on Sir Sidney Smith, 72
surrenders to Lewis, 120
at Toulon, 31
urges French naval development, 104
and war with Britain, 2
Napoleonic Wars (1803–15), 170, 173
Nauckhoff, Konteramiral Henrik (Swedish), 257–9
Navy Board, 11
Neale, Captain Sir Harry, 96, 131, 188, 215, 272
Nelson, Admiral Horatio, Viscount
activities in Mediterranean, 112, 114–15, 119, 121, 141
and attack on Spanish fleet, 190
at battle of Copenhagen (1801), 161–2
at Cape St Vincent, 95
career, 15
commands Mediterranean fleet, 171, 187, 189, 199
death at Trafalgar, 3, 200

early career, 5, 36
escorts Ferdinand to Palermo, 121
on Jervis, 81
and Lady Hamilton, 121, 142, 199
loses arm at Tenerife, 99, 127
loses prizes, 80
mobilised for war, 6
pursues Villeneuve to West Indies and back to Mediterranean, 196–8
reputation, 72
resents Sidney Smith's appointment in Levant, 121–2
returns to England: (1800), 142; (1805), 199
Trafalgar campaign and victory, 171, 196, 199–200, 209
on US Navy, 168
Netherlands (and Dutch)
attacked in East Indies, 69, 115, 180, 235–6
British expedition to (1799), 123
British successes against, 145
Camperdown defeat, 95
and Cape of Good Hope, 9
colonies taken, 162
conflicts with Britain, 4, 6, 53–4
forced from Ceylon, 61
France declares war on (1793), 6
France exploits, 80
French invade and occupy, 53, 169
losses in West Indies, 244
ships seized in British ports, 53
signs Peace of Amiens, 163
warships limited in size, 81
see also Dutch East Indies; Dutch Ships; Dutch West Indies
Neville, Lieutenant Martin, 152–3
Newfoundland, 82, 215
Newman, Captain James, 109
Nicolls, Lieutenant Edward (Royal Marines), 181
Nielly, Contre-Amiral Joseph-Marie, baron, 36, 42–3
Nisbet, Josiah, 15
Noirmoutier Island, 14
Nore mutiny (1797), 93
North Cape, 219
North Sea: British trade protection in, 221
Norway, 211, 260
Nova Scotia, 82
Nuku Hiva, Marquesas, 312

Occa Bay, battle of (1806), 217
O'Connor, Arthur, 83
Oliver, Captain Robert, 48, 225–6
Omnium scandal (1814), 274
Orde, Vice-Admiral Sir John, 196
Ortegal, Cape, 204
Osborne, Captain Samuel, 49–50
Ostend: Popham raids, 104
Oswald, Captain James, 221
Otranto, Strait of, 253
Otto, Louis Guillaume, comte de
    Mosloy, 77
Owen, Captain Edward, 189

Pacific Ocean: Porter in, 311–12
Paddon, Midshipman Silas, 148
Paget, Captain the Hon. Charles, 263
Paget, Captain the Hon. William, 44
Paine, Thomas, 54
Pakenham, Captain Edward, 114
Pakenham, Captain Thomas ('Mad-
    Pack'), 55–6
Palmer, Captain Nesbit, 251–2
Palmer, Commander Thomas, 79
Palmerston, Henry Temple, 2nd
    Viscount, 163
Papin, Capitaine André, 47, 105
Parish, Lieutenant John, 234
Parker, Admiral Sir Hyde, 133–4, 136,
    161
Parker, Captain Sir Peter, 252, 260,
    329
Parker, Captain William, 216
Pasquaglio, Capitano (Venetian), 253,
    255
Pastor, Don Gaspar el, 277
Paul, Tsar of Russia, 161, 164
Peake, Commander William, 307
Peard, Captain Shuldam, 141, 157
Pearson, Lieutenant (of
    Diamond), 71–3
Pearson, Captain Richard, 174
Pellew, Admiral Sir Edward, 1st
    Viscount Exmouth
  befriends Bergerac, 77
  captains Nymphe, 21, 24–7
  career, 21–3, 28
  with Channel Fleet, 172
  commands in Mediterranean, 250,
    328
  commands squadron in
    Indefatigable, 65–6, 73–6, 84–5

  on court martial of Hermione
    mutineers, 136
  on Culloden, 57
  Far East command, 231, 235, 285
  harries Brittany coast, 147
  helps rescue Sampson, 67
  investigates Scilly Isles as
    anchorage, 100
  learns of Peace of Amiens, 165
  praises Coghlan, 148
  prize money, 236
  promoted admiral, 155
  qualities and character, 21–2, 28,
    155, 235–6
  recaptures Hyène, 98
  recaptures Lord Nelson, 178
  serves in Arethusa under
    Warren, 38–40, 47–8, 59
  sits in Parliament, 165, 169
  supports French royalists in
    Brittany, 139, 144
  suppresses mutiny, 120
  thwarts French invasion attempt on
    Ireland, 87–91
  transfers to Impetueux, 120
Pellew, Captain Fleetwood, 231, 236
Pellew, Rear-Admiral Israel, 25–8, 93,
    328
Pellew, Pownall, 328
Pellew, Samuel, 22, 27
Pellowe, Richard, 26
Penang, 231
Peninsular War see under Spain
Perez, Capitán Pablo, 127
Péridier, Capitaine Jean, 253–5
Perraud, Capitaine Jacques, 177–8
Perrée, Contre-Amiral Jean-Baptiste-
    Emmanuel, 122–3, 141
Peruvian Ship: Nereyda
    (privateer), 312
Pétion, Alexandre, 244
Pévrieux, Capitaine Etienne, 39–40,
    79
Phélippeaux, Colonel Antoine de, 122
Philibert, Capitaine Pierre, 330
Pierrepont, Captain William, 132–3
Pigot, Captain Hugh, 94, 133–4, 184–5
Pillnitz, Declaration of (1791), 4
Pillon, Capitán Don Antonio, 133
Pine, Lieutenant Horace, 70–1
Pinsum, Capitaine Jacques, 226, 241–
    2

Pitt, William, the younger, 4, 23, 169, 209
Plymouth Sound, 66–7
Pocock, Nicholas, 77
Point, Général, 103
Pointe de l'Aiguillon, 224
Pondicherry, India, 195
Ponée, Capitaine François, 330
Popham, Rear-Admiral Sir Home Riggs, 104, 145, 189, 229, 276–8, 283
Porlier, Juan Diaz ('El Marquesito'), 277
Port Louis, France, 147
Port Louis, Île de France, 49–50, 149, 283–7, 289–93
Port Mahon, Minorca, 150, 164
Porter, Captain David (USN), 297, 310–17, 323
Porter, Evalina (née Anderson), 311
Portugal, 9, 159, 162, 213
Portuguese Ship, Naval: *Minerva* (later French *Minerve*), 283–8, 293
post-ships, 10
Potosí, Bolivia, 98, 114
Poustouchine, Kontr-Admiral, 211
Poyntz, Captain Stephen, 151, 217
Preble, Edward, 167
press gangs, 12, 19
Preussisch-Eylau, battle of (1807), 210
Price, Commander Charles, 102–4
prize money, 9, 24, 43, 133, 207
Proby, Captain William Allen, Lord, 94, 146
Proteau, Capitaine Guillaume, 272
Prussia: Jean defeat, 210
Puerto Cabello, Venezuela, 133, 135–6
Puerto Rico, 200, 240
Pulteney, Lieut.-General Sir James, 144
Purchet, Capitaine, 96
pursers, 11–12
Pym, Captain Samuel, 283, 286–9, 293

Quiberon, 139–40
Quiberon Bay, 60, 71
Quota Acts (1795), 13

Ragersvik, near Tallin, 258–9
Raggio, Capitano (Venetian), 253

Rainier, Vice-Admiral Peter, 69, 113–16, 150, 172, 195
Rainier, Captain Peter (nephew of above), 231, 236
Ranelagh, Captain Charles Jones, 4th Viscount, 107, 110, 140
Rathbone, Captain Wilson, 204
Read, Lieutenant George (USN), 300
Red Sea, 54, 114, 150
Rees, Lieutenant Thomas, 251
Renaud, Commodore Jean-Marie, 49–50
Renaudin, Contre-Amiral Jean-François, 57–9
republicanism: British fears of, 4
Réunion (island), 227, 231, 280, 289–90
Rey, Général, 106
Reynolds, Lieutenant Carthew, 193
Reynolds, Captain George, 261
Reynolds, Rear-Admiral Robert, 73, 84, 88–90, 257
Richer, Capitaine de Vaisseau Jean-Baptiste-Edmond, 116–18
Richery, Contre-Amiral Joseph de, 82–3
Riga, 261
Rivington, Commander Robert, 149
Rochambeau, Général Donatien de Vimeur, vicomte de, 179
Rochefort
    Allemand escapes from, 203
    blockaded, 120, 172, 223
    Cunningham reconnoitres, 129
    French fleet flees Gambier to, 271–2
    French ships at, 57
    Missiessey breaks out from, 196
    *Régénérée* and *Africaine* escape from, 145, 150
    supplies to, 97
    Villeneuve makes for, 198
Rodgers, Commodore John (USN), 296–9, 301, 308, 323
Rodney, Admiral George Brydges, 1st Baron, 130
Rodriguez (island), 283, 285, 290, 292
Romana, Marquís de la *see* La Romana, Marquís de
Roncière, Capitaine Nicolas de la, 272
Rondeau, Commodore Jacques, 44
Rosily-Mesros, Amiral François-Etienne, comte de, 199

Rowley, Commodore Josias, 202,
    283–4, 286–91, 293
Royal African Company, 51
Royal Navy
  Baltic fleet, 210
  categories of ships, 10–11
  character and career of officers, 14–
    17
  conditions and pay, 12–13, 92, 222
  convoy system, 8–9, 11, 308
  corruption and reforms in, 168, 171
  cruiser warfare, 213
  desertions, 236–8, 295–6
  discipline and punishments, 13–14,
    55, 94, 238
  disposition after resumption of war
    (1803), 171–2
  lacks accurate charts, 65
  logistical and communications
    improvements, 82
  manpower and strength, 69
  Parliamentary vote (1794), 35
  post-war conditions for officers and
    men, 332
  reduced after Peace of Amiens, 164–
    5
  reforms, 5, 14, 274
  role and responsibilities in wars with
    France, 2–4, 7–10, 214, 247, 326
  ships' companies and
    organisation, 11–12
  ships lost in heavy weather, 124
  strength and condition in war with
    USA, 297, 307–8
  success in war with France, 331–2
  supports Wellington and Spanish in
    Peninsula, 276–7
  surveying and charting, 332
  unrest and mutinies in, 54–6, 91–4,
    97, 100, 120
  see also British Ships, Naval
Royal Trinity House Volunteer
    Artillery, 188
Rudnov, Kapitan (Russian), 258
Russell passage (Channel Islands), 46
Russia
  alliance with France, 212
  in Armed Neutrality, 161
  and British dealings with
    Turkey, 211
  British trade with, 261
  conflict with Britain, 6

conflicts with Anglo-Swedish fleet in
    Baltic, 257–8
  Lemnos victory, 247
  Napoleon advances against, 210,
    212, 261, 279
  occupies Ionian Islands, 121
  resumes war with France, 256
  ships join British, 53
  war with Sweden, 256–8
Russian Ship, Naval: Sevolod, 258–9
Russian Ship (Other): Rose
    (merchantman), 222

Saba (West Indies), 244
Sables d'Olonne, Les, 265
Saint-André, Amiral André
    Jeanbon, 35
St Eustatius (West Indies), 244
St George's Channel, 77
St Groix (island), 240
St Helena, 331
St Lucia (West Indies), 49
St Marcou, Îles (Baie de la
    Seine), 102–4, 164
St Martin (West Indies), 244
St Thomas (island), 240
St Vincent, Admiral Sir John Jervis, Earl
    of
  appointed First Lord of
    Admiralty, 151
  Bruix avoids, 120
  Cape St Vincent victory, 94–5
  earldom, 94
  at Gibraltar, 91
  invests Brest, 139
  loses office to Melville, 206
  loses ships, 82
  naval reforms, 168–9, 171, 197
  naval successes, 69, 79
  Nelson on, 81
  posts Nelson to blockade
    Toulon, 112
  praises Markham, 209
  prejudice against Cochrane, 206
  promotes Cochran, 165
  promotes Coghlan, 148
  severe discipline, 57, 93–4
  suppresses mutiny, 93–4
  in West Indies, 49
  on younger sea captains, 172
St Vincent, West Indies, 68
Saintes, Les (West Indies), 242–3

Salamanca, battle of (1812), 213
Salcedo, Almirante Don Josef, 213
Saldanha Bay, 69
Sampson, Commander (of
        *Dutton*), 66–7
San Domingo (Haiti)
    acquires *Améthyste* (earlier French
        *Félicité*), 244–5
    actions at, 181–2
    battle of (1806), 3
    blockaded, 181
    captured by Anglo-Spanish
        force, 243
    as French base, 57
    French expedition to, 163, 172
    French reinforce (1805), 215, 217
    French retain, 240
    rebels against France, 157, 178–9
    retains independence, 244
San Ildefonso, Treaty of (1796), 80,
        82, 189
Santander, Spain, 277–8
Saratoga, New York, 21
Saulnier, Commodore, 142–3, 150
Saumarez, Rear-Admiral Sir James,
        Baron
    alarms King George at Weymouth, 46
    Baltic command and actions, 211,
        235, 247, 256–7, 259, 261
    blockades Cádiz, 159–60
    commands Channel Islands
        squadron, 174
    escapes in Channel Islands, 45–6
    in Nelson's 'Band of Brothers', 112
    pursues Linois at Algeciras, 159–61,
        165
    qualities, 262
    returns home on death of
        daughter, 262
    serves under Warren, 38
Saumarez, Mary, 262
Savary, Commodore Daniel, 105–7,
        110, 116
Sayer, Commander George, 231
Scandinavia: provoked by British
        convoy interceptions, 145, 161
Scandril Kichuc-Ali, Albay, 248–50
Schelde, river, 7, 164, 173, 276, 279
Scilly, Isles of, 100
Scoresby, Captain William, 220, 222
Scotland: and French invasion
        plans, 173

Scott, Thomas, 114
scurvy, 5, 13, 221–2, 297
Seagrove, Lieutenant James, 329
Searle, Commander John, 80
Sebastiani, Général Horace François
        Bastien, comte, 211
second masters, 10
Ségond, Capitaine Adrian-Joseph, 109
Selim III, Ottoman Sultan, 122, 211
Senegal, 51, 225
Senez, Capitaine André, 105
Seniavin, Admiral Dmitri
        Nikolaevich, 211–12
Sept Îles, Les, 146
Sercey, Contre-Amiral Pierre-César-
        Charles-Guillaume, marquis de
    activities in Indian seas, 80, 99, 113,
        128
    based in Île de France, 69
    flees from Hargood, 115
    and proposed attack on India, 111
    relinquishes command, 150
    in West Indies, 20
Seringapatam, battle of (1799), 115
Seven Years' War (1756–63), 5
Seychelles, 150–1
Seymour, Captain Michael, 225, 241,
        264, 282
Shortland, Captain John, 243
Shovell, Admiral Clowdisley, 125
Sicilian Ship: *Vincitoire*
        (privateer), 256
Sicily, 119
Sierra Leone, 51
Sinclair, Lieutenant, 117
slave trade, 51
sloops, 10
Smith (master's mate of
        *Blanche*), 181–2
Smith, Captain John (USN), 297
Smith, Captain Matthew, 49–50
Smith, Captain Sir Sidney
    actions, 31, 38, 47–8, 58–9, 64, 70–
        2, 102
    character and career, 72–3
    command and position in
        Levant, 121–3
    commands quadron in Thames
        estuary, 171
    in Dardanelles, 211
    in defence against invasion
        threat, 189

escape from captivity, 121
imprisoned, 73, 77
leads seamen in battle in Egypt, 145
in Mediterranean, 212
thwarts Napoleon in Egypt, 116,
    139
Smith, Midshipman William, 320
Soleil, Commodore Elénore
    Jean, 226–7
Sombrero (island, West Indies), 183–4
Soult, Marshal Nicolas, 127
South Africa, 9
Spain
    amalagamates Mediterranean fleet
        with French, 80–1, 120, 160
    Anglo-Portuguese army in, 9
    'Armament' (1790), 6
    Cochrane harasses coast, 238–40
    fleet prepares for invasion of
        Britain, 173
    France declares war on (1793), 6
    insurrection against Napoleon, 212
    peace treaties, 54, 80
    Peninsular War in, 9, 212–13, 234,
        276–8
    quality of navy, 81
    resumes war with Britain
        (1804), 189.195–6
    signs Peace of Amiens, 163
    treasure ships intercepted and
        captured, 98–9, 114, 131, 133,
        207, 236
    war with Britain, 5, 80–1
Spanish Ships, Naval
    Argonauta, 144
    Caroline, 207
    Ceres, 131
    Clara, 190–1
    Diana, 131
    Esmeralda, 131
    Europa, 115
    Fama, 190–1
    Gamo, 153–6
    Hermione (earlier HMS Hermione ;
        later HMS Retribution), 94, 133–
        7, 188
    Mahonesa, 80
    Medea see British Ships: Impérieuse
    Mercedes, 131, 190–2
    Montanes, 115
    Ninfa, 99
    Pomona (later HMS Cuba), 232

Proserpina, 125
Real Carlos, 144, 160
Salvador del Mundo, 95
San Agustín, 161
San Antonio, 144
San Fernando, 144
San Hermenegildo, 144, 160
San Joseph, 95
San Nicholás, 95
Santa Brigida, 132–3
Santa Elena, 99
Santa Teresa, 125, 127
Santissima Trinidad, 95
Thetis, 132
Spanish Ships (Other)
    Fortuna (merchantman), 207
    San Iago (merchantman), 23
    San Raphael (treasure ship), 236
Sparrow, Captain Benjamin, 73, 84–5
Spencer, George John, 2nd Earl, 53,
    72
Spithead mutinies: (1794), 55–6;
    (1797), 91–3, 97
Spitsbergen, 220
Spottiswoode, Commander
    Robert, 177
Stephens, Captain Philip, 94
Stevens, William, 319
Stewart, Captain Charles (USN), 325
Stewart, Captain James, 261
Stewart, Captain John, 248–50
Stirling, Captain Charles, 65, 198
Stopford, Captain Sir Robert, 60, 130,
    264–6
Stott, Captain John, 21
Strachan, Rear-Admiral Sir (John)
    Richard
    in attack on Ferrol, 144
    commands frigate squadron, 64–5,
        215
    promotion and knighthood, 206
    pursues and defeats Dumanoir, 203–
        5
    in search for Willaumez, 215, 217
    serves under Warren, 38–40
    supports French royalist rising in
        Brittany, 140
    thwarts Muskein's attack on St
        Marcouf, 103
    on Walcheren expedition, 276
Street, Lieutenant Benjamin, 286–7,
    291

Stuart, General Charles,  119
Suez,  145
Suffren Saint Tropez, Amiral Pierre
    André de,  25, 35
Sulivan, Commander Thomas,  234
Sunda Strait,  219
Surcouf, Robert,  149, 172, 285, 308
surgeons,  11–12
Surinam,  145, 192
Sutton, Captain Samuel,  190
Sweden,  145, 210, 256–8
Swedish Ships, Naval
    Camilla,  259
    Frederic-Adolphe,  258
    Tapperheten,  258
Swilly, Lough,  107, 110

Talavera, battle of (1809),  213
Talleyrand, Charles-Maurice de,  111,
    164
Tandy, Napper,  106
Tappanooly, Sumatra,  283
'tarpaulin captains',  11
Tate, William,  96
Taylor, Captain Bridges,  221
Taylor, Captain John,  307
Tenerife: Nelson attacks,  99, 127
Ternate,  162
Thames, river: mouth cordoned,  188
Thévenard, Capitaine Henri-
    Alexandre,  48, 68, 82
Thomas, Capitaine Guillaume,  68, 82
Thompson, Captain Sir Thomas,  112–
    13
Thomson, Lieutenant John,  28
Thornbrough, Vice-Admiral
    Edward,  107–8, 223–4
Tilsit, Treaty of (1807),  210–11, 234,
    240, 247
Tipu Sultan,  115
Tone, Wolfe,  81, 83, 105, 108, 111
Tor Bay,  100, 125–6
Torris, Capitán Don Francisco
    de,  155–6
Touffet, Capitaine Claude,  204–5
Toulon
    blockaded,  112, 140, 171, 189,
        250, 328
    Britain abandons as blockade
        station,  81, 213
    British evacuate,  31–2
    Bruix in,  120

    as French base,  7, 57
    Ganteaume returns to,  158–9
    Hood and Juno escape from,  32–4
    Smith at,  31, 72–3
Toulouse, battle of (1814),  213
Tourneur, Lieutenant de Vaisseau
    Laurent,  188
Toussaint-Louverture, Pierre-
    Dominique,  157, 178
Townshend, Captain Lord James,  298
Trafalgar, battle of (1805),  3, 7, 171,
    173, 200, 202, 209
Tréhouart, Capitaine Pierre,  49–50
Trincomalee, Ceylon,  61
Trinidad: captured from Spain,  99,
    164
Trinity House,  12, 188
Tripoli,  166–7
Trolle, Captain (Swedish),  259
Trollope, Captain Henry,  80
Troubridge, Captain Sir Thomas,  42,
    55–6, 95, 112, 121–2, 169, 231,
    235
Troude, Commodore Amable,  242–3,
    263–5
Truck, Bill (pseudonym),  2
Truguet, Vice-Amiral Laurent,  83
Tucker, Commander Thomas,  313–15
Tullidge, Lieutenant Joseph,  290
Tunis,  166
Turkey (Ottoman),  122–3, 211–12,
    247–8, 250
Turkish Ships, Naval
    Alis Fezzan,  248–50
    Badere-I-Zaffer,  248–50
Turquand, Commander William,  111,
    146
Twysden, Captain Thomas,  109

Ulm, battle of (1805),  210
United Irishmen, The,  81, 90, 105,
    111
United Provinces see Netherlands
United States of America
    achieves independence,  5
    British blockade of,  308–9, 323
    commerce-raiding against
        British,  309–11
    conflict with Tripoli,  166–8
    harasses Royal Navy,  214
    naval strength,  296–7
    and Peace of Amiens,  165–6

peace settlement with Britain
  (1814),  324
war with Britain (1812–14),  2, 4,
  238, 247, 280, 295–321, 323–6
welcomes Royal Navy
  deserters,  237–8, 295–6
United States Ships, Naval
  *Adams*,  184, 323
  *Argus*,  167, 301, 309–10
  *Bonhomme Richard*,  166
  *Chesapeake*,  166, 237, 296, 316–21
  *Congress*,  167, 297, 301, 309
  *Constellation*,  167, 310
  *Constitution*,  167–8, 298–300,
    303–6, 310, 321, 323, 325, 329
  *Enterprise*,  166–7, 323
  *Essex*,  166, 167, 237, 297, 302–3,
    310–15, 317
  *Essex Junior* (earlier whaler
    *Georgiana*),  312–13
  *Experiment*,  310
  *Hornet*,  303–4, 306–7, 309–10,
    316, 325–6
  *Nautilus*,  167, 298
  *Peacock*,  323, 325–6
  *Philadelphia*,  166–7, 310
  *Pike*,  330
  *President*,  166–7, 296–7, 301, 309,
    323–5
  *Siren*,  167
  *United States*,  297, 301–3, 309
  *Vixen*,  167
  *Wasp*,  301, 323
United States Ships (Other)
  *Barclay* (whaler),  312
  *Spitfire* (merchant brig),  296
  *Wasp* (privateer),  329
  *William* (merchantman),  304, 306
Upton, Captain Clotworthy,  241
Ushant,  60, 73–4, 84–5, 91, 100, 173
Ussher, Captain Thomas,  329

Valparaíso,  311–14, 316
Vandermaesen, Général Edmé-
  Martin,  293
Vanstabel, Contre-Amiral Pierre-
  Jean,  35
Vashon, Captain James,  41
Vaubois, Général Claude H.B.,
  comte,  140, 140–1, 143
Vendée: revolt in,  80
Venetian Ships, Naval

*Bellona*,  253–5
*Carolina*,  253–5
*Corona*,  253–5
*Eugenio*,  253
*Lodola*,  253, 255–6
*Principessa Augusta*,  253–5
*Principessa di Bologna*,  253
Venice,  252–3
Villaret-Joyeuse, Contre-Amiral Louis-
  Thomas,  35–6, 43, 57, 59–60,
  83, 242
Villeneuve, Captain Jean,  143
Villeneuve, Vice-Amiral Pierre,  83, 85,
  196–9, 209
  death,  200
Villéon, Capitaine Pierre,  39–40
Villon, Capitaine,  253
Vitoria, battle of (1813),  213, 276
Vrignault, Capitaine Joseph,  193, 216

Walcheren expedition (1809),  275–6,
  279
Wallis, Commander Provo,  321
Wallis, Quartermaster,  152–3
Walpole, Lieutenant the Hon.
  William,  174
Warren, Rear-Admiral Sir John Borlase
  in attack on Ferrol,  144
  attacks French convoys,  97–8
  captures two corvettes,  47–8
  in command of North American
    station,  209
  commands frigate squadron,  37,
    39–40, 47–8, 58–9
  delegates to subordinates,  59
  and French movements in
    Mediterranean,  157–9
  harries Brittany coast,  147
  pursues French fleet to West
    Indies,  215
  supports French royalist
    expedition,  60–1
  thwarts French invasion of
    Ireland,  107–11
Warren, Midshipman Robert,  153
Warrington, Captain Lewis
  (USN),  326
Washington, George,  171
Waterloo, battle of (1815),  330
Watkins, Captain Frederick,  63–4,
  145, 192
Watling, Lieutenant John,  287, 289

Watt, Lieutenant George, 319–20
Webly, Third Lieutenant William, 33
Wellington, Arthur Wellesley, 1st Duke
  of, 9, 210, 213, 234, 261, 276–8
Wells, Captain Thomas, 38–40
West Indies
  actions in, 49, 68, 133, 215, 217,
    231–4, 241–5, 263
  at war's end, 330
  British attempts to recover
    colonies, 192
  British forces in, 172
  colonies restored to former owners
    (1802), 172, 192
  corsairs in, 240
  Danish/Swedish colonies seized, 161
  enemy possessions seized, 244
  French possessions in, 240
  supposed French move to, 158
  see also individual places
Western Squadron (RN) see Channel
  Fleet
Wetherall, Commander Frederick, 243
Wexford, 105
Whinyates, Commander Thomas, 301
Whitby, Captain Henry, 253–4
White, Commander John, 106–7
White, Captain John Chambers, 158,
  215

Whitworth, Charles, Earl, 161, 169
Whitynow, Lieutenant (French), 29–
  30
Willaumez, Contre-Amiral Jean
  Baptiste, 177, 214–18, 229, 263–
  6, 272
Williams, Captain Sir Thomas, 77–9
Willoughby, Captain Sir Nesbit
  Josiah, 179–83, 192, 211, 283–9,
  291, 293–4
Wilson, Lieutenant Andrew, 251
Winter, Vice-Admiraal Jan Willem
  de, 95
Wintle, Lieutenant Frederick, 301
Wolfe, Captain George, 272
Wood, Captain Sir James, 232–4
Worsley, Commander Richard, 43
Worth, Captain James, 328
Wright, Commander John Wesley, 71–
  2, 121–2, 188–9, 200
Wulff, Kaptajn (Danish), 260
Yeo, Captain Sir James, 244–5
York, Frederick Augustus, Duke
  of, 124
Yorktown, 171
Young, Captain James, 132–3, 158
Young, Admiral Sir William, 207, 273

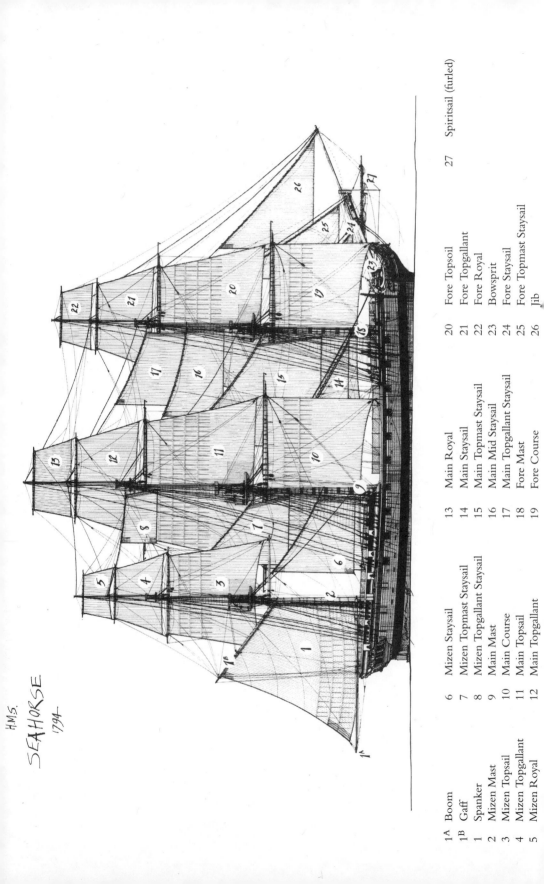

H.M.S.
SEAHORSE
1794

1A Boom
1B Gaff
1 Spanker
2 Mizen Mast
3 Mizen Topsail
4 Mizen Topgallant
5 Mizen Royal

6 Mizen Staysail
7 Mizen Topmast Staysail
8 Mizen Topgallant Staysail
9 Main Mast
10 Main Course
11 Main Topsail
12 Main Topgallant

13 Main Royal
14 Main Staysail
15 Main Topmast Staysail
16 Main Mid Staysail
17 Main Topgallant Staysail
18 Fore Mast
19 Fore Course

20 Fore Topsoil
21 Fore Topgallant
22 Fore Royal
23 Bowsprit
24 Fore Staysail
25 Fore Topmast Staysail
26 Jib

27 Spiritsail (furled)